ANIMALS AS LEGAL BEINGS

Contesting Anthropocentric Legal Orders

In *Animals as Legal Beings*, Maneesha Deckha critically examines how Canadian law and, by extension, other legal orders around the world, participate in the social construction of the human-animal divide and the abject rendering of animals as property. Through a rigorous but cogent analysis, Deckha calls for replacing the exploitative property classification for animals with a new transformative legal status or subjectivity called "beingness."

In developing a new legal subjectivity for animals, one oriented toward respecting animals for who they are rather than their proximity to idealized versions of humanness, *Animals as Legal Beings* seeks to bring critical animal theorizations and animal law closer together. Throughout the book, Deckha draws upon the feminist animal care tradition, as well as feminist theories of embodiment and relationality, postcolonial theory, and critical animal studies. Her argument is critical of the liberal legal view of animals and desirous of an animal-friendly cultural shift in the core foundations of anthropocentric legal systems.

Theoretically informed yet accessibly presented, *Animals as Legal Beings* makes a significant contribution to an array of interdisciplinary debates and is an innovative and astute argument for a meaningful, more-than-human turn in law and policy.

MANEESHA DECKHA is a professor and Lansdowne Chair in Law at the University of Victoria.

Praise for *Animals as Legal Beings*

"Finally! – a comprehensive analysis of animal law that does not rest upon anthropocentric liberal assumptions, but instead advocates for 'beingness' as a new legal subjectivity for animals. A must-read for anyone who cares about more-than-humans."

Irus Braverman, Professor and William J. Magavern
Faculty Scholar, The State University of New York at Buffalo

"Animals as property or animals as persons? This dichotomy has consumed scholars debating the legal status of animals. Esteemed feminist and postcolonial scholar Maneesha Deckha breaks through this dichotomy with her argument that animals should occupy the novel legal category of 'beingness.' Her conclusions land in surprising places and must be confronted by anyone seriously concerned with the legal status of animals."

Dale Jamieson, Professor of Environmental Studies and
Philosophy and Director of the Center for Environmental and
Animal Protection, New York University

"*Animals as Legal Beings* is an impressive model of research and theoretical literacy. Its breadth is astonishing; Maneesha Deckha is well versed across traditions and theorists. The book's engagement with complex theory is detailed and sensitive to nuance. It is an important contribution to critical thinking about law."

Margot Young, Peter A. Allard School of Law,
University of British Columbia

"Well written and highly readable, *Animals as Legal Beings* is an excellent piece of scholarship. Maneesha Deckha offers a clear theorization of animal legal subjectivity using 'beingness' as her core theoretical value and notes the limitations or unanswered puzzles related to her theorization, as one might expect of such an intellectually humble – in the best sense – scholar."

Anna Grear, School of Law and Politics, Cardiff University

"Maneesha Deckha has emerged as a leading voice in law scholarship which crosses animal studies with feminist and postcolonial theory. This book offers a new contribution to thinking about animals as legal subjects beyond the current impasse between personhood and property. Deckha's innovative approach proposes a new third status – 'beingness' – representing an original attempt to solve a practical dilemma."

Dinesh Wadiwel, School of Social and
Political Sciences, The University of Sydney

Animals as Legal Beings

Contesting Anthropocentric Legal Orders

MANEESHA DECKHA

UNIVERSITY OF TORONTO PRESS
Toronto Buffalo London

ISBN 978-1-4875-0844-9 (cloth)   ISBN 978-1-4875-3825-5 (EPUB)
ISBN 978-1-4875-2587-3 (paper)   ISBN 978-1-4875-3824-8 (PDF)

Library and Archives Canada Cataloguing in Publication

Title: Animals as legal beings : contesting anthropocentric legal orders /
    Maneesha Deckha.
Names: Deckha, Maneesha, 1972– author.
Description: Includes bibliographical references and index.
Identifiers: Canadiana (print) 20200345443 | Canadiana (ebook)
    20200345516 | ISBN 9781487525873 (paper) | ISBN 9781487508449 (cloth) |
    ISBN 9781487538255 (EPUB) | ISBN 9781487538248 (PDF)
Subjects: LCSH: Animal welfare – Law and legislation – Canada. |
    LCSH: Animals – Law and legislation – Canada. | LCSH: Animal
    welfare – Law and legislation. | LCSH: Animals – Law and legislation. |
    LCSH: Feminism.
Classification: LCC KE3676.D43 2021 | LCC KF3841.D43 2021 kfmod |
    DDC 344.7104/9–dc23

This book has been published with the help of a grant from the Federation
for the Humanities and Social Sciences, through the Awards to Scholarly
Publications Program, using funds provided by the Social Sciences and
Humanities Research Council of Canada.

University of Toronto Press acknowledges the financial assistance to its
publishing program of the Canada Council for the Arts and the Ontario
Arts Council, an agency of the Government of Ontario.

Canada Council **Conseil des Arts**
for the Arts **du Canada**

ONTARIO ARTS COUNCIL
CONSEIL DES ARTS DE L'ONTARIO
an Ontario government agency
un organisme du gouvernement de l'Ontario

Funded by the   Financé par le
Government   gouvernement
of Canada   du Canada

To my dear parents whose love and dedication continue to lift me up

And to all animals who never had the chance to bond with their mothers and family like I did and experience the security and beauty in life that follows

Contents

Contents

Acknowledgments

I wish to extend my sincere appreciation to Daniel Quinlan at University of Toronto Press for his unwavering enthusiasm for this manuscript and for everything he did to carry it forward. I would also like to offer profuse thanks to Angela Fernandez for inviting me to workshop two earlier chapters as part of the University of Toronto's Animals in Law and Humanities workshop. I remain extremely grateful to the participants who attended and forwarded those two chapters to Daniel. I also extend my deepest thanks to Will Kymlicka, who invited me to present a previous iteration of chapter 2 at Queen's University at a time when the completion of the manuscript was still a few years away and who supported me thereafter in bringing the manuscript to publication and a wider readership. Other chapters also benefited from exposition at New York University, the University of Basel, the University of Denver, and the University of Victoria, and I am grateful for those invitations and the comments received from participants.

This monograph germinated during directed reading studies I was able to carry out as a third-year law student at the University of Toronto thanks to Craig Scott, who embraced the idea of exploring animals' legal status from a critical theory perspective and who warmly encouraged publication of the final product as a monograph. I never thought it would be so many years before that work found its updated expression as chapter 1. The generous feedback I received all those years ago kept the completion of this manuscript as a consistent goal as other publishing and life priorities came along. The works of Carol Adams, Josephine Donovan, and Gary Francione were foundational departure points for the socio-legal analysis I undertook then and now, and I thank each of them for their inspiring work and unfailing dedication to transform the lives of animals.

I am equally grateful to senior feminist theorists who encouraged and generously supported my own scholarly growth as a critical animal scholar. Jennifer Nedelsky convinced me as a third-year law student that I had what it took to pursue a graduate degree when I seriously doubted it and supported me with reference letters and ongoing career advice for many years thereafter. I attribute my professional landing at the University of Victoria Faculty of Law to the enthusiasm Hester Lessard had for my candidacy, an enthusiasm she warmly maintained as the years went by. Her presence at the faculty was always a keenly felt comfort to me. I was fortunate enough to connect with Marie Fox at a Gender, Sexuality, and Law conference at Keele University when I was a few years into my position. It was rare to find then a feminist legal scholar whose intersectional vision included animals, and I am deeply grateful for the role Marie has also played as referee and friend.

My heartfelt thanks to those who make up the core of my feminist and critical animal studies research network, providing rejuvenating opportunities for scholarly exchange, as well as friendship and mentorship that have nurtured this manuscript to completion: Anurima Banerji, Mathilde Cohen, Jessica Eisen, Angela Fernandez, Will Kymlicka, Justin Marceau, Kelly Struthers-Montford, Chloë Taylor, and Dinesh Wadiwel. I am also appreciative of the general intellectual camaraderie and scholarly interaction with other colleagues over the many years in which this book was coming to fruition. Thank you, Constance Backhouse, Stephanie Ben-Ishai, Kim Brooks, Gillian Calder, Richard Delgado, Sue Donaldson, Elizabeth Adjin-Tettey, Gary Francione, Donna Jeffery, Rebecca Johnson, Freya Kodar, Hester Lessard, Mary Jane Mossman, Val Napoleon, Jennifer Nedelsky, Lincoln Shlensky, Christine St. Peter, and Jean Stefancic. And a different type of support but one that was instrumental to my academic and writing life was the security that came from being able to turn to colleagues at work when I needed help at home. Thank you, Gillian and Lincoln, for that priceless feeling over multiple years when I was caring for my father largely on my own. And thank you, Elizabeth and Paul, for your unfailing hospitality to my parents and larger family on many occasions.

I am grateful to the Social Sciences and Humanities Research Council of Canada, the US-Canada Fulbright Program, and the University of Victoria for supporting various parts of the present project. As part of my Fulbright support, I wish to thank the late Sally Merry for graciously hosting me as the Fulbright Chair in Law and Society at New York University. I also deeply appreciate the research and citation assistance provided by Alexa Powell and the secretarial assistance provided by Gail Rogers in polishing the manuscript in its final stages.

My academic career and the writing of this book would not have been possible without my parents, Anuradha (Vijaya) and Dayanand

Deckha, who inculcated a reverence for education in their children from the get-go and gave us everything they could, whose unconditional love and sacrifices I appreciated only later, and who I will always hold in my heart. I wish they had been able to see their youngest grandchild grow up and had more time with all of us. I am also deeply indebted to my brother Nitin, whose careful and patient guidance was an abiding part of my childhood and early university years and who started me on my journey to critically thinking about gender, interspecies relations, and personal dietary change. And I feel so fortunate to have met Rima as an undergraduate at McGill. Those days marking our critical intellectual coming of age were formative to my professional path, which is reflected in this work, and to my overall sense of purpose, and I cherish the friendship that has lasted and evolved into sisterhood.

Finally, to Rajesh, my number one fan and confidante, for loving me as much as my parents did, caring for them as much as I did, giving me hope when I had none, and finding the magic that empathy and attachment bring. And to my darling Bodhan, my deepest joy. You gave me the exquisite gift of motherhood, of nursing another being into and through life, and of more sharply comprehending the magnitude of embodied despair for mothers of all species when children are taken from them never having received the milk, comfort, or affection that should be theirs. My fervent hope is that you will know a world in which children are no longer separated from their mothers, loving family bonds are respected and sustained no matter what the species or difference at issue, commodifying animal life becomes unthinkable, and interspecies and global justice are norms rather than aspirations.

ANIMALS AS LEGAL BEINGS

Contesting Anthropocentric Legal Orders

Introduction

It seems to me that every time we humans announce that here is the thing that makes us unique – our featherless bipedality, our tool-using, our language – some other species comes along to snatch it away. If modesty were a human trait, we'd have learned to be more cautious over the years.[1]

Karen Joy Fowler, *We Are All Completely Beside Ourselves*

I. Property, Personhood, and Beingness

A. Sustaining Anthropocentrism through (Legal) Culture

In the first half of 2019, Canada took some bold policy and legal steps in favour of animals that would have seemed improbable just a few short years earlier. The first, taking effect in January, was the long-awaited revision of Canada's *National Food Guide*, a policy document published by Health Canada that, for the first time since its 1942 inception, recommended that Canadians follow primarily a plant-based diet to ensure good health.[2] The guide also downplayed the importance of drinking (cow's) milk. It never once mentions the word "veganism," and its ultimate effect in changing Canadians' dietary habits may be negligible; even so, it is a high-profile governmental statement about the benefits of plant protein and as such may reduce the number of farmed animals that are exploited and killed for human consumption. Canada's new approach promoting a diet rich in plants and low in animal-based foods aligned with an influential global study published in *The Lancet* recommending the same.[3] The second development, occurring near the end of June, was the enactment of a law banning the keeping of cetaceans (whales, dolphins, and porpoises) in captivity and their breeding and use for human entertainment.[4] With the promulgation of this law,

Canada became the first country in North America to join a handful of countries worldwide that have similarly prohibited holding cetaceans in captivity and breeding them to maintain captive populations.[5]

From one perspective, these policy and legal developments are clear victories for animals and ethical vegans and are rightly celebrated by animal advocates. From another, however, the January and June developments reveal a much more sobering account of human-animal relations in Canada insofar as they mask intensely fought ideological battles regarding the proper place of animals. It is no secret that Health Canada officials faced intense resistance not only from corporate lobbies representing animal agricultural interests but also from their own colleagues in Agriculture and Agri-Food Canada in charge of promoting the country's animal agricultural industries.[6] Similarly, the eventual success of the cetacean bill must be read as an instance of public opinion, aided by widely watched documentaries and years of advocacy and debate, finally changing in favour of a small group of megafauna whom a sufficient majority of Canadians now recognize share many human-like capacities and should not be treated as they have been in the entertainment industries. Meanwhile, scores of other types of animals are kept captive and bred into short-lived and immiserated existence each year in Canada in the hundreds of millions for human and corporate use.

I posit that the latter, more sobering perspective is the reasonable one to adopt toward Canada's new *Food Guide* and the cetacean anti-captivity law as we take stock of the state of human-animal and interspecies relations in Canada – and in almost every other country on Earth. Despite increasing awareness of the abject living conditions faced by most domesticated animals on this planet, of the horrors and unsustainability of intensive farming, of the damage these practices are doing to the earth's climate, and of the accelerated rate of species extinction and commercial plundering of the oceans for fish and other life, violence against animals is increasing. A snapshot of human consumption of farmed animals worldwide demonstrates this trend in terms of sheer numbers: global per capita animal flesh consumption was at 43 kilograms per person in 2013, up from 23 kilograms in 1961, with the richest nations in the world eating by far the most per capita and two of the world's most populous countries – China and Brazil – demonstrating the highest levels of per capita increase.[7] Presently, conservative estimates indicate that 65 billion land animals are farmed every year and between 2 and 3 *trillion* creatures are trawled from our oceans for human consumption. These figures are set to rise to 130 billion land animals by 2050, while the global collapse of all *taxa* currently fished is projected to occur by 2048.[8]

A complicated picture emerges when we try to comprehend why more public exposure to the drawbacks of animal consumption for human health and the environment, the conditions in which farmed and other animals live, and the mass species extinction currently under way have not curtailed the rate at which industries and humans exploit and kill animals and undertake activities that cause them serious harm. One prominent factor no doubt relates to cultural narratives of human exceptionalism – epitomized in Western modernist thought and now widely (although not yet universally) globalized through imperial and capitalist forces – that encourage us from childhood to see ourselves as different from and superior to animals. For example, when we trace the number of human explanations for the human-animal divide that have unfolded over the last few centuries of Western intellectual thought, we arrive at a list as long as it is varied. Deficiencies or absences (real or imagined) related to reasoning capacity, language, tool use, and emotions were among some of the earlier candidates proffered in the eighteenth century to sustain the cultural truism that a sharp line divides human animals from more-than-human animals.[9] These arguments about reason and other ostensibly demonstrable capacities, and who had them, performed two types of cultural work. First, they provided secular reasons to supplant the religious justification that earlier prevailed (i.e., that only humans had souls). Second, in the face of the growing ascendancy of Darwin's theory of evolution with its emphasis on continuities and blurred boundaries across species, these reasons shored up an entrenched sense of human exceptionalism.[10]

These anthropocentric cultural narratives still circulate today. Yet even while scientific studies repeatedly proved that animals too exhibited capacities for reason, language, tool use, and the ability to emote, newer justifications for human uniqueness materialized. These newer entrants included the ability to make tools from tools, express higher-level emotions, participate in cultural meaning-making, profess faith or spirituality, and so on.[11] As these goalposts continue to shift to accommodate new knowledge about animal capacities and traits heretofore "undiscovered" in animals,[12] those heavily invested in the divide's validity will likely instantiate newer "distinctive" human capacities such as creativity, efficient information transmission across generations, and so on.[13] To this end, it may be tempting for the legally minded to claim law as a definitive feature of human uniqueness on the basis that no other animal species organizes itself by a set of codified legal rules or provides opportunities for judicial review. In this argument, law serves as the newest explanation for why we as a species are different from

other species and thus entitled to the privileges our current anthropocentric social, cultural, and economic order affords us.

While this use of law to justify the human-animal divide may seem
novel, it is certainly not the first time that law – by which I mean doctrinal cases and legislation and also unwritten codes and customs regarding legality, justiciability, and subjectivity – has acted to support this
divide and the claims of humans' superiority and animals' inferiority
that underpin it.[14] In fact, law has been a principal component of the
institutional cultural infrastructure that buttresses the cultural stories
we are told early on about why humans can use animals. This book
critically examines how Canadian law, understood as state or settler-
colonial law – and, by extension, the many other legal jurisdictions
worldwide premised on human exceptionalism borne from the British
common law tradition – participate in the social construction and ongoing cultural maintenance of the human-animal divide and the abject
rendering of animals as property that attends it.[15] This book calls on
us to replace the exploitative property classification for animals within
these jurisdictions (hereafter referred to as "anthropocentric legal systems") with a new, transformative legal status or subjectivity, which I
term "beingness."

*B. Turning the Law toward Animals and Animality,
and Away from the "Human"*

In developing a new legal subjectivity for animals oriented toward
respecting animals for what they are – rather than for their proximity to
idealized versions of humanness – this book is situated within the "animal turn" in academia that has occurred across campuses in the United
States and, to a lesser extent, in other countries since the start of the new
millennium.[16] Precisely what the "animal turn" denotes is difficult to
articulate due to the variety of authorial motivations, subject matter, and
political impacts of the scholarship. At the very least, however, the "animal turn" points to the scholarly interest in non-human animals as serious and meritorious subjects of academic study and intellectual effort –
an interest that has given birth to the interdisciplinary field of animal
studies in the social sciences and humanities.[17] And within animal studies, there is a growing subfield of scholarly work that examines animal
issues from an intersectional perspective. Indebted to earlier feminist
work, especially ecofeminist analyses of the continuities between the
domination of women and the domination of nature and non-human
animals,[18] a growing cohort of scholars are turning their attention to the
nexus between the human, the animal, and other more-than-humans.

Theorists harnessing a range of critical frameworks have highlighted multiple ways in which ideas of animals and animality, and processes of animalization and speciation, are related to questions of civilization, racialization, sexuality, gendering, ability, and age, and are thus imbricated in human rights and critical theory discourses typically viewed as unaffected by "the animal question."[19] Many studies have also shown how ideas of humans and humanness, as well as humanization projects, give shape not only to animal exploitation and abjection but also to human experiences of violence and other injustices.[20]

Yet only a fraction of this scholarship critically attends to law and its norms and outputs.[21] Law schools in what is now known as the United States and Canada, among other places, have themselves witnessed an "animal turn" since the mid-1990s – a turn that has produced the now consolidated field of animal law. But with only a few exceptions of the feminist, postcolonial, posthumanist, and biopolitical kind, animal law scholarship is decisively doctrinal and liberal in orientation.[22] This book seeks to address this disconnect and bring critical animal theorizations (defined as those theoretical frameworks that are critical of liberal humanism and are primarily identity-based and directed at social justice and anti-oppressive ends) and animal law closer together for practical and transgressive effect. It articulates the intersectional racialized, gendered, and species valences of dominant legal understandings of and assumptions about the terms human, animal, and personhood, as well as humanization, dehumanization, animalization, and animality, as a means to unpack and take aim at the anthropocentric response (or lack thereof) to animals in anthropocentric legal systems.

This book uses what many would apprehend as an intersectional analytic that draws heavily from the feminist animal care tradition, as well as feminist theories of embodiment and relationality, postcolonial theory, and critical animal studies, to unpack these understandings. These theoretical frameworks help explain why anthropocentric legal systems today are so poorly equipped to do anything about systemic violence against animals even when intentions to help animals are present. These theoretical frameworks also provide the lens through which I suggest how the law in these systems can move forward for animals in an impactful and non-reductive way despite its anthropocentric foundations. My argument, which is critical of the liberal legal view of animals (see part II of this book), is invested in innovating a transgressive legal subjectivity for animals, one that is attentive to their embodied vulnerability and relationality and desirous of bringing about an animal-friendly cultural shift at the core of anthropocentric legal systems.

C. Beingness as a Solution to the Animal Law Chasm between Welfarism and Abolitionism

This book thus contributes to a long-standing debate in animal law circles as to the best legal pathways and strategies to follow to ameliorate the conditions of animals. It implicitly weighs in on the "welfarist" versus "abolitionist" debate (the former defined as an approach to advocacy that is tolerant of a property classification for animals in law and that attempts to seek positive change for animals from within this paradigm, the latter defined as an approach that seeks to abolish animals' status as property as a preliminary and fundamental element of law reform).[23] "Beingness," as the new legal subjectivity I argue for, is directed at eliminating the property paradigm for animals. Thus, my departure point is decidedly not welfarist in perspective.

Yet this book also takes issue with the "abolitionist" side of the debate insofar as it resists abolitionism's classic desired legal end point: personhood status for animals. Personhood is the legal category or subjectivity that is supposed to protect an entity from being treated as property – that is, as subject to instrumental use by others – through the assignment of rights.[24] In the present day, personhood as a legal subjectivity is ascribed only to human beings, corporations, and ships.[25] In the law's binary outlook, according to which almost all worldly entities/beings are categorized either as property or as persons, it is clear that it is much better to be the latter rather than the former. Leading advocates of the "abolitionist" approach to animals such as Gary Francione and Steven M. Wise have thus championed personhood for animals, deploying reasoned liberal argumentation and using current jurisprudential frameworks to achieve this coveted end point.[26] Of course, given the violence against animals that their property status produces, it is obvious why those who object to animals' instrumentalization would seek personhood as a comprehensive legal remedy. I advance the argument, however, that personhood is not the appropriate legal status for animals, not because animals don't deserve the same legal protection as humans, but because personhood is not an animal-friendly category. We can do better in the struggle for law to assign a new legal status or subjectivity to animals. The central contribution of this book is to explicitly argue the following: (1) personhood, while it would obviously be an enormous improvement for animals to be classified as such rather than as property, is still a decidedly anthropocentric model; and (2) the alternative, "beingness," as a more animal-centred, animal-friendly replacement for property, would be a better goal.

In advancing this argument, this book extends critical theory into the domains of animal law to generate an innovative and more animal-centred/animal-friendly legal subjectivity for animals that does not bear the imprint of either liberal humanism or anthropocentrism (the former defined as an intellectual outlook premised on liberal values in which the human, who possesses rationality and speech, and is also the most detached from bodily preoccupations or associations, is exalted as the ideal subject;[27] the latter defined as a belief system and wide-ranging material network centred on human exceptionalism, and exalting and maintaining a certain type of paradigmatic or fully human being at the apex of a hierarchy of beings).[28] Beingness thus offers a theoretical innovation as well as a practical solution to evading the impasse that currently encapsulates the core debate in animal law circles. Furthermore, it pragmatically responds to the call from a rising cohort of critical animal law scholars to create "more-than-human legalities" – that is, to find a way forward in law for animals that does not reinscribe law's humanist premises and that invites contemplation of other legal pathways for perceiving, representing, and (sometimes) being-with animals that do not deny their alterity, expressions, and relationality.[29]

As a secondary but still important focus, this book seeks to demonstrate the material and symbolic relevance of the marginalization of more-than-human animals and animality to critical theorizations of law and injustice, in general, through a critically oriented legal analysis. It extends critical animal studies and animal law's pleas to interrogate anthropocentrism into the domains of critical theory, which is still overwhelmingly humanist. It advances the view that injustice against animals should matter not only to those who actually care about animals, but also to those seeking to attend and respond to human suffering, vulnerability, precarity, invisibility, subalternity, and marginality of all kinds. This project joins a growing literature that seeks to illuminate why an anthropocentric focus on human rights and the continued emphasis on the wrongs of dehumanization in the discourse of human rights both backfire against vulnerable human groups and will not create a just world even by anthropocentric metrics, let alone non-anthropocentric ones.[30] As a *critical* account of the *legal* treatment of animals, this book hopes to persuade more socio-legal scholars to consider "the animal question," given the overall relative silence of socio-legal scholarship in this area.

II. A Legal Subjectivity That Resists Liberal Legalism and Liberal Humanism

Research into law reform measures concerning the legal status of animals is becoming more common, and while animal law as a subject of student inquiry in law schools has become mainstream in the United States,[31] issues of gender, race, and non-species difference have not been central in these analyses.[32] Most scholars writing in this area approach the question of changing animals' legal status from philosophical vantage points that do not question liberalism; instead, these approaches generally reside within liberal deontological and utilitarian schools of thought and ultimately press forward animals' similarities with humans.[33] This book does not review the many arguments as to why animals are similar to humans in terms of traits and capacities we normally believe qualify humans for special ethical and legal regard.[34] These arguments are no doubt important in many contexts. I do not rehearse them here because they are well-established already and because my argument for changing animals' status from property to beingness is not rooted in respecting animals out of sameness to humans and human benchmarks, but rather pivots on difference and alterity understood relationally. The book thus seeks to instantiate a new legal subjectivity that is not rooted in the liberal tradition.

A. Why Are Liberal Approaches to Law Problematic?

There are, of course, many forms of liberalism.[35] Discussing features common to most such forms to summarize the problems with currently available legal subjectivity options for animals in anthropocentric legal orders will necessarily be reductive. It is not my intent to caricaturize liberalism; rather, I mean to convey what many scholars have identified as typical core features of liberal worldviews and why such features impede the attainment of a just end point for animals. Liberalism, broadly scoped, is sourced in Enlightenment ideals about civilizational progress. Critical indicators of liberalism include (1) the rule of law and other state institutions to which individuals consent, (2) reason and rational, publicly justified deliberation about society's allocation of resources, and (3) individual freedom and equality.[36]

A central concern with animal law theories that implicitly or explicitly adopt liberal worldviews in their argumentation is that they foster a robust faith in modern legal institutions. Liberal animal law theorists assume that liberal legal orders will eventually render justice through the conferral of personhood to animals, at which point animals will be assigned equal moral worth and afforded liberty – two key features of personhood that prevent instrumentalization and commodification.[37] Liberalism generally allows an expansive role for law and adopts a favourable disposition toward it, faulting it only for not being inclusive enough in ensuring that the principal justice-related rights of equality, autonomy, and dignity are granted to all and respected.[38] Liberal legal thinkers accept that liberalism is marred by its exclusive past but generally assume that the basic contours of the liberal subject – an individual fully in control of himself, non-relationally autonomous, normatively rational and guided by reason, unmarked by identity or social location, and representative of a universal human – are not ethically suspect or defective.[39] They are also not generally troubled by liberalism's normative outlook – namely its "abstract rationalism," "moral individualism," and "narrowness or insufficiency (of its ideas) of distributive justice" – as a constitutive feature of the legal order.[40] This normative outlook, along with the features delineated above of the classic liberal subject, produces, in the legal order shaped by liberalism, the legal system known as "liberal legalism."[41]

Many feminist and postcolonial legal critics articulate a sharp critique of liberal legalism. They can be sceptical of law as a liberatory agent and of the *rule* of law as a benevolent and equalizing force.[42] Feminist legal theorists have specifically questioned the public/private divide on which liberal legal orders pivot as well as the method of reasoned proof that liberal legalism presumes is the sole basis of authority and evidence.[43] Feminist legal theorists, including those who apply their theories to highlight animal suffering, have also contested reason's privileged place in legal method and its discrediting of emotion, care, and relationality as principles and values to guide our assessments of what just relationships with animals would look like.[44] For their part, postcolonial legal scholars have located law and liberal legalism as agents of imperialism that facilitate colonial rule and influence postcolonial legal institutions at the global level.[45] Indeed, postcolonial legal scholars have pointed out that it is through liberal legalism that other nations' peoples are disciplined "towards liberal modes of self-articulation"[46] or, even worse, rendered into "states of exception" and indefinitely denied conventional liberal legal protections associated with the rule of law.[47]

Postcolonial feminist legal theorist Ratna Kapur captures the essence of this layered dissatisfaction with legal liberalism as a model for equality and dignity when she writes that "the liberal house is burning – it cannot be fixed by a mere lick of paint. The intellectual tradition incorporates arguments not only about freedom and equal worth but also about civilization, cultural backwardness, and racial and religious superiority."[48] Kapur is fiercely sceptical that liberalism is capable of adjusting in any significant way to abide by postcolonial or other alterity concerns.[49] She does not believe liberalism can transcend its customary limits. For her, liberal legal systems are doomed as pathways to just societies.

B. Contesting Liberal Humanism along with Liberal Legalism

Although Kapur and other scholars typically focus only on humans, we can easily see too that liberal legalism is a particularly unwelcoming home for animals. On the surface, liberal legalism's present-day commitment to inclusiveness formally extends to all humans. But the guarantee of equal moral worth really only applies to those humans who can resemble, in sufficient content and form, the classic liberal *humanist* subject at the heart of law: a human who is self-sufficient, independent, and fully rational and who needs no positive assistance from the state to get on in life.[50] Animal law theorists who work in this tradition do not decode the liberal subject as always already a paradigmatic human agent with a privileged mind, body, race, gender, and class status; they merely object to a homogenously imagined human limit to the liberal subject. Herein lies the second problem with liberal approaches to animal law reform: their goal is incomplete, that goal being to eliminate anthropocentrism from the liberal legal order by transforming animals from legal objects in which humans and corporations have rights (property) to legal subjects (persons). Incomplete, for it does not account for the residual anthropocentric imprint and other limits of liberalism for animals (or other types of beings whose bodies and minds are far removed from the liberal subject at liberalism's core) because of the particular meaning of "human" that liberal humanism promotes.

This liberal humanist approach to animal law precludes a full accounting of the origins and dynamics of violence against animals because it conflates anthropocentrism with speciesism without considering that anthropocentrism is actually a construct given shape by a confluence of multiple historical structural exclusions, including racism, colonialism, and sexism. Matthew Calarco defines anthropocentrism as "a set of ideas, structures, and practices aimed at establishing and reproducing the privileged status of those who are deemed to be fully and quintessentially human."[51] Owing to racism, colonialism, sexism, and other entwined structural exclusions, as I discuss in this book, the signifier "human" has traditionally had a very narrow scope. Calarco distinguishes anthropocentrism, with its very narrow meaning of "human," from "speciesism," which he defines as "a prejudice that aims to justify discrimination and exploitation of members of nonhuman species simply because they are members of other species." Calarco contends that it is anthropocentrism, rather than speciesism, that better accounts for the staggering levels of violence that animals experience, adding that only an intersectional perspective can tap into and undo its complicated workings.[52]

Liberal animal law theorists miss this distinction, seeking to point out the law's *speciesism* (and not anthropocentrism *per se*) in denying autonomy, dignity, and equality to animals and to correct it through personhood.[53] Traditional animal law scholarship does consider other social differences, but it is usually to point to parallels between the claims of the animal rights movement and those of other social movements. The women's, anti-slavery, and civil rights movements in the United States are commonly invoked to convey that the animal rights critique of speciesism – as an oppression based on cultivated social understandings of biological difference – shares much with the feminist, abolitionist, and civil rights movements' concerns with sexism and racism.[54] By this analogy, in each case beings are discriminatorily excluded from equal moral worth and full dignity because of their perceived biological status.[55]

These animal law accounts persuasively interrupt long-standing narratives about radical discontinuities between humans and all other creatures and can be intuitively and logically forceful; yet they also assume separate historical trajectories of formation between gender, race, and species. Animal law analyses situated in a liberal humanist worldview do not consider or emphasize that species difference comes into being through other socially constructed differences, nor do they incorporate critical theory to fully decode the human/nonhuman species divide and the anthropocentrism that underpin law.[56] This "silo" approach to social axes of difference is problematic for any analysis committed to an intersectional intellectual worldview, as this book is. Calarco's differentiation between speciesism and anthropocentrism exposes a vital need to understand species and speciesism, as well as the constructs of anthropocentrism, human and animal, as deeply racialized and frequently mediated by other cultural understandings of difference.[57]

This has led some animal law scholars and animal ethics theorists who do not question liberal humanist premises to adopt sameness logics in their personhood projects as an extensionist approach to convincing sceptics that animals should matter.[58] Here, then, is a third problem with liberal approaches in animal law. The gravitational pull of liberal legalism and its liberal humanist ideologies toward sameness rather than difference means that animal advocacy campaigns that strategically privilege "sameness with humans" arguments to bring about personhood create a hierarchy among animals even when the legal advocates behind such campaigns themselves believe that all animals, and not just human-enough ones, should matter. The sameness strategies are justified as a way of "opening the door" for all animals – even those very dissimilar to the paradigmatic human subject at liberalism's core – to enter law's zone of visibility and matter as legal persons.[59] But it seems optimistic to hope this strategy will work since these arguments reinforce human benchmarks and anthropocentric valuations about who can properly be considered a legal subject.[60] Even where animal law scholars emphasize sentience as the capacity that entitles a being to become a legal person – as Francione importantly does – rather than sameness *per se* to humans, it is assumed that personhood can work sufficiently for animals to protect them against instrumental use.[61] But as we know from critical theorists writing about alterity, whether it is through the prominent critical conceptual frames of "bare life," "states of exception," "grievability," or the "subaltern," personhood has not sufficiently protected many vulnerable *human* Others to whom it formally applies today.[62] It would seem that legal arguments in favour of animals must succumb to reinforcing human benchmarks and reinscribing anthropocentrism as a path to achieving a legal status. In the end, this does not bode well for animals.

Critical animal law scholars go beyond such work to excavate the humanism at the heart of legal liberalism and identify it as a form of anthropocentric violence. They do not uncritically celebrate theories of difference – often presented as the corrective to liberalism's flaws.[63] In their view, liberalism is not the main or only culprit in efforts to reconsider animal legal subjectivity. The culprit, instead, is the ingrained liberal humanist valuation of the (paradigmatic) human. As such, critical animal law scholars question legal reform premised on proving animals' sameness to (paradigmatic) humans not just because it eclipses difference *per se* but also because it bolsters anthropocentric benchmarks. They thus contest the liberal legalism and liberal humanism, and the anthropocentrism attending both, that inhabit the law.[64] Feminist legal theorists who write on animal ethics, for example, are wary of law's normalizing and taxonomizing tendencies, which demand conformity to pre-existing androcentric and anthropocentric valuations regarding which lives matter.[65] Instead of requiring that animals conform to human norms, they argue for more animal-centred alternatives when we redraw our moral and legal horizons, calling for legal analyses that would imagine animals in less humanistic terms and would address in contextual rather than universal ways to ethically and legally respond to animal relationality and vulnerability.[66] Rather than degrade relational or affective-inflected responses as part of sound legal decision-making, critical animal legal scholars have sought to respect the affect-laden nature, reasoning, and intentionality of beings in both groups, which liberal legalism and liberal humanism posit as worlds apart.[67]

I say more about problems with personhood in chapter 2. For now, I simply emphasize that critical theorists, in contrast to liberal ones, reject sameness arguments and are more realistic about personhood's limits insofar as they are more circumspect about what the law can deliver through the vehicle of personhood, pointing to law's chronic shortcomings in terms of how it distributes power and creates vulnerabilities.[68] Given the above concerns about liberal legalism and liberal humanism, this book proposes a transformation of animals' legal subjectivity in Canadian and other anthropocentric legal systems by means of critical theories that assail the discourses and legacies of liberal humanism and its expression in law as legal liberalism. I seek to build upon the above-noted emergent critical literature in animal legal circles to address these two matters: how we can alter animals' legal status in law in a way that is most favourable to them; and how we can steer the law's basic tenets toward a less anthropocentric, less humanist, and generally less oppressive outlook.[69] I say "less" in all these instances because the law is still a human and liberal institution. There are pitfalls to pursuing social change for animals through legal reform – I will elaborate on this later on – but even so, I assert that it is possible to proceed with a project, such as this one, to reconceptualize animals' legal subjectivity in a productive, critically oriented manner despite law's foundational liberal and exclusionary premises.[70]

III. Alterity-Based Theoretical Frameworks as the Foundation for Beingness

In this section I introduce and justify the primary theoretical influences I will be drawing upon in discussing the problems with liberalism and its humanism, and also in assessing and reshaping human-animal relationships within anthropocentric legal systems. These influences are feminist animal care theory, postcolonial feminist theory, and critical animal studies.

A. Feminist Animal Care Theory, Ecofeminism, and Linked Oppressions

This book is built on the premise that ideas about animals, humans, animality, and humanity that permeate law's non-response to animals today, as well as human-animal relations in Western societies more broadly, are closely connected to gendered imperial logics and their striations. Among the critical epistemologies that link the oppression of the more-than-human world with the oppression of humans, ecofeminist theory stands out. The following analysis draws closely from this framework, which attends to injustices across species borders. As leading ecofeminist theorists Carol Adams and Lori Gruen have recently described, "ecofeminism addresses the various ways that sexism, heteronormativity, racism, colonialism, and ableism are informed by and support speciesism and how analyzing the ways these forces intersect can produce less violent, more just practices."[71] Erika Cudworth has further stated that "ecofeminism can most simply be defined as a range of perspectives that consider the links between the social organization of gender and the ways in which societies are organized with respect to 'nature.'"[72]

Vegetarian ecofeminism, also called feminist animal care theory, is a multipronged ethic that has been particularly instructive in highlighting the structural discursive similarities and interconnections between sexism and speciesism.[73] Adams propelled this literature forward by coining the term "sex-species" system to describe the intertwined nature of gender and species constructs.[74] She and other feminist animal care theorists have discussed at great length how the "human/nonhuman animal dualism functions in ways that parallel the culture/nature, reason/emotion, and masculine/feminine dualisms"[75] as well as how "speciesism is a form of oppression paralleling and reinforcing other forms of oppression."[76]

Ecofeminist theory (including its vegetarian iteration) gained renown during its formative years in the 1980s but fell out of favour thereafter. While internal conversations within ecofeminism regarding gender essentialism productively took place and "offered a well-grounded corrective to the essentialism of the unitary category 'woman,'"[77] mainstream feminists and non-feminists upbraided ecofeminism for being irremediably essentialist and ethnocentric. These charges were fuelled by distortions and misconceptions about ecofeminism's core principles[78] and generated associations that were difficult to shed.[79] Ecofeminists have since rebutted accusations of essentialism and ethnocentrism by pointing to ecofeminism's long-standing commitment to exploring "multiplicities of domination"[80] and to vegetarian ecofeminism's track record in addressing issues that centrally engage race and class.[81] Greta Gaard has traced the stigmatizing charges of ethnocentrism to mainstream feminists' resistance to vegetarian feminism's critiques about speciesism and concomitant objection to eating animals – critiques that would cause feminists who did not include more-than-human animals in their ethical worldviews to revisit fundamental dietary and other lifestyle choices.[82] Gaard notes that others may be sympathetic to ecofeminism but are worried that ecofeminism's proponents and audience are still largely white and otherwise elite.[83] Indeed, as Sue Donaldson and Will Kymlicka have argued, leftist scholars largely resist embracing anti-speciesism because of the misperception that animal rights is a privileged white issue and that advocating on behalf of animals necessarily endorses ethnocentric, culturally imperialist and/or racist discourses.[84]

This viewpoint glosses over the incredibly rich non-Western traditions in the global South that favour vegetarianism and non-anthropocentric worldviews, as well as the multispecies ethos of many Indigenous cultures in Western settler-colonial states. As Kymlicka and Donaldson have noted, "the idea that the treatment of animals could be invoked to support Western superiority is puzzling, given that the West is responsible for inventing and then diffusing the techniques of industrial-scale animal exploitation, whereas many non-Western societies have historically had more respectful relations with animals."[85] The tendency among leftist scholars to associate more-than-human activism with whiteness, racism, and imperialism is situated within a Western frame. That tendency selectively applies otherwise legitimate concerns about white normativity to social movements that populate the global North – for example, as a reason to exclude more-than-human causes but not anthropocentric ones.[86] The case can be made that *all* social movements in the global North normalize/reinforce whiteness, as well as dominant racial norms, and are racist or ethnocentric, given the ubiquity of whiteness in most of these spaces.

Besides being unfairly maligned on cultural and racial grounds, vegetarian ecofeminism (or feminist animal care theory) has not received sufficient credit even where it has been influential. Susan Fraiman has discussed the tendency among male animal studies scholars to dissociate themselves from "scholarship marked as feminine" and their efforts to position the field "in opposition to emotionally and politically engaged work on gender, race, and sexuality."[87] Here we see not so much a discrediting of the more-than-human focus and challenge to speciesism, but a devaluation of its feminist moorings. In identifying feminist animal care theory as a formative theoretical undercurrent for the analysis that follows in this book, I acknowledge the generative contribution it has made to theorizing the links between multiple oppressions and understanding speciesism and anthropocentrism as indelibly formed by androcentrism and patriarchy. I will be harnessing this theory's insights about linked oppressions, and about care and compassion, to propose a new legal subjectivity for animals that attends to animals' vulnerability, embodiment, and relationality and to suggest how Canadian law can adopt a post-anthropocentric outlook in general.

B. Postcolonial and Other Feminist Thought

However much this book's analysis will owe to the insights of feminist animal care theory and ecofeminism in general, it is necessary to introduce other frameworks. Notwithstanding ecofeminists' multilayered approach and their recognition of the importance of paying attention to multiple hierarchies of power,[88] in theorizing injustice toward the "natural" world, gender retains a primacy that eclipses the impact of other systems, discourses, and narratives in shaping ideas about animality.[89] Ecofeminists in general have not focused on cultural and racial Othering except to suggest shared dualistic premises to oppressions and to note the partiality of Western intellectual traditions vis-à-vis animals.[90] Whether situated as part of ecofeminism or not, only some feminist animal care scholarship – most of it in the humanities – moves beyond gender to consider species difference or that the "human" and the "animal" as social constructions are inflected by gender, class, sexuality, ability, and race.[91]

Thus, this analysis also enlists postcolonial feminism to establish the relevance of race, culture, and imperial ideologies to anthropocentrism and the latter's manifestation in law's foundations and subjectivities.[92] It is instructive to examine the entwined dynamics of cultural, racial, and gendered Othering – this last examination being a signature approach to postcolonial feminism – in order to understand law's anthropocentrism, the limits of personhood as a legal subjectivity for animals, and the promise of beingness in this regard. This book also integrates insights regarding the body, relationality, vulnerability, subjectivity, response ethics, and the law from a range of feminist authors working in critical fields outside of feminist animal care theory to help demonstrate its claims regarding the anthropocentric landscape of law, the imprint this landscape leaves on the category of the legal person, and the benefits for animals of adopting a new legal subjectivity with a specific type of content.

C. Critical Animal Studies, Preventing Exploitation, and Interspecies Power

In integrating feminist animal care theory with postcolonial feminist theory and other critical feminist scholarship, my intention is to develop a new legal subjectivity that can reduce if not end the unbearable forms of violence that many animals experience. That being its goal, this book may be situated in the burgeoning academic-activist field known as "critical animal studies." That field prioritizes an intersectional approach to critically evaluating human-animal power relations, striving to showcase how power circulates across multiple axes of difference in intertwined ways.[93] Within academic animal circles, it is a subset of the better-known fields of posthumanist studies and human-animal studies;[94] it is also a distinct branch of these, in that scholarship under its purview raises the question of the animal with the explicitly politicized purpose of educating others about animal exploitation for the purpose of ending it.[95] Thus, while both posthumanist and human-animal studies engage with animals and animalities, it is critical animal studies that focuses on the exploitative dimensions of animal lives and that presses scholarship to be in the service of social change.[96] Many critical animal scholars are frustrated by posthumanist scholars who vociferously critique liberal humanism and claim to be animal-friendly yet subordinate animal interests to those of humans or endorse animal-use industries.[97] In taking issue with this complicitous iteration of posthumanist intervention, critical animal studies aligns with feminist animal care theory. The latter has long aimed to generate an ethos of non-violence and care for animals rather than simply critique humanism or animal-inflected concepts without any corollary commitment to acknowledge or respond to the material conditions of the violence animals experience.[98]

It is on this point, too, that critical animal studies diverges from the Continental philosophical tradition as it has applied to animals. Within Continental analytical scholarship on animals, the deconstructive work of Jacques Derrida has loomed large.[99] Like critical animal studies scholars, Derrida championed a difference-based approach to revisiting human-animal relations and other human–non-human relations, inviting us to question our anthropocentric precepts and norms and to disavow the binary hierarchical structure that privileges humans over all other beings.[100] His work emphasizes the need to destabilize conventional human-animal relations and to respond to the vulnerable animal Other rendered abject by standard liberal humanist formulations of self and subjectivity; it also demands that critical theory attend to the social construction of the human through animals and animality.[101] The present book is very much influenced by Derridean deconstruction in its analysis of difference across multiple registers and, in particular, in it its ability to distil and discern "anthropocentrism, logocentrism, and phallocentrism in pro-animal discourse and practice"[102] so as to adopt a logic of sameness as opposed to alterity.[103] Yet I hesitate to situate the subsequent chapters more firmly in Derrida's body of work because it consistently turns away from questions of political and legal reform.[104] As Calarco notes, "even on the most charitable reading of Derrida's work, it is difficult to reconstruct anything like a robust account of strategies for developing a more nonanthropocentric politics."[105]

My argument, however, is indebted to Derrida's "animal-friendly reformulation of response ethics"[106] and the concepts of vulnerability, relationality, and responsibility that response ethics prioritizes. My discussion of these concepts, however, in relation to legal reform is meant to reflect a critical animal studies ethos. I take critical animal studies' non-exploitative stance toward animals (and marginalized humans) as an implicit undercurrent of my proposals to fashion a better legal response to animals. All my proposals in this book are aimed at productively theorizing how a change in legal classification for animals from property to what I call beingness, and the enculturation of different foundational norms in law, can cultivate human and corporate responsibility toward animals that can dramatically alter their present, often horrific, conditions of existence.[107]

IV. Liberal Legalism, Animal Sovereignty, and Social Change through Legal Reform

I am mindful in executing this project of Carol Smart's powerful caution against turning to the law for transgressive legal reform. In *Feminism and the Power of Law*,[108] Smart implores legal feminists not to see the law as a cure-all to what precludes full justice and equal citizenship for women. While she sees the debates legal feminists have engaged in over the masculinist nature of law and the sameness/difference debates over how to accommodate the differences women represent rather than penalize them for those differences as important and necessary, she views these concerns as limiting. Smart argues that feminists, by turning so eagerly and optimistically to legal institutions for social change, eclipse the possibility of better activism through other venues – indeed they undermine their own cause when they do so. As Smart says, "put simply, in accepting law's terms in order to challenge law, feminism always concedes too much."[109] She argues that law needs to be decentred from the hegemonic position it enjoys and that clamouring for legal reform will simply reinforce its exalted status.[110] Smart, of course, does not counsel feminists to ignore the law; rather, she calls on them to change their focus and strategy from one of fighting for gains for women through the narrow options that the present terms and conceptualizations of law allow to "the task of deconstructing the discursive power of the law,"[111] for the "law must also be tackled at the conceptual level if feminist discourses are to take a firmer root."[112]

Many of the contributors to Yoriko Otomo and Edward Mussawir's *Law and the Question of the Animal: A Critical Jurisprudence* (one of a handful of animal law texts that take a non-liberal departure point) make a similar argument about the focus and direction of animal law. As earlier remarked, traditional animal law scholarship does not question law's legitimacy in any notable way, and it is this theoretical gap that their collection sets out to redress. Contributors to the volume seriously question whether law as a legal institution and norm-setting body is able to properly subjectivize animals (i.e., in a way that truly respects their alterity and sovereignty from human domination). Accordingly, the volume is deliberately not aimed at developing policy or law reform initiatives, seeing this agenda as too aligned with traditional animal law contributions and their "narrow (i.e., liberal) ideological starting point."[113] Yet they are also sensitive to the reasons why animal law scholarship has focused to date so heavily on reform, given the systemic violence done to animals that law facilitates, and they acknowledge that law reform proposals can be productive. Still, they strive to introduce "an alternative voice … that … engages with law relating to animals and the question of the animal in law at a critical, creative and theoretical nexus."[114]

Indeed, the critique about "conced[ing] too much" and fortifying law's hegemonic position is arguably heightened in the cross-species context. Applied to animals, this critical lens about the imperial imbrications of law elicits reservations about law's ability to deliver animals from their abject status in industrial captivity (slaughterhouses, research labs, etc.).[115] The critical disposition of rule-of-law discourse also creates an awareness within critical animal scholarship of the imperial gestures that the law, no matter how radically reshaped and benevolently intended, can enact vis-à-vis animals.[116] Law, whatever its shortcomings and marginalizing effects on various human groups, is still an institution designed by humans. The extension of law to humans, then, does not seem particularly problematic as long as meaningful assent is given. This, of course, is why the postcolonial dynamics in settler-colonial nations such as Canada are so contentious: the imposition of one nation's law on another without consent is an act of violence that permanently stains not only the legal system but the social fabric as well.[117] When such laws, however "animal-friendly" in design, are extended to animals, they may be properly perceived as violently colonial in nature vis-à-vis animals, whose ancestors were also colonized by colonial human settlers,[118] and they still subject animals to a form of human governance they never assented to or even requested and are responsible for their brutal and fragmented conditions of existence in a violent capitalist order.[119] Worse still, the law is a form of governance that exalts argumentation and debate, both of which are arguably anthropocentric and masculinist and teach us to value our minds, control our emotions, and generally be ashamed or derisive of our bodies and the abjected bodies and experiences of others that we are taught have little if any mind or capacity for debate.[120] Although one of many human institutions, law seems particularly complicitous in valuing the reason and rationality that are at the heart of liberal humanism.

Dinesh Wadiwel alludes to this conundrum when he shifts the focus of human-animal relations in law from a welfare and rights focus to one of sovereignty. For Wadiwel, to examine human sovereignty is to "question the fundamental assumption that humans have a right of domination over non-human animals, and establish sovereignty recognition as a starting point for dialogue between human and non-human animal perspectives."[121] The extension of law to animals, then, is an extension of human sovereignty into animal worlds and thus can be read as an act of domination whatever the benevolent purposes.[122] Victoria Ridler concurs.[123] She seeks to interrupt animal lawyers' attempts to legally subjectivize animals through personhood or another equivalent status by focusing on the absence of consent – so critical to models of political liberalism – on the part of animals to obey a human-made legal order:

> Whether we look to social contract theory, concepts of equality and democracy more generally, or the idea of the emancipatory subject, the non-human animal in every instance remains that which is subjected to law, entrenching the very hierarchy of being we sought to overcome by escaping the *dominium* of the category of property. Through the legal subjectivation of the non-human animal we have replaced *dominium* with *imperium* – the right of rule.[124]

Ridler's critique of law for animals recalls Smart's in relation to legal feminist reform. Both command our close attention in any attempt to engage with law in the hope of producing social change. Yet neither advocates the abandonment of law to obtain a more just society for animals or women. Ridler also concedes that law reform for animals is desirable even where the move proceeds in a manner that fully embraces the law's power to protect animals through an appropriate alternative status.[125] She simply asks for more nuance and reflection from animal law advocates in their engagement with law, which for Ridler signifies a starting point of injustice rather than justice.

This process would not rely on arguments from sameness or start from a principle of justice and then reach out to animals through an extension of legality. An alternative legal status for animals, such as the reimagined relational interspecies beingness model I advance in chapter 4, should thus be acceptable to law's critics as long as it governs relations among those who have accepted it (presumably most humans and corporations) and does not compel animals to do anything or suggest that humans have any rights in animals. Abjuring a sameness ethic, I posit the new legal subjectivity of beingness I develop here as a more responsive and contextual remedy for injustice even if it does subsist in an overall capitalist, imperial, and humanist system.

Relatedly, by suggesting reform of anthropocentric legal systems, I align this project with legal pluralist efforts to decolonize settler-colonial legal systems. Such efforts to shift core liberal legal values inherited from European intellectual and political traditions and secure widespread public recognition of multiple legal orders as constitutive of a nation's constitutional foundations.[126] As indicated above, and as I discuss in later chapters, to contest the anthropocentrism of the law is also to contest its imperial origins and its degradation of Indigenous epistemologies.[127] In terms of how civilizational backwardness hinged heavily on how societies treated animals, wherein a respect for animals and a refusal to objectify them was an indication of civilizational inferiority, and in terms of how European farming practices deployed animals to settle colonized land, colonial violence is also anthropocentric violence.[128]

Some theorists who lament the anthropocentric worldview of such societies and the toxic human–non-human relations it produces may nonetheless view an engagement with settler-colonial law, even for the purposes of reform, as seriously misguided. For example, Indigenous "resurgence" theorists in Canada worry about the continued colonizing and domesticating effects of state law and frameworks on efforts to revitalize Indigenous legal orders and to press forward for self-determination.[129] As Michael Elliott has described, "for proponents of resurgence, continued attempts to resist and transform the settler-colonial order from within – through the channels, arenas and discourses it makes available – can neither ensure Indigenous survival nor realize genuine progress towards decolonization and might in fact prove counterproductive on both counts."[130]

The present analysis may thus find more support from Indigenous "reconciliation" theorists who are also committed to revitalizing Indigenous legal traditions, and to creating sovereign Indigenous societies, but also desirous of engaging with present colonial orders for the purposes of decolonizing the worldviews expressed by present systems, such as the common law legal system. As a law-based example of this, Indigenous and feminist legal scholars have called for the teaching of Indigenous legal traditions in Canadian law schools despite the "risks of engaging with Indigenous laws in state or non-Indigenous environments."[131]

I raise this divergence in positions between resurgence and reconciliation theorists in Indigenous legal and political scholarship in order to recognize a further, postcolonial layer in the critical scholarship that debates the value of engaging with the dominant and colonial legal order and also to further explain my reasons for such engagement in the context of critical animal law. A real risk exists that if Canadian law ever recognizes animals as legal subjects, it will still covertly advance human exceptionalist norms and premises that subordinate animals. However, the consequences of not engaging with the law are too great for animals. For them to continue as legal objects subject to complete commodification and immense levels of pain, violence, and trauma in multiple animal-industrial complexes (agriculture, aquaculture, research, entertainment, the military, etc.) is not an acceptable option.[132] Animal cultures and communities cannot survive, resurge, and thrive until humans and corporations stop exploiting and subordinating them. For this to happen, Canadian law must assign a non-anthropocentric, non-instrumental legal subjectivity to animals; engagement with the law is thus critical.

In making this parallel, I am mindful of the critique that a new legal subjectivity for animals, as much as it is meant to disrupt colonial understandings and treatment of animals, might also impinge on Indigenous cultural practices and legal orders that view animals more relationally and that already contest anthropocentrism even while condoning the killing of animals or treating them as resources. Would a new legal subjectivity have the collateral effect of undermining Indigenous rights, laws, or sovereignty? There are no simple resolutions to this question, and the literature emerging on this point, including some of my own, provides a variety of answers.[133] The intricacies of this important question demand a stand-alone monograph, which is a main reason why I do not address the question further in the present book. This project focuses on why a new legal subjectivity other than property or person-hood is needed for animals in dominant legal orders and what it should look like.

V. Otherness, Alterity, and Improved Interspecies Relations

While the concept of the Other emerged out of postcolonial analy-ses and so is more associated with theory focused on West/non-West power relations,[134] it has also permeated a range of critical theory to cast a lens on relations of oppression and domination along other axes. This book takes animals' Otherness as a given, seeking to understand and remedy the ways in which the law creates animals as Others. It is motivated by a desire for the law to value animals not as human-ity's Others but as beings of value that can exist outside of instrumental relationships with humans and other legal persons and be protected against instrumentalization and commodification. Simply put, it is our negative understanding of the Otherness of animals, borne out of and sustained through gendered imperial narratives and other binary log-ics, that I wish to unsettle so as to eventually place animals in "coeval engagement" with humans, so that their alterity is viewed as merely different rather than inferior.[135] At the same time, I seek to affirm the always already nature of our relational imbrication with animals in rei-magining legal interspecies relations.

In drawing from theories of both alterity and relationality, my approach is a blend of two of the three different modalities by which animal theorists and activists advance their arguments and cam-paigns.[136] The first are those that proceed through what I earlier called a logic of sameness and what Matthew Calarco terms identity-based arguments, that is, those arguments that seek to convince others that certain animals share what are presumed to be typical human traits and thus deserve equivalent ethical and legal protection.[137] The second advocacy modality, according to Calarco, champions difference and is thus classified as a difference-based model.[138] Advocates in this group resist assimilationist logic. Instead, they seek to expose the anthropo-centrism of Western intellectual traditions by deconstructing the pur-ported differences established within these traditions that prop up the human-animal boundary on the one hand, and by affirming the wide spectrum of differences both animal and human groups exhibit on the other.[139] Difference-based theorizations seek to destabilize conventional understanding of why humans are exceptional and animals are not.[140]

Calarco discusses the benefits and shortcomings of these first two modalities, which he says have dominated advocacy efforts.[141] The criticisms he presents of the identity-based model overlap with what I have argued in relation to sameness logic.[142] His chief criticism of the difference-based approach, of which he takes Derrida's deconstructive work on animals as the most influential theoretical iteration, is its disinclination to articulate a concrete proposal for reform of any kind. The value in the work instead lies in its ability to illuminate inconsistencies, contradictions, fissures, and pressure points in the hegemonic stories told about the sharp divide between humans and animals, which can then be applied to inform concrete reform efforts.[143] Of course, as Calarco further notes, the difference-based approach can also help reveal "lingering forms of anthropocentrism, logocentrism, and phallocentrism in proanimal discourse and practice" that follow the identity-based sameness approach.[144]

Calarco presents the third model, which he terms an "indistinction" approach, not as a corrective to the shortcomings of the first two but as encapsulating an emergent and eclectic array of initiatives that provide an opportunity to think and move more innovatively through the project of reconfiguring interspecies relations.[145] Initiatives housed under the indistinction approach do not pursue sameness logic; nor, as Calarco argues Derridean difference-based theories are wont to do, do they "underscore endlessly the reductionism of traditional discourse on the difference between humans and animals."[146] Instead they offer us opportunities to expand our repertoire as we engage with non-humans "along lines that enable alternative modes of living, relating, and being with others of all sorts [human and non-human] ... The other approaches are left behind, or rather are placed temporarily to the side, in order to find out what else might be done in terms of establishing forms of resistance and living differently."[147] As such, Calarco would like to see indistinction approaches that consider new post-anthropocentric ontologies receive more sustained attention by all types of animal advocates.[148]

I suggest that the new legal subjectivity of beingness that I propose for animals as a replacement for their current property classification qualifies as such an indistinction initiative. My arguments as to how law plunges animals into a legal abyss through their property status and why a legal subjectivity other than personhood is needed to ensure for animals a non-exploited status in the social and cultural order are clearly situated in the difference-based approach. But my arguments also overlap with the "indistinction" approach insofar as a relational shift in legal culture that cultivates human and corporate responsibility toward animals is meant to complement beingness as a new legal subjectivity for animals. A chief contribution I see of the present work is that it does not merely expose the anthropocentric workings of the law and how it creates animals as Other, but also (1) theorizes a new subjectivity for animals in law that is conceptually shaped by features emblematic of the more-than-human world (and relevant to humans as well), namely, vulnerability, embodiment, and relationality; and (2) encourages an orientation in law that affirms the deeply relational interspecies nature of our lives and the ethical responses the law should reflect to honour these relations. I say much more about this new subjectivity and the larger relational shift toward responsibility in chapters 3 and 4. I raise this contribution of the work at this point in order to explain how I see my work fitting into the typology Calarco has identified and, particularly, how I see it being responsive to his primary criticism of difference-based approaches.

VI. Drawing Lines and Establishing Connections

This book draws a line in terms of subject matter to the extent that it focuses on animals. It does not, however, draw sharp lines as to what types of beings should matter morally. I say this to pre-empt what is in my experience the common question when animal issues are raised: "What about plants?"[149] The focus on animals should not be read as excluding those beings positioned even lower in the evolutionary hierarchy such as plants and bacteria; nor is it meant to dismiss the possibility that humans owe ethical obligations to inanimate yet relational robots. Indeed, many of the continuities I identify between animal subordination and human subordination would apply to the marginalization of other non-human beings. What is more, cultural narratives about multiple kinds of difference, including those relating to animals and animality, influence how we treat non-animal, non-human beings.[150] The matter of what injustice looks like in relation to these beings is no doubt complex (as it is for humans and animals), and I do not fully address it here.[151] Again, this is not because these questions fall outside "the animal question" or are unimportant. This book addresses the cultural and legal marginalization of more-than-human animals because that is its focus. Nothing that follows in these pages is meant to establish another type of demeaning or subordinating hierarchy. To the contrary, this book calls attention to the line-drawing within animal law and animal studies between different animals and between animals and other non-humans in order to point out the problems with such practices and to consider why types of distinctions surrounding capacities (sentience, animacy, non-conscious response) might be permissible.

Although this book does not aspire to draw lines, it does draw connections to intra-human hierarchies, a move some may find even more problematic. I do not have in mind here the expected anthropocentric response that disavows such comparisons due to human exceptionalist views.[152] Instead, I anticipate that critical scholars open to questioning anthropocentric traditions may nonetheless worry that establishing connections between marginalized groups (animal or human) may be executed in a reductive manner that eclipses the seriousness, history, or uniqueness of an issue.[153] Drawing analogies to highlight a presently more invisible or obscure form of injustice is a popular and pragmatic move not just in animal rights campaigns and animal law and ethics literature, but also in social justice literature in general.[154] Notably, feminist work routinely considers race and sex analogously in order to illuminate the extent of patriarchy and heterosexism.[155] Postcolonial and critical race feminists, however, have noted the potential pitfalls to doing so even where intentions are fully on side not to eclipse the experience of one group when relating it to another.

For example, Malini Johar Schueller identifies the problematic use of analogies between race and gender theorizing in the work of prominent white Western feminist scholars. She discusses the influential boundary-crossing work of Donna Haraway, one of animal and feminist studies' most influential theorists (though not a feminist animal care scholar), as well as Gayle Rubin's and Judith Butler's genre-defining work on sexuality and heteronormativity. In both cases Schueller discusses a dynamic in which race is brought in primarily to illustrate the workings of sexual oppression – a move that makes the racial dynamics the little sister to the gender and sexuality ones – although all three theorists purport to be discussing problems relevant to all women, not just white women.[156] Schueller is also concerned that their influential essays presume that the social axes of race, gender, and sexuality have more in common than not and that they sublimate significant components of racism and racialization as means to highlight gender/sexuality injustice.[157] She argues that "racial analogy in white feminist/gender/sexuality studies functions as a colonial fetish that enables the (white) theorist to displace the potentially disruptive contradictions of racial difference onto a safer and more palatable notion of similarity"[158] and as such, that it "helps whiteness retain its privilege by being uninterrogated."[159]

If media accounts are a reliable gauge, I anticipate that a similar set of concerns may arise here for the anti-racist postcolonial/decolonial/anti-colonial feminist reader. J.M. Coetzee, two-time Booker-winning novelist, has drawn heavy critique for several high-profile animal-human comparisons he has made in his writings, which connect systemic violence against animals with the Jewish Holocaust and South African apartheid.[160] Prominent animal rights campaigns by People for the Ethical Treatment of Animals (PETA) that have compared factory farming to the Holocaust and animal captivity in zoos and circuses to slavery have also attracted outrage.[161] Indeed, PETA's strategically generated litigation that challenged (unsuccessfully) the captivity of five whales at SeaWorld on the basis of the Thirteenth Amendment that abolished slavery in the United States drew the ire of some prominent African-American groups.[162] Even critically staged art exhibits *against* colonialism and racism have generated controversies for merging Black bodies with animal signifiers to provoke contemplation of the animalization at the root of the colonial mission and contemporary forms of violence against humans and animals both.[163]

Comparing animal and human suffering to incite human empathy and action for animals is nothing new. Anna Sewell's 1877 novel *Black Beauty* is perhaps the earliest still-famous fictional story that adopts the slave narrative genre to allow Black Beauty to narrate his own experience of suffering and thus comment on the violent condition of animals more generally.[164] Of more recent vintage is celebrated Black American novelist Alice Walker's short story, "Am I Blue?," which suggests to the reader that the complete obliteration of the relationships and kin networks that animals have by animals' ongoing commodification and sale today is equivalent to what African-Americans experienced as slaves.[165] Again, disavowal of these "dreaded comparisons"[166] is a response to the "dehumanizing" association of marginalized human groups with even more abject non-human animals. Such a perspective is both reflected in and distorted by an anthropocentric mindset that presumes that animals are unequal and thus generates the "dehumanizing" reaction.[167] The response is simple to apprehend. As John Miller notes in objecting to the slave analogy in this context: "The topic is 'dreaded' because slavery's dehumanization of millions of Africans surely necessitates a vigorous restatement of human status rather than its apparent, continuing erosion through association with the suffering of animals."[168]

Yet the contextual unpalatability of the association should not erase the legitimacy of careful comparisons and multifocal analyses that affirm the ongoing and systemic nature of racism while trying to highlight animals' plight as they endure unrelentingly atrocious conditions of living and dying that most humans ignore or deny, and expose the shared animalizing narratives that sustain violence across species lines.[169] We should be mindful that this resistance to comparisons with animals is the symptom that anti-exploitative animal theories and activism are trying to address. We should also consider that controversies over comparisons "may be yet another instance of deflection, another instance of the refusal to see or care about ... the animals [that] continue to suffer the cruelty and indifference of the vast majority of their human animal kin."[170]

Moreover, it is not at all clear that Miller's conclusion that humanization is the corrective for dehumanization is accurate. Critical theorists who resist thinking about animals as ethically important or who object to cross-species connections or associations no matter how nuanced, particularly in relation to race and racism, must confront the prospect that the concepts of "the human" and "human rights" are not innocent categories. Indeed, such categories generate "axes of inequality, violence, and biological essentialism" that are damaging to non-humans, certainly, but also to racialized and otherwise marginalized humans.[171] As more and more social psychological studies about the nature of human prejudice have shown, drawing a sharp line between humans and animals in our moral compasses *increases* prejudice and dehumanization against racialized peoples, women, and other marginalized groups.[172] Dubbed the "interspecies model of prejudice," studies in this growing literature indicate that teaching children to rank humans over animals builds racist views and that teaching them instead about continuities between humans and animals builds more empathy for marginalized human groups.[173]

Of course, we should be mindful that analogies and parallels not become "strategies of equivalence" that eclipse and misguide or, even worse, are superficial, overstretched, or opportunistic in either direction.[174] This issue seems particularly accentuated given the real and imagined whiteness of those who take up animal issues in North America as academics and advocates.[175] And we also need to attend to how laws, norms, and discourses protecting certain animals in certain contexts are mobilized to exacerbate intra-human hierarchies and promote violence against marginalized human groups.[176] The analysis in this book tries to keep both these concerns in view without losing sight of the violence that animals experience or otherwise privileging human animals over non-human animals.[177] It thus takes seriously the "interspecies model of prejudice," on the basis that we cannot hope to make headway on structural exclusions and oppressive norms and attitudes against dehumanized humans without also contesting human exceptionalism and anthropocentrism. This book explores the deep entanglements among multiple axes of difference rather than positing simple analogies or equivalencies among them.[178] Following my earlier body of work as well as other scholarly interventions in this conundrum of representation through comparison,[179] this book presumes that there are synergistic continuities, overlays, and co-emergences between the ideologies that sustain animal subordination and those that sustain various forms of human oppression.[180] I also discuss the importance of ideologies surrounding species to understandings of race, gender, and culture and the hierarchies they sustain, emphasizing the co-constitutive nature of these differences, which for so long have been commonly imagined as discrete, and the myriad ways they inflect one another. This approach very much models the multifocal theorization that postcolonial feminists such as Anne McClintock and Eve Darian-Smith have charted in their influential work,[181] the major difference in my project being the attention I pay to race, gender, and culture in relation to species and animality.

The argument here thus aligns with Megan H. Glick's recent proposal surrounding the "infrahuman," a term she offers to conceptualize the mutually iterative process by which race and racism, and species and speciesism, emerge from American historical scientific, popular cultural, and political discourses.[182] It also joins with other critical scholarly works on race and species that call for a "multidimensional" and "multi-optic" analysis that can uncover how the tropes of human, humanity, animal, and animality, and the human-animal divide in general, are foundational to racism and how race is encoded into anthropocentrism.[183] In a similar vein, just as postcolonial feminists believe that feminist reform today would be "unthinkable without a critical awareness of the co-constitutive nature of race and gender,"[184] this book suggests why it is also impossible to understand feminist, anti-racist, or postcolonial critiques of the law and injustice without interrogating forces of animalization and species differentiation. The relational basis for the law reform the last part of this book addresses incorporates this amplified focus.[185] I do not pretend that the analysis will do full justice to all nodes of difference at all times; intersectionality as a methodology has difficulty living up to the full extent of what the theory implies, and inserting animals and animality into a framework and overall humanist academic arena makes attempts to do so even more challenging.[186] But as I write against the presumption that species ideologies are uninformed by other ideologies of difference, and that the legal and corresponding material abyss into which billions of animals are placed is an isolated social phenomenon that has no impact on other iterations of violence, I can ensure that the analysis does much more than reason by analogy. That is how this work differs from traditional liberal animal law accounts that advert to race and gender oppression.

VII. Terminology and More-than-Human Animals

Somewhat related to Calarco's concerns about indistinction approaches versus difference-based ones are questions of terminology. While this book is shaped by theoretical influences that eschew binaries as well as by essentialized understandings of terms within those binaries, it invariably employs terms constitutive of those binaries – for example, West and Western, and non-West and non-Western, as well as self, Other, and Otherness. One reason it does so is that critique about colonial hierarchies simply cannot proceed without using the categories under dispute that established these hierarchies and moved them intelligibly forward.[187] I use concepts such as the West, non-Western, and the Other to generalize for the sake of critique and not to eliminate the heterogeneity, fluidity, or fragmentation within these categories. Yet, following Farah Godrej's additional defence of these terms for her project challenging the Eurocentrism of cosmopolitan political theory, I also want to "insist that the history of domination and exclusion in global politics and in knowledge-production makes it important for us to rely on the West/non-West distinction" as well as the trope of Otherness to which it gives rise.[188]

Perhaps, however, objection will surface most actively in relation to the terms used to discuss the book's main objects/subjects. It is difficult to know how, as humans, we should refer to those beings caught under the human (English) signifier "animal." As a baseline, when I say "animal," I am referencing the dizzying array of life forms that comprise the biological kingdom Animalia, including vertebrates and invertebrates, as well as those animals, except the human, that most of us do not think of as animals, such as insects but also sea creatures such as sponges, corals, and anemones. But it is precisely in dropping the qualifier "non-human" that an author misses the opportunity to subvert the cultural denial – what Frans de Waal has called "anthropodenial"[189] – that humans are also animals, taking science as our authority; instead, we perpetuate the culturally entrenched view that "we" are different from "them."[190] Referring to any non-human as an "animal" sublimates the incredible diversity among animals by applying a category that purports to encapsulate them all at once. Recalling feminist anti-essentialist debates about the signifier "women," the term "animal" suggests that animals such as jellyfish and elephants have more in common with themselves than either of them do with humans. The term fuels harmful myths about human uniqueness and exceptionalism that most animal theorists wish to dispel as well as the impression that the concept contains an internal coherence when humans are excluded from it.[191]

More worrying still, as Erica Fudge notes, the word "animal" enacts a type of epistemic violence against animals, thus reducing them to a presumed unity and shared identity.[192] This epistemic violence has material implications. As some scholars seeking to account for the tremendous violence suffusing animals' lives have argued, "the use of the word 'animal' or 'the animal' to refer to any and all living creatures is a conceptual violence that expeditiously legitimates our actual violence."[193] Adopting this perspective, the use of the term can never be benign because "it is the foundation, if not the origin, of all practices of Othering – of claiming and justifying, first, human exceptionalism and, then, of claiming the superiority of particular groups who are seen as belonging legitimately in the category of 'human.'"[194] "Animal" effects a symbolic animalization that scaffolds all the violence to follow.

We cannot escape this problem by simply adding a qualification. There are also pitfalls to keeping the "non-human" modifier by using the term "non-human animal." Just as feminists and queer theorists have encountered their own definitional issues with the terms "women" and "non-heterosexual," the term "non-human" reinforces the dominance of the signifier this book seeks to legally displace. Others have thus turned to the terms "more-than-human" animals (as I have used above in several places) and "other-than-human" animals, terms united by the hope that they can help decentre the human subject. Some, however, reject terms using "non" or "other" because of the binary problematic they entrench.[195] I appreciate Lisa Kemmerer's term "anymal" for its ability to create teachable moments about our impoverished language around animals and the human exceptionalism it yields.[196] As Kemmerer herself acknowledges, however, the term retains a dualistic logic. Finally, many scholars still employ the term "animal" the way I do in this book – as convenient and intentionally neutral shorthand – though I occasionally refer to those scholars' use of "more-than-human" or "other-than-human" to recall for the reader their theoretical commitments.[197]

I do not have another signifier to propose that will circumvent the ethical and imperial quagmire that the question of signifier and signified brings forth when humans like myself talk and write about animals. I do wish, however, to acknowledge before moving forward that through my use of the word "animal," I am reinforcing linguistic conventions that create conceptual and epistemic violence that enables actual violence against animals. I see no way to avoid this paradox, given that my intention in writing this book is to theorize a new and implementable legal subjectivity that will end human and corporate violence against animals. In this work, I will move between referring to animals as "more-than-human animals" and just plain "animals," using the latter term more often for the sake of brevity.

VIII. How This Book Unfolds

Part I is titled *Beyond Property and Personhood: Contesting Legal Objectification and Humanization*. It traces the abject rendering of animal subjectivity in contemporary Canadian jurisprudence. Chapter 1, "No Escape: Anti-cruelty Laws' Property Foundations," explains the non-subjectivity of animals in the law as a whole due to their legal status as property and reveals the extent to which this status renders animals invisible in law even where animal interests are purportedly paramount or, at least, elevated above routine commodification. Put differently, this chapter lays bare the common law's legal erasure of animals through their commodification as objects, even in those doctrinal spaces where a different standard might be expected, namely, in the realm of anti-cruelty statutes. Chapter 2, "What's Wrong with Personhood? The Humanizing Impact of *Anthropos*," considers law reform campaigns promoting personhood that animal advocates have initiated to challenge the typical legal stance toward animals. Primarily, it considers the effectiveness of personhood as an alternative way for law to relate to animals and concludes that it is a reductive category for animals and is too tethered to anthropocentric constraints. Chapter 2 further argues that a reconceptualization of personhood will not separate it from its more objectionable iterations to the extent that personhood as a legal status for animals cannot be compatible with feminist, postcolonial, and critical animal studies' analytics as to why animals should matter in the first place. I focus here on the debate within critical theory as to the reductive nature of liberal legal concepts even when placed in the service of emancipatory ends, articulating why law's understanding of personhood cannot be meaningfully extended to animals. Chapter 3, "Toward a Post-Anthropocentric Legal Ontology," considers the additional legal cultural shifts that are required beyond implementing a new and more animal-centred legal subjectivity for a legal order in general to become more animal-friendly and multispecies-oriented. Chapter 3 engages with broader feminist and other critical calls to ethically and productively engage with the suffering (and joys) of animal Others. This layered analysis sets up the discussion for part II, which contemplates a new type of law reform in relation to animals – one that rejects personhood.

Part II, on *Animals as Beings: In Pursuit of a New Post-Anthropocentric Legal Order*, proposes a new legal status for animals in Canadian law: beingness. Chapter 4, "Beingness: A New Legal Subjectivity for Animals," charts the features of an alternative legal subjectivity for animals that can help generate a post-anthropocentric legal order. Beingness as a new legal subjectivity is meant to carry the same high level of protection for animals that personhood is intended to provide by the latter's proponents, but without personhood's anthropocentric limits. It is thus proffered as a transgressive category, and I outline its immersion in feminist understandings of embodiment, vulnerability, and relationality (particularly relational and response ethics theorizations). In chapter 5, "Liberal Humanism Repackaged?," I consider the limits of beingness as a model, exploring various anticipated objections coalescing on the point that beingness is also tainted by anthropocentrism and liberalism and thus shares some of personhood's defects so that it does not actually provide a satisfactory alternative for animals. The final chapter concludes this book by providing a roadmap with examples outlining the preliminary legal action that would need to occur for anthropocentric legal systems to switch to a beingness model.

I hope that the reader will emerge from this analysis with a deep and sustainable sense of why animals matter to critical pursuits of justice, whether activated within or outside the legal arena, as well as how the law can better attend to the vulnerabilities, embodiment, and relationality of all animals. Also, where we might be quick to imagine conflict between animals and humans in claims of justice, this book invites readers to consider the synergy and even harmony across justice claims. As its signal contribution, it maps out a legal status that aims to be respectful of animal alterity and responsive to animal subordination, but without exacerbating intra-human hierarchies, promoting human benchmarks, or denying interspecies relating. The hoped-for result is not simply the critical enrichment of animal law, but the promotion of a new legal subjectivity for animals that is viable and intelligible to the current dominant legal imagination and that has the potential to stop the systemic anthropogenic violence and routine brutalities and traumas that the vast majority of animals presently endure.

PART I

Beyond Property and Personhood: Contesting Legal Objectification and Humanization

1 No Escape: Anti-cruelty Laws' Property Foundations

The animals should be healthy, comfortable, well nourished, safe, able to express innate behavior without pain, fear and distress. They are entitled to justice. The animals cannot be treated as objects or property.[1]

Karnail Singh and others v State of Haryana, India,
2019, per Justice Rajiv Sharma, para 93

The law treats animals as property even where we would expect otherwise. Although the cultural understanding of animals as property resonates unevenly given human emotional attachment to "companion" animals and our reverent awe of certain "wild" animals, the law categorizes these and other animals as property.[2] It is a general principle of property law that domesticated animals are the private property of their human or corporate owners and that all other animals, whether defined as stray, feral, abandoned, or wild, are amenable to propertization once properly "possessed" according to laws of possession; owners thus have a "bundle" of rights in animal bodies.[3] Reviewing the ways in which the law assumes the property status of animals would be an exercise without end, for the property status of animals is ubiquitous. There are numerous provincial and federal statutes in Canada alone, not to mention subordinate legislation such as underlying regulations and municipal codes, that govern the human use of animals as property.[4]

This chapter takes one context – anti-cruelty law as a subset of criminal law – as illustrative of the law's dismal treatment of animals due to animals' categorization as property. What Canada's *Criminal Code* has to say about animals is particularly instructive, since the *Code* is the repository not only of mundane categorizations of animals as property but also, critically, of federal *anti-cruelty* laws. It is commonly assumed that anti-cruelty laws protect animals from harm and focus on animals' interests as sentient beings rather than on their status as property. This chapter questions that assumption by exposing the devastating impact that animals' status as property has on the protections they receive under anti-cruelty laws. The analysis draws upon Gary Francione's influential theory of legal welfarism to explain the severe anthropocentric shortcomings of the law's understanding of the concept of cruelty when it applies to animals.[5] Canadian criminal law is analysed here as a case study of a larger symptom in anthropocentric legal systems whereby the institutionalized exploitation of animals is perceived as legitimate violence or as not violence at all. Throughout, the analysis contributes to animal law scholarship critical of the welfarist logic of anti-cruelty legislation by elucidating the racialized aspects and imperial origins of legal welfarism's anthropocentrism and their particular dynamics in the Canadian legal system.

I. The *Criminal Code*'s Overall Instrumentalist View of Animals

In general, the *Code* repeatedly confirms the property status of animals. It explicitly declares their property status by housing most animal-related crimes under parts of the *Code* that pertain to property rights, namely, Part IX: Offences Against Rights of Property, and Part XI: Wilful and Forbidden Acts in Respect of Certain Property.[6] In Part IX, references to property interests in animals are found in subsection 322(5) (theft of a wild animal in captivity) and section 338 (fraudulently taking cattle or defacing brand of ownership). Subsection 322(5) permits the captor of a wild animal to claim a property interest in it.[7] Section 338 deals with acts to steal or fraudulently assert a property interest in cattle "found astray" without the consent of the owner, either by physically taking, concealing, or trading the cattle or by tampering with the brand of the cattle – an indication of ownership.[8] The harm perpetrated by the committed offences is understood primarily as injury not to the animal's well-being but to the human owner's property right.[9] The lives of animals are held to be devoid of intrinsic value and instead are assigned a market value based on their alienability. Their propertied being is an emblem of domination branded, sometimes literally, on them.

Under Part XI, which makes clear by its title that the offences at issue are property ones, we find much the same thing in long-standing sections 444 (injuring or endangering cattle, recently repealed)[10] and 445 (injuring or endangering other animals, recently amended to incorporate section 444).[11] Before sections 444 and 445 were melded into one, the former prohibited the killing or injuring (including poisoning) of cattle; the latter prohibited the same acts with respect to "dogs, birds or animals that are not cattle and are kept for a lawful purpose."[12] The distinction between cattle and other animals was not arbitrary but betrays these provisions' purpose, which is to secure property rights rather than attend to animals' interests or needs. When one traces the legislative history of these offences, the possible penalties for injuring cattle were highest. Cattle were economically more important vis-à-vis other animals, and thus offences interfering with owners' property rights against these animals were more seriously addressed.[13] Although the disparity in the penalties has now been levelled for the current amalgamated version of these offences, and the *Code* now includes a new offence specifically directed at the killing or wounding of on-duty "law enforcement" or "military" animals or "service" animals at any time,[14] they are still presently understood as violations of property rights and not as violations of the right of animals.[15]

Furthermore, as even a cursory review of case law attests, these offences are explicitly declared to be crimes against the animals' owners and not against the animals themselves. For example, many cases under then-existing section 444 involved accused persons who killed or castrated wandering male animals to protect their economic interest in the breeding of their female animals. They either are acquitted for taking proper and reasonable responses to protect their (female) property/ animal (as is their property right)[16] or are convicted for failing to take a reasonable alternative, such as impounding the animal, which would have saved the other person's (male) property/animal.[17]

II. Implicit Property Categorizations

At first glance, it seems that the *Code's* main anti-cruelty provision (s.445.1) is a reprieve for animals. But on closer examination it becomes transparent that the general prohibition against animal cruelty also affirms animals' property status. What is more, the doctrinal interpretation of the provision erases animals' interests from legal assessments of what constitutes "cruelty." This instrumentalism may seem discordant, for anti-cruelty legislation is the one area of law where one would expect to find the greatest protection for animals in spite of their property status.[18] But the provision is interpreted through an anthropocentric filter. This Part details how animals' legal classification as property inhibits any meaningful consideration of their interests in anti-cruelty jurisprudence when socially acceptable human uses of animals are at stake. The analysis unpacks the common law understanding of "cruelty," which is a term the *Code* does not define. It reveals the anthropocentric content ascribed to it through judicial interpretation that permits virtually all culturally dominant and economically directed human use of animals

no matter the suffering involved as long as normative cultural or industry means are used. In this Part, I focus on the anthropocentric foundations of anti-cruelty legislation and the implicit classification of animals
as property on which these statutes rely.

A. A Skewed Balance: Legal Welfarism and Anti-cruelty Law

In *Animals, Property, and the Law*, Gary Francione carefully analyses how
the property status of animals in the United States grossly attenuates the
impact of anti-cruelty legislation that is meant to protect animals from
"unnecessary suffering," a concept on which such statutes typically turn.[19]
After surveying anti-cruelty statutes in all fifty American states, Francione
argues that American law, even when it allegedly ascribes ethical consideration to animals via anti-cruelty legislation, will privilege all but the
most trivial human interests over any animal interest, regardless of the
life-and-death import of the animal interest.[20] The animal's suffering thus
becomes "necessary" under this anthropocentric framework. Francione
refers to "the current regulatory structure"[21] in America "as it pertains to
animals as *legal welfarism*, or the notion, represented by and in various
legal doctrines, that animals, which are the property of people, may be
treated solely as means to ends by humans as long as this exploitation
does not result in the infliction of 'unnecessary' pain, suffering, or death."[22]

Francione carefully details how legal welfarism "permits any animal
exploitation that is not wholly gratuitous."[23] He acknowledges that
judges who interpret anti-cruelty laws in light of unnecessary suffering
do in fact take into account animal interests when deciding what constitutes cruelty and unnecessary suffering. He argues, however, that this
weighing of interests is heavily skewed in favour of humans because
American courts begin from the premise that humans are persons and
animals are their property. Furthermore, maximizing the value of property for the proprietary right-holder is an ideal to be safeguarded.[24] Animal interests as other than the private property of a human, a corporation, or the state are unrecognized by the courts.[25]

The legal ideology of instrumentalism saturates anti-cruelty jurisprudence to the extent that actions will only be characterized as cruel
if they do not serve any socially legitimate human end.[26] Conversely,
actions are considered illegitimate that cannot be reasonably said to
serve any human desire at all or when they impair the normative economic exploitation of animals. Hence:

> legal welfarism interprets "cruelty" to refer to animal use that, for the most
> part, fails to facilitate, and may even frustrate, that animal exploitation.

For example, we tolerate practices in animal agriculture, such as castration and branding without any pain relief, and we do not label these practices "cruel," because they facilitate our institutional use of animals for food. We do not, however, permit farmers to starve these castrated and branded animals to death merely because the farmer does not wish to be bothered to feed the animals. The difference in treatment is not attributable to any differences in the *quality* of treatment. Rather, castration and branding are regarded (by those who own animals used for food) as "necessary" and are, as a result, permitted by the legal system, whereas allowing animals to starve for no reason other than neglect does not facilitate the exploitation of the animals for food or any other purpose.[27]

Francione's theory explains how the legal and popular support of current social institutions of animal exploitation and the staggering rates of violence against animals are completely consistent with anti-cruelty statutes. Despite the horrors to which animals are subjected, animal suffering is virtually non-existent in legal terms.

The historical backdrop to these statutes sheds light on their grave limitations. Although anti-cruelty statutes were viewed as championing animals' welfare over and above owners' property rights – in contrast to the similar malicious mischief offences, which applied only to another's inanimate property[28] – anti-cruelty statutes remain deeply informed by animals' property status.[29] Notwithstanding the purported concern for them, animals are viewed instrumentally because the underlying rationale behind anti-cruelty offences is to avoid the degrading effect that cruelty to animals would have on human moral development, which is an anthropocentric as well as imperial concern.[30] Historically, we find that the crime of "cruelty to animals" was never meant to target the normalized practices of human ab/use of animals. As I've discussed elsewhere, these laws developed amid a climate of British empire-building wherein it became important for Europeans to signal civilizational status and superiority vis-à-vis other nations and peoples through certain metrics. Exhibiting kindness to animals (which were nevertheless, according to Judeo-Christian tenets, properly subject to human dominion) was a principal metric of appropriate/civilized character.[31] Another key metric was how societies were perceived to treat women.[32] Thus it is fair to characterize these laws as primarily motivated by imperial civilizational ideologies that stratified peoples abroad but also "at home" along gender, race, and class lines. Without impugning the passion that individual advocates may have had for improving animals' lives, a critique of anthropocentrism, speciesism, or the instrumental individual or institutional use and ownership of animals was never the purpose of anti-cruelty laws.[33] This background helps illuminate the compelling nature of Francione's critique that anti-cruelty legislation is anthropocentric in purpose and design and thus welfarist in nature. It also helps uncover the imperial nature of legal anthropocentrism.

B. *Legal Welfarism in Canadian Anti-cruelty Law*

What about Canadian anti-cruelty jurisprudence? Does legal welfarism define it as well? If so, would it lead to a similar outcome, that except for actions which are wholly gratuitous, suffering is permitted because the law is guided by the ideal of private property protection and the premise that animals are always already property? In a review essay of *Animals, Property, and the Law*, Robert Adams posits that Francione's compelling thesis would be fortified by a comparative study of foreign jurisdictions with similar anti-cruelty provisions.[34] Lesli Bisgould has reviewed Canadian anti-cruelty cases in *Animals and the Law*[35] to explore the protections available for animals at the federal and provincial levels. In this section I build upon Bisgould's work by highlighting the welfarist but also imperial nature of this legislation, taking the federal provisions as a model.[36]

1. THE ANTI-CRUELTY PROVISIONS

Presently, there are four "anti-cruelty" provisions in the *Code*: ss.445.1, 446, 447, and 447.1 (see Appendix). Most federal cases are triggered by an alleged violation under s.445.1 (Causing Unnecessary Suffering) and/or s.446 (Causing Damage or Injury),[37] since these protections are more general in scope and do not target a particular practice as s.447 does in concentrating on animal fighting. Indeed, cetacean breeding and the captivity of cetaceans (prohibited by s.445.2, with some exceptions), along with trap-shooting/other release and shooting of captive birds (prohibited by s.445.1(1)(d)), and animal fighting/baiting in general (s.445.1(1)(b)), are among the few uses of animals Canadian society has absolutely outlawed because these practices are now considered morally repugnant.[38] The exceptional status of, first, cockfighting, and then other forms of animal fighting within animal anti-cruelty legislation, may be explained by British and American empire-building projects that aimed to cultivate "civilized" and virtuous character among so-called lower classes and racialized groups.[39] Socially stratifying meanings of race, gender, and class continue to shape discourses around and representations of animal fighting today.[40] I say more about the cetacean provisions below.

Blood sports and cetacean captivity and breeding being exceptional instances of animal cruelty, the "necessity" of the suffering of animals

used in them is not an element of these offences, and there is no attendant inquiry into their purpose for or their necessity to the humans
who engage in them. In contrast, the other offences in ss.445.1 and 446
are filtered through the "necessity" framework and operate from the
premise, through the words of the offence or the jurisprudence that has
interpreted them, that animals are property, that they may be legitimately used by humans, and that this use will often entail suffering.[41]
Revealing the inadequacies of the jurisprudence generated under these
general anti-cruelty sections, then, is the best means to dispel the common misunderstanding that anti-cruelty measures effectively protect
animals.

First, however, we can make several observations about these provisions from a textual reading. According to s.445.1, cruel actions
include the wilful causation of unnecessary suffering (note that the
meaning of unnecessary is left open), the aiding or abetting of animal
fighting or baiting, the poisoning or administering of another harmful substance to one's own or another's animal without a reasonable
excuse, and the broadly defined participation in trap-shooting activities. Supplementing this provision, s.446 prohibits, at subsection 1,
the injury of an animal in transport as well as the neglect of the basic
needs of one's domestic or captive animal.[42] Violations of s.445.1 carry
a maximum potential prison sentence of five years if the conviction
follows an indictment. Penalties for s.446 are considerably less, with
the offence carrying a maximum incarceration period of two years on
indictment and no fine for a summary conviction. For both categories of offences, s.447.1 enables a court to prohibit a convicted person
from residing with or owning or otherwise having custody or control
of animal for "any period that the court considers appropriate but,
in the second or subsequent offence, for a minimum of five years."[43]
It is also instructive to note the evidentiary presumptions that apply
to offences that trigger ss.445.1(1)(a) (causing unnecessary suffering)
and 446(1)(a) (causing damage or injury during transport).[44] These
presumptions ease the Crown's burden by letting neglect be evidence
of intent to harm.[45]

2. LIMITED REACH OF THE PROVISIONS

Despite these positive features, ss.445.1 and 446 are hampered in their
effect in reaching animal suffering by the social and cultural interpretive frame through which they are interpreted, which excludes from
scrutiny most acts against and uses of animals. As Francione has demonstrated with respect to American anti-cruelty statutes, and as we
shall see below in Canadian judicial interpretation of such statutes of

the *Code*, implicitly, most human uses of animals are legally accepted as natural and necessary.[46] Since institutionalized exploitation of animals is deemed socially acceptable, it rarely attracts anti-cruelty attention. Scores of injurious activities against animals are engaged in every day but are never subject to ss.445.1 and 446.[47] Animals are slaughtered and exploited routinely for their flesh, milk, and eggs, cut, burned, and deliberately infected with disease for research, held captive for so-called entertainment or education, and hunted for sport, yet these activities are promoted and, at least in the case of hunting, licensed rather than condemned.[48] Francione's thesis that anti-cruelty laws have more to do with human moral elevation and human property interests is well illustrated by the Quebec Court of Appeal in *R. v Ménard*.[49]

3. *R. V MÉNARD*: LEGAL WELFARISM ENTRENCHED

This 1978 decision is significant because it remains the highest-level judicial precedent discussing the meaning of Canada's federal provision against animal suffering.[50] As Bisgould notes, the case is unusual because it is one of the rare instances within anti-cruelty jurisprudence that an institutionalized practice was subject to an anti-cruelty prosecution and, furthermore, a conviction was secured.[51] This is ironic, since the case confirms a narrow remit for animal cruelty as a legal concept. In *Ménard*, Lamer J.A. (as he then was) undertook an inquiry into the rationale for the anti-cruelty offence (then s.402(1)(a)) and the meaning of cruelty. The respondent accused operated a business in Longueil, QC. The business disposed of animals found dead in public spaces and caught animals "found straying within the meaning of the municipal by-law" and killed animals that had not been claimed by their owners within three days.[52] To kill the animals, the respondent placed them "in a small metallic chamber five feet in length by four feet in width and of a height of a little less than three feet." The air-tight chamber was connected to a motor, and loss of consciousness did not take place until after the animal had injested carbon monoxide for at least thirty seconds.[53] Expert evidence about this procedure revealed that the intense heat and carbon particles generated by the combustion engine normally caused pain, suffering, and burns to the mucous membranes and respiratory tracts of the animals.[54]

The killing of stray unclaimed animals – or "euthanasia," as the court euphemistically called it[55] – is permitted by law, and the legality or morality of such killing was not engaged in *Ménard*. What *was* at issue was the procedure used to effect this legal purpose; accordingly, the accused was charged under s.402(1)(a) (the subsection that incorporates the element of necessity into the offence). Mr Ménard was initially found guilty by a Judge of the Sessions of the Peace and ordered to pay a fine of $200 and costs; failure to do so would have resulted in imprisonment for thirty days.[56] The respondent successfully appealed to the Superior Court, which followed the precedential definitions and concepts of standards of pain and unnecessary suffering as they had been applied in *R. v Linder*,[57] a case decided in 1950, and *Ford v Wiley*[58] and *Swan v Saunders*, cases decided in the late 1800s.[59]

(a) "Substantial" Quantification for Suffering Formally Eliminated. It is worth reviewing the facts in *Linder*, which was heard at the British Columbia Court of Appeal (BCCA), to understand the significance of the *Ménard* decision.[60] In *Linder*, the BCCA reversed the accused's conviction at trial for causing unnecessary suffering to an animal under the 1927 *Criminal Code* equivalent of s.446.1(1)(a), which was s.542(a).[61] The accused had used a bucking flank strap on a horse for purposes of a bucking contest rodeo event. The trial judge found that "the use of the strap does at least excite or irritate the horse to more strenuous bucking in its struggle to unseat its rider, and that is an abuse of the horse."[62] The appellate court reversed the judgment on the ground that the Crown had not shown that the horse had *substantially* suffered. *Linder* affirmed a threshold of "substantial suffering," following the late 1800s cases of *Ford* and *Swan* that incorporated the qualifier of "substantial" in defining pain and suffering.[63]

In *Ménard*, Lamer J.A. reviewed these authorities but did not follow them in requiring that the suffering meet a quantifiable threshold. He interpreted the 1953–4 legislative amendments to the *Code* as eliminating a threshold requirement. Lamer J.A. authorized the proposition that to establish a cruelty offence, it is sufficient if the Crown can show that suffering existed without demanding that it reach a certain "substantial" level; if it was caused unnecessarily and wilfully, then the elements of the offence under s.445.1(1)(a) were present.[64] This positive legacy of *Ménard* is not to be dismissed, given the prior jurisprudence, but its impact is virtually theoretical. In reality, the cases that come before the courts involve intense suffering.[65] It is the narrow interpretation of suffering "without necessity" that Lamer J.A. proceeded to articulate that accounted for this converse result.

(b) Extremely Narrow Interpretation of "Cruelty." After minimizing the quantity of suffering that must be present to qualify as an animal cruelty offence, Lamer J.A. addressed what he saw as the heart of the matter: the meaning of "necessity" as it relates to animal suffering, upon

which the concept of cruelty pivots.[66] After reviewing the holdings in these older cases, Lamer J.A. concluded:

> ... [a] reading of ss.386(1) and 400 to 403 reveals a legislative policy which seeks to recognize the protection of animals in accordance with the place which is theirs in the hierarchy of our "world" and the responsibilities that we impose on ourselves as their "masters." Within the hierarchy of our planet the animal occupies a place which, if it does not give rights to the animal at least prompts us, being animals who claim to be rational beings, to impose on our ourselves behaviour which will reflect in our relations with them those virtues we seek to promote in our relations among humans. On the other hand, the animal is inferior to man, and takes its place within a hierarchy which is the hierarchy of the animals, and above all is a part of nature with all its "racial and natural" selections. The animal is subordinate to nature and to man. It will often be in the interests of man to kill and mutilate wild or domestic animals, to subjugate them and, to this end, to tame them with all the painful consequences this may mean for them and, if they are too old, or too numerous, or abandoned, to kill them. This is why, in setting standards for the behaviour of men towards animals, we have taken into account our privileged position in nature and have been obliged to take into account at the outset the purpose sought. We have, moreover, wished to subject all behaviour, which would already be legalized by its purpose, to the test of the "means employed."[67]

In reasoning that the legislature intended that cruelty be contingent on purpose and method viewed from a certain hierarchical worldview, Lamer J.A. tells us several things that confirm Francione's thesis about the purpose and scope of anti-cruelty laws. Notwithstanding Lamer J.A.'s assertion that "s.402 was enacted for the protection of the animals themselves,"[68] Francione's argument that anti-cruelty laws treat animals instrumentally and still primarily respect the owner's property rights are evident in Lamer J.A.'s reasoning.

First, it is clear from the first two sentences of the excerpt that the rationale for the law is human moral elevation for the purpose of better human social relations. We see that the concern is not for the well-being of animals but for the cultivation of human virtue. Animals' inferior position is presumed by the familiar religiously laced appeal to the laws of nature and serves to justify the assertion that animals are at the service of humans. Animals are presumed to be lower creatures; treating them without cruelty is mainly for the purpose of cultivating desired moral sensibilities regarding the treatment of other humans.

Lamer J.A. echoes the common claim that a concern for animal welfare is a mark of civilized status. A few paragraphs later, in comments that contain both anthropocentric, gendered, and imperialistic meaning,[69] he writes that "the animal is inferior to man, and takes its place within a hierarchy which is … a part of nature with all its *racial and natural*' selections." This perpetuates the imperial teachings of Social Darwinism, in which non-white, non-Western societies were placed on the lower rungs of the ladder of civilization and progress, with ideal societies (i.e., white, Western) perched on the higher rungs. There is a continuum of domination in the hierarchy he constructs: "man" is superior to animals, and certain races of men (read: white) are superior to other races of men.[70] Lamer J.A.'s remarks expose the imperial civilizational logic that has shaped anti-cruelty legislation. As noted earlier, anti-cruelty legislation arose as part of a deliberate imperial agenda to civilize non-white and non-Western peoples; thus the existence of such legislation on the books became a mark of civilized status. The benefits to animals that accrued through such efforts were secondary to the ones that accrued to humans; animals' suffering did not matter in the anti-cruelty calculus if it did not arise from activities deemed morally objectionable from imperial, gendered, and classist hierarchical worldviews.[71]

The exercise of long-standing property rights rarely fell into the category of morally objectionable activities. *Ménard* does not alter this historical purpose of the law. The Canadian framework that *Ménard* develops does not prioritize animal suffering over human – specifically, property – interests. Instead, as per Francione's theory of legal welfarism, the owner's interest in the animal is weighed against the interest of a legal non-subject, the stray animal, which leads to a result whereby almost every interest of the owner is permitted. The court embeds legal welfarism when it reasons that "man's" use of animals is determined by his "privileged position in nature" and his attendant interest in subjugating animals. This welfarist attitude receives legal expression through the means/purpose test that Lamer J.A. entrenches, whereby Judeo-Christian cultural and religious suppositions about human superiority and exceptionalism result in affirming comments about the "necessity" of almost every human activity that involves animals. Justice Lamer condones the view that humans have the right to exploit animals "given to them by their position as supreme creatures"[72] even when this is "unnecessary":

> "Without necessity" does not mean that man, when a thing is susceptible of causing pain to an animal, must abstain unless it be necessary, but means that man in the pursuit of his purposes as a superior being, in the pursuit of his well-being, is

obliged not to inflict on animals pain, suffering or injury which is not inevitable
taking into account the purpose sought and the circumstances of the particular
case. In effect, even if it not be necessary for man to eat meat and if he
could abstain from doing so, as many in fact do, it is the privilege of man
to eat it.[73]

The test that Lamer J.A. devises is a valuation of necessity contingent on
the particular purpose that gave rise to the animal's suffering and the
surrounding circumstances – for example, social priorities, the alternative available means, and their accessibility and affordability for the
user.[74] Within this assessment, animals are conceptualized from the
outset as property, and not, for example, as sentient beings capable of
suffering. The discordant reference to the privilege of meat-eating confirms that the test for necessity is premised on the normalized exploitation of animals. Regarding unreflective privilege claims, no justification
is proffered for why the suffering inherent in meat-eating is "necessary." In fact, Lamer J.A. concludes that the term "does not mean that
man ... must abstain unless it be necessary."

The requirement that surrounding circumstances be taken into
account does not overturn the anthropocentric privilege in which
Lamer J.A. embeds the meaning of "without necessity." Instead, where
context triggers an inquiry into the accessibility and affordability of
alternative means as it did in *Ménard*, the animal's interest is still considered secondary to the unfair competitive advantage the property
owner or other claimed human animal user may enjoy vis-à-vis others in the same industry. Justice Lamer engaged in a cost–benefit pain
analysis of different methods of animal euthanasia.[75] In terms of pain
relief, or the animal's well-being the expert evidence adduced suggested the use of anaesthesia; but because of the prohibitive costs of
this for "those who use the method regularly," the court held that this
was an unreasonable alternative.[76] The court, however, did take notice
of a system that eliminated the harmful carbon and lowered the heat
to a "tolerable" level.[77] Because the system was relatively simple to
install, inexpensive, and already an industry standard, and because
the respondent knew of its availability, the court concluded that the
respondent "could *easily and at reasonable cost* have equipped himself so
that the animals to be killed need not be subjected to the pain, suffering
and injuries that the method which he used necessarily involved."[78]
Viewed from this perspective, the fact that the animals "won" in this
case in fact offers no reason for celebration or optimism. The court was
simply following an industry standard that kept Ménard's operations
economically in line with his industry. Ménard's property rights were

only impugned to the extent they had a negative effect on the economic interest of his competitors.

4. CASE LAW AFTER *MÉNARD*

Ménard is significant because it explicitly authorized a legal welfarist interpretation of the federal anti-cruelty law in Canada. Although, being an appellate court judgment from Quebec, it is technically binding only on Quebec courts, *Ménard* has been consistently cited in many Canadian provinces as well as in intervener submissions at the Supreme Court of Canada as the authority on the meaning of "unnecessary ... suffering" in s.445.1(1)(a) or its historical antecedents.[79] It is still regarded as the leading case in this area.[80] It has thus done much to generate the attendant property framework that has been heavily criticized by Francione, which expunges from the concept of "cruelty" and "unnecessary suffering" any meaning independent of anthropocentric purposes.[81]

Indeed, when one looks at the seventy-three cases reported after *Ménard* until 2018 in which an accused stood trial for allegedly violating s.445.1(1)(a),[82] in none of those cases is the animal harm at issue attributable to institutional practices.[83] Moreover, if we look closely at the facts in the cases involving for the vast majority individual acts of physical aggression, and also in some instances neglect, they confirm Francione's argument that anti-cruelty prosecutions target socially deviant acts and not what mainstream society considers socially acceptable animal (ab)use. The facts in these cases overwhelmingly involve abuse of domestic dogs and cats and leave little doubt that the *Code*'s catchall anti-cruelty provision has only been effective in condemning socially deviant acts against companion animal dogs and cats entailing extreme suffering for animals.[84]

It may seem that the cases involving neglect of domestic animals are more redemptive of anti-cruelty law in the *Code*. After all, injuries that occur to domestic or captive wild animals either through neglect of basic needs of food, water, shelter, or care (s.446(1)(b)), or abandoning the animals in distress (s.446(1)(b)), or while animals are being transported (s.446(1)(a)), are not subject to a test of necessity. We may infer that these subsections aim to secure the provision of basic needs for animals. But the purpose of s.446(1) is only properly understood if we recall that anti-cruelty legislation first centred on economically significant domesticated farmed animals and the harm that *third parties* did to the owner's interest in these animals through behaviour adjudicated to be "cruel."[85] Anti-cruelty legislation eventually evolved to include in its ambit the actions of *owners* who neglected or abandoned their own animals, as the current *Code* provisions attest. We might conclude that this extension finally created a law that expressed concern about animals apart from their status as someone's property – a law whose provisions, moreover, are not at risk of dilution through a necessity test. Francione cautions us against such a hopeful interpretation, however. He argues that instead, the criminalization of neglect and abandonment is an expression of the law's distaste for the "socially undesirable destruction of property"[86] rather than an affirmation that animals' basic needs should be protected.[87] Even if one disagrees with Francione on this point, or applauds the end result of basic needs protection for animals that nevertheless can result despite the law's original disappointing purpose, the overall anti-cruelty regime in the *Code* still leaves much to be desired in that it criminalizes only deviant acts involving intense suffering.[88]

C. Any Bright Spots at All?

Although Canada's anti-cruelty provisions reflect a deeply legal-welfarist approach, one favourable element of s.445.1 is the presumption found in s.445.1(3) that enables a court to presume wilfulness on the part of the accused in committing the violating act absent any contrary evidence. The advantage provided by this wording, however, is in danger of being eclipsed by a line of reasoning that had circulated in lower court judgments and has recently been articulated by the BCCA, which advances a subjective standard for *mens rea* that defeats the codified presumption against the accused.[89]

Recall that to prove intent, the prosecution must prove that the offence occurred "wilfully." *R. v McHugh* is not considered to be an authority on the test of "unnecessary suffering," but it is often referred to by courts in anti-cruelty cases in order to ascertain the meaning of "wilfulness."[90] *McHugh* held that "wilfully" meant "deliberately" and thus did not require the additional element of malicious or evil intent. *R. v Radmore* adopted this broad understanding to convict a former veterinarian for causing unnecessary suffering by failing to provide suitable and adequate food, water, shelter, and care for his horses.[91] The court held that the accused's honest belief that he was taking care of the horses did not exonerate him because he was nevertheless careless. Thus, carelessness, helpfully for animals, became another indication of wilfulness.[92]

The prospect of *McHugh* and *Radmore* laying the foundation of legal doctrine and setting a low prosecution-friendly threshold to prove wilfulness, however, may be faint. In *R. v Higgins,*[93] the court adopted the broader understanding of "wilful" as articulated in *McHugh*, yet it *raised* the threshold of proof. Mr Higgins was charged under a previous version of s.445.1(1)(a) for injuries sustained by his cat, Sammy, who desperately took refuge in the furnace room to escape being chased through his whole house with a broom for the purported purposes of discipline.[94] It was not until the accused's daughter found Sammy, hours later and severely injured, that Mr Higgins admitted that Sammy had been harmed as a result of the pursuit.[95] The principal issue before the court was the wilfulness of the offence. As noted above, wilfulness for the purposes of proceedings under s.445.1 is determinable by reference to s.429. This section deems that someone has acted "wilfully" when he "causes the occurrence of an event by doing an act or by omitting to do an act that is his duty to do, knowing that the act or omission will probably cause the occurrence of the event and being reckless whether the event occurs or not."[96] The trial judge interpreted this definition to mean that the accused needed to be aware that the act would likely result in the event in order to be found guilty.[97] The accused claimed that he was not at all aware that his actions might injure the cat and thus did not have the requisite awareness for a wilful act; the judge agreed.[98]

The prosecutor appealed the decision on four grounds; the submissions all alleged errors in the trial judge's interpretation of "wilfully" and in the handling of the presumption regarding s.446(3). The prosecution pressed forward an understanding of both that did not require an accused to hold a subjective view regarding knowing his act or omission would result in harm or that he was being reckless.[99] The Newfoundland Supreme Court Trial Division, as a summary conviction appeal court, disagreed with all four grounds, thus confirming the subjective nature of the *mens rea* requirement despite the necessary presumption of wilfulness absent evidence to the contrary.[100] The trial judge had completely ignored the presumption.[101] The Newfoundland Supreme Court hearing the appeal accepted the accused's "explanation of his motivation for his actions and concluded that he did not intend to injure the cat and that he did not have an awareness that his actions might have injurious consequences" as sufficient "evidence to the contrary" under s.445.1(3) to rebut the presumption that failing to exercise reasonable care will constitute wilfulness.[102] Since the Court found that an accused can effectively rely on self-proclaimed ignorance as a ready defence, *Higgins* has rendered the presumption of wilfulness in subsection (3) virtually meaningless. Instead of subjecting the accused to a contextualized objective test of reasonability, or requiring corroborated testimony to rebut the presumption of s.445.1(3), *Higgins* advances a subjective threshold for *mens rea* that is ripe for opportunistic use by accused persons.[103]

Regrettably, the 2016 BCCA case of *R v Gerling* gave appellate stature to this interpretation when it held that the meaning of wilfulness in s.429 of the *Code* includes a subjective element such that "knowing that suffering was a likely result or that a reasonable person would realize that this was a likely result," as the trial judge had held, was an error.[104] Instead, the court held that s.429(1) "engages a subjective element: knowing that the act or omission will probably cause the occurrence of the event and being reckless whether the event occurs or not."[105] The BCCA held that the presumption in s.445.1(3) only works to effect an objective standard for "willfulness" (i.e., "an absence of reasonable care or supervision")[106] where there is no evidence to the contrary;[107] otherwise s.445.1(a) referentially incorporates from s.429(1) a subjective *mens rea* definition of "willfulness."[108] Unfortunately for animals, the threshold for what constitutes "evidence to the contrary" for animals is low: it "is simply evidence raised by the accused which raises a reasonable doubt about her willfulness."[109] Credible assertions that the accused believed they were adequately caring for their animals (no matter how unreasonable to an objective person) could qualify as "evidence to the contrary."[110]

A second line of reasoning that preserves a livelier role for the animal-friendly presumption in s.445.1(3) is present in other jurisdictions and is advanced by the 2016 Ontario case of *R v Way*,[111] decided after the BCCA's decision in *Gerling*. The court addressed the *mens rea* element of s.445.1(a) head on:

> This case turns entirely on a proper understanding and application of the required *mens rea* of the offences charged. Essentially, it comes down to this: Does the Crown need to prove that the accused intended the consequences of her failure to care for these animals? Or, must the Crown only prove that she actually knew that her conduct was causing suffering, and failed to act accordingly? Or, is it sufficient for the Crown to simply prove that she was aware of the circumstances that existed and ought to have foreseen that her conduct would cause the prohibited consequences, the suffering inflicted on these animals?[112]

The court held that it was the last, objective standard, option that applied. Citing precedent that characterized s.445.1 as housing offences that relate to duties of care, it found that a subjective *mens rea* was not intended.[113] Rather, "[t]he mens rea of these offences is measured by a modified object test" requiring the court to inquire into whether a reasonable person would have foreseen the criminal harm had that person taken the same actions or omissions as the accused.[114] The Ontario approach is much more favourable to animals, but as an appellate case, the *Gerling* decision has the potential to persuade other jurisdictions to adopt the BC subjective interpretation.

D. Summary

Since Canadian anti-cruelty case law is entrenched in a property paradigm that measures the interests of the animal in whose body the property rights of legal persons inhere against those very same property rights, the overwhelming bulk of painful/distressing and suffering-inducing acts are not outlawed absolutely. Instead, they must endure a test of necessity because of a hegemonic willingness to sacrifice animal interests, no matter how compelling, for a competing human one. The only activities that are treated as cruel by their very performance, without an inquiry into reasons, justifications, or excuses, are captive-shooting and fighting. Everything else, even killing one's companion animal, must first be characterized as unnecessary before it is considered cruel.[115] The primary rationale for this position is that the exercise of property rights, which includes owners' decisions to kill their animals, is not to be interfered with by anti-cruelty law.[116] And because institutional and otherwise instrumental use of animals is socially accepted, it is overwhelmingly only those acts deemed culturally aberrant by dominant cultural standards that are prosecuted under anti-cruelty statutes.[117] From this review of Canadian anti-cruelty jurisprudence, we can conclude that the doctrine of legal welfarism that Francione identifies in American case law is a vibrant doctrine with respect to Canadian anti-cruelty law as well.[118] The leading Canadian case, *Ménard*, has entrenched a legacy of the skewed balancing test that has naturalized human superiority and animal instrumentality. Legal reform efforts have not been able to challenge the anthropocentrism of the common law. A survey of the proposed and accepted amendments to anti-cruelty legislation shows that this skewed balancing of interests has sullied law reform efforts to "modernize" the law in this area.

III. Amendments to Anti-cruelty Law

Animal cruelty laws at the federal and provincial levels in Canada have been the subjects of attempted – and sometimes successful – amendment over the past few decades. Although the scope of the laws and the breadth of the proposed amendments vary between levels of government, the changes proposed all have a number of things in common. In each case, the amendments were inspired by the public reaction to stories of animal abuse.[119] They also had the potential, at least to a slight degree, to discursively contest the propertied status of animals in Canada. When one examines the few amendments that were enacted and the bulk that were rejected, the formative undercurrents of anthropocentrism and the cultural Othering in conceptualizing cruelty against animals become visible. This section discusses these amendments and the anthropocentric, racialized, and cultural norms that determined their fate. The analysis explains how the legal welfarist logic that defines anti-cruelty law has caused such efforts to meet with little success despite their modest goals.

A. Federal Amendments

As discussed above, criminal prohibitions on animal cruelty in Canada are administered at the federal level through the *Code*.[120] The anti-cruelty laws thus establish offences and penalties for the country as a whole, and as a result, more than any of the various provincial anti-cruelty statutes, they can provide a national remit for the concept of "animal cruelty." However, by the early 1990s this section of the *Code* had been stagnant for more than a century.[121] The provisions reflected ideas about non-human animals that were grounded in the nineteenth century rather than more modern views.[122] Awareness of this disconnect through media stories of sadistic animal abuse prompted the federal Liberal government from the late 1990s through the early 2000s to attempt to amend the century-old anti-cruelty provisions. Although animal advocacy groups had been lobbying for amendments to the *Code* many years before this,[123] it was news stories detailing graphic abuse of companion animals that appeared over a few months in the summer of 1998 in national and local newspapers that galvanized the government to take action. These articles described painful acts against animals that did not fall into any of the dominant cultural and thus legal practices against animals (dragging dogs behind cars, torturing cats, etc.) as well as the slim legal repercussions housed in the *Code* for such crimes.[124] The media reporting caused a public outcry that attracted government attention, and in 1998 the Department of Justice released a report titled *Crimes against Animals* that had solicited input from the public on how to amend the anti-cruelty laws.[125] It is reported that the government had received more public input in the form of letters for this consultation than for any previous consultation it had conducted.[126] The legislative result of all of this was the introduction of Bill C-17 in the House of Commons in December 1999.[127]

1. LIMITED SCOPE OF AMENDMENTS

It perhaps comes as no surprise that the changes Bill C-17 proposed were minimal. Nothing in the proposed amendments to the *Code* would have changed the definition of cruelty that the case law had created; "cruelty" would continue to be understood as "unnecessary suffering."[128] On the contrary, the government sought to reassure hunting, farming, and research groups worried about the effect of the amendments that the proposed law would not illegalize any industry that was currently lawful.[129] The bill did not aim to change the legal status of animals as property or disturb the practices of any animal-based industries. Instead, it subscribed to the view reflected in the case law that violence against animals was episodic in Canada, rather than routinized in various industries, and was the result of the aberrant actions of a deviant few.[130] The background report even claimed that the government had been motivated to update the anti-cruelty provisions by growing scientific research linking animal abuse to aggression against humans.[131] It was this type of culturally aberrant violence against animals that the bill sought to curtail.[132] Consequently, Bill C-17 altered the distribution of property rights only minimally, as explained below.

(a) "Property or Not"? Notwithstanding its traditional approach to conceptualizing "cruelty," Bill C-17 did include a few provisions that sought to alter the association of animals with property, although they did not go so far as to change animals' propertied status. While modest, these provisions were not without symbolic and even substantive effect, given the anthropocentrism that saturates anti-cruelty jurisprudence and law in general. The primary revision that would have accomplished this contestation of animals' property status was a change in the placement of the new anti-cruelty offence within the *Code*. Recall that the anti-cruelty provisions were and still are housed in Chapter XI of the *Code*, "Wilful and Forbidden Acts *in Respect of Certain Property*."[133] Bill C-17 would have placed the provisions in a brand-new section titled "Cruelty to Animals," in Chapter V, then and still titled "Sexual Offences, Public Morals and Disorderly Conduct." Bill C-17 would have changed this to "Sexual Offences, Public Morals and Disorderly Conduct *and Cruelty to Animals*."[134] This move sought to affirm that animals are sentient and that their current placement in the *Code* undervalued their capacity for suffering in favour of ownership interests.[135] The move was also meant to recognize the ways in which human relationships with companion animals transformed animals into more than property in the eyes of their human guardians even though the legal relationship would remain one of ownership.[136] The bill conveyed

the growing sensibility that animals were different from inanimate forms of property, and that, as companion animals, many had obtained the cultural status of a family member.[137] The bill sought to respond to this new cultural view through the symbolic gesture of the new chapter heading.[138]

The second way in which Bill C-17 gently questioned the property status of animals was through the substantive measure of including wild animals under the purview of anti-cruelty offences.[139] The existing anti-cruelty provisions had betrayed their ownership orientation by focusing on animals that were already owned rather than by treating all animals equally as possible subjects of cruelty.[140] Again, without challenging the overall legal status of animals as property, Bill C-17 would have ascribed a valuation to an animal's suffering irrespective of harm to the animal's owner. The change would have connoted that the harm was to the animal herself – a new component of "cruelty" – rather than to the property interest of the animal's owner.

(b) Non-property Changes. Other proposed changes did not contest the property classification but were nonetheless notable in terms of altering the reach of the provisions. First, the bill would have more precisely identified animals as vertebrates.[141] While this centring of the capacity to feel pain may be read as a progressive move on the part of the government to value all sentient life,[142] it must be remembered that the existing provision does not define "animal" at all; its open-endedness could potentially be read as including invertebrate animals as well.[143] A second change expanding the category of animals to which the bill would have applied related to one specific practice only: organized animal fighting. Bill C-17 would have extended the existing cockfighting prohibition so that it applied to all other organized animal fighting, a measure that clearly would have broadened the ambit of the then existing section.[144]

Third, Bill C-17 would have widened "cruelty" to include the act of killing an animal "brutally or viciously, regardless of whether the animal dies immediately."[145] Due to the wording of the existing section, only those practices that killed animals in non-normative ways where the animals actually suffered before dying (instead of simply dying) were caught by the offence.[146] This revision was a response to the public's revulsion that it was possible to sadistically attack animals (again, we have to read "sadism" here as the non-dominant manner of violating animals rather than normalized violence against them) but not be charged with cruelty if the animal died upon the first blow and thus did not suffer.[147]

Finally, in terms of substantive changes, fines and incarceration periods were increased. For the first time, the Crown would have been able to proceed by indictment, which, if resulting in a conviction, could entail incarceration for five years. The bill kept the option of proceeding summarily but would have increased the incarceration period from a possible six months to eighteen; the maximum fine for a summary conviction would have remained $2,000.[148] Whether the Crown proceeded summarily or by indictment, however, the bill included a new provision that would have enabled a court to institute a lifetime prohibition on a convicted party from owning animals, a marked increase from the existing restriction of only two years; in the case of a second or further offence, the court would have to impose a minimum ban of five years.[149] As well, Bill C-17 would have permitted a judge to order an accused to compensate an individual or group for the reasonable expenses incurred for caring for the abused animal after it came into their custody,[150] as well as apply general provisions regarding restitution orders in the *Code* to animal cruelty-related orders.[151]

(c) *Summary of Amendments.* It may be argued that two of the non-property substantive changes – defining animals as "vertebrates" (if we believe the governmental purpose of this change was to signal a value for all sentient life), and raising the penalties that could attach to a conviction – signalled a new approach to valuing animal life, however mired that life was in anthropocentric and subordinating worldviews. When combined with the property-related substantive change of extending the reach of the section fully to unowned (i.e., wild) animals and the symbolic removal of the provisions from the property section of the *Code*, one can perceive a conceptual shift, however modest, in attitudes toward animals underlying the bill. It thus becomes apparent why so many animal advocacy organizations endorsed this bill and similar successor bills through various sessions of Parliament despite their limited application to a nominal fraction of the violence against animals and the government's repeated statements of support for the normalized industries that enact this systemic violence.[152] It is this same internal limit to the bills that enabled such widespread support from a public that believed in consuming animal products and researching on animal bodies.[153]

2. RESISTANCE TO THE AMENDMENTS

Despite the bill's acceptance of the division between legitimate and illegitimate violence against animals as well as the considerable support from a similarly oriented public, the bill encountered strong resistance from industry.[154] Bill C-17 died when Parliament was dissolved in October 2000 due to an election call. Its successors, either identical to or closely reminiscent of it, also encountered various forms of industry resistance that translated into parliamentary resistance. In the eight years after Bill C-17 died, various bills proposing to amend the anti-cruelty provisions, all of them closely reminiscent of Bill C-17, were introduced both in the House and in the Senate.[155] They were all unsuccessful.[156] This dismal result may be attributed to the high number of federal elections called during this time, but also to the disagreements, generated by industry lobbying against the more substantive bills, that emerged between the political parties as well as between the House and the Senate over the necessary amendments and their wording.[157]

(a) By Industry. While the Liberals were in power, they continued to re-introduce bills that were close iterations of Bill C-17, but their consistent statements that the amendments would not impinge on normative uses of animals and existing industries did not quell anxiety among animal industry stakeholders.[158] Industry stakeholders claimed that the changes to the existing law would harm "human rights" as well as trigger a slippery slope that would eventually favour the position of animal "extremists" seeking to humanize animals and outlaw their industries.[159] The farming, research, and hunting and trapping communities were particularly vocal in expressing this view.[160]

John Sorenson has written about the politics of the consultations as they coalesced around Bill C-10B, an early reincarnation of the original Bill C-17, introduced by then Liberal Minister of Justice and Attorney General Anne McLellan in November 2002.[161] Through a critical discourse analysis of the governmental committee deliberations, Hansard debates, and media reports surrounding the various forms of the bill until 2002, Sorenson elucidates the "deliberate and misleading attempts to exaggerate the implications of the[ir] modest amendments and to vilify animal rights advocates."[162] Sorenson details the numerous negative responses by representatives of the animal agriculture, research, and hunting industries, which were "disproportionate to the scope of the legislation."[163] Despite the government's repeated assurances regarding the scope of the legislation, these industry representatives maintained that the proposed legislation was a "human rights bill for animals"[164] and constituted a "fundamental, even revolutionary reconfiguration of the human/animal boundary."[165] Both industry representatives and conservative politicians claimed that the bill would undermine "normal" animal-based industries and convert ranchers, researchers, and hunters who love "their" animals into criminals.[166] The bill was identified as a "weapon" of "animal rights extremists"[167] that would undermine the anthropocentric normative order as well as human health, economic prosperity, Indigenous rights, national identity, and society as we know it.[168]

What is more, these distorting views were expressed in a relatively industry-friendly environment. As Sorenson reveals, expressions of support for the proposed legislation were hampered by the parameters set for the government deliberations – only national organizations were invited to participate.[169] This privileged large-scale, well-resourced organizations as opposed to smaller grassroots organizations more critical of animal exploitation. More animal welfare organizations qualified (that were accepting of animal use but critical of industry conditions) than animal rights organizations (that sought an end to the commodification of animals); thus, the bill's animal welfare proponents validated the normalized exploitation and killing of animals in an effort to reassure industry actors that the bill focused on uses of animals that are not culturally acceptable (i.e., sadistic or "barbaric" uses of animals).[170] At the same time, such comments were prefaced or followed by assurances that opponents were all "animal lovers."[171]

Bill C-10B died in November 2003 upon prorogation of Parliament after having passed all three readings in the House as a government-supported bill only to encounter resistance in the Senate over the issue of Indigenous rights. Industry opponents had succeeded in opportunistically mobilizing discourses about Aboriginal rights to bolster their own for-profit exploitation of animals.[172] Industry advocates argued that the transfer of the anti-cruelty provisions outside of Part XI of the *Code* addressing property offences and the elimination of any distinction between domestic and wild animals would be detrimental to Aboriginal rights to practise traditional hunting, fishing, and trapping.[173] It is telling that only one Indigenous organization raised the same concern.[174] Nonetheless, non-Indigenous industry advocates vigorously argued that the changes would expose traditional Indigenous hunting, fishing, and trapping in relation to wild animals to criminalization because such practices might not be the least painful means of hunting, fishing, and trapping animals when compared to more technologically astute methods.[175] Some senators seemed to be more sincere in their insistence that the amendments not be passed without an exempting provision for Indigenous cultural practices protected as Aboriginal or treaty rights under the Canadian Constitution.[176] The House refused to incorporate the exemption, insisting on a universal standard for all Canadians.[177]

This last point of contention in the legislative drama over Bill C-10B reveals how the force of hierarchical civilizational racialized logic that shaped legally welfarist views of cruelty toward animals from the outset continues to inform legislative debates about the meaning of cruelty. The animal anti-cruelty offence has been shaped by the colonial context in which it originally arose that saw the offence apply to non-Western practices abroad in British colonies and animal uses associated with the lower classes domestically at home.[178] The racial logic that inflects the offence's application may also be identified in current cases, as we have seen in *Ménard*.[179] That the practices of Indigenous Canadians might have been subjected to more anti-cruelty scrutiny had the amendments gone through to eliminate the distinction between wild and domestic animals is not a fanciful prospect. What reveals the cultural Othering embedded in the legal concept of anti-cruelty is the invisible premise that informed most of the parliamentary exchange about the exemption, namely, that normative Western practices of hunting, fishing, trapping, and otherwise appropriating animal bodies are superior and obviously are not cruel.[180] As Andrew Brighten has argued, legislative debates surrounding the exemption permit "the dangerous inference ... that Aboriginal hunting, fishing and trapping would by definition constitute criminal behavior absent an exemption – i.e., that traditional practices *are* 'unnecessarily' painful and that 'adjustments' *would* be inconsistent with Aboriginal culture."[181] Once again, it is the non-Western cultural Other from whom animals need saving by a Western liberal legal intervention.[182]

Brighten draws our attention to the perversity of this inference when we consider that Indigenous worldviews of human-animal relations do not follow Cartesian hierarchies that have proven so disastrous for animals but instead recognize animals as kin, as agentic and sentient beings, as co-participants in community, and, critically, as persons.[183] Instead of attracting mainstream attention as a repository of ideas, knowledge, and models for vastly improving human-animal relations as Brighten advocates,[184] the exemption feeds cross-cultural misunderstanding – linked to imperial ideology – that non-Western cultures are less animal-friendly and, indeed, dangerous to animals.[185] As Brighten points out (despite his awareness of the risk of overgeneralizing regarding Indigenous legal orders and cultures),[186] it is commonplace among Canada's First Nations to regard animals as persons.[187] Personhood in the Indigenous context arises from "the idea that animals are active individuals capable of intentional social interaction that can be understood via the same basic relational concepts used to conceptualize human social interaction – such as reciprocal exchange"[188] and are "conscious, sentient beings who possess volition, plan and deliberate, interact socially and communicate with each other and with humans."[189] Brighten argues that the effect of this ontological view of animals is to produce codes and rules in Indigenous legal orders that mandate minimizing pain when killing animals[190] and that generate an overall ethos of respect and reciprocity toward them.[191] Legislative debates that reach an impasse over anti-cruelty exemptions for First Nations risk distorting such alternative human-animal ontologies and the cultural norms that already may be said to be more than compatible with *Ménard's* narrow conceptualization of cruelty.

Legislation at the provincial level addressing cruelty toward animals carries exemptions for dominant Canadian industry practices. Thus, in addition to the dominant cultural view embedded in the common law that does not perceive factory farming, animal experimentation, non-cetacean animal captivity, or the animal skin trade, for example, as "cruelty," let alone "violence," but simply "normal," it is common for provincial anti-cruelty legislation to *explicitly* exclude industry practices from its purview.[192] It may be argued that these exemptions recognize that non-Indigenous dominant Canadian practices are cruel toward animals, thus requiring an exemption to permit them to continue. Although this view is plausible, it is fair to say that most Canadians do not know the content of provincial anti-cruelty statutes, let alone that an exemption has been tucked into these documents. No doubt that there has been a parliamentary deadlock between the House and the Senate over the Aboriginal exemption may also have escaped the attention of most Canadians even though it has happened on a national stage. It is telling, however, of the racialized double standard informing anti-cruelty law – and, as we see, legislative reform – that a proposal suggesting exemptions for mainstream practices was not considered a solution to the impasse.[193]

(b) Through Senate Dilution. The influence of the Senate in preventing substantive legislative change for animals, however modestly designed, from succeeding was also felt from a different direction. By 2005, Senate bills had started to compete with the House bills, offering a diluted version of the changes outlined above. These bills essentially left the substance and placement of the anti-cruelty provisions intact but increased the penalties.[194] In October 2007, Liberal senator John Bryden introduced Bill S-203.[195] It went through the Senate without debate, received first and second readings at an accelerated pace in the House, and, a month later, in November 2007, was referred to the Committee on Justice and Human Rights. Over opposition from several animal advocacy groups that recommended that the more robust version be enacted, Bill S-203, supported by industry,[196] received Royal Assent a few short months later, in April 2008.[197]

The bill's success where fourteen other bills since 1999 had failed is explained by the absence of any substantive changes in its provisions. Industry advocates were wary that the more substantive changes of Bill C-17 and its ilk might harm the rights of animal exploiters, though they also approved the increased penalties for what they saw as animal abuse.[198] The bill transformed animal cruelty into a hybrid offence. The amendments increased jail times and fines; it also provided more judges with more sentencing options. Specifically, prison sentences under indictment went as high as five years; also, a fine of up to $10,000 could now be imposed upon summary conviction.[199] Also, in terms of enhanced sentencing options, judges can now ban convicted persons from owning, possessing, or even residing with animals and compel them to pay restitution to organizations that incurred expenses in treating the animals post-abuse.[200]

From one perspective, the increases in penalties are noteworthy, given the meagre penalties that existed previously and how greatly the amendments raised them (most notably, five years replacing six months as a possible incarceration period upon indictment). As one judge noted in sentencing an accused after the amendments had come into place: "Such a dramatic change in a penalty provision is virtually unheard of in our criminal law."[201] Animal Justice, a legal advocacy group, reviewed the sentencing results pre and post the 2008 amendments (up to 2012) and found that judges have by and large imposed harsher penalties, although these penalties are still on the lighter side given the fines and the terms of incarceration now available.[202] The amendments have inspired at least one appellate-level court in Canada to affirm the difference between animals and other types of objects and to refuse to reduce the length of an appealed sentence.[203] In the 2015 case of *R v Alcorn*, the Alberta Court of Appeal held that "Parliament recognized, and intended that courts also recognize, that cruelty to animals is incompatible with civilized society."[204] In this case the accused had contested the length of his twenty-month sentence for the act of stringing a cat up by her hind legs, slitting her throat, and forcing the cat to bleed to a slow death from that position so that the blood could drip onto the accused and his female sexual partner, who were having sex on the garage floor below.[205] The court conceded that the appellant's sentence was high relative to other offences, but rejected his appeal, affirming that the sentences expressed in the case law so far do not "establish ... a range, let alone a cap. The case law has not revealed an overall policy strategy for animal cruelty cases as yet."[206] The court followed this reasoning with the observation that "[s]entient animals are not objects"[207] and cited the dissenting judgment from the Chief Justice in a previous decision of the Alberta Court of Appeal emphasizing animals' vulnerability.[208]

From another perspective, however, the pared-down "law and order" bill left much to be desired. Animal advocacy groups opposed it.[209] At least some MPs lamented the loss of the substantive provisions. According to the Canadian Federation of Humane Societies, which had appeared at the committee's hearings on the bill to oppose it and promote a more robust version, while "many committee members acknowledged the weaknesses in S-203, they felt that something was better than nothing."[210] As a result, despite the "staggering" number of bills that had been introduced, the animal cruelty laws in the Code remained essentially as they had been when the federal government in 1998 first began the public consultations.[211] And for the most part, the trend documented by Animal Justice in cases reported between 2008 and 2012 – increased sentences for offenders, but still far short of the five-year maximum – is evident in the cases since 2012 as well despite judicial recognition of Parliament's intent to create harsher penalties in these later cases.[212]

Indeed, in only one of the cases reported between 2012 and 2018 has the Crown proceeded by indictment, thus triggering the possibility of a five-year maximum penalty. This case, R v Perrin, involved the "brutal slaying of a healthy domestic cat that belonged to Mr. Perrin's girlfriend."[213] Sentences are typically higher where they occur in the context of intimate relationships and domestic violence cases as retaliation against the partner.[214] Yet even in other cases where an intimate partner or domestic violence was involved and the level of extreme violence against animals was comparable, sentences have ranged between a mere ninety days and two years and three months, with the majority under twelve months.[215] Indeed, even in Perrin, the accused received only thirty days in jail, which the accused could serve intermittently, plus twelve months' probation.[216] The court reached this sentence after careful consideration of the sentences meted out for animal cruelty prior to the 2008 amendments and afterwards.[217] Perrin was also a case where the court agreed that Mr Perrin's actions were "egregious" and "repugnant, horrendous, despicable, cruel, and malicious."[218] The court emphasized these aspects of Mr Perrin's actions in rejecting a conditional sentence that would not have involved jail time, but it declined to impose a "federal period of incarceration" – something that the charge brought under indictment would have allowed it to do.[219]

A review of other cases confirms the trend toward higher but still markedly light sentences post-2008. In *R v Camardi*, 2015 ABPC 65, 2015 CarswellAlta 536, the accused was to be sentenced for killing a dog and a cat. Justice G.J. Gaschler reviewed eleven cases for precedential guidance. The longest sentence was two years plus three years' probation (beating a family dog until presumed dead and throwing it into a dumpster; the dog survived).[220] The next closest sentence was twenty months plus three years' probation (for the *Alcorn* case discussed above, where the cat was hung from rafters, stabbed, and bled out for sexual gratification).[221] Only one other case had a sentence longer than one year – this one for sixteen months (for killing a family dog to retaliate against a woman).[222] The rest of the cases save two resulted in sentences ranging from six to twelve months (twelve months for torturing a girlfriend's two dogs over the course of one month, killing one;[223] ten months for stealing the family cat of acquaintances, stabbing and breaking the neck of the cat, and dismembering and attempting to cook the cat;[224] nine months for choking a cat and partly drowning and throwing two cats with great force against a wall;[225] eight months for throwing a twelve-week-old puppy down a flight of stairs, and picking up and throwing the puppy again after an argument with a girlfriend;[226] six months for a drug-induced two-day attack on a girlfriend's dog involving hitting the dog on toes, head, and elsewhere with a hammer;[227] and six months for the brutal killing of a friend's dog).[228] Of the last two cases, one led to a ten-month conditional sentence (threw the family dog from second floor and then beat the dog to death outside).[229] The lightest custodial sentence was ninety days (assault on the family cat out of frustration against an intimate partner).[230] After this review, Justice Gaschler imposed a custodial sentence of thirty-eight months.[231]

When the reasoning processes of courts in sentencing decisions are examined, it is apparent that judges weigh, as they are statutorily required to do for all offences per s.718 of the *Code*, the need for denunciation and deterrence against more rehabilitative goals.[232] To point out the light sentences that have been delivered even after the 2008 amendments and the judicial recognition of Parliament's intent to modernize penalties in this area is not to lament the lack of long incarceration periods for offenders, given the systemic racial and class inequities of the criminal justice system and the violence within prisons themselves. The pattern of light offences, however – well short of five years, a maximum sentence that reflects an anthropocentric valuation of animal life[233] – is cause for concern, given the benchmarks it suggests for future cases that judges may feel compelled to follow even as we can contest carceral outlooks and the hierarchies they exacerbate.[234] Furthermore, sentences on the lighter end may be said to reflect an ongoing welfarist interpretation of the anti-cruelty offence.[235] Indeed, the court in *Perrin* affirmed the historical Kantian-inspired justification for criminalizing cruelty against animals in the first place, namely due to its links to violence against humans.[236] In this regard, it is revealing that Parliament thought it fit to amend the sentencing principles in the *Code* in 2015 to instruct that where military, police, or service animals are involved (i.e., sentences made pursuant to subsection 445.01(1) of the *Code*), "the court shall give primary consideration to the objectives of denunciation and deterrence" over other considerations in section 718 of the *Code* that point away from incarceration.[237]

The ubiquitous presence of cats and dogs in the above list is not anomalous.[238] The extreme violence in the actions leading to the prosecutions and court decisions is also no coincidence.[239] Because it did not incorporate any substantive change regarding which actions qualify as animal cruelty, the 2008 amendments did nothing to broaden the remit of anti-cruelty laws. It is sadistic animal violence (i.e., harm to animals undertaken for no commercial or legitimate social purpose) that was targeted.

(c) More Recent Proposals. Shortly after the "law and order" legislative amendments were enacted in 2008, NDP MPs as well as Liberal MPs (then in Opposition) introduced private members' bills in yet another attempt to pass the more substantive changes. These changes were all reminiscent of Bill C-17 from years past; all of them were unsuccessful.[240] Most recently, in October 2016, a Liberal private member's bill C-246 failed at second reading. Had it succeeded, it would have introduced three significant substantive changes to animal protection law.[241]

First, that bill would have banned shark finning as well as the importation of shark fins detached from the rest of the shark into Canada; this would have brought Canada in line with international standards.[242] Second, it would have banned the sale and importation of cat and dog furs[243] and required source labelling of animal hair and cat and dog fur.[244] Again, this would have caught up with bans in other Western liberal democracies, which was its stated intent.[245] Third, the bill proposed amendments to the *Code* to strengthen and modernize animal cruelty offences. These included several long-standing proposals traceable to C-17 introduced almost two decades earlier (moving animal cruelty offences out of the section dealing with offences against property and into the section regarding public morals; adding "vicious or brutal" killing as an offence; changing the standard of wilful negligence to gross negligence for anti-cruelty offences; and introducing lifetime bans on ownership for convicted animal abusers) as well as new proposals (broadening the definition of bestiality and amending animal fighting laws to prohibit profiting in any way).[246]

The bill failed second reading in the House; even so, it is worth analysing the legislative debates it generated, for several reasons. For one, in targeting shark finning and the use of cat and dog fur for textiles, the amendments proposed two new substantive prohibitions that the series of bills following C-17 in 1999 did not include. Perhaps more importantly, however, examining the legislative debates about Bill C-246 elicits an appreciation of the tenacity of legal welfarism in shaping purported attempts to modernize legislation. That is, despite the fresh topics in the bill, the objections to the modest changes to anti-cruelty law included in Bill C-246 followed the same legal welfarist logic articulated juridically in *Ménard* almost four decades ago. When we calibrate overall support for Bill C-246, we find that it designated as "cruel" only culturally aberrant acts, understood as individual sadism or coded as (non-Western/ racialized) cultural backwardness. Despite the support for targeting these culturally aberrant practices, the legislation was defeated by the spectre that the proposed changes to the generic anti-cruelty provisions in the *Code* would apply to what by today's cultural standards is the legitimate use of animals. An entwined logic of species, culture, and race thus informed the support for different parts of the bill.

How can we see these dynamics at work? Consider first that almost all MPs supported the ban on the importation of shark fins. In speaking in support of the shark fin provisions in the bill, MPs cited concerns about the impact that shark extinction would have on marine ecosystems and decried the inherent cruelty of allowing live sharks to drown after their fins are removed.[247] Although some members felt that the ban was unnecessary or redundant, given that the act of finning itself is already illegal in Canada, there was no outright opposition to the ban from these quarters.[248] The ban on cat and dog fur sales and importation, along with the labelling amendments, fared even better, receiving no criticism in the House.[249] The lack of controversy over the targeting of these specific practices is of little surprise. They are widely presumed to be foreign practices not constitutive of Canadian (read: white) cultural sensibilities and economic realities.[250] Dogs and cats have been strongly humanized as companion animals and family members in Canada, so one would expect to see support for a proposed law to ban their use in textiles.[251] Sharks, by contrast, enjoy no such cultural endorsement. Yet parliamentarians were still in support of laws to discourage shark finning – a discordance that makes sense once we grasp the racialized cultural coding of shark finning. To be sure, there had been multiple defeats of anti–shark-finning initiatives before this victory, which speaks to the sobering reality that even non-culturally dominant exploitation of animals can encounter resistance.[252] It also shows how advocacy efforts in favour of certain racially or culturally coded animal-use practices can invoke ideals of multicultural and racial equality to work against animals.[253] Yet it is notable that the shark fin campaign eventually succeeded (see below).

In fact, the failure of Bill C-246 resulted from opposition to the generic amendments to the *Code* that were perceived to impinge on normalized *Canadian* animal uses. This opposition rested yet again on fears that lawful activities involving animals, such as hunting, fishing, and farming, would be swept into the new regulations. In particular, those opposed suggested that proposed s.182.1(1)(b), stating that "everyone commits an offence who ... kills an animal ... brutally or viciously, regardless of whether the animal dies immediately," would open all lawful killing to prosecution.[254] This fear arose from the fact that "brutally or viciously" is not defined in the *Code* and has not been interpreted by the courts, leaving the realities of this provision's application unknown.[255] The opponents suggested that a list of exempted activities be added to protect legal animal use.[256] The opposition to the move to change wilful negligence to gross negligence stemmed from a similar fear that such a change would make any accident, such as hitting an animal with one's car, criminal.[257] There was also objection, to a lesser extent, to moving animal offences out of the section dealing with property and into a section that deals with offences against persons. It was suggested that such a shift would create a slippery slope that could ultimately pit persons against animals in law.[258] It was also noted that placing purported animal rights in a section with rights of persons would afford animals human-type rights and thus inevitably threaten hunting, fishing, and farming.[259]

The support the *Code* amendments did attract stemmed from agreement to limit legal loopholes that had allowed acquittals in animal cruelty cases in the past without disrupting lawful and socially acceptable animal use in Canada. For example, the Supreme Court of Canada had recently ruled that a man was not guilty of bestiality for engaging a dog in acts of oral sex with his stepdaughter because there had been no physical penetration.[260] The amendment to broaden the definition of bestiality to include all sexual activity involving an animal was seen by supporters as a solution to this loophole.[261] Similarly, some supported adding "brutal and vicious" killing to remove the loophole that allowed an owner who killed his dog with a baseball bat to be acquitted because the animal died immediately and therefore did not suffer.[262] The proposed amendments to animal fighting laws were also supported to close loopholes that shielded from prosecution those who profited from breeding, training, and fighting animals.[263] The amendment moving the standard of wilful negligence to gross negligence was likewise supported to make it easier to prosecute animal abuses involved in puppy mills.[264] The gross negligence standard is also the standard employed in the remainder of the *Criminal Code,* and it was therefore argued that the standard should not be lower for crimes involving animals.[265] There was also some support for more stringent criminal laws for animal abusers generally, based on evidence that animal abuse is a precursor to other violent offences against humans.[266] Once again, far from suggesting that these types of amendments would impact the legality of current animal-use industry practices, MPs who spoke in favour of these amendments affirmed that they would not and also commonly affirmed these normalized uses.[267]

Reading the parliamentary debates on this most recent attempt at "modernizing" animal cruelty reveals the entrenched legislative commitment to legal welfarist views regarding which uses of animals should be illegal. Through repeated affirmations in the House by its supporters that the bill would not apply to the socially legitimate use of animals, this relatively recent round of debates on amendments first proposed now almost twenty years ago reveals the rigid anthropocentric parameters that continue to limit change for animals through the federal anti-cruelty law. Resistance from influential industry stakeholders and deference to industry activities among virtually all stakeholders have been formidable obstacles in effecting any substantive change beyond amplified penalties and judicial remedies. Majority support for substantive reform regarding what qualifies as cruelty has only been galvanized where activities are imagined as culturally deviant or culturally Other to normative Canadian sensibilities about human-animal relations.

The most recent reform measures – this time successfully adopted – confirm the above reading of the role of culture and race in determining human-animal relations. After an intense animal advocacy campaign that galvanized broad public support through petitions and letters to MPs to counter marine mammal industry lobbying, Canada has become the first country in North America to establish a national ban on keeping cetaceans in captivity.[268] This most recent proposal to alter the *Code,* emanating from the Senate this time as Bill S-203, culminated in the *Ending the Captivity of Whales and Dolphins Act,* which received Royal Assent on 9 June 2019.[269] Introduced in early 2015 by a senator influenced by the CNN documentary *Blackfish,* which chronicled several main harms of captivity to orcas through the case study of an orca named Tilikum, the now enacted bill has amended the *Code* by insert-ing a provision, s.445.2, that bans the captivity or breeding of cetaceans (whales, dolphins, and porpoises) in Canada.[270] Exemptions remain for cetaceans already in captivity or those who are confined in order that they may receive assistance, care, or rehabilitation;[271] the act is also not to derogate from existing Aboriginal rights.

The new law is underpinned by the high cultural status whales and dolphins enjoy as megafauna and "honorary humans" due to their appearance as well as their high levels of social, emotional, and intel-lectual complexity.[272] The act thus adds to the list of human uses of ani-mals that are prohibited outright without regard to necessity. At present, there are only two facilities in Canada that display and breed cetaceans: the not-for-profit Vancouver Aquarium in Vancouver (where one dol-phin is still captive after the Vancouver Aquarium lost several legal battles and endured negative publicity after municipal action to curtail cetacean captivity), and the commercial enterprise of MarineLand in Niagara Falls, Ontario (where one orca, five bottlenose dolphins, and fifty-three beluga whales are captive). Remarkably, despite cetaceans' special cultural status and the fact that other municipal and provincial governments have already passed similar initiatives curtailing these facilities' ability to display cetaceans,[273] the fate of the bill was far from clear, given industry resistance to it; the bill received only a lukewarm reception and required a substantial and sustained advocacy effort to pass.[274] A Senate bill to ban the import of shark fins was also proposed again in 2017, and in contrast, passed with little resistance in either the Senate or the House.[275] And, as referenced in the Introduction, as part of this animal reform trifecta, Canada has also closed the above-noted loophole regarding bestiality and strengthened its capacity ability to combat animal fighting and baiting;[276] the only real debate on these pro-visions was why the current Trudeau government had taken so long to close the loophole.[277]

B. Provincial Amendments

Has legislative reform at the provincial level escaped a doctrinal welfarist conceptualization of cruelty? Every Canadian province and territory has its own stand-alone animal cruelty legislation.[278] The provincial statutes range widely in content in terms of the pro-tections afforded to animals and the penalties imposed on offend-ers.[279] However, even the strongest legislation – such as the *Ontario Society for the Prevention of Cruelty to Animals Act*, which defines stan-dards of care for animals and includes comparatively high penalties, restitution provisions, mandatory veterinary reporting of suspected abuse, lifetime prohibitions on animal ownership for offenders, and a strong enforcement regime[280] – has done little to challenge the legal status of animals or limit industrialized abuse that enjoys some modicum of social support. As noted above, Ontario recently banned the captivity and breeding of cetaceans, but hunting, fishing, agriculture, and animal research all receive exemptions from the prohibition on causing distress or are exempt from complying with the regulated standards of care.[281] The killing of an animal meets the standard of care as long as it is done by a "method that produces rapid, irreversible unconsciousness and prompt subsequent death,"[282] potentially permitting a violent killing to escape penalty where the animal dies immediately. Other provinces provide even wider exemptions for industrialized violence against animals. In Alberta, the prohibition on causing distress does not apply to "animal care, management, husbandry, hunting, fishing, trapping, pest control or slaughter."[283] As with the *Code* provisions, only episodic violence is covered by the legislation. The provinces, however, have tended to amend their animal cruelty provisions more frequently than the federal government, and there have been some minor gains for animals. Yet even when public outcry has prompted legislative change, and quickly, the legal welfarist understanding in which cruelty is embedded has prevented anything further.

1. AMENDMENTS IN BRITISH COLUMBIA

For example, in early 2011 the government of British Columbia committed to a proposed series of amendments to the *Prevention of Cruelty to Animals Act* ("PCAA").[284] As with Bill C-17 at the national level, the impetus for the amendment was public outcry after intense media coverage of a particular incident of animal abuse.[285] Unlike the incidents that prompted the federal response, however, the acts of cruelty in British Columbia took place within an animal-based industry. The subsequent attention, and some of the amendments, focused a spotlight specifically on the industrialized treatment and economic status of animals.

The media coverage, which began in February 2011, described the deaths of about one hundred dogs killed in Whistler by a dogsled touring company apparently facing a drop in tourist demand after the end of the 2010 Vancouver Winter Olympics.[286] The killings, which took place on 21 and 23 April 2010, came to public attention as the result of a WorkSafeBC claim for posttraumatic stress by the employee who killed the dogs.[287] The claim provided horrific descriptions of the deaths of these dogs, all of which had been healthy (a veterinarian had in fact refused to euthanize them on this ground).[288] The dogs were either killed in a mass shooting, many "execution-style" (held down underfoot, gun to head), or had their throats slit. One dog escaped after having her cheek and one eye shot off and could not be recaptured; she was eventually shot with a scoped rifle. Another dog was found alive twenty minutes after being shot, crawling through the mass grave.[289] There were multiple mass graves at the end of the two-day massacre, which had been undertaken by an employee who considered the dogs his friends, the same as "pets," and in whom the dogs had placed their trust.[290] The alleged economic impetus, the sheer number of dogs killed, the witnessing of the deaths by other dogs that were slated to die and by those that were not, and the brutality of the killings all attracted intense public attention.[291]

As a result, the BC government quickly formed a Sled Dog Task Force in early February 2011. This task force, asked to recommend changes that would limit the possibility of similar killings in the future,[292] released a series of recommendations aimed at the sled dog industry specifically as well as at animal cruelty laws in the province generally.[293] These included the regulatory definition of specific standards of care for animals, particularly in the unregulated sled dog industry; an extension of the limitation period under the PCAA; enhancements to the enforcement and investigative capacity of the British Columbia Society for the Protection of Cruelty to Animals; mandatory veterinary reporting of suspected abuse; and an increase in penalties for offences committed.[294] The government announced it would act on all the recommendations, emphasizing the introduction of the "toughest animal cruelty laws anywhere in Canada."[295] The penalties for animal cruelty did rise to $75,000 and twenty-four months imprisonment for serious offences, and investigative capacities were increased.[296] Also, veterinarians are now required to report abuse when they reasonably suspect that "a person responsible for an animal is, or is likely, causing or permitting the animal to be in distress" as defined by the PCAA.[297] Perhaps most critically, the care requirements, although they do not transcend the traditional legal welfarist provisions related to adequate food, water, shelter, space, ventilation, light, and medical care, along with requirements for transport and the minimization of pain and distress during death, do set out specific standards for such care rather than leave these standards up to the industry itself, as is typically the case.[298] The response included a $100,000 grant to the BC SPCA for it to bolster its investigatory resources.[299]

2. POTENTIAL IMPACT OF BC'S AMENDMENTS

The main amendments to the PCAA – particularly the increase in penalties and the creation of regulatory standards of care for sled dogs in subordinate legislation – are arguably steps forward for the province.[300] At the same time, the amendments do no more than bring BC's animal cruelty laws in line with those in other provinces that are already hampered in their effects by a logic of legal welfarism. Perhaps most tellingly, the amendments do not meet the stated goal of preventing similar acts, for it is still permissible to kill sled dogs en masse.[301] They simply encourage owners not to kill healthy dogs, and if they do, the regulations attempt to avoid gruesome killings of the type that prompted the public outcry.[302] The industry-specific focus of the report that was a critical part of the legislative background explains the regulations' shortcomings.[303] Furthermore, the task force paid little attention to the ramifications for other industries.[304] The formation of the task force, the production of the report in response to the killings, and the resulting regulation all suggest that other industries will come under scrutiny and increased regulation only where an incident falling far outside the norms of industrialized abuse and cruelty comes to public attention and prompts a widespread outcry.

The one step the report did take toward challenging the property status of animals, at least within the dogsledding industry, is nowhere reflected in the resulting amended legislation. Buried in a discussion of the role of sled dogs – and not reflected by any specific recommendation – the report made the statement that there is "no acceptable reason to end the life of a healthy, socially amenable dog simply because it may no longer be suitable for use in the industry."[305] It further suggested the creation of "an appropriate long term plan for the dogs after they have been retired."[306] The suggestion that a business create retirement plans for the dogs appears to theorize animals as employees rather than as property. Regulation requiring retirement for older sled dogs would go beyond "treatment of animals exclusively as means to human ends"[307] and remove entirely the property owner's right to destruction.[308] If animals are seen as legal property, the company will have the right to dispose of them just as they would outdated machinery; the report suggests that where animals are involved, that right should be curtailed in favour of the animals' interests. These positions were not integrated into the regulation or in the guidelines that followed.[309]

3. SOME HOPE? CHALLENGING THE STRUCTURE OF ANTI-CRUELTY (UNDER)ENFORCEMENT

One promising development out of Ontario was a 2018 successful challenge to the tepid law enforcement structure of anti-cruelty legislation in general. These laws are enforced not by fully publicly funded police departments but by private charitable organizations commonly known as SPCAs, which are underfunded and whose primary source of revenue for their enforcement activities is community donors.[310] SPCAs are thus not subject to the same transparency and accountability measures that governmental bodies are. In *Bogaerts v Attorney General of Ontario*, the court held that this arrangement was unconstitutional.[311] The judgment eventually convinced the Ontario SPCA to stop enforcing animal cruelty legislation at the end of its funding agreement with the Province of Ontario; this forced the government to step in and administer and enforce its own legislation.[312] The ruling has been embraced by animal law advocacy organizations as a positive one inasmuch as it may catalyse a permanent change in law enforcement in this area, so that it would take on a decidedly public and government identity with the accountability, transparency, and funding measures that would presumably entail.[313] It remains to be seen whether this expectation will be realized.

IV. Conclusion

The *Code*, as an example of one significant area of the legal treatment of animals, is deeply influenced by their status as property. This legal status is most explicit in criminal offence provisions where the law declares animals to be property that can be stolen. Yet the complete commodification of animals is also demonstrated in legal doctrine that purports or appears to consider the welfare of animals. Canadian anti-cruelty law reflects the same legal welfarist bias found in American anti-cruelty jurisprudence in the weighing of the animal's interest as property against the human's interest as a property rights holder. As a result, animal interests judicially prevail only where there is no tangible human interest that is respected by majoritarian sensibilities. This makes animal suffering actionable only in an extremely narrow set of circumstances – a state of affairs confirmed by BC's inability to charge a man who had adopted a rescue pig from the BC SPCA only to kill and eat her a few short weeks later, an act that generated intense public outrage.[314] While the provincial and federal governments in Canada face different challenges in amending and updating their anti-cruelty laws, with the exception of orcas, both levels of government have so far failed to mount any substantial challenge to the property status of animals or to the massive industrialized violence they endure. Furthermore, the willingness to modernize penalties over even modest substantive change is revealing of the hold that legal welfarism exacts on the legal meaning of cruelty.[315]

This legislative rigidity is not surprising. Attempts to modernize legislation were never intended to dislodge the original anthropocentric, imperialist, and culturally contingent perceptions of what amounts to cruelty/illegitimate violence against animals.

This chapter has demonstrated that the non-contestation of the property classification of animals and the industries that rely on this status to instrumentalize them strips the legal concept of cruelty from all but the most culturally aberrant acts. Property status consigns animals to a legal abyss that anti-cruelty statutes cannot ameliorate. Even the rare court decision, such as Justice Rajiv Sharma's 2019 judgment from India extracted at the outset of this chapter, which states that animals should not be treated as property, cannot undo the built-in legal welfarist logic of these statutes. The next chapter considers whether property as a legal concept may be productively revised to respond to animals' needs and produce non-welfarist protective results for animals against exploitation, and, if not, whether personhood is an ideal replacement.

Appendix (Section 445.2 on cetaceans omitted)

445.1 (1) Every one commits an offence who
    (a) wilfully causes or, being the owner, wilfully permits to be caused unnecessary pain, suffering or injury to an animal or bird;
    (b) in any manner encourages, aids, promotes, arranges, assists at, receives money for or takes part in
        (i) the fighting or baiting of animals or birds, or
        (ii) the training, transporting, or breeding of animals or birds for the purposes of subparagraph (i);
    (c) wilfully, without reasonable excuse, administers a poisonous or an injurious drug or substance to a domestic animal or bird or an animal or a bird wild by nature that is kept in captivity or, being the owner of such an animal or a bird, wilfully permits a poisonous or an injurious drug or substance to be administered to it;
    (d) promotes, arranges, conducts, assists in, receives money for or takes part in any meeting, competition, exhibition, pastime, practice, display, or event at or in the course of which captive birds are liberated by hand, trap, contrivance or any other means for the purpose of being shot down when they are liberated; or

     (e) being the owner, occupier or person in charge of any premises, permits the premises or any part thereof to be used for a purpose mentioned in paragraph (*d*).

(2) Every one who commits an offence under subsection (1) is guilty of

     (a) an indictable offence and liable to imprisonment for a term of not more than five years; or

     (b) an offence punishable on summary conviction and liable to a fine of not more than $10,000 or to imprisonment for a term of not more than two years less a day, or to both.

(3) For the purposes of proceedings under paragraph (1)(a), evidence that a person failed to exercise reasonable care or supervision of an animal or a bird thereby causing it pain, suffering, or injury is, in the absence of any evidence to the contrary, proof that the pain, suffering, or injury was caused or was permitted to be caused wilfully, as the case may be.

(4) For the purposes of proceedings under paragraph (1)(b), evidence that an accused was present at the fighting or baiting of animals or birds is, in the absence of any evidence to the contrary, proof that he or she encouraged, aided or assisted at the fighting or baiting.

446 (1) Every one commits an offence who

     (a) by wilful neglect causes damage or injury to animals or birds while they are being driven or conveyed; or

     (b) being the owner of the person having the custody of a domestic animal or a bird or an animal or a bird wild by nature that is in captivity, abandons it in distress or wilfully neglects or fails to provide suitable and adequate food, water, shelter and care for it.

(2) Every one who commits an offence under subsection (1) is guilty of

     (a) an indictable offence and liable to imprisonment for a term of not more than two years; or

     (b) an offence punishable on summary conviction.

(3) For the purposes of proceedings under paragraph (1)(a), evidence that a person failed to exercise reasonable care or supervision of an animal or a bird thereby causing it damage or injury is, in the absence of any evidence to the contrary, proof that the damage or injury was caused by wilful neglect.

447 (1) Every one commits an offence who builds, makes, maintains or keeps an arena for animal fighting on premises that he or she owns or occupies, or allows such an arena to be built, made, maintained or kept on such premises.

(2) Every one who commits an offence under subsection (1) is guilty of

   (a) an indictable offence and liable to imprisonment for a term of not more than five years; or

   (b) and offence punishable on summary conviction and liable to a fine not more than $10,000 or to imprisonment for a term of not more than two years less a day, or to both.

447.1 (1) The court may, in addition to any other sentence that it may impose under subsection 445(2), 445.1(2), 446(2) or 447(2),

   (a) make an order prohibiting the accused from owning, having the custody or control of or residing in the same premises as an animal or a bird during any period that the court considers appropriate but, in the case of a second or subsequent offence, for a minimum of five years; and

   (b) on application of the Attorney General or on its own motion, order that the accused pay to a person or an organization that has taken care of an animal or a bird as a result of the commission of the offence the reasonable costs that the person or organization incurred in respect of the animal or bird, if the costs are readily ascertainable.

(2) Every one who contravenes an order made under paragraph (1)(a) is guilty of an offence punishable on summary conviction.

(3) Sections 740 to 741.2 apply, with any modifications that the circumstances require, to orders made under paragraph 1(b).

2 What's Wrong with Personhood? The Humanizing Impact of *Anthropos*

But how do we engage with "others" responsibly? Instead of asking how, whether, and when animals should be included in existing models of subjectivity, I argue that they already underline the core of that subjectivity – that definitions of self-consciousness, rational agency, the capacity to use language are foundationally underwritten by an understanding of "the human" as emerging in relation to "the animal" and that we need to go the other direction and envision viable forms of alterity that are neither appropriative nor oppressive.[1]

Colleen Glenney Boggs, *Animalia Americana: Animal Representations and Biopolitical Subjectivity*

In accordance with its duty to reexamine the common law in light of scientific discovery, evolving standards of morality, public opinion, and experience, this Court should recognize that Happy is a "person" with the common law right to bodily liberty protected by the common law of *habeas corpus* as a matter of liberty, equality or both, and order her immediate release.[2]

Elizabeth Stein and Steven M. Wise, "Memorandum of Law in Support of Petition for Habeas Corpus"

We have seen that the legal classification of animals as property is incompatible with ameliorating the vast majority of animals' lives through other reform measures. Property is a legally debilitating category, and the association of animals with property is so entrenched that animalization has become synonymous with propertization and the loss/denial of legal personhood. Given this situation, scholars and advocates have sought to extend personhood and the core life and bodily integrity rights this legal status denotes to animals. In 1993, philosophers Peter Singer and Paola Cavalieri launched the Great Ape Project, an initiative meant to generate worldwide support for the protection of rights to life, liberty, and security of the person for non-human great apes (chimpanzees, gorillas, orangutans) by tapping the expertise of biologists, psychologists, ethicists, philosophers, and other scholars.[3] Although all of these experts approached the question from the unique frames of their own institutional disciplines, they all advanced the view that non-human great apes are sufficiently close to human great apes in cognition, emotional expression, social organization, and sentience that they warrant the core fundamental rights of life, liberty, and security of the person that humans enjoy.[4] By signing on to the Great Ape Declaration – the crux of the initiative – country signatories and individuals would be signalling their support for including non-human great apes in the "community of equals"[5] and for recognizing them as legal persons. The project has enjoyed some significant successes; as of this writing, more than twenty countries have signed on to the declaration.[6]

As might be expected, however, the initiative has drawn criticism from those who believe that humans are fundamentally different from animals and that animals could never qualify as legal persons.[7] It has also drawn critique from those who, while sympathetic to the cause, nevertheless are concerned that any endorsement of similarity between humans and other animals, let alone an affirmation of personhood, might lead to the "animalization" of an already precarious human status for marginalized groups of humans.[8] The Great Ape Project has also drawn criticism from a perhaps less expected faction – scholars and animal advocates concerned about its exclusionary and anthropocentric parameters. Voices from that quarter have challenged the decision to exclude all animals except non-human great apes from the purview of the declaration and larger initiatives. They have also impugned the rationales given for why chimpanzees, gorillas, and orangutans deserve the three core rights, grounded as these are in the emphasis on proximity and/or sameness to humans.[9]

The Great Ape Project and the debate it has generated within animal circles brings into sharp relief the lack of consensus as to how to move forward legally for animals, given the spectre of the "human" as the benchmark deciding which other animals warrant legal protection and status. This debate has been revivified by new high-profile litigation in the United States. The Nonhuman Rights Project is an organization dedicated to securing legal personhood for non-human animals, "beginning with some of the most cognitively complex animals on earth, including chimpanzees, elephants, dolphins, and whales."[10] The organization has pursued groundbreaking litigation in this regard for captive chimpanzees in New York and elephants in Connecticut that has attracted considerable media attention[11] and raised new questions that have exposed divisions among scholars and advocates,[12] such as, Is legal personhood necessary to liberate animals or can meaningful protection against exploitation accrue through less radical, more incremental legally welfarist measures? If not, and if animals' property status must be abolished, how is such a disposition among jurists to be instilled? Should abolitionist legal reform be strategic and focus on the animals that are most likely to pass through the otherwise tightly closed legal door? If so, is personhood the legal status that animals should have?

This chapter takes up these questions about how animal law should move forward through the lens of critical theory. In it I argue against working within a property paradigm *and* pursuing a personhood model for animals. I demonstrate the limits of a personhood model for animals through the lens of critical theory. The opening section briefly addresses, however, the first question in this set of cascading queries: Must animals' legal status as property change for their condition to improve in any notable and lasting way? As the literature here is well developed, I briefly examine the main contours of the debate before indicating, again, quite summarily, why the answer to this question must be "yes" for any critically informed engagement with the question.

I. The Property/Personhood Debate

A. Property as a Bar to Animal Rights: The Abolitionist Position

The property/personhood debate is closely related to the welfare rights debate. Scholars have divergent views as to whether animals' property status must change in order for us to launch improvement in their lives and bring about anti-exploitative living conditions. Gary Francione is well-known as a passionate and resolute proponent of the abolitionist position, so-called for its insistence that the property status of animals in law must be abolished before any meaningful change can occur. Everything else for Francione is window-dressing: the very urgent material reality is that until property status for animals ends, violence against them will continue. Any other approach will merely assuage people's consciences.[13] As David Delaney stresses, "to own an animal is to have virtually complete dominion over the life and experiences that the being is to have."[14] The legal nature of property being what it is – that is, it orients the law toward owners' rights vis-à-vis legal objects rather than toward their duties to beings that lack legal subjectivity – a continued "owned" status will not give animals the trump cards they need to challenge how their owners choose to treat and use them.[15] This seems especially so, as Delaney points out, given the mind/body, subject/

object, and culture/nature binaries that are still so central to liberal legal humanist visions of human-animal relations today, which cast humans as superior in kind to animals.[16] This dynamic inheres even in the ideal companion animal situation, in which we may assume that animals command the love and respect of their human owners.[17] According to Francione, animals, being property and thus without rights, are vulnerable to shifts in their owners' emotional dispositions toward them and cannot avail themselves of the protection of law over those who hold rights in them.[18] Under the abolitionist view, animals need rights via legal personhood to protect them from instrumental use.

B. *Property as Incidental to Progressive Law Reform: Welfarism*

Those who seek liberal justice for animals but who disagree with Francione's abolitionist position offer two main arguments. The first emphasizes strategy and the efficacy of law reform. Theorists here contend that the abolitionist position is too idealistic and utopian and that if advocates concentrate their efforts solely on that position no change for animals will result.[19] They disagree with Francione that welfarist measures are ineffectual, insisting that they *can* have tangible suffering-reducing effects on animals' lives even if animals' overall exploitation within a given industry continues.[20] These effects can be experienced by animals in the here and now despite their eventual death in whatever industry is exploiting and consuming their bodies. The divergence of opinion on this point was clearly articulated, for example, in relation to Proposition 2 in California, the referendum that banned veal and sow gestation crates as well as battery cages for chickens in California on 1 January 2015.[21] When Francione was asked whether he supported Proposition 2, he replied that he did not since the initiative did not abolish factory farming or the tremendous suffering it entailed but merely made its existence more palatable to consumers.[22] His welfarist critics disagree, arguing that while the proposition is modest in scope, it is still a "step forward."[23]

A second common welfarist reply to the abolitionist stance in the property debate adopts a different view of the implications entailed by the legal status of property. Cass Sunstein has argued that it is not animals' property status that impairs the operation of animal welfare laws but poor enforcement.[24] For Sunstein, owners' duties to provide the basic necessities of life that these laws typically provide translate into rights for animals and the defect in the system is lax enforcement. If animal welfare laws were applied properly, animals would enjoy cruelty-free lives. The human and corporate service to which animals' lives would still be put is not a problem for Sunstein.[25]

C. Property as Amenable to Law Reform: The Rehabilitative Position

Other critics of the abolitionist approach accept Francione's egalitarian departure point for animals (or concede it for the sake of argument) but disagree with his appraisal of the subordinating effects of property; they see more potential in recuperating property from its normalized owner-oriented connotations and transforming it into a concept that demands more from owners in relation to their living yet objectified charges. They thus seek to rehabilitate property from its usual owner-obsessed connotations.[26] David Favre has developed this view most robustly in a series of articles dedicated to advancing animals' interests without waiting for a revolutionary change in law, which he sees as highly unlikely.[27] He has offered the concept of "living property" for domesticated animals as a new legal category that would entail, in his view, more duties on owners than they currently have under anti-cruelty statutes or otherwise.[28] Favre has also suggested that current property rights in animals be reconceptualized through the prism of equitable principles that have supplemented the common law for centuries.[29] He presents the idea of giving animals equitable title to themselves through the long-accepted practice of dividing legal from equitable ownership rights when equity calls for it. The most relevant contemporary use of equitable principles is through the vehicle of the trust, which separates legal title (which resides in the trustee, who manages the trust fund but is unable to benefit from it) from equitable title (which resides in the beneficiary, who does not get to direct her money but gets the benefits of it once the trustee sees fit to disperse it). Crucial to the trust dynamic is the principle that the legal owner must act in the best interests of the equitable owner.[30]

Once these equitable principles and the trust dynamic were transposed onto the situation of domestic companions, the human owner would be legally required to act in the best interests of the companion animal. That animal would still be owned, but she would now possess the equitable title, not the human owner, who presently holds both forms of title.[31] This is an innovative solution, but it is perhaps revealing that Favre only applies this theory of equitable self-ownership to certain groups of animals – those kept for companionship rather than profit.[32] In the more corporate realm of ownership where animals are bred, confined, and slaughtered routinely to turn a profit, it is highly debatable whether any amount of tweaking of the property concept would divest it of the power it gives to owners to control, maim, kill, and generally exploit the items they own and in which they hold rights. Favre does not address this shortcoming to his theory.

D. Assessing the Positions through Critical Theory

Without discounting the importance of the property/personhood debate and the nuanced positions that have been articulated by its participants, I believe that critical theory offers us a more decisive and satisfying answer as to whether property is a problematic category for animals.[33] In all the critical theoretical examinations of human injustice it is virtually impossible to encounter any theorist who accepts that the situation of owning a human being is compatible with justice for that individual or group of individuals. For all the richness of opinion across and within these theoretical frameworks, ownership of one person by another is never entertained as a viable option for conditions of justice.

This is the case even in scholarship guided by liberalism and economic theory where the issue is *voluntary* human slavery and servitude (i.e., where an adult agent chooses to enter into a contract of servitude because he believes the arrangement to be a better option than what current impoverished life circumstances allow). Notwithstanding strong commitments to individual adult agency, free markets, capitalism, globalization, and market efficiencies, scholars here have argued that it is immoral to permit a human being to enter into a servile relationship with another.[34] As Debra Satz has noted in arguing against the legality of such contracts, "even those who have defended the economic rationality of such relationships have noted the 'ugly power relations' involved in the phenomena."[35] If it is so basic to human justice (whether understood as freedom, autonomy, dignity, or equality) that persons are forbidden to sell themselves, how can the same type of servile relationship with all its "ugly power relations" (at least in the industrial context, in which the vast majority of owned animals exist) pass muster when the living beings at issue do not choose to be owned? Even if we were to switch this last premise and accept that animals do consent to their domestication and subordination to human and corporate owners,[36] the argument Satz advances would still hold. As suggested by the title of her monograph, *Why Some Things Should Not Be for Sale: The Moral Limits of Markets*,[37] consent by someone to adopt a completely commodified position vis-à-vis another is irrelevant. Satz, like many others, maintains this position even where the "thing" at issue is dispensable body tissue and not the entire person.[38] When animals are owned it is their entire body that is propertized. Because of their absolute commodification, there has been little debate about whether it is acceptable to commodify parts of animals. This is what property status in the law entails.[39]

Both critical theory and more classically oriented liberal theories instruct that this status – the status of being owned – is ethically unacceptable for human beings. This prompts the question why the same conclusion has not yet been reached about animals. The now entrenched association between property and animality that Delaney highlights (see below) provides an instructive explanation. Yet it is precisely that association that critical researchers need to investigate and dismantle. The implications of not taking up this work are too dismal and violent. As property, animals occupy a commodified and objectified social status that only cherished and respected companion animals have any hope of transcending. All animals, though, occupy a position of legal invisibility due to their propertized status; this is the case also for wild animals, which are always already amenable to propertization schemes. As we have seen, the negligible protections under anti-cruelty statutes do not yield anything remotely approximating legal subjectivity. If the desire is to inaugurate a legal system that prevents animal exploitation, the declassification of animals as property is a necessary step. What new legal status should prevail can then emerge as the more pressing question.

II. Personhood as an Alternative to Propertization: Its Origins and Contours

By far, the most common alternative legal status proposed for animals by abolitionist scholars, as well as advocates seeking non-incremental change (as instanced in present personhood projects for animals such as the Great Ape and Nonhuman Rights Projects), is personhood. Personhood, understood in common law and civil law systems as a Western legal concept, in fact originated in ancient Roman theatre.[40] A *persona* was a mask worn by an actor in Roman classical drama.[41] That mask conveyed a *persona* to audiences, and it was this concept that eventually inspired the idea of personhood as a means to encode legal subjectivity in an entity in the common and civil law systems.[42] David DeGrazia provides a helpful abbreviated explanation of the development of the concept:

> The word "person" traces back at least to the Latin persona: a mask, especially as worn by an actor, or a character or social role. The concept evolved into the Roman idea of a bearer of legal rights – so that, notably slaves did not qualify as persons – before broadening into the Stoic and Christian idea of a bearer of moral value; perhaps this transition involved broadening the relevant conception of law from human legal systems to

"natural" law. The modern concept, as exemplified in John Locke's writings (Locke 1694: Bk 2, ch. 27), understands persons as beings with certain complex forms of consciousness.[43]

Although personhood initially applied only to human actors, in law it was extended (without fuss) to corporations and ships in the nineteenth century.[44] Animal advocates often make much of this point to illustrate that personhood does not correlate with an innate biological species status and, moreover, does not require a living being or even a tangible and material entity to ground its application.[45] If personhood can operate at such a high level of abstraction so as to accommodate the "interests" of corporations, which do not think, feel, or breathe, then surely it can extend to animals without serious controversy.[46] With such arguments, lawyers for animals draw upon what Ngaire Naffine terms the legalist perspective on how law should define persons – that they are a pure construction of law and thus do not mandate any pre-existing biological form or physical or mental capacity.[47]

Francione was the earliest legal scholar to deliberately and comprehensively argue for the extension of personhood to sentient animals, and his stance in this regard remains the most influential.[48] For him, personhood naturally flows from the abolition of property that must occur if we are to treat all sentient beings equally. If we are committed to the principle that humans should not suffer from exploitation due to their sentience and grant them rights to protect them from such suffering, then on the principle of equal consideration, we should treat animals in a similar way, for they too have an interest in not suffering.[49] Legal personhood will permit animals to be the rights-bearers they deserve to be as sentient beings and they will thus be entitled to protection from the state against those who wish to violate their rights.[50] The status will communicate full moral status, but more importantly, if working optimally, it will trigger the state to enforce the application of the equal consideration principle.

Other abolitionist scholars make the same argument but extend it to all conscious animals. In *The Animal Question: Why Nonhuman Animals Deserve Human Rights*, Cavalieri meticulously argues that human rights may logically extend to all animals expressing consciousness, thus implicitly endorsing personhood for animals so that it corresponds with human rights.[51] Cavalieri defines "consciousness" as the ability "to have experiences and to care about these experiences. It means to have at least the interest in avoiding pain and experiencing pleasure."[52] Cavalieri does note some concerns with the personhood model but accepts it nonetheless.[53] By these accounts, personhood, then, appears to be a viable and desirable concept that can sensibly extend to non-human animals both morally and – more importantly for our purposes – legally. Given the current choice between property and personhood, legal personhood (which encompasses the rights protections inherent to it) is the only legal status that will actually protect animals and help them flourish. Yet, as a rising chorus of critical scholars have noted, we need to consider whether it is possible to reach the abolitionist end points of Francione, Cavalieri, and like-minded scholars with respect to non-instrumental treatment without promoting the problematic liberal humanist affinities entailed by personhood. The next section addresses these problems.

III. Personhood's Exclusionary Imprint and Its Implications for Animals

It is perhaps no surprise that many animal law scholars and lawyers would endorse the aims of the Great Ape Project and the Nonhuman Rights Project insofar as they champion personhood for animals that possess the cognitive and other capacities for which (paradigmatic) humans have been valued.[54] The problematic outcome of focusing on those animals that humans recognize as similar to themselves is that all the others continue to be legally invisible and their exploitation justified.[55] It would be a mistake, though, to presume that the problem with this type of personhood litigation would disappear if personhood litigation were suitably revised to include *all* animals. This section explains why this option is unavailable and discusses the ongoing problems in accommodating alterity that personhood presents.

A. Exclusionary History and Mould – Law's Person as Paradigmatically "Human"

As with all entrenched legal terms, contemporary invocations of Western understandings of personhood to denote legal subjects flow from a particular historical trajectory. A primary concern with personhood as developed in the British common law and extended to settler-colonial legal systems like Canada's is the hierarchical nature of this background. While the open-ended, non-biologically rooted legalist accounts of legal personhood circulate in jurisprudence, it is clear that another vision – one that Naffine terms rationalist – of the legal person dominates in legal jurisprudence.[56] The rationalist vision of who qualifies as a legal person privileges the intelligent human agent who can make decisions as well as accept accountability. As Naffine underscores, the underlying narrative about the creation of rational actors engaged in legal transactions and encounters is the social contract theory inspired by seventeenth- and eighteenth-century Lockean and Kantian political philosophy as well as by Cartesian dualistic thinking.[57] This narrative imagines a fully formed adult human who is independent, autonomous, and intelligent, who can be held accountable due to these qualities, and who freely enters into society in this state in order to take advantage of law's ordering power to maximize his self-interest in staying this way.[58] Critical to this path of self-actualization and self-maximization is the ability to contract to acquire property.[59]

In this narrative, it is obvious that personhood was reserved for an elite sector of humanity: white, able-bodied, cisgender heterosexual men of property. This concept accentuated stratifications of class, sexual orientation, gender, race, ability, and age at the time when these stories of creation were formulated and advanced.[60] As Anna Grear adeptly explains, it is these "human hierarchies of being,"[61] disavowing the feminine and the embodied,[62] that are embedded in "law's central subject,"[63] the *anthropos*. Tracing a "critical legal reading of its genealogy," Grear outlines how law's rationalist person was central to European capitalist and imperial expansion, colonial Othering, theft of Indigenous lands, and environmental devastation occasioning the current phenomenon of the Anthropocene as well as global neoliberal governance.[64] All those not residing under the aegis of the white, able-bodied, property-holding masculinity to which the *anthropos* correlated were devalued as feminized, close to nature, and of the body.[65] Indeed, law's person houses a vision of "the human ... that was always intended selectively to bring within its orbit only those beings who fit a relatively narrow set of criteria for inclusion in the circle of humanity proper."[66] Grear identifies this mainstay figure of "liberal legal anthropocentrism" as a "cipher bearing only attenuated resemblance to a living human being."[67] Moreover, this vision of the "human" was not unique to law; this very particularized idea of the "human" has been similarly partial historically and even today vis-à-vis certain dehumanized/animalized populations that nonetheless biologically belong to the human species.[68]

But it is not just the exclusionary historical origins of this concept and the marks it has left to this day that are concerning. Returning to the examples of the Great Ape Project and the Nonhuman Rights Project, we can now more clearly apprehend a further element of the criticism that followed the initiative, namely, that a focus on great apes and other culturally popular or revered animals will reinscribe humanism and anthropocentrism. The problem is not simply that an initiative that privileges certain human-like or human-enough animals as persons excludes all other animals, but that the exclusionary historical imprint of personhood inclines the concept in the present to *systemically* disfavour those that do not match the Western, able-bodied, propertied, human male identity through which personhood was first consolidated. In other words, it is not just that animal advocate petitioners make an encumbered choice "to convert 'otherness' into 'sameness'"[69] in campaigns in which personhood or classic civil and political rights for an animal or animals are sought. The personhood model in fact encourages a route that inevitably highlights the differences and putative inferiority of the excluded animals that fall outside the litigation's parameters as well as the included animals whose residual embodied non-humanness, despite this latter's group "honorary human" status, haunts the category itself. According to elitist, masculinist, racialized, and able-bodied understandings of what humans are, all animals are not, and likely never will be, "human" enough to either "merit" personhood as a protective legal status or to receive adequate legal protection once deemed "persons"; that the substandard treatment of dehumanized humans persists despite their personhood is a persuasive indicator that similar substandard treatment will befall animals if they become "persons."[70]

Law is still anthropocentric, yes, and extends personhood to all biologically designated humans, but its understanding of the human and thus legal person is delimited by a "Cartesian/Kantian tradition of Western philosophy that exalts human minds and excises the body and all things associated with nature as *exterior* to this rational mind."[71] Thus, even if personhood campaigns on behalf of animals avoided sameness discourses, and were potentially or actually theoretically inclusive of all animals, personhood as a category would still be premised on a sharp mind/body split that exalts a certain type of reasoned cognition. Fitting beings that the law has traditionally disavowed as legal subjects because of their location in these Cartesian/Lockean/Kantian dichotomies as "mere bodies" into the coveted category of personhood that is still tightly correlated to anthropocentric exaltation of human minds, and thus "the foundations of modern liberal legal subjectivity," will be difficult.[72] As Sheryl Hamilton has also argued in her work canvassing an array of liminal humans and non-humans,[73] the push to encapsulate these beings can result in an awkward fit into a category that has a clear culturally constructed originating and exclusionary identity.[74] A central part of this identity is the degradation of embodiment that the concept has entailed, making it nearly impossible for those whose current-day corporeal manifestations do not cohere with the "white, property owning, acquisitive, broadly Eurocentric masculinity that acts upon a world constructed as a juridically striated, territorialized *extensa*"[75] to qualify as legal persons.

B. *Personhood and Animality as Mutually Exclusive*

Colin Dayan's work adds a strong historical current to Hamilton's argument by charting the multiple ways in which personhood cannot be counted on to secure the protections one would wish because of the cultural narratives in which the law is embedded and from which it draws strength – narratives on which jurists and legislators are quick to rely. In *The Law Is a White Dog: How Legal Rituals Make and Unmake Persons*,[76] Dayan reveals the "sorcery of law" in creating persons and things.[77] In doing so, she also importantly illuminates personhood's steadfast reliance on the concept of animality and the figure of the subhuman. Dayan's entire book considers law's agency in defining personhood – how it assigns personhood to some, denies it to others, and withdraws it when social forces coalesce to make withdrawal acceptable.[78] In this latter regard, Dayan discusses at length the concept of civil death – where one is legally alive but no longer a person in law; her main examples come from American slavery, but she traces the residue of slave law in contemporary examples of prisoners in the United States and "detainees" at Guantanamo Bay.[79] Dayan considers how personhood can be so quickly lost and reveals the law's role in, as she puts it, creating these "negative" and "disfigured" models of personhood for human beings.[80]

Dayan's work exposes how heavily definitions of legality and illegality are bolstered by cultural narratives, among them the familiar narrative of dehumanization through animalization.[81] The efficacy of dehumanization discourses in legitimating slavery is well-known. Dayan helpfully stresses the same point in relation to contemporary penal politics: "Before the state can punish, it must appear to know what is being judged. The rules of law and leeway within them enact and enable a philosophy of personhood and create the legal subject. They also recognize forms of punishment that are activated for people of a certain 'nature' or 'character' – those labeled unfit, barbaric, subhuman, or 'the worst of the worst.'"[82]

Dehumanization thus emerges as an extremely popular strategy to legitimate the stripping away of rights from human beings that then enables treatment and violence that would otherwise be unacceptable.[83] It has been used over many centuries and in many instances of war and ethnic conflict and, as Dayan demonstrates, in homegrown domestic policies when the state intervenes in the bodies of its subjects through its biopolitical projects.[84] It is through dehumanization that personhood is lost; discursively and materially, humanization becomes a prerequisite for personhood. To be a person, one has to be *seen* as human. Put differently, animal personhood is an oxymoron in anthropocentric legal systems.

Samera Esmeir highlights the same associations between property/personhood and animality/humanity but from the obverse angle. She elucidates the tight entwining of legal personhood with human identity such that any violation of this legal status is immediately perceived and represented as a loss of humanity:

> Contemporary liberal assertions equate illegal oppression and practices of expulsion from the juridical order with exclusion from humanity. It is often argued that violence ensuing from the abandonment of persons beyond the pale of the law not only violates their humanity but also, and perhaps more crucially, dehumanizes them or constitutes them as less than human. While the objective of these critical assertions is to expose the radical evil that illegal violence can institute, they also establish an equation between the protection of the law and the constitution of humanity, effectively granting the former a magical power to endow the latter.[85]

Esmeir argues that law, particularly British colonial law and modern international human rights law, constitutes the human through the conferral and respect of rights-bearing status – so much so that the predominant frame advanced when a person's or people's rights are violated is not depersonification but *dehumanization*. Esmeir terms this understanding of humanity, as dependent on and sublimated to the legal status of personhood, a "juridical humanity."[86] She is dismayed by the hold that law exacts on our understanding of what it means to be human and is further concerned that the narrative of dehumanization that attends stories about human rights violations in the global South continues a colonial legacy whereby racialized non-Western subjects are forever waiting to be saved by the magical powers of Anglo-American law to humanize them.[87] In this postcolonial critique of law, personhood is not a justice-conferring category but rather a vehicle that constitutes the human and that claims to protect human rights through long-standing colonial premises about the humanizing and enlightening effects of Western legal systems on the rest of the world.[88] Is it thus part of a set of "imperial narratives," whereby force is narrated as a gift, as if empire is what gives the Other freedom, what brings the Other into modernity.[89] In other words, colonial law makes humans through the assignment of personhood. One has to be a person to be a human *because that is what personhood signifies*.

This colonial humanizing function of personhood is perceptible in contemporary human rights contestations. When we want to recognize the personhood and human rights of groups today, we humanize them. Importantly, this means ascribing the traits associated with dominant masculinist and Western understandings of what it means to be human canvassed above: rationality and the capacity and desire for independence and non-relational autonomy. Conversely, when the desired outcome is the depersonification of purportedly human subjects, the strategy elected is to dehumanize these subjects. This entails the ascription of traits associated with dominant understandings of what it means to be less than or non-human: animality, the subordination of the mind to the body, and the rejection of Western values. Liberal legal subjectivity cannot escape the power of the human–non-human binary in creating its preferred legal subjects and their corresponding masculinist and colonial exclusions. As feminist, postcolonial, and queer theory scholars discussing violence at Guantanamo Bay and Abu Ghraib and other contemporary "states of exception" have commented, this masculinist and colonial and humanist logic of legal personhood and rights is not exceptional, but "symptomatic of the very nature of the predominant liberal democratic system and of the liberal notion of human rights."[90] Liberal humanism's traditional exclusions in mapping out the category "human" that generated law's understanding of the "person" have not disappeared;[91] they are still at work in shaping legal subjectivity, its extension and denial.[92]

Viewed within this frame, personhood is further and irrevocably tainted as a viable option for respecting animals, and all their alterity, as legal subjects. Animality is a contra-indication for personhood because persons are made through proving their humanity and unmade when that humanity is called into serious question. So it is not simply the case that animals are legally property and thus need only to be moved outside of this category and made persons for legal benefits to flow.[93] Instead, animal law advocates are facing a situation where the *very category of property is defined through animality*. Returning to Delaney again, we see the force of these associations between property and animality:

A being, a baboon, a dolphin, a pit bull, is doubly objectified, doubly reduced by prevailing discourses of power. First, it is reduced to "animality" and all that that means and doesn't mean. Second, it is reduced to property and all that that entails. It is positioned within forms of meaning, and so positioned within circuits of power vis-à-vis the legal subject and vis-à-vis the state as the guarantor of the rights of ownership. Its figurations as animals, as nature, as body, on the one hand, and as property on the other hand, are mutually reinforcing and neither can be severed from the other. Because it is "an animal" it can be treated like property; because it is property it can be treated like an animal.[94]

If we accept that in general, "animality is not simply outside of the social order and its mechanisms of subjectification [but] is foundational to it," the sheer magnitude of the influence of the human/non-human divide to law's foundational divide between property and personhood that Delaney outlines is obvious.[95] In law, it is this animalized underpinning of property that constitutes property's real and imagined polar opposite: personhood, which itself is rendered indissociable from humanity for living beings.[96] How can animals be legally represented through a legal category that has traditionally repelled them and constituted itself against them? Furthermore, how can animals then move easily into a new legal category that is virtually synonymous with humanity (and problematically relies on subordinated alterities to shore itself)?

Personhood campaigns, especially those like the Nonhuman Rights Project that actively deploy sameness logic to be persuasive – but also, critically, campaigns that do *not* do this – thus intensify existing hierarchies. This intensification occurs among humans and animals but also across these categories as well. When advocacy efforts concentrate on those animals most like humans (in the hope that decision-makers will be persuaded of the injustice of the disparate treatment between subjects that are otherwise alike due to certain shared capacities), they implicitly grant honorary human status to those animals.[97] These animals are invariably what Cary Wolfe, in discussing the species grids that organize societies, has called the humanized animals.[98] Wolfe asserts that every stratified society encodes a hierarchical species grid that contains four categories organizing human-human and human-animal relations. In descending order, these categories are: humanized humans, animalized humans, humanized animals, and, at the bottom, animalized animals.[99] Although humanized animals are still subordinated to humanized and animalized humans, they are still culturally superior to the animalized animals in any given culture. Personhood campaigns seeking to envelop humanized animals in the protective cover of personhood by emphasizing these animals' similarity to humans may benefit humanized animals – not an insignificant achievement by any measure – but they also reinforce cultural attitudes about why law can continue subordinating animalized animals.[100] And it is the latter category into which most animals (consider farmed animals and trawled fish) are placed.[101]

C. Binary Reinforcement

Ciméa Barbato Bevilaqua educes a final critique of the personhood model: its reinforcement of the binary vision of legal subjects and legal objects. Personhood proceedings do not disrupt the dichotomy at the heart of the legal system, which problematically forces virtually every type of entity into one of two categories.[102] Indeed, the seemingly intractable presence of the term in the law is a reason why some animal scholars who might otherwise abandon the term given its theoretical resonance opt to tolerate it for animals.[103] If we allow personhood to continue, however, aspirations toward personhood will always already rely on the Otherness of things, all of them non-human. As much as legal strategies downplay animal difference in the hope of humanizing animals, some level of difference will always remain, making humanizing strategies always already precarious and unpredictable. As Bevilaqua notes, this is the case even for animals that are doubly humanized – first, by their genetic similarity to humans, like the chimpanzees at the heart of the Nonhuman Rights Project litigation in New York, and second, by their living arrangements in close proximity to humans, like the chimps Lili and Megh at the heart of Austrian personhood litigation. The latter have been infantilized through care practices (sleeping in children's beds, being fed through a bottle, having a "nanny" as their caregiver) despite their adult status in chimpanzee lifespans.[104] In litigation, the similarities of chimpanzees like Lili and Megh to humans in genetic heritage, sociality, and the ability to impart culture intergenerationally can be stressed,[105] but the non-humanity of the chimpanzees can never be fully erased. This insight should lead us to the same conclusion that the discussion in this part of the book has repeatedly drawn – personhood as a legal concept fits at some levels but not others, and attempts to pursue it for even humanized animals merely entrench the paradigmatic human identity that defines it.

Efforts to personify some animals will thus necessarily accent the *thing*ness of other beings, again not merely excluding other animals from the argument but pushing them deeper into the realm of the property/thing. For Bevilaqua, the legal status for animals that is most consonant with this critical appraisal of personhood for animals is one that can recognize that animals are not things without insisting they be persons.[106] Whether she would endorse Hamilton's model of personae as a better alternative to personhood is an open question, but these two theorists are united in their rejection of personhood for liminal beings – and, in the case of Bevilaqua, for animals – as a route to granting full legal protection for these beings.

D. Personhood outside of Western Liberal Legalism?

I have been arguing that personhood is inherently an exclusionary category given its origins, which have imprinted on the concept a certain mould into which previously excluded others fit badly. Personhood's contraindications for animals are particularly stark, given the extent of overlap between personhood and human as coterminous concepts; personhood exerts a humanizing force that is not easily banished. The foregoing discussion, of course, has highlighted the problems with the term as it is understood in Western liberal legal orders. Personhood as a legal (and moral) term also exists in other legal traditions and societies unencumbered by anthropocentric or binary worldviews or foundational species-based hierarchies. Consider various Indigenous legal traditions worldwide, for example, as well as African and Asian cosmologies.[107]

Certainly, changing the core attributes of personhood to signal a relational, socially connected, reciprocating actor who may or may not be human – features often ascribed to persons in many non-Western cultures where interspecies relations are visible and normalized[108] – would likely be a momentous and welcome development for most of the beings concerned.[109] What if personhood as it operates in settler-colonial Canadian law could be stripped of its current content and supplanted with these new associations to denote something altogether different from the rational, culturally unencumbered, socially dislocated, wealth-maximizing human actor? And what if this could be done without personhood being defined in a binary fashion against the category of property? As much as some non-Western understandings of personhood would be a thorough disavowal of dominant colonial understandings of personhood inherited from European worldviews, I worry that personhood even robustly reimagined, and thus distanced from its current roots in Canadian law, would never fully shed the dominant traditional (and problematic) associations embraced by mainstream jurists and legal actors. If we are going to supplant the Western liberal legal understanding of personhood in settler-colonial jurisprudence with a completely different understanding of personhood, why not aim for a new term altogether rather than retaining personhood? The next chapter discusses a replacement for personhood that could be applied to animals once their propertied status has been eliminated. As will become apparent, multiple points of overlap exist between my proposed replacement – beingness – and Indigenous and other non-Western understandings of personhood as outlined earlier.

IV. Summary

For obvious reasons, personhood is a preferred legal alternative to property for animals, but it is not without significant limitations. The tethering of personhood to human benchmarks is evident in the Great Ape and Nonhuman Rights Projects and part of an understandable strategy to "get a foot in the door" that will open more broadly for all animals in the years to come. But the promotion of personhood in its dominant liberal legal sense for animals today invests in a colonial and otherwise exclusionary logic. Also, the concept of personhood contains anthropocentric valuations at its core such that a simple extension of personhood to animals will not destabilize the concept's anthropocentric parameters. Given this investment, it is worth devising an alternative legal subjectivity for animals that does not bear the imprint of the hierarchical stratifications that are central to modernity and its colonizing impulses.

Indeed, the critique of personhood canvassed in this chapter presages the work of those critical animal scholars who have called for a different model of subjectivity for animals, one that decentres the human and the thinking subject. Calls for such subjectivity have centred on valuing animals on account of their vulnerability, embodiedness, and relationality. To be sure, one need not resort to critical scholarship to encounter arguments for ending animal exploitation based on a relational account of animals' vulnerability.[110] But the concepts of embodiment, vulnerability, and relationality I seek to cultivate and combine into a new juridical recognition for animals is heavily indebted to the mappings they have received in such scholarship. Chapter 4 outlines these proposals and, harnessing their insights, assembles a transgressive alternative to personhood as a new legal subjectivity for animals that can nonetheless still signal an anti-exploitation stance vis-à-vis animals. Before delineating beingness as that new legal subjectivity, it will be instructive to set out several changes required to a liberal legal foundation on which any new subjectivity for animals would rest.

3 Toward a Post-Anthropocentric Legal Ontology

If we are serious about not rehabilitating humanism, or recognizing that a brutal humanism exists as a form of speciesism that cleaves not only raced and sexed humans from other humans, but also complicates any human/nonhuman animal divide and puts under duress our contingent relations to other animals, plant life, and ecologies of matter and material, can we think of precarity "beyond" the human? What would an interspecies politics or vision of precarity entail? What kinds of tentative relationships of interdependency and vulnerability should we attend to if the human is just one actor among many lively and not-so-lively actors that compose "a struggle to establish bonds that sustain us"?[1]

Jasbir Puar, ed., "Precarity Talk: A Virtual Roundtable with Lauren Berlant, Judith Butler, Bojana Cvejic, Isabell Lorey, and Ana Vujanovic"

To develop an ethic of nonharm to all living beings is to redefine the place of human/man in Western metaphysics, and that is why, among other reasons, it is aligned with a feminist project.[2]

Irina Aristarkhova, "Thou Shall Not Harm All Living Beings: Feminism, Jainism, and Animals"

Beingness (explored at length in the next chapter) provides law with a new way of conceptualizing animals, namely as legal "beings" that are defined by their embodiment, relationality, and vulnerability in much the same way that law's person is presently (and problematically) defined as rational, independent, and autonomous. Beingness is meant to be an alternative to both property and personhood. As a new legal subjectivity for animals, it forms one part of a larger ontological foundation for state law to become post-anthropocentric. By itself, however, it can only accomplish so much. A new legal foundation is still required that can shift law from its liberal legalist humanist values toward an overarching framework that is anti-anthropocentric. This chapter provides a theoretical treatment of what this foundation underlying beingness should be. It expands on the concept of post-anthropocentric legal ontology introduced in the Introduction as shorthand for a gold standard in creating a legal response to animals that does not ask them to comply with (dominant) human norms.

The modernist autonomous subject is, to be sure, "an incredibly powerful abstraction" in mainstream law structuring the concept of property.[3] The possessive and colonial individualism that the common law, colonialism, and capitalism have entrenched in the dominant social order is not easily undone. The discussion in this chapter is not meant to suggest otherwise. Law's liberal orientation and the multiple dispossessions and marginalizations it entails will likely be with us for a very long time to come. This sobering situation need not foreclose, however, the project of imagining alternative orientations, or what some have called other worldings,[4] and the decisional legal aptitudes that would need to be cultivated to shift law in that direction. The present chapter identifies at least some of these aptitudes or features for a post-anthropocentric legal foundation.

This chapter significantly enlists the work of feminist animal studies philosophers. The first part presents three different but related approaches to interspecies ethics advanced by leading animal ethics scholars. I comparatively identify the features of their interspecies *ethea* that should infiltrate the law. I first turn to the work of feminist animal care theorists Carol Adams, Josephine Donovan, and Lori Gruen to argue that feminist animal care theory's caring and empathetic interspecies orientation should shape a post-anthropocentric legal response to animals. I address the main criticisms of that framework regarding its care orientation as well as its heightened respect for emotions-based reasoning. I then explore the insights from Kelly Oliver and Cynthia Willett's respective proposals for interspecies relations that would helpfully supplement a feminist animal care approach. Oliver's and Willett's works combine to create what they term a "call and response" ethics toward animals that emphasizes human responsibility and biosocial awareness in apprehending and responding to animals' needs. I argue here that Oliver and Willett's call and response ethics reinforce the non-anthropocentric, non-masculinist, and non-colonial commitments of feminist animal care theory while adding valuable insights about human responsibility for and accountability to animals and their biosocial needs that the law should also incorporate.

As a third and final approach to interspecies ethics from which law can learn, I showcase two closely aligned phenomenological approaches that emphasize the centrality of the body and flesh as a means to understand and recast human-animal relations. Here, I first discuss the feminist work of Jennifer McWeeny, who urges the adoption of "topographies of flesh" when analysing oppressive conditions across difference. I then look at the transhuman ethic of shared bodiment, conviviality, and corporal compassion articulated by Ralph R. Acampora. My purpose in this first section is to argue that all three feminist/feminist-inspired frameworks provide critical ingredients for shifting the way law perceives animals, and makes sense of and responds to their needs, and thereby clear a path toward a post-anthropocentric legal ontology.[5]

I. Laying the Groundwork for Reorienting Legal Reasoning

A. The Feminist Animal Care Tradition and Reasoning from Emotions

For law to advance into post-anthropocentric terrain, reason must lose some of its powerful hold. In particular, reason must cease to be viewed as a capacity in denoting who counts as a legal subject. The critical insight that reasoning, including legal reasoning, is an emotion-based process must become normalized among legal decision-makers. That it is important to embrace emotions in our response to animals and use emotions to guide decision-making about our relations with animals is a key insight of vegetarian ecofeminist theory,[6] also known as the feminist animal care tradition (see this book's Introduction).[7] The feminist animal care tradition is responsive to animal suffering not through abstract rationalizations but rather out of sympathy, empathy, and compassion for animals as well as recognition of their ability to emote and feel.[8] Feminist animal care theorists[9] contest the classic theories in animal ethics as well as those of new posthumanist scholars who rely solely on reasoned and abstract arguments to persuade their audiences of the validity of non-exploitative end points for animals.[10] They have long impugned the devaluation of emotions that occurs in these theories[11] and the resulting alienating effects that such traditional theorizing has on those it seeks to motivate.[12] Critically, feminist animal care theorists urge us to richly contextualize ethical questions, including those that touch on the relationships involved and the emotions that circulate when we confront pain and suffering.[13]

From the writings of prominent animal ethics theorists such as Peter Singer, Tom Regan, and Steven Wise, who have attempted to advance claims for animals through reasoned argumentation, we observe and can infer that they were/are keen to meet the standards of their disciplines, which expect as much and frown upon appeals to emotion.

Nevertheless, as feminist animal care theorists emphasize, it is difficult to deny the androcentrism that resides in arguments that aim to uplift animals through a vehicle (reasoning capacity) that has served as the crux of the stories we tell and that in the West, for generations, has been making the case for animals' categorical inferiority to humans as well as for women's and other marginalized groups' subhuman status.[14] Keenly aware of how we are shamed into denying or minimizing our sympathies for animals who suffer – a gendered hegemonic move that stigmatizes emotions as feminine[15] – these theorists prompt us to recover our emotions in relation to animals and mobilize them into a widespread political project.[16]

Critical to this emotional rehabilitation is the cultivation of certain caring dispositions toward animals, namely attentiveness, but also responsiveness and respect. Some feminist care theorists have proposed a framework of sympathy to mobilize these emotional dispositions.[17] Josephine Donovan has suggested that sympathy is first cultivated by encouraging humans to imagine themselves in the shoes of the particular suffering animal they encounter through a spirit of attentive love.[18] Attentive love, a concept developed by Simone Weil and incorporated into care theory by Iris Murdoch, directs our focus to what another is experiencing and, in particular, suffering.[19] This state of emotional resonance having been achieved, feminist animal care theory calls on us to extend this sympathy to animals that one has not personally encountered but that are similarly suffering.[20] This should lead to awareness and understanding of human-animal power imbalances in the broader culture and to a desire to undo these asymmetries.[21] Donovan is clear that practising sympathy is a cognitive as well as emotional faculty in that it involves "strong powers of observation and concentration, as well as faculties of evaluation and judgment."[22] She proposes a dialogic ethic of care that asks humans to attend to animals through love, listening to what animals are communicating, and being responsive to those needs and feelings. This is a ground-up approach that cautions against the appropriation of animal voices through predetermined anthropogenic knowledge claims.[23]

Other feminist ethic-of-care theorists single out empathy rather than sympathy as a primary caring mobilizer. In *Entangled Empathy*, Lori Gruen draws from more than a quarter of a century of activism and academic scholarship regarding empathizing with animals to outline her theory promoting "entangled empathy" to radically improve animals' lives.[24] She writes: "Entangled empathy is a type of caring perception focused on attending to another's experience of wellbeing. An experiential process involving a blend of emotion and cognition in which we recognize we are in relationships with others and are called upon to be responsive and responsible in these relationships by attending to another's needs, interests, desires, vulnerabilities, hopes, and sensitivities."[25]

Gruen insists that we are always in relationships with animals (many of these relationships are, of course, bad for animals).[26] She argues that simply informing people that animals suffer is not enough to motivate them to act in favour of animals; rather, an affective connection must be made to stimulate care, compassion, and, ultimately, responsibility.[27] Gruen proposes a model of entangled empathy to achieve this type of connection. In contrast to the standard emphasis in deontological and consequentialist approaches that disavow empathy or omit particularized attention to the perspective of a particular animal being in favour of advancing more "abstract," "generaliz[able]," and "interchangeable" claims, extending empathy for Gruen means adopting the perspective of the particular animal in need through careful listening and attention.[28]

Gruen is keen to move toward a form of empathy in which the empathizer is able to distinguish self from other in order to avoid a situation where an empathizer subsumes the other into the self, projecting her own account of what the other is experiencing.[29] Gruen is further aware that championing empathy generically can saddle those socialized to care (i.e., women) with disproportionate responsibility to care and act.[30] As a response, she, and other care feminists, have stressed the need for men to adopt caring dispositions as well.[31] Like sympathy, empathy is a means for directing attention and channelling responsiveness to animal others that we should be able to apply despite our gendered social locations. Within this framework, we all have responsibility toward animals simply because we exist in relationships with animals.[32]

There is much to commend in feminist animal care theory's emotions-guided approach to responding to animal suffering. As Kamalini Ramdas observes, "[feminist animal care theory] emphasizes the relational, dependent and non-voluntary nature of care relationships and the inequalities of power implied in these relationships."[33] It motivates us to care by teaching us that "moral selves emerge through our relations of responsibility and care for particular others."[34] We are invited to cultivate our capacities for attention, responsiveness, and respect in this regard.[35] In addition to its valuable recuperative insights into why emotions must guide how we respond to animals, the teachings of care theory foreground the important values of embodiment, vulnerability, and relationality (discussed at length in the next chapter).

At a pragmatic level, feminist animal care theory proffers the affect-laced capacities of empathy and compassion to motivate people to care about animals and act on their behalf. Even those who question whether empathy is required in order to stimulate moral regard for animals and / or who assert that other emotions, such as anger, are more effective in mobilizing resistance to the status quo in the case of animals[36] affirm that empathy, when present, does increase human concern for animals.[37] The law should thus adopt feminist animal care theory's insights about valuing emotional cues in general – and, in particular, emotional-laden responses to animal suffering – to become more emotion-based when resolving animal cases. Specifically, the law should attend to the emotional (and physical) suffering of animal beings as well as allow human emotions about animal suffering to prompt action and guide decisions regarding how to respond to this suffering. This is not to say we should abandon reason in advancing animal-friendly claims or arguments. Reasoned argumentation is indispensable. Indeed, the critique of reason is a reasoned analysis itself that allows us to understand why the privileged place reason holds in our cultural imaginaries about who counts and why should erode. Reasoned argumentation is of value, particularly when we understand that emotions form part of reasoning and that we should be guided by our emotional responses to animal suffering, including, of course, to animals' emotional vulnerability.

This call for legal decision-makers to value emotions by recognizing their role in shaping human reasoning and their proper place in public deliberation is echoed by the growing field of law and emotions, which rehabilitates the status of emotions in law and also endorses legal and judicial reasoning that embraces emotion-based reasoning.[38] Indeed, the scholarship on law and emotions has clearly demonstrated that adjudication is always already an emotion-laden project.[39] Of course, feminist animal care theorists seek to cultivate widespread valuation of emotional responses to non-human animals in particular.[40] Notwithstanding its elision of animals from its purview, the findings of law and emotion scholarship regarding the extent to which "emotion pervades the law,"[41] including extant decision-making, bolsters feminist animal care proposals for acknowledging and embracing the role of emotions in ethical deliberation and my specific proposal here for doing so in legal decision-making.

1. CONTESTING AN ETHIC OF CARE

I have argued thus far that the feminist animal care tradition offers valuable insights about emotions that can help direct law toward a post-anthropocentric outlook. Many feminists are wary, however, of adopting any form of care theory. It seems there are several reasons for this reluctance. First, a care ethic still signals to many a focus on privatized and personal relationships rather than broader social relations of power. While feminist animal care theorists have responded convincingly to the critique that their focus is problematically embedded in private relationships, and have shown that the feminist animal care approach clearly does consider social relations of power,[42] the privatized connotations of care frameworks linger, which troubles some feminists.[43] A second connotation of care theory that concerns some feminists is its tight association with maternalist thinking. Care theory has traditionally foregrounded the care a mother gives to her child as a model for public life and social governance in general.[44] As much as some care theorists have sought to escape the gendered and romanticized connotations of maternalist thinking, in order to advocate for a care ethic that men, nonbinary people, and women can all adopt in public and private life, the associations are not easily avoided.[45] This leaves feminist care theorists in the difficult position of trying to politicize a degendered care ethic when care is still so tethered to gender roles for women and prone to further exploit women's caring labours.[46]

A third and related reason for discomfort with ethic-of-care theories is the essentialist ontological vision of women that traditionally grounds them and the perception that women's caring, cooperative, loving, compassionate, peaceful, empathetic, responsibility-oriented, and nurturing nature is in sharp contrast to how men behave.[47] As Maria Drakopoulou has traced, second-wave feminist legal scholarship traditionally embraced care theory as a guide for legal reform.[48] The rise of the essentialist critiques in the 1990s, however, persuaded many feminists to abandon their belief in a unified caring female subject.[49] Certainly, Carol Gilligan's groundbreaking work in articulating an ethic of care – arguing that women make decisions to resolve conflicts through an ethic of care as opposed to an ethic of justice[50] – from which the feminist care paradigm grew, merited the anti-essentialist interrogation it received.[51] Despite the dislodging thereafter of essentialist visions about women in much of feminist legal scholarship informed by care theory, care-inspired feminist jurisprudence continues to carry essentialist associations.[52]

Taken together, these concerns have done much to convince feminists to avoid care ethics.[53] Yet as noted above, these objections have largely to do with misperceptions about the richness and nuances of contemporary care theory today in contrast to its original formulation as a moral theory.[54] These misperceptions shouldn't taint the insights of feminist animal care theorists today who seek to cultivate care and compassion toward animals at a personal but also, critically, institutional and community level. These theorists maintain that caring responsiveness to animals is a disposition equally available to humans of all genders who seek widespread human behavioural change toward animals.[55]

A more legitimate critique of care theory is that the desire to engage with animals, learn about their desires, and respond to them normalizes a level of interaction that may actually breed harm. In her writings seeking to infuse feminist animal care theory with Jain sensibilities of non-harm, Irina Aristarkhova notes that animal care theory depends on engaging and learning from animals, a process requiring proximate relations.[56] Aristarkhova urges feminists to consider the Jain concept of non-harm, which encourages adherents to cultivate not so much care per se but rather carefulness.[57] Such an orientation demands prudent action only after deliberative reflection, given that human activities toward animals, even those of benevolent intent, are fertile ground for anthropocentric effects to merge. Given this predilection humans have to harm non-humans due to the former's hegemonic position, or at least to keep animals close to us so that we can learn from them,[58] Jain's views on non-harm counsel distance wherever possible at the same time that they affirm our co-evolution and shared daily intimacy with animals.[59] We can accept this plea to mainstream an ethic of carefulness into feminist animal care theory as a friendly modification of its ethical core.

2. THE SUBJECTIVITY OF EMOTIONS?

Another set of concerns may arise apart from objections to care-inspired theories. For some, any framework for animal subjectivity shaped by emotions – both our emotional responses to animals and their emotions in suffering – is a treacherous pathway to achieving actual results for animals. This objection diverges from the traditional objection to emotions, which counsels their exclusion from "public discourse on the grounds that [they are] chaotic, unpredictable, and can therefore too easily lead us into error."[60] While there is much to commend in the feminist animal care tradition and other emotionally anchored theories that feminists have proposed to reconfigure our responses to animals, the argument may proceed that there is potential for such theories to privilege animals that humans like and can easily care about,[61] or worse, actually defend commercial uses of animals. Indeed, a recent feminist argument about relating to animals through love demonstrates that emotionally constituted theories for assessing how we should treat animals can engender much less than desirable end results for animals.

In *Loving Animals*, Kathy Rudy calls for a new type of animal advocacy and mode of theorizing – one based on and informed by the love we have for animals in our lives.[62] Rudy speaks passionately about the incomplete and thus ineffectual nature of current Enlightenment-based modes of theorizing in animal ethics (deontological, utilitarian, welfarist) as conceptual underpinnings for the animal advocacy movement; she contests their ability to generate widespread concern for animals and for the animal movement.[63] Like feminist animal care theorists, Rudy wants animal ethics to prioritize the emotions we as humans have for animals rather than disavow or marginalize them.[64] Her specific focus, however, is on the bonds of love that many animal advocates have for particular animals, which, if illuminated to the mainstream, Rudy believes, will prompt compassion for those animals that languish unloved in animal industrial complexes.[65] Rudy thus calls for theoretical underpinnings for the animal advocacy movement that foreground "the emotional and spiritual connections" humans have with animals, a cluster of connections that she encapsulates under the umbrella term of love.[66] So redirected, this "more sophisticated understanding of the role of affect and emotion"[67] will result in "a more viable social movement."[68]

Rudy is committed to promoting a relational worldview "where animals are subjects, agents, and actors in their own right."[69] She argues that theory that foregrounds how humans and animals interrelate and thus co-constitute each other's subjectivities can enable such a worldview to emerge.[70] Despite this commitment, an ethic of love toward animals does not prevent animals from being killed for human uses in food, research, or even entertainment industries under Rudy's analysis of how such industries need to be reformed.[71] Rudy's ethic of loving animals, even ones treated like family, does not operate as a barrier to their non-consensual use and death in these industries.[72] Hers is a clear example of a theory that allows emotions to direct our response to animals so as to dilute the protections they receive.

Rudy's ultimate conclusions about how various industries should be reformed in favour of animals are clearly disappointing from a non-instrumental perspective,[73] but that does not mean that all feminist or otherwise critical accounts championing the importance of emotions in animal ethics (and law) will settle at similarly weak positions for animals or justify privileging those we love over those animals that might repel us or make us squirm or retreat. Clear examples exist in feminist theorizations of animals that do not accept the commodification of animals or differentiate among species, the feminist care tradition epitomized by Adams and Donovan being an obvious example. Conversely, reverting to purely reason-based theorizing (presuming that such theorizing is even possible) that either stigmatizes emotion-based reasoning or consigns it to secondary status will not guarantee that desirable results for animals will prevail. There are plenty of animal ethics arguments that privilege reason yet exclude some animals from their purview altogether or otherwise permit animal bodies to be appropriated for commercial ends. Welfarist and utilitarian arguments easily come to mind here, but capabilities and rights-based arguments also qualify.[74] Emotion-based theories like Rudy's should not be discounted because they, too, can fall short in their application. To ensure against limited results in either theoretical context, a clear vision of power relations is required, guided by a sustained commitment to subverting anthropocentric reasoning. I now turn to feminist writings on ethical responsibility to animals for this clear vision mandating accountability toward animals.

B. Call and Response Interspecies Ethics

The feminist care tradition for animals gives us reasons to validate our emotional responses of empathy and compassion toward animals as ethical cues and legitimates the emotion-based deliberation that it counsels should flow from this validation. As I argued earlier, legal decision-makers should take their own cues from this literature to endorse care, empathy, and compassion toward animals as legitimate values as well as legitimate guides to inform the resolution of legal disputes and the creation of policy involving animals. This outlook will help set a relational and responsive orientation in law toward animals as beings.

It would also be useful for law to heed the insights of feminist philosophers who endorse a caring and compassionate stance toward animals but who take our relationality with animals even further than feminist animal care theorists do by presenting *our relationality* with animal Others as the trigger for our ethical responsibility toward animals and the Earth in general. Working in the tradition of response ethics, but forging a distinctive sense of "call and response ethics," these feminist philosophers also illuminate the anthropocentric deficiencies in law's concept of the sovereign individual by showcasing the claims that infants (human and nonhuman) make on us ethically even though their subjectivity is not yet formed. In this section, I discuss the work of Kelly Oliver and Cynthia Willett in this regard to signal how their reflections on interspecies relations amplify our understanding of the relationality between humans and animals and also connect this relationality with non-violent responsibility for and accountability to animals. In these two respects, call and response ethics affirms but also extends the insights of feminist animal care theory in ways that are helpful to the overall project in this chapter of developing a post-anthropocentric legal ontological foundation that protects animals from exploitation.

1. KELLY OLIVER AND ENABLING RESPONSE-ABILITY

In *Animal Lessons: How They Teach Us to Be Human*,[75] Oliver canvasses the work of leading Western philosophers of difference/otherness from the eighteenth century onward to explore how animals both literally and figuratively figured in their theories. What Oliver finds is an undeniable centrality of ideas/projections about animals and animality and their alterity to the construction of man, human, humanity, politics, and ethics in this era of the Western intellectual tradition even as these philosophers objected to strict Cartesian thinking about animals and its teachings about the links between rationality, autonomy and subjectivity.[76] Oliver traces a pattern among multiple thinkers of defining humanity against animality and rejecting our interdependence with animals; at the same time, these philosophers unpacked naturalized differences among humans and exposed the fiction of previous thought about the unified and stable nature of the human subject.[77] From this exposition, Oliver argues that the human-animal divide remained a fundamental premise in philosophical pronouncements in European theories of Otherness from Rousseau onward, foreclosing any attention to animals as subjects of ethics.[78]

As Oliver shows, animals' alterity is perceived as so radical and other that even anti-humanist theories of Otherness cannot attend to it and, furthermore, cannot acknowledge how much their understandings of humanity depend on animals. By denying this ambivalence, Oliver argues, eighteenth-, nineteenth-, and twentieth-century theorists of Otherness repress how animals enable them to articulate what, they insist, it means to be human.[79] Yet, as she goes on to demonstrate, it is the animal and corresponding ideas of animals and animality that allow these philosophers to state what they want to say about humans, humanity, and subjectivity; animals enable their teachings, but this reliance on the animal is denied.[80] As she succinctly puts it: "By uncovering the latent humanism in antihumanist texts, we continue to witness the ambivalence toward animality and animals that has defined Western philosophy and culture."[81]

Oliver includes in her capacious discussion the response ethics that emerged in European post-structural thought from the mid-twentieth century onward, following the atrocities of the Holocaust and Western colonization. Catalysed by the writings of Emmanuel Levinas, this tradition turns away from moral theories that require the ability to reason or speak for beings to qualify as moral patients and orients itself "to the pathos of the vulnerable Other."[82] It does not demand sameness, but calls on us to value otherness and alterity by responding to the Other even where radically different.[83] As Cynthia Willett observes, "response ethics resides in a nonjudgmental stance of generosity and compassion"[84] (we can see, here, its alignment with feminist animal care theory). But, as Oliver notes, even Levinas, for all his insistence on responding compassionately to the Other in all her alterity, does not extend the ethical response to animals.[85]

As a corrective to anthropocentric response ethics, Oliver seeks to inaugurate what she calls a "sustainable ethics."[86] To replace the conservatism she repeatedly observes in Western theories of Otherness when it comes to animals, Oliver calls for a response from humans that rejects the human-animal divide and embraces our interdependence with animals and our dependence on them.[87] It is a call to abjure sameness logic, but instead of positing radical otherness, it emphasizes shared relationality and interdependence with all living beings so as to refuse as best we can, given our privileges, domination over them.[88] In this way, Oliver's ethical orientation differs from that of the post-structural theorists who have taken up Levinasian response ethics and applied them to animals. Here, the influence of Jacques Derrida's writings on animals weighs heavily. Derrida remonstrated Levinas for his anthropocentric line-drawing, calling on scholars to acknowledge the foundational yet untenable socially constructed chasm between humans and animals to Western thought; the latter's key features he captured with his highly influential term of "carnophallogocentrism."[89] But whereas Derrida emphasizes the alterity of animals, Oliver emphasizes our interrelatedness with them. As she puts it: "What we need is to move from an ethics of sameness, through an ethics of difference, toward an ethics of *relationality* and *responsivity*."[90] The ethical imperative is "to share resources and life together on this collective planet."[91]

In advancing these insights, it is evident that Oliver's sustainable ethics is allied with feminist animal care theory. An important innovation Oliver offers, however, is to call for the development of a capacity in ourselves and others, which she terms response-ability, that is meant to cultivate animals' "ability to respond"[92] but also, critically, human responsibility toward animals and all living beings. "Response-ability" is a capacity to attend to the needs of others (and ourselves) through a non-domination ethos; when directed toward animals, our response-ability replaces a domination sensibility over nature with a willingness to share our earthly space and resources with animals for mutual well-being.[93] We respond because we affirm rather than disavow our dependence on animals.[94] Adopting a posture of response-ability, then, motions us forward to an ecological subjectivity that constitutes a "transformation from the traditional image of man as conquering nature to one of human beings nourishing it."[95] Part of this posture is to be humble about the limits of our knowledge and to redouble efforts to understand the needs of others.[96] As Oliver puts it: "The ethical question that asks us to confront our own responsibility to animals is not whether they can suffer but how we respond to the suffering of others."[97] How can we care for them to help them respond as equal "inhabitants of a shared planet"?[98]

2. CYNTHIA WILLETT AND MULTISPECIES
AND INTERGENERATIONAL ETHICS

Cynthia Willett's work on interspecies relations affirms Oliver's insights about what post-anthropocentric relations should mean from a response ethics tradition. Like Oliver, Willett distinguishes her approach from Continental response ethics and North American reason-based animal ethics, epitomized by Jacques Derrida and Peter Singer respectively,[99] on the basis that they emphasize our differences from animals rather than our connections to them.[100] Willett is not unaware of vast differences among species but emphasizes "that underlying the spectacular differences among species are the common capacities of creatures who in fact have coevolved in shared habitats and multispecies communities."[101] She introduces a more communitarian aspect to our relationality with animals and the types of shifts in understanding and relating that will be needed to bring about ideal interspecies relations. In terms of widespread institutional change toward animals, Willett directs our attention to (1) the importance and transformative potential of preverbal and non-verbal communicative exchanges in reading preferences and reorienting ethics, (2) the importance of viewing animals as social agents that use their own social codes to govern themselves and maintain (mostly) peaceful relations, and (3) the potential for past trauma to manifest itself in current individual and group behaviour and the corresponding need for a multigenerational perspective in order for us to understand and heal human-animal relations.

Her vision of interspecies ethics, then, is one that supplements the response ethics of animal scholars influenced by alterity scholars such as Levinas and Derrida with "call and response" ethics – that is, an interspecies ethics aimed at responding to the vulnerability of animals but without eclipsing their active, playful, resisting, and norm-building communications and contributions or forgetting the intergenerational causes of community well-being or dysfunction.[102] Animals, even infant ones, including human infants, "call" on us actively, and it is these calls that we need to acknowledge and attend to, grasping that they are situated in broader biosocial relations.[103] Willett is cognizant that her call for a "communitarian resituating of response ethics into histories and agencies rooted in communicative exchange will require critical vigilance against imperialist, predatory, and neoliberal modes of power."[104] Embrace of alterity thus continues to be critical to her version of call and response ethics, as is the need to confront skewed representations of difference and anthropocentric, racist, sexist, etc., base points of understanding.[105]

3. UPTAKE FOR LAW

Call and response ethics as outlined by Oliver and Willett provides several non-anthropocentric signposts for law to follow. Such ethics promote many of the same insights as feminist animal care theory regarding extending care and compassion toward animals, eschewing sameness logic, and valuing alterity approaches while underscoring relationality and connection. Call and response ethics also brings animals into the centre of response ethics aimed at attending to the needs of Others, but without presuming what those needs are in advance or presuming to ever "know" the Other. In this way, such ethics abide by the insights of postcolonial theory and feminist care ethics to avoid "epistemic imperialism."[106] Call and response ethics also proceeds cautiously in how it describes animals, emphasizing the differences among animals and not the difference between humans and animals. Here, too, the influence of postcolonial thought is discernible, namely with regard to avoiding homogenizing claims about Others and interrupting the dualistic standard metrics by which Others are perceived and known.[107] Perhaps most critically, the vision of Oliver and Willett joins feminist animal care theorists in dispelling myths about human exceptionalism and recognizing the multiple capacities of animals, without taking a capacity-based approach for why animals should matter, but also taking an ethical stance against exploitation of animals in animal-based industries.[108]

Call and response ethics as represented by Oliver and Willett ultimately settles on a deeper sense of relationality than that articulated by feminist animal care theory to anchor its approach to human-animal relations. Here, its insights regarding the deeply relational nature of our lives with animals merit specific mention and legal attention, as does the ethical responsibility that directly flows from this relational status. To reiterate, call and response ethics maintains that our subjectivity develops *through* relations with others. Furthermore, it is this feature of subjectivity that mandates our responsibility to other beings and the cultivation of response-ability.[109] Call and response ethics thus makes us accountable to animals at a foundational level, including to animals we may not even recognize as subjects yet (such as infants), as well as to intergenerational animal kin/social groups. Willett's specific emphasis on biosocial networks and "affect clouds" reminds us that in order to repair human-animal relations, we need to attend to dynamics beyond the individual level and the current temporal period. This is illuminative of a different aspect of collective causality beyond the now routine call in feminist animal care theory (and other critical theories) to address the larger institutional factors that undergird oppression and marginalization. With its focus on response-ability and communal well-being, call and response ethics provides attractive theoretical supplementation to feminist animal care theory to jointly create a new ontological foundation for law.

C. Flesh Forward

As a third and final feminist/feminist-inspired philosophical approach to reconceiving human-animal relations, I turn to those writers who affirm that we exist in "thick embodied relationship with those around us"[110] but who accentuate the role played by our physicality and bodiment with regard to our capacities to care and respond.

1. JENNIFER McWEENY AND TOPOGRAPHIES OF FLESH

Jennifer McWeeny's work on the interrelatedness of bodies and the ethical dictates that flow from this integrates feminist animal care theory, postcolonial theory, and feminist phenomenology to develop the concept of a topography of flesh to ground feminist politics.[111] I turn to her work in this section because I see the charting of what McWeeny calls "topographies of flesh" as a useful way to practise in law the blended insights from feminist animal care theory and call and response ethics. Topographies of flesh are meant to be intersectional analyses of how we (humans and animals) are invariably related through intercorporeal exchanges.[112] The purpose of such analyses is to enable feminist identification of the asymmetries of power that permeate these exchanges along cultural, racial, species, gender, and other mutually constituting lines,[113] as a way of permitting feminists "to think our ontologies without essentialism, individualism, disembodiment, oppressor-centrism, or other reductions of the complexity of lived experience."[114] McWeeny harnesses the geographical concept of topography as a way to map these bodily relations and the "social, material and economic relationships (they) present in a given locale at a particular point in time."[115]

McWeeny insists on drawing our attention back to the experiences that we and other animals have through our flesh because of what this focus can illuminate. She credits ecofeminist and other intersectional theories of human and animal oppression with providing analyses of how animals are oppressed through a "racist-speciesist-heterosexist-colonial imaginary."[116] Yet she argues that in focusing their lens on the multiple ideologies that have been built up to render animals ontologically inferior, these analyses fall short in uncovering the actual lived experiences of animals. She worries that ecofeminist and other intersectional accounts of animals have the potential to portray animals in a non-agentic way solely as objects of oppression.[117] But her main goal is to supplement critical accounts of how ideologies normalize oppression against animals with a discussion of how animals act through their bodies in these conditions. She "reject[s] the idea that oppressive ideologies and practices are determinative of the ontologies of the oppressed."[118] For McWeeny, an "ontological concept of flesh allows us to affirm the relationality and complexity of lived experience, which does not present beings as either mind or body, active or passive, self or other, oppressed or privileged, but as both of these aspects at the same time."[119] Charting a topography of flesh, then, can provide "a three-dimensional landscape of bodily, material relationships of exchange and asymmetry, exploitation and solidarity, oppression and resistance."[120]

McWeeny offers the concept of topography of flesh as a new and better anchor for feminist intersectional analyses that would unpack anthropocentrism and species privilege and eliminate violence and other oppression.[121] She describes the layers of this mapping as follows:

> To chart a topography of flesh is to look for what you cannot see from your perspective, that is, it is to make visible the myriad perspectives-fleshes-that constitute a world, despite our personal investments in concealing them. It is to look for whose bodies sustain our own through their flesh, labor, and sociocultural position: Whose hands prepared this meal? Whose eyes sewed this shirt? Whose sweat cleaned this university bathroom, this hotel room, this apartment? Whose resources are my profit? Whose inferiority enhances my superiority? Whose milk is this that I drink?[122]

By asking these questions about the economy of and material impacts on bodies, McWeeny envisions a feminist analysis that reveals how bodies cluster together on some registers and disaggregate on others to expose the complex landscapes of intercorporeal exchange we all inhabit. It is an approach that motivates feminists committed to non-violence and anti-oppression to attend to these flesh-based positionings for humans and non-humans alike that the topography discloses.[123] Whether such new awareness will catalyse efforts to undo asymmetry remains to be seen – a point McWeeny emphasizes herself.[124] She urges all of us to chart our own topographies to illuminate the asymmetries of power from which we benefit and to work toward "crafting a topography where the bodily exchanges, substitutions, and asymmetries constitutive of sexism, racism, speciesism, and other oppressions are inoperative and unthinkable."[125]

2. RALPH R. ACAMPORA AND CORPORAL COMPASSION THROUGH SYMPHYSIS

I suggest that McWeeny's flesh-focused approach is closely aligned with Ralph Acampora's body-focused theory of symphysis, which is also heavily informed by phenomenology and, specifically, by Merleau-Ponty's teachings.[126] Acampora is deeply sympathetic to feminist pushback against rationalism in animal ethics.[127] He seeks, however, to excavate even further the role of non-rational elements of how humans live and interact with the more-than-human world. Specifically, he insists that it is the physical body, our animate existence, that undergirds our capacity to be, and, furthermore, that it is through our bodies that we engage with the animals around us. Acampora aptly observes that articulations of why animals should be included in the moral sphere problematically accept the parameters of Western humanist metaphysics that establish a starting point that animals don't matter; animal advocates then have to justify why they should, with such justifications typically marshalling sameness logic to succeed.[128] This way of drawing the terms of the query, Acampora attests, is backward.[129]

Like Willett, Acampora takes as a base point for ethics the social nature of human beings and other social mammals, emphasizing that this sociality – what Acampora terms "somatic sociability"[130] – brings us into immediate physical connection with the more-than-human world. Furthermore, it is only "through this interaction with other animate bodies" that we experience and make sense of our own bodies.[131] He thus argues for a "corporally restorative reformation of moral philosophy."[132] His theory of "symphysis" is meant to perform this recuperation by valuing all beings with "live bodiment."[133] As he explains, the term "is meant to convey the sense of sharing with somebody else a somaaesthetic nexus experienced through a direct or systemic (inter) relationship. In this way the concept comes to signify a pattern of more densely physical orientation – i.e., by contrast to the more airy, psychic notion of sympathy frequently utilized by moral sense theorists."[134] It is the animal's capacity for being in somatic sociality with humans, also called "conviviality," that qualifies her as a moral subject.[135] Perhaps these descriptors makes symphysis sound more complicated than Acampora intends. Seemingly addressing this point, he tells us that in essence the biophilic ethos he urges us to adopt is not a new ethos; it can be found within other (colonized) cultures but also in childhood before dominant Western norms instruct us not to care too much about most animals or envision ourselves as embedded in joint development with them.[136]

Symphysis is not just a descriptive concept. Normatively, it directs us to be responsive to the vulnerability of the bodies that are in relation with us,[137] seeking to strike a balance between responding to animals as individuals on the one hand, and affirming the collective ties that bind us together and form us as individuals in the first place on the other.[138] Being in relation does not include only those animals we view as family. Acampora has a much broader remit for his theory. He suggests that we can be in relation and intersomaticity with animals we do not know personally and gives the example of squirrels in a park. Furthermore, symphysis does not depend on bodies touching. We can share bodily experiences through other means. Regarding observing squirrels in a park, Acampora identifies shared experiences of climaticity, auditory engagement, and consumption that humans have with squirrels if we simply "note the passage of seasons in the bushiness of squirrels' tails ... aurally attend to their clucking barks as they play or mate ... watch them forage for food"[139] as we also snack. Our predisposition to view squirrels as "related others" and not simply as rodents, or worse, as pests, inclines us to value and protect them rather than control or regulate them through violent means. Caring about squirrels in a respectful way makes us more inclined to respond to their vulnerabilities and otherwise attend to their suffering.[140] Thus symphysis produces an interspecies ethics of "corporal compassion" – it is our threefold recognition of our "own vital status as animate zoomorphs," the sharing of this status with other animals, and the vulnerabilities that can then flow for all beings in this category, that broadens our care horizons.[141]

Wither empathy?

It is because he champions "transpacific intersomaticity"[142] as an ethical base point that Acampora objects not only to the hyperrationalism of animal ethics and the corresponding devaluation/suppression of emotional connections to animals, but also to the proposed alternative suggested by feminist animal care theorists – that empathy toward animals is the fulcrum of an ideal interspecies ethics.[143] Acampora argues that the empathetic experience "is originally mediated by physical sensibility."[144] Since empathy is normally translated as the ability to perceive the mind of the Other, it is too divorced from the primordial state of physical connection that Acampora presses us to acknowledge.[145] As he puts it, "cultivating a bodiment ethos of interanimality is not a matter of mentally working one's way into other selves or worlds by quasi-telepathic imagination, but is rather about becoming sensitive to an already constituted 'inter-zone' of somaaesthetic conviviality."[146] Indeed, Acampora uses the unique term "bodiment" because he views the traditional term "embodiment" as too invested in a sense of self as exterior to the body.[147] Acampora is further wary of empathy and sympathy because advocates often wish to credentialize empathy by pointing to its cognitive dimensions in its more advanced state.[148] Acampora also finds empathy problematic because it assumes a relationship between a discrete self and an other instead of visualizing a "jointly held form of bodily consciousness."[149]

Feminist animal care theorists do indeed discount the ethical potential of empathy when it is not infused with cognition.[150] However, some feminist animal care theorists have approached with scepticism the purely affective response that Acampora applauds. Gruen, for example, acknowledges that empathetic response includes a precognitive reaction. Yet for her idealized version of empathy to occur, empathizers must think reflexively and evaluate the other's position from their own reflective position, a task that requires the empathizer to collect, identify, and prioritize relevant information[151] and that, Gruen argues, "motivates the empathizer to act ethically"[152] in a way that sympathy does not.[153] Gruen is aware of Acampora's concern that her theory of empathy requires a split between self and other that in Acampora's view maintains a problematic separate subjectivity rather than symphysis.[154] Gruen defends the split, noting that for those marginalized humans for whom the public affirmation of a sense of self is still comparatively recent, abandoning the self to celebrate blending with others in shared bodiments is not necessarily prudent or necessary.[155] On this latter point, Gruen attests that retaining a distinct sense of self "need not be one of distance, need not require dominance and subordination and thus can be maintained in ethical ways."[156] For his part, Acampora permits some separation to mediate his argument. As an alternative to the dominating anthropocentric gaze with which humans typically view animals when we seek them out for biophilic encounters – a fraught pursuit exemplified by the spectatorship activities that occur at zoos – Acampora adopts feminist Marilyn Frye's concept of the "loving eye"[157] as a vehicle to perceive animals from a position of epistemic humility. He thus doesn't jettison empathetic engagement and the capacity for moral imagination that inheres in it. Indeed, he admits "that feminist philosophy's retrieval of bodily consciousness has inspired the present work and that its theories deserve credit for calling animal ethics to account on the use of caring's centrality to moral thought and practice."[158]

3. UPTAKE FOR LAW

How, then, can a convivial intersomatic ethics as proposed by Acampora and the mapping of topographies of flesh as proposed by McWeeny ameliorate legal culture? How can they help shift law toward a post-anthropocentric ontology? For one thing, if it became *de rigeur* to identify the intercorporeal exchanges that shape legal disputes through the topographies of flesh that McWeeny promotes, it would become second nature for legal decision-makers to grasp how the constellations of power involved give rise to a particular dispute. They would develop the sensibility to understand the vulnerabilities of fleshy bodies, as well as a skill set to identify hierarchies of power. Jurists and other lawmakers could then proceed to ascertain how the law should respond to the power constellations in which a particular legal dispute is enveloped. If the law were to take Acampora's symphysis concept seriously, it would start from a base point that is radically different from the present one – that of a "jointly held form of bodily consciousness" between animate lives, particularly those of social animals.[159] Hierarchical rankings exalting paradigmatic mental states and human beings who possess them would disappear. As Acampora puts it: "No one is first. What must come first from us is compassion."[160] Arrogant and dominating speciesist norms would also fade. All animate life would matter morally and also be seen to be constitutive of human beings. The law would also be primed to meditate on the twin capacities of vulnerability and togetherness, for being in symphysis with other animals would make these more transparent. A predisposition to real protection for animals through a caring and respectful outlook would then follow.[161]

II. Conclusion

Abolishing animals' status as property in the law would not fully change Canadian law's foundations or cultural suppositions. To move state law toward a post-anthropocentric ontology, a more robust reorientation is required. Feminist writing on animals helps us comprehend what these further modifications could be. Feminist animal care theory helps us understand the need to attenuate reason's exalted status as part of any legal paradigm shift for animals and to avow the mainstream valuation of emotions in the law. In particular, it demonstrates the need to extend care, empathy, and compassion when we encounter vulnerability and suffering. Feminist applications of call and response ethics to animals help us understand how deeply our own subjectivities are constituted through Others, how this compels responsibility toward animals, and why healing human-animal relations require not only responding to suffering but also viewing animals as agents with their own social lives, social codes, and histories. Feminist-inspired phenomenology theories transport us back to the physical undercurrents for this responsiveness, challenging the rationalist nature of moral and legal considerability and exposing the physical elements of empathetic connection. Through the concepts of topographies of flesh and symphysis, our attention is directed most fully to our bodies and the ways we are always already in physical and hierarchical connection with other beings. These theories' combined tenets about emotion, care, empathy, compassion, witnessing, response-ability, and attention to flesh and materiality can collectively provide an alternative foundation for Canadian law, which at present is deeply anthropocentric.

I am not claiming that any one of these three approaches on their own, or even all of them combined, provide a perfect normative view of interspecies ethics or that other epistemological traditions are not also useful repositories for teachings as to how law needs to change. I am thinking here particularly of important critiques by Indigenous legal scholars assailing the anthropocentric norms and effects of Canadian law.[162] But as the permissibility of "respectfully" killing animals per Indigenous legal orders is generally left unquestioned or at least explained and thereby justified according to time immemorial traditions based in reciprocity and kinship in such critiques, my own preference is to situate this argument in feminist animal care theory, which takes a more critical view of all killing of animals even where the cultural rights of colonized peoples and other marginalized groups are at stake.[163] In doing so, I have argued that feminist writing on animals presents theories whose salient and core features would help Canadian law to shift from its anthropocentric, imperial, and gendered foundations. Canadian law should endorse care, empathy, and compassion toward animal bodies as legitimate values as well as legitimate guides for informing the resolution of legal disputes or the creation of policy involving animals. The law should recognize the shared somaticity we have with animals, lament the vulnerabilities they face, and seek to remove the causes of their suffering. The dominant legal order should also normalize human responsibility toward animals because of our dominating power. In short, the present dominant liberal legal culture should absorb these insights to generate a relational, compassionate, and responsive orientation in law toward animals as vulnerable, embodied, and relational beings. It should also create a new legal subjectivity that does the same. The next chapter explores my proposal for such a new legal subjectivity and explains why it sensibly applies to animals.

PART II

Animals as Beings: In Pursuit of a New Post-Anthropocentric Legal Order

4 Beingness: A New Legal Subjectivity for Animals

The problem raised by the demands of recognition of non-human living beings as legal subjects is precisely how to define – and thereby bring into existence – a kind of difference that is in itself different to the mode of differentiation conveyed by the principle of (human) agency which, embedded in one of the two poles of the person/thing opposition, governs their mutual relations.[1]

> Ciméa Barbato Bevilaqua, "Chimpanzees in Court:
> What Difference Does It Make?," in *Law and the*
> *Questions of the Animal: A Critical Jurisprudence*

I am referring not only to humans not regarded as humans, and thus to a restrictive conception of the human that is based upon their exclusion. It is not a matter of a simple entry of the excluded into an established ontology, but an insurrection at the level of ontology, a critical opening up of the questions, What is real? Whose lives are real? How might reality be remade?[2]

> Judith Butler, *Precarious Life: The Powers of Mourning and Violence*

If property is inherently exploitative and personhood is inherently anthropocentric, anthropocentric legal systems seeking to shift toward a multispecies orientation must respond to animals through a new transformative legal subjectivity, one that doesn't merely refine personhood's parameters or take paradigmatic human ontologies as its model. I call this new legal status, with apologies to Martin Heidegger, "beingness." Beingness is a status that is meant to provide, at a minimum, the legal recognition that personhood is meant to afford, but it would be a legal subjectivity that caters to the ontologies of breathing, embodied creatures.[3] Beingness would undercut the traditional account of who counts in law – the white, male, property-owning actor – and its residual emphasis on independence, wealth maximization, disembodiment,

Table 1 Principal constitutive features of contrasting legal subjectivities

Personhood model	Beingness model
Disembodied	Embodied
Independently autonomous	Relational
Rational	Vulnerable
Legal impact: Western law conceptualizes a "person" to be disembodied, independently autonomous, and rational. These are the attributes that are paradigmatic of persons, prized, and legally supported/promoted.	*Legal impact*: If beingness were to be implemented instead, the law would conceptualize beings as embodied, relational, and vulnerable. The law would value embodiment and relational experience and recognize that these attributes of living experience create vulnerability to which the law must respond.

and rationality despite the gradual expansion of personhood to absorb humans traditionally excluded. In contrast to legal personhood, legal beingness does not glorify these elusive features of the proper legal subject. Rather, it replaces them with concern for capacities and values meant to shatter the existing parameters of who matters to law to allow animals (and, very likely, other non-humans, of which I say more in the next chapter) to count as legal subjects. As such, beingness will allow animals to receive legal protections against the instrumental use their present property status permits.

As table 1 reveals, the main elements of beingness are embodiment (and the revaluation of the body and emotion this entails), relationality (and the social embeddedness and attention to power relations but also interdependence this entails), and vulnerability (and the materiality and attention to pain and suffering this entails). Beingness is thus directly oriented toward salient features of animals' lives that personhood does not easily accommodate and that property presently disavows. It is a better alternative than either as a protective legal subjectivity for animals. To support this claim, this chapter (1) expounds upon and draws together beingness's three main constitutive elements into an analytical tapestry to explain the orientation of a legal subjectivity based on these interrelated features, and (2) explains why animals descriptively and normatively qualify as embodied, relational, and vulnerable beings whose corresponding needs obligate anthropocentric legal systems to respond.

Specifically, I deploy feminist understandings of relationality along with contemporary social theories of the body, vulnerability, and precarity to argue that the law should draw attention to the vulnerability and precarity that animals experience as embodied and relational beings due to the fact that they are legally situated as property. My discussion of *embodiment* reviews why critical theorists across the board demand the discursive and material rehabilitation of the body – marginalized bodies in particular. I explain why animal bodies fit into this critical repertoire as a type of marginalized body requiring rehabilitation. My discussion of *relationality* invokes feminist argumentation for such a reorientation of law and ethics in how we understand subjectivity as well as animal-focused relational accounts to demonstrate why animals should be considered relational beings and the corresponding value of a legal system that classifies them as such. Finally, the discussion of why the law should embrace *vulnerability* as a foundational concept forefronts Judith Butler's influential understanding of vulnerability and precarity to scaffold legal subjectivity and applies it to animals.

This chapter thus details the three principal elements of beingness and builds upon the anti-anthropocentric reformulation of law's foundational architecture in the previous chapter. My aim is to synthesize multiple strands of feminist philosophy, social theory, and legal analysis to develop/articulate a new, more animal-friendly legal subjectivity that can concretely create legal change for animals while avoiding pressing animals into the anthropocentric and otherwise exclusionary mould of personhood. This chapter articulates why a new legal subject position for animals grounded in embodiment, vulnerability, and relationality can better respect animals as social and material beings than personhood would.

I acknowledge at the outset that a valid criticism of the legal being proposal is the complete novelty it poses for the Canadian legal system. Personhood, while still a remote possibility for animals, is at least a concept that is currently intelligible within the common law and civil law and to legislators (notwithstanding the paradoxes in how it is interpreted by jurists).[4] Yet other jurisdictions and legal systems suggest that the concept of beingness, at least in name if not in the full meaning I wish it to convey here in terms of protections equivalent to legal personhood, could be intelligible to law. Germany and Austria have inaugurated fellow-beingness status for animals in their jurisdictions.[5] As Sabine Lennkh notes, the concept was inaugurated to recognize dignity, humanity, compassion, and justice in animals, bestowing them with inherent value, dignity, and identity.[6] Although it sounds path-breaking for animals, anthropocentric interpretations of beingness have precluded any revolutionizing impact.[7] Applications of beingness so far are thus quite distant in scope and ambition from the aim of legal beingness: a legal end point for non-human animals that can serve as a route "to resistance that breaks through human/animal bipolarism and redresses continuities between all violated bodies."[8] Yet the existence of the term in existing legal systems in some jurisdictions signals some level of receptivity to creating new legal categories for animals beyond personhood. This chapter explores what a considerably more substantive definition of beingness could look like.

I. Embodiedness

A signal contribution of feminist theories broadly conceived is their focus on the body, its discursive formation as well as its material registers. Feminist theory has migrated from a focus on gendered difference to take embodied difference as its central organizing principle.[9] The tenet that the body matters to ethical formulations and the conceptualization of subjectivity has also prompted scholars committed to queer, disability, postcolonial/anti-colonial/decolonial, anti-racist, and anti-ageist frameworks to argue that an ethics derived from the body, and thus taking embodiment as central to subjectivity, is crucial for widespread and transformative social change.[10]

Law needs to be a central locus for such change. It has been largely inhospitable to marginalized bodies.[11] Kelly Oliver has written about "a growing disconnect between our conception of law and our bodily experiences,"[12] which she locates in Western law's continuing placement of bodies in the realm of nature and thus outside law and the realm of culture and so-called civilization.[13] Oliver points to the centuries-old political exclusion of natural bodies from the body politic in the Western tradition and the logic of exception this occasions that enables political elites to determine who can live and who can die.[14] Oliver's claim here is not that the law does not interface with bodies. Her body of work demonstrates her abiding awareness of the ways in which the law constructs, criminalizes, and otherwise interferes with marginalized bodies.[15] Rather, hers is a call for the law to respond more affirmatively to these marginalized bodies, an undertaking that requires a legal overhaul of ideas of the body itself. As one feminist legal scholar aptly puts it, "it is as though when the body does come to the foreground of attention the subject status [of the person] recedes."[16] Cartesian-derived intellectual traditions have generated cultural norms about the body that have infected the law that regard the body disproportionately as a source of disgust and other negative attributes, which must be transcended in favour of a life lived by reason.[17]

These cultural and legal norms teach that certain beings are more mired in their bodies than others, incapable of such a life and thus inferior.[18] Those who are routinely identified with their bodies are marginalized because of how their bodies diverge from the normative embodied subject that the law pretends has no body and is universal – the body that is coded as white, without disability, heterosexual, and male.[19] As Anna Grear observes, "the tales of the violence of law's engagements with those subjects whose embodied presence is constructed as being somehow 'problematic' to 'progress' – those whose bodies are 'in the way' – are legion."[20]

The negative discursive construction and reception of the body has had a negative impact not only on humans but on animals and other beings as well, but it is a logic of animalization that unites them.[21] As Laura Henson reminds us, "as the representation and embodiment of nature, the animal becomes the marker of bare life. Whereas human subjectivity must be respected, animal bodies can be killed without crime."[22]

In this worldview, animals are synonymous with their bodies, and this enables a logic of animalization to reduce certain groups of humans to their bodies and a lesser, violable status.[23] Despite the centrality of embodiment in new critical theorizations of social justice – a feature distinguishing them from their more historical counterparts that privileged dichotomous and hierarchical understandings of reason and the mind – the vast majority of critical theory of the body misses this insight and adopts an anthropocentric outlook.[24] We may "have come a long way from a Platonic world where the body is a threat to virtue, from a Cartesian world where my personhood is reduced to the cogito, from a Kantian world where ethics is a matter of disembodied universal principles, and from a Rousseauian world where only men possess the requisite rationality for moral and political action,"[25] yet most critical theory is still immersed in a humanist paradigm that takes the human body as an innocuous foundation for ethics. The critical impetus to respect, protect, and even celebrate marginalized bodies has not transcended the traditional anthropocentric mindset in Western traditions. The vast majority of scholars who attend to how gender, race, culture, age, class, disability, and queerness are coded on bodies to deny humanity to so many, do not apprehend the role of species difference in these codes. Even in critical race theory and postcolonial theorizations, a body of scholarship that highlights the spectrum of dehumanization that gives rise to civilizational heirarchies and their resulting violence, animals have figured primarily symbolically, with little attention to animals' embodied experiences. The literature has overlooked the co-constitutive nature of racial, cultural, and civilizational ideologies with anthropo-centrism and animal abjection, as well as how animalization logics have functioned in civilizational ideologies in terms of the expansive and damaging reach of the tropes of "animal" and "animality" since the transatlantic slave trade and European colonialism.[26] The response is one that contests liberal humanism's racial exclusions but does not apprehend that the speciesist limits of humanism are what permit an ongoing qualified account of (white) humanity.[27]

Indeed, it is no small task to bring the abjected body and marginal-ized bodies into law, given this general anti-body and anthropocentric backdrop.[28] Despite the monumental nature of the challenge, a core priority for a legal subjectivity that can attend to marginalized bodies, particularly those of animals, must be to de-emphasize the rational and affirm the body, including recognizing what we experience at the bodily level.[29] As discussed in chapter 2, the premium that law places on rea-son and the mind in terms of who matters is problematic on a whole host of critical registers whether focused on gender, race, ability, class, or other axes of analysis.[30] Recall that feminist, postcolonial, and critical disability theorists especially have revealed how the Western exaltation of reason privileges a hyperrational human as paradigmatic, resulting in partial and impoverished representations as it devalues other ele-ments of human life and experience.[31]

If the problem in exalting reason is of concern in the human realm to conceptualize who humans are and why we are important, it is even more acute in the case of animals, which are still explicitly and openly held deficient on this metric and widely subordinated because of it. Many animals farmed for their flesh are presumed to be cognitively inferior and are not even seen as whole bodies, but merely as body parts (breasts, thighs, legs, ribs, rumps, and other "cuts"). Farmed ani-mals overwhelmingly are valued insofar as their body parts, fertility, and reproductive capacities are profitable and thus "productive," and their lives are controlled and terminated for pure economic motives. Scholars working at the intersections of critical animal studies and critical disability studies have discussed how human ableism and its devaluation of embodied differences are imbricated in the industrial regulation of animal life, harnessing genetic breeding protocols as well as lethal measures against animals that are perceived to be "disabled" or "non-productive." Farmed animals that are "spent," "downed," or "diseased" require unusual medical care, or they cannot enter the food chain because they are deemed "unhealthy," and are killed even as the agricultural industry routinely breeds animals for disabling conditions in order to maximize profits and further maims theirs bodies once they are born.[32] Sunaura Taylor notes how the cultural ableist aversion to dependency in humans not only works to animalize those humans whose bodily differences cast them as "excessively" dependent on others, but also serves to marginalize animals.[33]

A legal subjectivity that embraces embodiment would not devalue humans or animals because they cannot reason to a certain level or at all. It would not animalize animals or human bodies due to other cognitive or physical differences since animality and embodiment would not be stigmatized.[34] Instead, the body would receive higher valuation in the law. That beings have a body through which they have the capacity for sensory experience is a more palatable and ethical criterion for who counts and why, although it need not be framed in such stark and exclusionary terms – that is, that only those embodied beings that have sensory experience count. I will say more about this "line-drawing" problem in the next chapter. My present purpose here is to press the importance of embodiment to how we see others and ourselves and to argue for what the law should value when it encounters marginalized bodies.

The discourses that humans enculturated into prevailing Western norms generate about animals and their bodies morally and legally legitimate the violence animals endure. If we inaugurate an understanding of animal bodies as sufficient in form, capacity, and impacts to matter, rather than deficient in one or more ways, a new starting point for law will emerge, one in which the law is positioned to remedy the relationality and vulnerability in these relations as a matter of human responsibility. It is to the concepts of vulnerability and relationality that the discussion now turns.

II. (An Embodied) Relationality

A second feature of beingness is relationality, meaning the quality of being in relationships with others both at a personal level and, more critically, at a systemic level. Relationality is meant to displace the individualism and individual autonomy inherent in the conceptualization of the modernist legal subject. Jennifer Nedelsky illuminates the harm this individualism does and the benefits of a relational legal subject in her body of scholarship, particularly in *Law's Relations*, in which she offers the metaphor of "creative interaction" – an overarching concept for the ability to interact with others and with phenomena around us and to respond to them – as a way for law to value autonomy in a relational manner.[35] To be clear, the body is imperative to this call for relationality in the law. Although we may conceive of our bodies as an interior experience, so that individualized outcomes and thus legal rights pertain to bodies as individuated self-determination claims (in areas such as reproductive rights or the right to assisted suicide), this view of the body lacks a presence in public and social life. Judith Butler illuminates this point when she writes:

> The body implies mortality, vulnerability, agency: the skin and the flesh expose us to the gaze of others, but also to touch, and to violence, and bodies put us at risk of becoming the agency and instrument of all these as well. Although we struggle for rights over our own bodies, the very bodies for which we struggle are not quite ever only our own. The body has its invariably public dimension. Constituted as a social phenomenon in the public sphere, my body is and is not mine. Given over from the start to the world of others, it bears their imprint, is formed within the crucible of social life.[36]

Butler calls attention to the public resonance of the body, implicitly linking this insight to her own scholarship discussing the discursive construction of bodies along hierarchical registers of normality and conformity and the benefits and risks this portends for differently situated bodies.[37] Like Nedelsky, Butler cautions against a classic liberal understanding of autonomy over our body in favour of a vision that acknowledges the "social conditions of ... embodiment"[38] and relationality "as an ongoing normative dimension of our social and political lives, one in which we are compelled to take stock of our interdependence."[39]

A. Relationality and Animals

Although Butler and Nedelsky have suggested that their work on relationality and subjectivity can extend to non-humans, both focus on humans when expounding on the importance of conceptualizing life as relational.[40] To more fully demonstrate the validity of such an extension of feminist relational theory to animals, we can turn to animal ethologists. In *Wild Justice: The Moral Lives of Animals*,[41] Marc Bekoff and Jessica Pierce "argue that animals have a broad repertoire of moral behavior and that their lives together are shaped by these behavior patterns."[42] The authors elaborate:

> Animals not only have a sense of justice, but also a sense of empathy, forgiveness, trust, reciprocity, and much more as well ... We show that animals have rich inner worlds – they have a nuanced repertoire of emotions, a high degree of intelligence (they're really smart and adaptable), and

demonstrate behavioral flexibility as they negotiate complex and changing social relationships. They're also incredibly adept social actors: they
form intricate networks of relationships and live by rules of conduct that
maintain social balance, or what we call social homeostasis.[43]

Bekoff and Pierce take aim at the perceived sense of a species divide
by showing that not only do animals exhibit the cognitive – including
emotional – capacities typically ascribed only to humans, but they also
abide by moral codes that manifest themselves notably through play
activities.[44] They also contest the notion that animals are more competitive than cooperative with one another,[45] noting that "cooperation is
everywhere in nature, and that it is [sic] serves to foster relationships
and societies in which morality blossoms."[46] The sociality of social animals like mammals is vital to the development of moral behaviours
because such animals are interdependent.[47] So it is sensible and accurate
to conceive of social animals as relational.

The feminist philosophers we encountered in the previous chapter
have taken up this work from cognitive ethologists regarding animals' sociality to argue for a relational orientation to how we think
of animals. Recall Cynthia Willett, who advocates rethinking human-
animal relations through the dynamics of "worldly engagement and
shared agency."[48] She relies considerably on the research of leading
primatologist Frans de Waal to augment her claims regarding human
and animal sociality and relationality.[49] Willett aims to create an interspecies ethics that better distances itself from the liberal humanist
individuated subject, is anti-anthropocentric in other respects, and is
also practical.[50] "Through multimodal social signaling,"[51] particularly
as expressed through play, and drawing also from Bekoff's work, Willett argues that mammals learn the ethical codes of our social group
and learn to live peacefully the vast majority of the time in our biosocial networks.[52] For Willett, "ethics becomes a matter of attending to
the rich networks in which biosocial selves are formed,"[53] a relational
network in which she squarely places mammals and other animals.

Feminist philosopher Lori Gruen, who it will be recalled has written
extensively about feminism, empathy, and human responsibility toward
animals,[54] stresses the relational nature of animals' lives using cognitive
ethology evidence.[55] Recall further that Gruen uses the term "entangled
empathy" to capture the inescapable entwinement of humans and animals in relationships, through which their subjectivities are shaped and
created.[56] She draws on Karan Barad's feminist material theory of "intra-
actions," which teaches that we are never discrete selves but instead
come into being through our encounters with other matter.[57]

Bekoff and Pierce as well as Willett and Gruen provide clear accounts grounded in cognitive ethology as well as feminist philosophy of why we should regard social animals as relational. As these works attest, relational theory is sensibly applied to animals because animals are relational. Acknowledging the profound relationality that sociality occasions in animals, however, should not efface the fact that non-social animals are also relational. Even animals that live individually outside of close kin networks form part of interdependent ecosystems. More importantly, perhaps, it is critical to remember that "being relational" does not simply mean that we live in social networks; we also inhabit relations of power, and so do non-social animals. Relationality is not simply about sociality; it also attends to the social hierarchies that structure our relations with one another – with those we affiliate with and recognize as kin or friends, and with those we do not know. It is about how we come into our selves through our connections to others.[58] The same principle would apply to our relations with social and non-social animals as well as to animal–animal relations.[59] It thus makes practical sense for law to conceive of all animals, social or not, as relational.

Conceptualizing animals as relational makes good empirical sense in that the law would finally reflect the reality of how animals live; it also reminds us that many animals lead deeply social lives that matter to their sense of well-being and that the relationships in which they are immersed are also relations of power. At the most basic level, the dominant legal discourse surrounding property narrates property as a right, not a thing, that exists between at least two people, thus indelibly structuring relationships.[60] As property, animals are caught or constantly at risk of being ensnared in extremely exploitative and paternalistic relationships where they are subject to the dominion of legal persons, human or corporate. Viewing them as relational legal beings brings these experiences into full juridical view at the same time that it stresses the enormous damage done to animals when they are denied their relations of childhood and other family bonds as they languish in exploitative relationships of commodification.[61] In highlighting the relationality of animals, beingness would direct juridical attention to the multiple ways in which animals are made vulnerable.[62]

III. Vulnerability

A third core feature of beingness as a new legal subjectivity for animals is vulnerability. Feminist care ethics has long held up human vulnerability as a reason to strive for non-violent and just relations.[63] The

preceding two sections on embodiment and relationality also demonstrate the vulnerability of animals. Indeed, it is our embodiment and
relationality as beings that together make us vulnerable to harm and
violence for all the reasons that vulnerability theorists suggest.[64] The
capacity to suffer, though not synonymous with vulnerability, is paramount here. Animals share their vulnerability with humans and all
other embodied beings.[65] In this section, I consider influential theories
regarding the promotion of vulnerability awareness, in the legal arena
and more generally, to compel legal and other institutional responses to
violence and suffering. I do so to consider whether there are any legitimate conceptual or practical objections or impediments to extending
such theories to animals.

A. Feminist Vulnerability Theorizations

Martha Fineman's formulation of the vulnerable subject has been
broadly influential in feminist legal theory.[66] This formulation subverts
the classic autonomous liberal subject by normalizing dependency and
relationality, affirming embodiment and social embeddedness, and
rejecting the possibility of impartial and neutral disembodied judgment.[67] In seeking to displace the law's autonomous rational subject
with the vulnerable human subject, Fineman's vision of vulnerability
affirms classic liberal egalitarian aims (such as equality and dignity
for humans only) and assumes the stability of subjectivity in general.[68]
Although Ani Satz has helpfully extended Fineman's "vulnerability thesis" to animals in the American legal context, and other critical scholars
have taken up the thesis to apply to non-humans more broadly,[69] some
may view Fineman's vulnerability theory and Satz's extension of it to
animals as too liberal in orientation.[70]

For the purposes of demonstrating why vulnerability is an appropriate trigger for ethical and legal response and should include animals as
vulnerable beings, I turn to the work of Judith Butler. Her writings are
widely embraced across disciplines as substantiating the importance
of vulnerability as an ethical catalyst for responding to Others.[71] Her
response ethics–inspired insights about which acts trigger vulnerability
also constitute a model more oriented to alterity and may be more palatable to critical theorists who appreciate Fineman's vulnerability thesis
but seek to substantially supplement or transcend its residual liberalism. To be clear, I showcase Butler's theoretical treatment of vulnerability here because it enjoys wide support within and outside legal circles
among feminist, queer, disability, and other critical theorists oriented
toward theories of alterity, in which I have thus far located my critique

of property and personhood as legal subjectivities. I invoke Butler's theoretical treatment of vulnerability to demonstrate why animals can fit into Butler's account and thus why critical theorists should welcome them as vulnerable beings to whom the law and other institutions should affirmatively respond. Put more simply, I demonstrate why it makes sense to conceptualize animals as vulnerable in these highly endorsed accounts of how law and ethics should be organized.

Butler's scholarship about vulnerability (and its closely related concept of precarity) is dedicated to understanding contemporary logics of neoliberalism and imperialism at the global, transnational, and local levels and the harms they produce. Her aim is to generate a non-violent world in which lives are not placed on a hierarchy of grievability.[72] In Butler's ethics, a shared "corporeal vulnerability ... is the source of the obligation to be non-violent towards one another."[73] Butler initially appears to stake a bold humanist foundation for her theorizations of both vulnerability and precarity when she asks: "From where might a principle emerge by which we vow to protect others from the kinds of violence we have suffered, if not from an apprehension of a common human vulnerability?"[74] Butler avows that humans are made vulnerable because of the harms their bodies can expose them to, what she calls their "corporeal vulnerability."[75] She posits that humans share a corporeal vulnerability but does not establish this condition as triggered by harm and "the ever-constant possibility of dependency"[76] (as Fineman does); rather, she sees it as emerging through *ethical interaction* with another. Here is one way Butler explains it:

> A vulnerability must be perceived and recognized in order to come into play in an ethical encounter, and there is no guarantee that this will happen. Not only is there always the possibility that a vulnerability will not be recognized and that it will be constituted as the "unrecognizable," but when a vulnerability is recognized, that recognition has the power to change the meaning and structure of the vulnerability itself. In this sense, if vulnerability is one precondition for humanization, and humanization takes place differently through variable norms of recognition, then it follows that vulnerability is fundamentally dependent on existing norms of recognition if it is to be attributed to any human subject.[77]

Fineman classifies vulnerability as an innate or constant human condition because it arises from the possibility of dependence and harm, which always surrounds us.[78] For Butler, in contrast, although she clearly views the body as easily amenable to violence and suffering, the trigger for vulnerability is its recognition and response by another.[79] It is in this public moment that vulnerability shifts from its private form to a crystallized social and relational one. As Butler herself indicates, this account relies heavily on feminist psychoanalytical and Hegelian theory.[80] The core of her concern, however, is a Levinasian one:[81] to emphasize the role played by recognition as the first step in an ethical response to the Other.[82] That there is an absence of recognition of another's vulnerability is the implicit premise of Butler's question of what makes for a grievable life, of whose life we can publicly mourn with approval and support.[83] Butler hopes that our "apprehension of life as precarious" – and here we can read her as emphasizing our embodiment and social relationality as producing the precarity – will mobilize us toward acting ethically with all Others.[84] This relational sense of the fluid ontology of bodies/selves diverges from the more coherent ideas of self and Other formation in relational theories of vulnerability such as Fineman's because it is meant to be more provisional and shifting.[85]

In discussing the precarity of human lives and the uneven assignments of precarity that are a consequence of global economic, political, social, and cultural forces, we can distil how Butler's explanation of precarity significantly departs from a liberal vision of subjectivity detached from difference. We also see from Butler more acknowledgment of the need to reject humanism. In my own view, then, we have to start from this shared condition of precarity (not as existential fact, but as a social condition of political life) in order to refute those normative operations, pervasively racist and ableist, that decide in advance who counts as human and who does not.[86] My point is not to rehabilitate humanism but rather to struggle for a conception of ethical obligation that is grounded in precarity. No one escapes the precarious dimension of social life – it is, we might say, our common non-foundation. Nothing "founds" us outside of a struggle to establish bonds that sustain us.[87]

Butler appears to nuance her earlier initial statements about a "common human vulnerability" as arising not simply from biological conditions of embodiment, but also through larger political forces that take up our embodiment. It would seem, then, to house critical purchase and scope for transformative impact for other species as well.

B. *Vulnerability, Precarity, and Animals*

Is there any reason why animals should be excluded from Butler's theory of vulnerability grounded in response ethics rather than liberal egalitarianism? Although critical of liberal humanism, Butler's own work may be read as explicitly excluding animals from its critical purview.[88] As Chloë Taylor observes,

> for Butler, the frame of the human must be interrupted, dislocated beyond the dominant (First World, heterosexist) model, in order to include human beings who are currently dehumanized, and yet Butler does not consider dislocating this frame – which determines which lives are considered grievable – beyond the human.[89]

Despite this criticism, Taylor goes on to

> argue that Butler's account of an ethics of interdependence, embodiment, vulnerability, and mourning is a compelling incentive for thinking about the lives not only of humans, but of animals more generally, and that there is nothing about Butler's ethics that would justify an exclusion of non-human animals.[90]

Butler and others, in a virtual round table of feminist scholars/activists who locate their work within precarity scholarship,[91] were recently questioned about this residual humanism by Jasbir Puar, a postcolonial queer theorist who has previously addressed issues pertaining to the human/non-human divide.[92] Puar asks Butler and other key interlocutors on precarity the following question (which opened chapter 3):

> If we are serious about not rehabilitating humanism, or recognizing that a brutal humanism exists as a form of speciesism that cleaves not only raced and sexed humans from other humans, but also complicates any human/nonhuman animal divide and puts under duress our contingent relations to other animals, plant life, and ecologies of matter and material, can we think of precarity "beyond" the human? What would an interspecies politics or vision of precarity entail?[93]

Butler's reply is nuanced and worth quoting at length:

> It is always possible to say that the affective register where precarity dwells is something like dehumanization. And yet, we know that such a word relies on a human/animal distinction that cannot and should not be sustained. Indeed, if we call for humanization and struggle against "bestialization" then we affirm that the bestial is separate from and subordinate to the human, something that clearly breaks our broader commitments to rethinking the networks of life ... But the critical task is to find a way to oppose that inequality without embracing anthropocentrism. So we have

to rethink the human in light of precarity, showing that there is no human without those networks of life within which human life is but one sort of life ... Indeed, the connection with nonhuman life is indispensable to what we call human life ... In other words, to be alive is already to be connected with, dependent upon, what is living not only before and beyond myself, but before and beyond my humanness. No self and no human can live without this connection to a biological network of life that exceeds and includes the domain of the human animal. This is why in opposing war, for example, one not only opposes the destruction of other human lives, but also the poisoning of the environment and the assault on living beings and a living world.[94]

In these remarks, we hear a clear denunciation of anthropocentrism on several levels. First, Butler addresses the deeper logic of dehumanization, a logic critical theorists often contest when it is applied to render human lives sub-human, but without remarking on the abject coding that dehumanization entails for non-humans.[95] Butler insists that we have to contest the subordination of non-humans as well. Second, Butler affirms the view that an ethics premised on a species divide between humans and animals is unsustainable not just because of the socially constructed nature of the divide but also because of the imbrication of human lives with non-human ones.

It is possible to read Butler's comments in the latter part of the extract as rehearsing a classically anthropocentric script: that we must reflect upon our actions on the non-human world due to this connectedness in order to prevent adverse implications for the human world. My sense is that this would be a misreading, given her earlier statement that our ethical impulses toward equality cannot be anthropocentric. Instead, Butler seems to be avowing the connectedness of all life to move her readers away from a view of the human subject as separate from and unshaped by non-human subjectivity. Indeed, she seems to intimate the mutual constitution of human and animal subjectivity through the interdependent encounter. With such a gesture, she approaches Colleen Glenney Boggs's relational interspecies view of subjectivity formation, namely, "there is no subject that predates the relationship with animals – subjectivity emerges in and remains unhinged by cross-species encounters."[96]

It is this recognition, derived from feminist, postcolonial, biopolitical, and post-structuralist orientations, of the relational vulnerability and precarity of embodied others that compels a response to animals. Animals are immensely vulnerable. The status of property to which the law relegates them creates this acute level of vulnerability, with attendant living conditions (even for beloved companion animals), that epitomizes precarity.[97] What is sought is a response to prevent, alleviate, mitigate, or stop the suffering that flows from injury and violence whether directed at human or non-human lives. As Taylor notes above, and as demonstrated through Butler's own words,[98] there is nothing in Butler's widely influential account to suggest that animals should be excluded from concerns about vulnerability.[99] Animal vulnerability conforms to the core meanings of Butler's concept of vulnerability.[100]

While I cannot further substantiate this claim here, other feminist accounts of why societies should be oriented around vulnerability logically extend to animals, whose bodies are also material, prone to wounding, and entrenched in relations of dependence and care.[101] Consider as just one example the summative statement by Wendy Rogers, Catriona Mackenzie, and Susan Dodds following their account of why vulnerability is universal for humans and why it matters ethically and politically: "As biological and social beings, we share much vulnerability – to ill health, to bad luck, to natural and human-generated disasters, and so forth. Although these and other vulnerabilities are not equally distributed, none of us is invulnerable; we all have some experience and understanding of what it is to feel vulnerable."[102] We would be hard-pressed to find a defensible reason to exclude animals from this description of what triggers vulnerability.

Indeed, prioritizing attention on the material effects of power on vulnerable bodies and precarious lives seems particularly important in the case of animals, given the immiserated conditions in which billions of animals are confined and the exceptional brutalities to which they are subject, as well as the far-reaching scope of the trope of animality to render any life of little or no value.[103] If beingness can help signal to judges, legislators, or policy-makers that they direct their attention to the vulnerability animals experience because of their embodiment and relationality, then there is a possibility of intervening in practices that normalize the degradation of animal bodies and the denial of their vulnerability. Presently, the property classification disavows animal vulnerability or minimizes it to the point of meaninglessness in the case of anti-cruelty legislation, as chapter 1 discussed. Personhood will not be a sufficient corrective to direct the law's attention maximally to vulnerability because its primary organizing legal subject is a disembodied, non-dependent, rational human thinker. In contrast, to institute beingness for animals would be to signal to all legal actors and the public at large the instantiation of a system that cares about violence and the suffering it causes irrespective of whether such suffering is "humane" or "necessary." It signals a system that mandates law's response in the face of such egregious, chronic, and disavowed harm.

IV. Some Objections

The preceding sections have explained why legal valuation of certain features is important, namely, (1) to rehabilitate animals' current mainstream legal position by unsettling the entrenched Western cultural and legal epistemologies that have rendered animals inferior and subject to commodification, and (2) to respond to the embodied and relational vulnerability animals face given current power arrangements. I turn now to consider two objections grounded in feminist and postcolonial ethics that point to drawbacks of this model, notably with the concept and permutations of vulnerability.[104]

A. Embodied Vulnerability as a Stigmatized Status

A legal subjectivity that emphasizes vulnerability troubles those scholars who view the focus on suffering that vulnerability entails (although, again, the two are not coterminous) as a potentially problematic resting point for law or ethics. In *Fruits of Sorrow: Framing Our Attention to Suffering*, Elisabeth Spelman identifies three archetypical ways in which American culture views those who suffer: "as the subjects of tragedy; as the objects of compassion; and as spiritual bellhops, carriers of experience from which others can benefit."[105] The risks of problematic responses to those who are vulnerable are intensified for those whom the public may already associate with perpetual victimhood and by stereotypes that disparage vulnerability as an undesirable, feminized, passive state.[106] As part of this cluster of concerns, Spelman highlights how our understandings of the complexity of sufferers' lives and the underlying social issues annexed to them may be further impoverished, given background cultural norms about the body and the tendency for a focus on suffering to overshadow all other capacities of sufferers.[107] Some feminist legal scholars have echoed this concern, noting that despite critical scholarly attempts to recuperate the term and attach positive associations to it, its long-standing negative connotations persist.[108] Such connotations continue to encourage victim-blaming in legal decision-making or to discursively force individuals into stereotyped or neoliberal subject positions in order to secure legal victories as "vulnerable subjects."[109] Focusing on suffering and its correlate, vulnerability, can thus be reductive.[110]

Taimie Bryant, borrowing from Spelman's work, has raised this point specifically in relation to animal law reform.[111] She is concerned that the devalued position of the body in Western intellectual traditions contaminates any plea to make suffering an ethical or legal trigger for rights and protection because it draws attention back to the devalued body. In this conceptual architecture, creating subjectivity for marginalized beings through a recognition of their capacity to suffer immediately places those beings at a devalued starting point and thus undermines the purpose for attending to suffering in the first place.[112] For Bryant, asking the law to affirm animals as vulnerable subjects compels highlighting their bodily experiences, thereby inviting an implicit devaluation of animals even as we try to affirm their value. Her second and related concern is that animals will be reduced to their suffering, leaving no room to present a more complex, hopeful view of what animals are and the rich lives they can lead.[113] As Alice Kuzniar intimates, representations of animals through tropes of poverty and privation are contested by those seeking to inspire a more agentic view of why animals matter.[114] Recall that Cynthia Willett also objects to the vulnerability/suffering frame. She contests the routine representation of animals as mere moral patients,[115] forever cast as "vulnerable, mute and suffering beings on the receiving end of human moral consideration and treatment."[116]

Animals are indeed much more than their vulnerability. They have capacities for so many other experiences and expression that a focus on the capacity to suffer might obscure. Doubtless, attending to suffering can generate political and legal responses that are comparatively meagre, simplistic, neoliberal, or opportunistic. But a main structural issue shaping the potential of vulnerability discourse to further marginalize those it is intended to benefit – at least as it is argued in the accounts of some feminists who raise this concern – is that vulnerability discourse in law or politics operates as an *exceptional* classification that largely leaves the broader liberal order intact.[117] Those to whom the "vulnerable" label applies thus stand out for a type of lack, or worse, deviance, for which they are blamed or typecast. But conceptualizing all animals as vulnerable is a much more destabilizing move against the liberal legal order in that *all* animals would be deemed "vulnerable," given how prone they are to human control and domination. Furthermore, characterizing animals as such should not incite the same concerns about "victim-blaming" humans as we do not presently impute moral agency to animals and then harshly judge them in a general way, as we do to other humans.

In any case, the question remains: Would the potential adverse outcomes of the legal ascendancy of vulnerability (notably, eclipsing agency or essentializing an entire group classified as vulnerable)[118] as an organizing concept for a new animal legal subjectivity entail abandoning vulnerability as a platform of ethical and legal relevance? This is not the end point that theorists who criticize the use of vulnerability as a lens call for; instead they advocate a more productive or nuanced response.[119]

One such notable response is found in the work of the feminist philosopher Kelly Oliver.[120] Witnessing is the frame she proposes to create a relational exchange that is respectful of difference and Otherness. By "witnessing," Oliver means to connote the classic juridical and lay sense of being an eyewitness to an event. She also, however, wants witnessing to signal the religious idea of "bearing witness" or acknowledging that there are aspects of experiences of Otherness that can never be grasped or seen but to which we nonetheless owe responsibility.[121] This position allows us to be humble yet still respond to the needs of vulnerable Others because we approach them as inhabiting multilayered experiences and not simply trauma or marginalized status.[122] If animals are approached only as victims, this ability to encounter them as partners in "reciprocally responsible relationships"[123] that constitute mutual subjectivity is thwarted.

Incorporating an ethos of "witnessing" vulnerability allays the criticism that viewing animals as vulnerable subjects will further marginalize them. Bryant, though, is insistent on a clean break from a suffering framework because of her worry about the devalued bodily associations that suffering will provoke. But if the law were to create a legal subjectivity that affirms not only animals' vulnerability but also their embodiment, as I have argued that it should, then this type of subjectivity could eliminate Bryant's concern. Asking the law to witness animals because of their vulnerability would bring animals onto our legal horizons as their own subjects. This move need not foreclose consideration of the multiple, more positively associated, capacities animals have beyond suffering and vulnerability or the transformative potential of properly framed vulnerability discourses.[124]

B. Embodied Vulnerability as a Problematic Universal

As I have added Butlerian vulnerability and precarity theory as a decolonizing and anti-humanist corrective to Fineman's vulnerability work, it is important to engage Malini Johar Schueller's analysis that Butler's ethics of vulnerability and precarity are part of a resurgence of the universal in critical theorizing on the world scale.[125] Schueller draws our attention to the enthusiasm with which influential critical scholars, seeking to intervene in the global reach of neoliberalism and the domination and oppression it entails, have revivified Western bench-marks in their universal claims about what it means to be human.[126] This, Schueller reminds us, runs against the basic teachings of postcolonial theory: "those of us who are wary of eighteenth-century Europe's racial projects and colonial missions have reason to be extremely wary of these current projects in which a West-centered humanism parades as universalism."[127] Schueller discusses several towering figures in contemporary "global progressive intellectual culture":[128] Michael Hardt and Antonio Negri, Giorgio Agamben, and Butler.[129]

Schueller helpfully encapsulates the core of Butler's writings on vulnerability and precarity in *Precarious Life* as an attempt, shortly after 9/11 and the global security, militaristic, and violent implications that followed, "to theorize an ethics of interdependence as the basis for a world without violence."[130] She quickly acknowledges that Butler is genuinely aiming for an anti-imperial ethics of Otherness that emphasizes human interdependence and empathy rather than fear, distrust, and violence.[131] Butler's urge to intervene in the present "imperial moment" through a theory of vulnerability derived in part from feminist commitments to relationality is not objectionable.[132]

What *is* of concern for Schueller is Butler's continuing resort to claims about what all humans experience – that is, loss and a relational state with other people from which we can cultivate an ethics of connection through empathy and recognition.[133] Schueller notes that Butler retrieves her sense of a universal vulnerable subject from Hegel; as mentioned earlier, for Butler, vulnerability crystallizes through a Hegelian concept of recognition as reciprocal exchange itself aimed at a Levinasian ethic of Otherness.[134] It is at this point that Schueller presses forward her postcolonial intervention via the following query: "But if a radical human vulnerability, dependent upon recognition, is to be posited as the basis for a tranformative [sic] ethical encounter, it is important to again ask whether this formulation of human vulnerability does not, in fact, depend on the erasure of unevenness that has been the basis for a West-centered humanism."[135] Schueller is worried about what universal claims, however provisionally situated, will obscure rather than reveal. She contrasts Hegel's work with Frantz Fanon's views on vulnerability, which contested Hegel's comparative undertheorization of domination in conceptualizing reciprocity and recognition, as an antidote to Butler's optimism about the benefits that a fixation on vulnerability will yield.[136] Schueller believes that recognition can obfuscate power relations that structure reciprocal exchange.[137] She maintains that she is "not suggesting that we throw out all possibility of human community, but that we maintain a vigilance about how we want to postulate community so that it doesn't re-inscribe imperialism."[138] In terms of Butlerian recognition, she proffers some revisions to soften its totalizing impulse, namely, by continually looking for the exceptions and contingencies to how recognition works and by foregrounding the conditions of inequality in which it develops or abates.[139]

I believe that Oliver's emphasis on witnessing that I have suggested here should be adopted to inform how we approach others in vulnerable states; doing so would solve the recognition problem Schueller identifies. I nevertheless welcome Schueller's proposed revisions, for they incline the Butlerian model of vulnerability and precarity closer to the anti-imperial intervention it seeks to be in terms of charting an ethics of alterity/Otherness. It is a revision I incorporate into the concept of vulnerability I have drawn here to give content to beingness as a legal subjectivity.

V. Conclusion

Elsewhere, Paola Cavalieri reminds us that "the inferior status to which animals are relegated is, like many other historical phenomena, really accidental. A different perception of animals could have prevailed had it not been defeated in some specific clashes of views."[140] If we depart from law's rationalist preferences – those that valorize a thinking, disembodied, and independently autonomous human person over every other kind of being as the proper subject of law – we can move toward this alternative perception. As demonstrated in chapter 2, personhood, a legal concept that prioritizes an independent rational agent and defines itself through the objectification of animals, is not an ideal vehicle through which the law can move toward this view regarding which beings matter. A different legal subjectivity is needed for animals. This chapter has argued that instead of embracing personhood, or a modified vision thereof, the law should recognize animals as legal subjects (and thus entitled to the protections against instrumental use that status is meant to provide) through a new vehicle I term "beingness." Beingness invites a different legal outlook on animals than property or personhood – one that emphasizes the embodied, vulnerable, and relational aspects of animals. Configuring a particular assemblage of feminist and other critical social and philosophical theory on why embodiment, relationality, and vulnerability are central to subjectivity, I demonstrated why such theories are sensibly extended to animals. Beingness would constitute a paradigm shift in anthropocentric legal systems because it would end the legal classification of animals as property and attend to animals' vulnerability by way of their embodied and relational nature.

The foregoing theorization of the principal constitutive elements of beingness does not settle this question: "Who or what counts as flesh and who does not?"[141] Nor does it fully address Butler's query – "Whose lives are real? Whose lives are grievable?," that is, the underlying questions of which entities ought to count as beings whose interests/needs/desires the law should try to consider. I imagine this question regarding the precise boundaries of the terms "animal" and "legal being" might by now be foremost in the reader's mind. I address this question next.

5 Liberal Humanism Repackaged?

As a new legal subjectivity, beingness is meant to establish a new, non-propertied status for animals that guards against their exploitation but also avoids what I have argued are the pitfalls with personhood. As is evident by now, the present project is committed to providing an alternative to the traditional dominant legal conceptualization of animals as property as well as to law reform proposals that have liberal humanizing precepts at their foundation. Beingness's theoretical formation as a feminist and critical animal studies legal intervention is a direct response to the problems that I have argued inhere in the current property status for animals but also in a liberal humanist vision of personhood as a replacement for that status.

A consistent concern thus carried through this work has been the exclusionary nature of theories and campaigns that rely on sameness logic to articulate claims for animal justice. As I've discussed, many animal theorists see within animal campaigns based on sameness a humanizing impulse that merely shifts the zones of inclusion and exclusion rather than eliminating exclusion altogether.[1] An animal theory that encodes the logic of humanizing sameness thus replicates the conventional liberal dynamic of trying to be more inclusive of who/what counts by extension rather than subversion of existing tenets.[2] In this section I take up the question of whether the standard of legal beingness conceptualized through the features of embodiment, vulnerability, and relationality as charted in the previous chapter avoids this fate. I consider which animals should count as legal subjects under this new category and thus confront the difficult and sparsely theorized issue of "line drawing" among animals as well as between animals and other non-humans. As these questions regarding non-animal non-humans are naturally broad, the theorizations in this latter section are necessarily brief. I include these brief discussions, however, to give the reader a sense of which entities in the non-human realm *could* become legal beings. I also answer the closely related question almost invariably posed to animal advocates – "What about plants?" – which then prompts further queries about other types of matter.[3] In taking up the matter of which animals and other non-humans count, this chapter anticipates and replies to the criticism that beingness is really a liberal humanist concept in disguise rather than an innovative and promising concept that is more animal-friendly in being much more responsive to animals' alterity, aspirations, and vulnerabilities.[4]

I. Which Animals Count?

A. Defining Animals

The concern with what many refer to as the "line-drawing" articulated by some animal theorists forces all of us to tackle a question that is not easily answered: What/who do we mean by "animal" when we discuss ethical or legal reform? I set out my definition of animal in the Introduction, stipulating that I was referring to all beings taxonomically defined as animal other than humans. While the expansive use of the term made sense when considering Canadian criminal law on anti-cruelty (chapter 1), and the problems with property as well as personhood (chapter 2), now a potentially confounding question presents itself: Which animals count as "beings"? Starting this second inquiry with a dictionary definition of "animal" points to the challenge posed by simple descriptors, let alone normative ones, for what would qualify as "beings" under a beingness model. The online *Oxford English Dictionary* offers the following definitions of "animal" in numbered order:

1. a living organism which feeds on organic matter, typically having specialized sense organs and nervous system and able to respond rapidly to stimuli
    1.1 any such living organism other than a human being
    1.2 a mammal, as opposed to a bird, reptile, fish, or insect
    1.3 a person without human attributes or civilizing influences, especially someone who is very cruel, violent, or repulsive.[5]

An animal is also defined through differentiation from plants:

Animals are generally distinguished from plants by being unable to synthesize organic molecules from inorganic ones, so that they have to feed on plants or on other animals. They are typically able to move about, though this ability is sometimes restricted to a particular stage in the life cycle. The great majority of animals are invertebrates, of which there are some thirty phyla; the vertebrates constitute but a single subphylum.[6]

It should be clear that no one in animal theory endorses definition 1.3. Also, it is implicit that most theorists have birds, reptiles, amphibians, and fish in mind when considering claims about animal justice and so would also not accept 1.2 as a sufficient definition. The exclusion of insects, however, may be more palatable to some. Does the concept of *legal* being advocated here capture insects as well, and is it so inclusive as to comply with the definition in 1.1 of "any living organism"? Does beingness have to align with 1.1 to avoid the charge of hypocritical line-drawing? Does it have to delve even deeper than 1.1 and include those beings that are living, like plants, or even those that are not living (or that dominant human culture typically perceives as such)? This chapter defends the assignment of beingness to all "animals" as I have been using the term in previous chapters – that is, to all mammals, birds, reptiles, amphibians, fish, and insects. In what follows, I justify this position on who would qualify to be a legal "being" by assembling and responding to critiques of sentientism, biocentrism, and all other capacity-based approaches.

B. Capacity-Based Approaches: Expanding the Circle but Always Already Exclusionary?

1. IS SENTIENCE THE NEW REASON?

Most animal theorists have avoided the potentially confounding question of how to define precisely which animals should count as ethical and legal subjects by implicitly emphasizing sentience and the corresponding capacity to suffer.[7] Sentience is viewed as a legitimate boundary marker to replace the illegitimate emphasis on rationality that presently serves as the general placeholder for legal personhood.[8] Some feminist animal scholars have endorsed sentience as the criterion for full legal subjecthood because of its correlation to embodied vulnerability. These arguments privileging sentience are understandable, yet sentience does not fully capture the features of embodiment, vulnerability, and relationality that the law should foreground. Specifically, it is possible to be vulnerable through one's body without being sentient. There are living beings that can die (a form of vulnerability) without going through what we normally characterize as sentient experience: plants and embryos (of all species) are ready examples. Another point to consider is that the animals we presume not to be sentient (say, insects or even plants) may in fact be sentient – our anthropocentric ways of perceiving simply blind us to that fact.[9]

More to the point, the drawing of a line at sentience to include all animals, however practical and normatively better than the existing line, may register an insupportable position and fate for those below the line. Consider bacteria, whether anaerobic or not. Bacteria are a form of non-animal and non-sentient life that would not count within many prominent animal ethical theories. Taimie Bryant notes how bacteria conceptually belong to those forms of life that we usually disavow completely in philosophical discussions.[10] She challenges the view that human entitlement to manipulate bacteria as we see fit is ethically benign; she questions whether such a view is anything but a problematic hierarchical claim motivated by our ability to only value in other beings what we value in ourselves (here, sentience).[11] A further point of reflection is to query whether size matters – would we be comfortable drawing a line at sentience if the animals we currently excluded on this ground were in fact much larger than the typically imagined category of non-sentient animals?[12] For Bryant, all approaches to line-drawing among living beings are problematic. Bryant urges activists, instead of trying to decide on what an "animal" is and which animals should receive moral and legal consideration, to redirect society's attention to claims that humans are entitled to violate all other beings, including bacteria and corals.[13]

Bryant emphasizes that all forms of life depend on one another for mutual well-being, thus pointing to the limits of a model that would protect some in this web from exploitative use, but not others.[14] John Miller endorses a similar position in commenting about the typically antithetical relationship imagined between postcolonial and environmental studies: "Ecological and human interests are better conceived, then, as community rather than opposition, a mutual involvement that vouchsafes the basis for both a more accurate appreciation of the realities of our ecological situation and also a more inclusive ethical commitment that imagines no being as the disempowered, passive side of an imperial either/or."[15] Both Bryant and Miller identify the limitations of an approach to line-drawing that would exclude *any* form of life. Symbolically and materially, line-drawing is a hierarchical/imperial/subordinating act. In practical terms, an ethics that does not presumptively seek to protect *all* forms of life discounts the relationality of all life on the planet, a move that will ultimately disadvantage *all* sentient beings.[16] From their perspective, sentience does not suffice as an ethical and legal anchor for subjectivity and recognition; all living beings in the relational web of life must count.[17]

2. IS BIOCENTRISM OR ANY "CENTRISM" STILL PROBLEMATIC?

I expect that many would see the logic in Bryant and Miller's arguments but find the task of actually casting the net of legal subjectivity as wide as they wish to do a daunting and unworkable prospect. Others, however, may question whether Bryant and Miller stop short of true inclusiveness. Here, questions arise about non-living beings – entities we normally classify as things – and whether it is permissible as a matter of ethics and law to exclude them. In "A Vindication of the Rights of Machines," David J. Gunkel answers this question in the negative.[18] Gunkel identifies the arguments of those, like Bryant, who would make all life forms matter but would not maintain non-living entities on the same plane, as biocentric and as susceptible to the same critiques that animal theorists would level against anthropocentrism.

Gunkel credits the animal rights movement (his focus appears to be on the movement in the United States) with catalysing the philosophical pressure that has been brought to bear on human exceptionalism claims.[19] He also, however, notes the problems that arise when animal theories and other arguments for inclusion continue a logic of line-drawing even if do they lower the bar to let more beings in. Gunkel reminds readers that the Cartesian view of animals that animal theorists soundly denounce is one that equated animals with machines; it is because animals were thought to be non-sentient and no more than machines that it was acceptable to inflict pain on them.[20] Gunkel observes that "despite this fundamental and apparently irreducible similitude, only one of the pair has been considered a legitimate subject of moral concern"[21] owing to the current prominence of sentience as a marker for ethical consideration. Feminist new materialist, posthumanist, transhumanist, and Actor Network theories, among other theories highlighting the entanglements that humans, animals, and plants have with the object world normally seen to be non-living in Western cultures, bolster Gunkel's argument. These theories direct us to the agency as well as interactivity, interdependence, and mutual constitution between animate and inanimate matter, compelling contemplation of the possible tenuousness of any biocentric ethical distinctions that rest on a life versus non-life distinction.[22]

But Gunkel wants to make a further critique still. Besides seriously entertaining the question of whether machines may be able to experience pain as one pathway for challenging the widespread disavowal of ethical regard for machines,[23] Gunkel challenges the logic he sees encrypted into *all* forms of line-drawing.[24] Biocentric theories do not succumb to traditional markers of human exceptionalism such as consciousness or moral agency, and they broaden the circle beyond sentient beings, yet they accept the widely held view that non-life forms, mere things, should not have equal moral significance. Bryant's appeal for us to consider all life forms in our ethical and legal purviews still reproduces, according to this view, a logic of exclusion and creates its own binary.[25] Gunkel acknowledges that more inclusive line-drawing through biocentrism or otherwise "inverts or 'turns over' the traditional arrangement," but maintains that "inversion of a binary opposition actually does little or nothing to disturb or to challenge the fundamental structure of the system in question."[26]

It seems that this binary and unproductive result is inescapable. It applies to theories that seek to surpass biocentric ones in defining who/what matters by including all non-living things as well.[27] In Gunkel's view, the consequence is a theory that rests on sameness no matter how far from the anthropocentric centre it has strayed:

> All of these innovations, despite their differences in focus, employ a similar maneuver and logic. That is, they redefine the center of moral consideration in order to describe progressively larger circles that come to encompass a wider range of possible participants. Although there are and will continue to be considerable debates about what should define the center and who or what is or is not included, this debate is not the problem. The problem rests with the strategy itself. In taking a centrist approach, these different ethical theories ... endeavor to identify what is essentially the same in a phenomenal diversity of different individuals. Consequently, they include others by effectively stripping away and reducing differences. This approach, although having the appearance of being increasingly more inclusive, effaces the unique alterity of others and turns them into more of the same.[28]

For Gunkel, as much as theories of amniocentrism (those inclusive of all forms of animality) or biocentrism (those inclusive of all forms of life) or even ontocentrism (those inclusive of all things) wish to mark their divergence from human exceptionalism, they cannot avoid being drawn into a difference-effacing vortex because of the premise of sameness that defines the group (even when, as in the case of ontocentrism, no entities are excluded). Caught up as we are in our anthropocentric perspectives, we are shut off from the rich entanglements and ways of interspecies relating in the wider non-human zones of life and matter.[29] Gunkel invokes the work of Emmanuel Levinas to suggest that this epistemic reduction of the Other to the same is the hallmark of Western philosophy.[30] The solution to this dilemma for Gunkel is not to find the most inclusive point of reference, whether human, animal, all living things, or simply all things, but to disavow the philosophical tradition that searches for and establishes a base and universal commonality.[31] For besides being binary and reductive, the inclusive gesture entails a forced appropriation of non-human others based on human decision-making as to who/what counts.[32]

3. RESPONSE ETHICS AND ALL MATTER

Gunkel turns again to Levinas for an alternative way of moving forward for animals "that does not continue to pursue a project of totalizing and potentially violent assimilation"[33] and that can also avoid a binary structure.[34] He credits Levinas for being unique among Western moral philosophers in his ability to radicalize rather than domesticate difference. This is attributed to the Levinisian directive that we are responsible to Others who are suffering no matter their degree of perceived alterity.[35] It is also attributable to the fact that we can never fully know the Other[36] – an insight that postcolonial theory has also made prominent[37] – and as such turns attention from the minds of Others to their faces. It is then the face of the Other that establishes our own ability to act as a "self" and that compels our concern about the Other's vulnerability.[38] Gunkel explains this relational subversion of traditional accounts of how self and other relate when describing what happens when we encounter the face of the other:

> [The self] does not [yet] take the form of an active agent who is able to decide to extend him/herself to others in a deliberate act of compassion. Rather it becomes what it is as a byproduct of an uncontrolled and incomprehensible exposure to the face of the other that takes place prior to and in advance of any formulation of the self in terms of agency. Likewise the Other is not comprehended as a patient who would be the recipient of the agent's actions and whose interests and rights would need to be identified, taken into account, and duly respected.[39]

Gunkel notes that Levinas's view of self/other interactions does not amount to a traditional form of ethics, but is more what other scholars have called a "proto-ethics."[40] For this reason, he states that it is very difficult to transport it into the world of law and politics to sustain a program of transformative change for animals or otherwise.[41] Those who have tried (as I did in chapter 3, when delineating required legal ontological shifts through feminist response ethics) have succumbed to the pressures – perhaps inevitable in law – of articulating the scope of an extended legal subjectivity and answering the question of who/what counts and why (again, as I did in chapter 4 to explain beingness and do in this chapter to identify who is eligible for this new legal subject classification).

The interventions of feminist new materialists also align with Gunkel's turn to Levinas to rehabilitate how humans view, represent, and interact with machines. Focusing on all types of matter, this school of feminist thought has advocated for a posthuman turn that would put an end to humanist representations of matter as passive, inert, and acted upon by humans. Instead, feminist new materialists call for a complete reset in human relations with "things" and other non-humans, seeing the latter as "lively and agential" and as entities that shape our becoming as selves.[42] Like Gunkel, they are likely to oppose any sharp lines or tightly bound categories in law or ethics as to who counts and why.

C. Mammals to Insects to Oceans: Ethical Mattering for Most, but Beingness Just for Animals and Some Bodies of Water

1. ADVERTING TO CAPACITIES TO GAUGE LEVELS OF VULNERABILITY

But is it possible to think otherwise in law, to altogether avoid specifying who or what counts based on traits and features and instead just presume that all entities qualify? One way to do this is to ask Bryant's question about human entitlement rather than fixate on who or what is under or outside of legal protection.[43] Recall that Bryant argues against capacity-based metrics for ethical and legal worth. The "goal of [her] approach is to stop categorizing animals by reference to whether they are worthy of protection and to encourage reduction in human entitlements to act in oppressive ways. Since the world as a whole is necessary, breaking the world into discrete elements that will or will not be protected misses the point of interrelationship."[44] Bryant's category-eschewing proposal is attractive in that it seeks to avoid sameness logic, but it perhaps has its limits. Even she runs afoul of Gunkel and feminist new materialists' caution not to privilege life forms over "mere" matter.

But even if a new legal subjectivity directed at detoxifying law's anthropocentrism were to be inclusive of all matter living or not, it is not clear that privileging living matter or sentient matter should be ethically discredited as subscribing to liberal humanism. Although feminist legal scholar Ani Satz adopts the "presumption against exploitation"[45] for all living beings that Bryant advocates (as do I), Satz queries the practical and lasting implications of a framework that does not inquire into capacities at all. Satz instead recommends a capabilities approach.[46] Indeed, it would seem that simply *adverting* to capacities and assessing legal outcomes based on capacities does not contradict the normative dictates of embodiment, vulnerability, and relationality that beingness as a subjectivity is meant to convey. *Ranking* capacities, however, and ordering entities in such a hierarchy would, so beingness does not suggest that any particular capacity in animals is more valuable or ethically pertinent than another. It merely recognizes that responding to the suffering of Others may yield diverse and divergent needs. If faced with a choice between protecting one vulnerable, embodied, suffering being at the expense of another, how are we to proceed if not based on capacities (or qualities, features, and characteristics)? Under such an approach, it is possible and desirable to respond to vulnerability occasioned by different capacities such as sentience, consciousness, or self-awareness without saying that some beings are more important than others because of their proximity to or distance from paradigmatic humans or privileging cognitive complexity.

After all, the purpose of adverting to these capacities is to apprehend, and after strenuous efforts to adopt, Other-centered views as best as we can through our inescapably human-centred lens so as to continually revisit our perceptions of what matters,[47] that is, the experience of embodied and relational vulnerability a particular entity is having or enduring because of those capacities. An entity that is conscious is likely to be much more troubled by its confinement. One that is also self-aware is much more likely to psychologically apprehend its deprivation in such a situation, desire to exit its captivity, and suffer when it cannot do so. One that is also sentient is made more vulnerable to the risk of physical injury the confinement poses. Beingness as a new legal subjectivity would permit legal decision-makers to advert to capacities among animals in such a way as to be more comprehensively attuned to the vulnerability at stake while maintaining a protective stance for all legal beings be they sentient or self-conscious (to be clear: "self-aware" humans or animals would not be privileged over humans or animals that were not "self-aware").

An approach that pays heed to animals' varying capacities would not completely contradict directives that, to avoid liberal humanist claims, we shift our focus from capacity and the corresponding question of who can suffer when considering who or what counts. Even those who counsel us to abandon all categories and inquiries into capacities deploy categories and capacities. Feminist new materialists encourage us to act ethically toward all matter, but they still have to identify "matter."[48] Other feminists who are most concerned with how we treat animals and who counsel against capacity-based arguments also invariably resort to capacities. Kelly Oliver, for example, after noting the humanizing impulse of capacity-based theories in animal rights campaigns, directs

us to this question: "How do we respond to the suffering of others?";
which she states "is a question of response and relationship rather than
a question of capacity or identity."[49] But Oliver is not so much objecting
to advertence to capacities in ethical assessments – after all, it is difficult
to see how "bodily vulnerability," which is Oliver's preferred focus for
animal advocacy, is not also a capacity.[50] Instead she is redirecting law
from its fixation on who has the capacities that we admire and reward
in humans toward an orientation that highlights our responsibility to
respond to suffering. Beingness does precisely that.

2. BACK TO SENTIENCE: IS IT ALWAYS ALREADY
ANTHROPOCENTRIC TO PRIVILEGE IT?

I indicated earlier that beingness considers capacities beyond sentience. At the same time, it likely privileges sentience in many
instances because of sentience's correlation with vulnerability and
suffering. Is a theory directed at "responding to suffering" understood as arising from a sentient capacity always already anthropocentric because it privileges a type of experience (physical or
psychological pain) that, while not exclusive to humans, is so easily
modelled after them? Does this presumption in favour of sentient
legal beings render beingness an anthropocentric model because
sentient beings resemble humans much more than entities such as
bacteria do? Myra Hird, drawing from posthumanist new feminist
materialism, intimates that this would be the case. In the course of
explaining why bacteria merit moral consideration, she charges animal rights scholars with anthropocentrism for ignoring bacterias'
needs and generally being preoccupied with the concerns of large
sentient mammals that – not coincidentally, according to Hird – are
most like humans.[51] In Hird's view, in morally respecting bacteria
we would be disrupting the animal rights norm regarding ethical vegetarianism and veganism; for her, the fact that bacteria will
invariably die despite their moral considerability should make animal advocates more comfortable with the ethical consumption of
other non-human animals.[52]

Zipporah Weisberg has called Hird's argument in this regard "ethically obscene" and "pornographic."[53] She valuably elaborates:

> Certainly, it is important to recognize that the earth is made up of diverse
> organisms of various sizes, and that there is more life and vitality around
> us than mechanistic science has acknowledged. Part of the interspecies
> emancipatory project is re-enchanting and re-animating the earth and its
> inhabitants. But Hird takes the vitalist or materialist perspective to the

point of flattening ethics beyond recognition. Ethics is purged of meaning if we start calling for rights for bacteria, and in the meantime abandon systematic efforts to boycott the torture of animals for human use and consumption. It is unacceptable from an ethical point of view to derail C[ritical] A[nimal] S[tudies] and animal liberation's current focus on the creatures ensnared in the animal industrial complex (and those ravaged by human hubris in the form of habitat destruction, environmental devastation, and so on) in order to account for the existence and ethical claims of bacteria.[54]

Weisburg does not dismiss legal consideration for bacteria. Rather, she assails posthumanist arguments that diminish the extent of animal exploitation and disparage critical animal scholarly/activist efforts to end such violence. She accepts that reworked concepts of non-human subjectivity and ethical considerability can strive to be more inclusive. She is simply and rightly concerned that such efforts not abandon distinctions in such a way that the intense levels of suffering and violence experienced by many sentient animals in various commercial sites of captivity and killing would be defaced. I agree that it is not anthropocentric to stay focused on or prioritize the ending of such intense suffering among those that qualify for ethical consideration. To reconceptualize (certain) non-humans as legal beings rather than property is to activate legal attention to their embodied vulnerability and relational needs. What these needs are will depend on the capacities that different living entities have. Sentience produces many opportunities for embodied and relational vulnerability. Adverting to the sentient needs of legal beings will create a presumption in favour of sentient beings over non-sentient ones whenever the interests of both types of beings cannot be accommodated together or equally.

Lori Gruen further suggests that privileging the needs of those animals with whom we can empathize with over, say, bacteria, trees, or plants, which we may care about but not empathize with, is a legitimate position to adopt.[55] One need not agree with Gruen's emphasis on empathy as our primary ethical navigator in order to acknowledge that it is possible to have "loving regard for and commitment to other-than-sentient nature"[56] even while prioritizing the physical, psychological, and affective needs of sentient beings.

3. WHAT ABOUT PLANTS (AND RIVERS, LAKES, AND OCEANS)?

To recap what I have argued thus far, legal beingness, because of its commitment to abating the vulnerability occasioned by violations to and intrusions on physical and psychological embodiment and interference with / severance of desired relationships, is amenable to including within its purview all living beings that are embodied and relational. At the same time, it would privilege sentient beings over those entities that are not sentient and thus not so vulnerable. Legal beingness is thus conceptually able to embrace plants whether or not one perceives plants as sentient, although it would generally privilege sentient animals' needs as more urgent, given their heightened vulnerability in a situation of conflict.[57] The important question remains: Should beingness apply to plants notwithstanding their conceptual suitability?

The work of critical plant studies scholars helps craft a preliminary answer. Such scholars have argued in favour of "vegetal life," "plant-thinking," "vegetal intelligence," and plants' "non-conscious intentionality" and offer other provocative yet compelling reasons besides to adopt a respect for plants that is currently absent in academic circles and beyond. For those of us seeking to supplant anthropocentrism in ethics and particularly in law, their philosophical excursions into the capacities and ontologies of plants provide ample cause for deep and sustained reflection.[58] While I cannot unearth the richness of arguments here as to why humans concerned about Othering and alterity should, as philosopher Matthew Marder terms it, adopt a praxis of "plant-thinking," I would like to give a sample of the reception Marder's provocative work in particular has evoked among leading animal law theorists.

It is recognized that anthropocentrism hurts both plants and animals, yet not all animal advocates agree that a shared position of subordination should lead to ethical or legal regard for plants. Marder has debated his pro-plant perspective with Gary Francione, who has insisted that "if plants are not sentient – if they have no subjective awareness – then they have no interests. That is, they cannot desire, or want, or prefer anything." Francione cites the lack of conscious intentionality in plants as their distinguishing factor, noting that the obligations we have to plants are indirect and are really only obligations to other sentient beings to share planetary "resources."[59] In reply, Marder notes that Francione's denial of plant awareness is misguided, contending that "plants are aware of their environment in a nonconscious way."[60] He invites animal advocates to consider the "residual violence against other living beings" rather than adopting a human-authored perspective as to what awareness or sentience looks and feels like that entrenches plants' presumed thinghood status.[61] He insists that such status reflects a speciesist valuation. Francione has countered this argument by stating that speciesism as a problematic only arises when we disregard interests based on species, and since plants do not have minds they do not have interests. He believes that Marder's claims mistake mere biological responses with actual intentional ones. He is similarly unmoved by Marder's reply that plants act intentionally when they respond in ways that benefit them and keep them alive (move toward sunlight, emit biochemical signals to neighbouring plants about insect or other dangers, etc.). Marder believes that such intentionality is real and obligates us to consider plants' "vegetal good" in how we treat them; he also mandates "paying attention to both the methods of their cultivation and their reproductive possibilities" when we consume them. Francione characterizes these supposedly intentional responses as mere "react[ions] to stimuli."[62]

Whether or not plants act intentionally and thus may have interests, Marder rightfully notes that they are "thoroughly instrumentalized by the same logic that underpins human domination over other animal species."[63] Moreover, one need not fully agree with either perspective to recognize that in terms of beingness's animating features of embodiment, vulnerability, and relationality, it is a legal model that should extend to all living beings. And in terms of being responsive to alterity and difference and undoing the premium of human rationality, not to mention the power of plants to reverse the planetary crisis that anthropogenic activities have caused, extending beingness to plants seems an obvious move. At the same time, we need to be mindful that beingness is meant to *replace* property, not coexist with it. In the eyes of the law, an entity cannot be property and a being simultaneously. So in order to extend beingness more broadly beyond animals to all living things like plants (or even bacteria), such things would have to cease to be property. In other words, if plants are beings in law, they must not be commercially traded or bought or sold.

Does this mean that humans and other animals, if already vegan, can only ever be fruitarians? No, but they must consume plants in a "respectful" way. Marder calls for a drastically different approach to our consumption of plants than we have today, one that establishes "a complete and concerted decommodification of vegetal life, a refusal to regulate the human relation to plants on the basis of commodity-economic logic."[64] He is opposed to the "capitalist agro-scientific complex" and its complete and devastating approach to harvesting plants that does not respect plants' own cycles of time or their abundant life-giving capacities.[65] He would permit human (and presumably animal) consumption of plants in the form of "fruit, roots, and leaves,"[66] though he is careful to add the proviso that "plant-thinking does not condemn the consumption of plants and their parts, unless in utilizing them we dim down and disrespect the other facets of ontophytology."[67] Thus it seems that plants can be deployed for animal (human and other purposes) as long as they exit out of for-profit market circuits.

But herein lies a sticking point for beingness to properly apply to plants. I agree with Marder when he insists that we need to decommodify vegetal life and move toward a world in which plants are not commodities, yet his present position allows humans to kill plants or otherwise instrumentalize them if this is done "respectfully." Given that beingness is meant to be a legal status that affords protection equivalent to what personhood would afford an entity against instrumentalization and exploitation by humans or corporations, it is not suited for an entity that would still need to be classified as property. Of course, we can understand why Marder settles on the position he does, given the vast challenges of sustaining animal life (human or animal) without consuming plants. Nevertheless, beingness is incompatible with "respectful" killing/slaughter/harvesting/consumption. For this reason, in answering the "the plant question," we can conclude that beingness should not apply to plants or other non-humans that would need to be consumed by humans and animals for these groups to sustain their lives.

By the same reasoning, other animate life forms can be cast as legal beings insofar as they are living yet also not amenable to being bought and sold or subject to instrumental use that depletes them. Bodies of water (liquid or frozen) such as oceans, glaciers, rivers, lakes, and streams, which are classified as common property in Western legal systems and thus not owned by anyone at present in these anthropocentric jurisdictions, could thus qualify as eligible for beingness. As several international jurisdictions have recognized in granting personhood to rivers and glaciers within their borders for anthropocentric but also intrinsic reasons, such bodies of water are "animate" in the sense that they are full of life and life-supporting even if they are not alive according to Western biological understandings.[68] Bodies of water fit into the beingness model because they are embodied (consider the term "body of water"), vulnerable (consider the harm anthropogenic plastics are producing),[69] and relational (consider all forms of animal and other life that bodies of water sustain). Indeed, it is possible to think of water itself as an ideal model for subjectivity.[70] Yet, like plants, some bodies of water (such as freshwater lakes and rivers) need to be consumed by humans and other animals for hydration. Certainly, such bodies of water deserve legal status as something other than property in order to be protected from (further) anthropogenic harm, but it does not appear that beingness is suitable because of the instrumental use of these bodies of water by humans and other animals. However, beingness could be suitable for those bodies of water that are not required in order to sustain humans and other-than-human animals not living in the water. Saltwater bodies such as oceans would be excellent candidates for beingness if we did not interfere with them (this would help protect oceans from plastic abuse and fuel pollution from ships and other vessels as well as protect sea creatures from anthropogenic harms from aquaculture or otherwise).

4. DOES MATTER MATTER?

We are now in a position to answer Gunkel's claim that biocentric theories marginalize non-living matter: beingness should not apply to matter (understood as non-living things). While a transgressive approach to legal subjectivity would not exalt reasoning abilities or higher-level consciousness, it would be legitimate for a new anti-anthropocentric subjectivity directed at being responsive to suffering and vulnerability to be more attentive to entities that are born and living (understood as generally breathing, but also feeding, sleeping, reproducing such as mammals, reptiles, birds, insects, plants) than to those entities that are not living (robots, other machines, buildings, artwork, other matter). Why? Because living bodies are more vulnerable to violence, to intense pain and suffering, and to death.[71] Entities such as robots and other forms of artificial intelligence, even when we ascribe them an agency and vitality as "vibrant matter,"[72] can be interfered with without inducing physical or psychological pain or prompting attempts to avoid the interference. Moreover, machines may be disassembled and reassembled and, in this way, continue to "live" forever. It is not clear that when humans do destroy or abandon or neglect robots or other machines that the latter are harmed in equal measure by this refashioning.

Gunkel and others thus may assail beingness as a legal model for being biocentric and thus perpetuating a problematic animate versus inanimate distinction as well as Cartesian and binary thinking at some level. Yet we need to recall that although beingness, if implemented in law, would denote a legal subjectivity that includes all animals, even insects, it does not stipulate that other entities do not merit legal protection. Ascribing beingness to animals today also does not mean one has to oppose some form of legal subjectivity for robots or other forms of artificial intelligence, or for other machines and inanimate entities that may arise in the future. Beingness is meant to be a legal concept that is accepting of alterity; it accepts the claim regarding robots, as well as their agentic and life-giving or life-supporting qualities, albeit without prioritizing their needs.

D. Summary

The exchange between Gary Francione and Michael Marder as to whether plants have interests that humans are obligated to respect illuminates the critique as to why animal ethicists and legal models that exclude plants from their purview or otherwise draw lines might be problematic.[73] Francione's abolitionism includes all sentient beings as moral subjects and thus, of course, is not benchmarked to the purportedly paradigmatic human actor. Marder's plant-based ethics go even further in distancing themselves from human benchmarks. Both thus retain a critical purchase that even a robust reworking of personhood does not. Yet both models still suggest that we establish who is worthy of legal subjectivity because of possession of a trait or capacity. As such, even Marder's "radical" view about plants succumbs to the pressure of a centrism that Gunkel criticizes as a form of epistemic violence against difference.

Clearly, any theory that draws a line based on a shared capacity is unresponsive to some forms of alterity. Yet it is difficult to know how to proceed in law without categories of some sort. I have proposed legal beingness as a new legal subjectivity that would be afforded to all animals to acknowledge the vulnerabilities that arise from animals as embodied and relational beings in a propertied system, with the goal of reducing their exploitation to such vulnerabilities by changing their legal status to something much more protective. I have argued that we can understand all living (i.e., breathing and/or moving) entities to be vulnerable in this sense and craft an ethical relationship to them. I have also argued that beingness should not presently extend to plants (or land or bacteria), given that the latter would need to be commercially sold and traded in a post-property world for animals. As we move to fully plant-based rather than animal-based societies within a larger capitalist system, humans and other animals will need plants and bacteria to live. Certain bodies of water would also be used by humans and other animals to live; for this reason, beingness is not a suitable fit for these entities either. In contrast, I have argued that beingness should be extended to animals that are "living" and intensely vulnerable to injury and have also suggested that applying beingness to saltwater bodies of water such as oceans that humans do not need to instrumentalize for drinking and household water would also make sense.

This restriction of beingness to animals and perhaps saltwater bodies does not mean that plants, freshwater bodies of water, or other living non-humans should be denied legal subjecthood and continue to exist as property. A different category specifically catering to plants or rivers, for example, should be devised that permits them to be consumed for human or animal use but rejects their representation as mere natural resources available for any type of human or animal instrumentalization. We can also learn to think of matter as "agential and lively" and as deserving of a much higher cultural regard than many things currently command to shape and mediate our legal relationship with them. Although legal beingness would thus favour animals over most other living beings, the model does not seek to discursively establish living entities as superior to non-living ones or to degrade the latter in any way.

What the capacities of legal beings are should make a difference as to how the law responds to their needs. The variations in capacities among legal beings should be a critical consideration when legal decision-makers are tasked with resolving legal disputes and setting policy choices where the needs and interests of different legal beings in avoiding suffering or exploitation diverge or conflict. The model is thus permissive and reliant on assigning certain types of valuations (but not rankings) that have the potential to privilege the needs of conscious and sentient animals over those of other types of legal beings, whether an animal or a body of water.[74] Such privileging is legitimate. The model aims to reduce exploitation and suffering for embodied and relational beings whose embodiment and relationality exposes them to heightened fear and suffering from exploitation because of their sentience or consciousness. Despite its general orientation to value the needs and interests of conscious and sentient beings over other entities, legal beingness is qualitatively different from legal liberalism's *anthropos* and is not simply, in the end, another form of liberal humanism.

II. Some Further Objections

A. Beingness for Humans

Some may query why the application of beingness only centres on animals and other non-humans. Aren't the critiques I have lodged against personhood equally applicable to *all* marginalized human subjects and, for that matter, the non-marginalized? Indeed, I would quickly allow that beingness could be a category for humans and posit for all the aforementioned reasons that it would be more responsive to vulnerability than personhood.

B. Beingness as Second-Best

A further issue surfaces when we consider the possibility that beingness will circulate in law as a second-best subjectivity. Here an analogy to the debate over same-sex marriage may help illuminate the issue.

One question in this debate is whether to legalize same-sex marriage as opposed to an equivalent but different category such as civil union partnerships. Proponents of same-sex marriage worry that any option other than marriage will always be perceived as second-best and operate in that way. This is because marriage exerts such dominance and normative sway in the culture and in law that jurists, administrative decision-makers, and others will be inclined to see civil unions as not equivalent to it. Extrapolating from this, some may worry that decision-makers will always perceive personhood as superior to beingness.[75]

This is a very legitimate concern and very likely to materialize given the anthropocentric moorings of Western law and Western cultures. An important point here, though, is that beingness is not meant to be a second-best category on the spectrum of subjectivities. As well, it is a category that does not derive from compromise. The civil union alternative to marriage, for many, operates to preserve the sanctity of marriage as a heterosexual project while formally recognizing and according benefits to same-sex long-term relationships. The impetus for the category is to preserve a critical component of heterosexual and heteronormative privilege and status.[76] In contrast, the impetus for beingness is not to appease those who are resistant to extending personhood to non-humans but to find a legal subjectivity for animals that is properly responsive to their needs. Doubtless, it remains possible and indeed probable that beingness will reside in personhood's shadow for a very long time. This likely secondary status, however, is not a sufficient reason on its own to champion personhood and nothing else for animals; after all, even as legal persons animals may be seen to command a lower personhood status than humans.[77]

C. Beingness Will Open a Pandora's Box

With beingness following conventional biological taxonomy to include insects as "animals," every legal jurisdiction would now contain untold billions of legal beings. Legal decision-makers would need to sort through what their needs and capacities are and determine some to be more important, so that the specific nature of the legal dispute involved did not inject an impossibly confounding process into legal decision-making. Generalizations could be made where need be when legal disputes involved groups and collectivities rather than individuals. Remember that conflicts abound today between human and corporate persons and that the prevailing personhood paradigm already sorts and ranks the various interests of formally equal legal persons. Prioritizing among legal beings will very likely be more difficult and complex owing to the strong interdependence of ecosystems and earthly relations. This increased complexity, however, is not a sufficiently compelling reason to reject beingness. Such complexity is a reality of multispecies societies and one that the law, in the age of the Anthropocene and the species and planetary devastation it entails, can no longer deny.

III. Conclusion

In this chapter I have responded to two anticipated criticisms of beingness as a new legal subjectivity for animals. These criticisms cluster around the question of whether beingness falls short of the mark as a critically informed, non-anthropocentric alternative to animals' current property status. They raise the possibility instead that beingness is not as distant from traditional legal subjectivity as I have claimed because beingness still contains significant anthropocentric and liberal undercurrents. A major criticism suggests that when pressed to identify precisely which animals come under its purview, beingness will invariably succumb to its own version of hierarchical line-drawing and speciesism. This criticism appreciates beingness's attempt to resituate difference in terms of how we think about who counts in law but expects that beingness, in the end, will be pushed to value only sentient animals, as most animal law reform theories have. In reply to this criticism, I defended beingness as a biocentric-oriented model that could conceivably accord legal subjectivity to all forms of breathing life and should extend to bodies of water. It excluded plants for the time being for practical reasons arising from a capitalist system.

It was conceded that beingness's residual biocentrism excludes inanimate matter and rests on its own tenuous divide regarding the separability of life from the world of machines and other non-living objects. It thus, arguably, commits its own level of difference erasure and perpetuates an in-group, out-group binary logic of Cartesian thinking. Beingness, however, does not malign the difference of non-living entities, nor does it participate in a discourse about the inferiority of these other worldly realms. Thus it may be an exclusionary framework but not an alterity-denying one. Moreover, it was argued that it is legitimate to prioritize the vulnerability of living and conscious life forms over non-living ones, given the sensory physical embodiment of living beings and their corresponding greater scope for injury and death. It is not clear that a critical approach to law should disregard these capacities of beings that compel our response to their Otherness when we consider new forms of legal subjectivity and conflict resolution among legal beings.

Furthermore, for the task at hand of trying to make that first dent in the property paradigm for non-humans in anthropocentric legal systems, it is legitimate to draw a line at animals, which are vulnerable to intense levels of pain and suffering, and to death, and which seek to avoid such states, and at some bodies of water, which are vulnerable to irreversible injury. Beingness is thus more defensible than the present way in which law draws a line. In assigning legal subjectivity that rejects the property paradigm for animals, beingness is a position far removed from liberalism's starting point of the white, rational, propertied male or even its current resting point of the human or corporate subject. Although a biocentric-oriented, heavily animal-centred legal subjectivity, beingness does not rely on the logic that the excluded entities (such as matter, which does not display embodied vulnerability or intentionality, or plants or bodies of water, which humans and other animals need to consume) are inferior, matter less, or can be consumed/exploited without end.

Conclusion

Nietzsche had it wrong; we are not human, all too human, we are animal, all too animal. It is only by avowing our animality that we can also avow our precariousness. To do this shifts everything. It changes the questions we ask about who gets to be bearers of rights, who are subjects of ethics, who are moral patients. All of these political and ethical questions never stray from mourning, from determining which lives get to count as life.[1]

James Stanescu, "Species Trouble: Judith Butler,
Mourning, and the Precarious Lives of Animals"

I live across a large pasture where about fifteen cows graze year round. In autumn they each give birth to one calf and for about nine months the joy of living is apparent in those calves. Kicking their hind legs up in play, butting heads and chasing each other along the pond, these animals are really no different from young dogs in displaying their joy. Their idyllic life however ends ten months later when the rancher arrives with truck and trailer to collect the calves (and any "spent" cows). The ordeal is dramatic for all members of the herd. The mothers are forcibly pushed away from their calves with the rancher's swaying hands and aggressive shouts. These docile giants, afraid and confused, do all they can to stay together. Distress and fear eventually manifest themselves as desperate cries, but the cows will inevitably lose this battle just like last year and the year before that. After the calves are herded into the trailer and driven away to an auction facility where they will be sold and transferred to either the dairy or beef industry, the mothers are left to bellow for days to come. A haunting echo fills the night sky and it affects me profoundly. In an exercise of moral imagination, I try to picture myself as if I was in the place of her body and try to imagine how she feels. I try to empathize with her grief and profound loss. Genuine care, with its call for empathic understanding, requires we transcend our own frame of reference to consider the point of view of the animal before us.[2]

Nancy M. Williams, "The Ethics of Care and Humane Meat:
Why Care Is Not Ambiguous about 'Humane' Meat"

To say that humans and corporations are at war with animals, as Dinesh Wadiwel does, is not to engage in hyperbole.[3] By almost any metric or angle we adopt (annual numbers of land and sea animals killed in farming, the rate of species extinction/genocide, the profits and processes of the trade in exotic animals, or simply hearing stories about individual animals),[4] the escalating levels of violence to which animals are subject is undeniably obscene.[5] Law facilitates this violence through the category of property, giving legal sanction and enforcement to a broader toxic culture that exalts human exceptionalism, normalizes anthropocentrism, marginalizes humans who do not conform to its paradigmatic person/human, brutalizes animals *en masse*, and instrumentalizes and devastates other non-human beings.[6] To alter this state of affairs, multilayered and wide-ranging interventions from all corners of society will be required. This is especially the case if we follow Lynn Worsham in her suggestion that human violence against other humans and, critically, against animals may be read as a symptom of posttraumatic stress built up in our epigenetic make-up from generations of past trauma. Worsham contends our ancestors' "prey" identity in the Pleistocene, and in more recent and ongoing human experiences with colonialism, sexism, disability, homophobia, and the like, has created in us a deep-seated fear of our own vulnerability, embodiment, and animality, which we manage through intrahuman violence and by subjugating animals.[7]

Given the long-standing psychosocial causes that may well be at the root of current levels of violence toward animals, the law's role in effecting social change may be comparatively modest. Yet law still has a role to play in symbolically affirming that animals' lives should matter and in materially altering property relations so that animals are no longer the object of property rights of the legal persons who own them or who could take ownership of them with the right legal claim. The sea change in legal relations fostered by a beingness model would be a promising element of the sorts of institutional reorientations required to end the brutalities that animals presently endure.

In this concluding chapter, I outline the difference a beingness model would make in the lives of animals by charting the first steps in its legal implementation. After reviewing the chief advantages of beingness as a legal subjectivity for animals over personhood through engagement with notable media coverage in Canada of animal deaths, I examine the ways in which beingness could begin to be implemented in the current Canadian liberal legal order. I discuss the effects of beingness on animal use industries. I then review how the other supportive features required for a post-anthropocentric legal outlook to emerge (ethic of care, empathy, embodied compassion, accountability, and responsibility toward animals) could enter legal decision-making thereafter. At the close of this chapter, I contemplate the residual and pressing concern about the risk of epistemic violence when humans represent animal interests to make decisions about animals' lives. This discussion engages with postcolonial teachings about representation to consider how animals' agency might be preserved under decision-making that is still executed by humans.

I. Beingness as a Corrective to Personhood's Affinity for Enlightenment Humanism

Judith Butler's oft-invoked query in critical circles regarding "What makes for a grievable life"? encourages critical acknowledgment of the social marginalization that occurs when dominant social mores are not responsive to the mourning we may feel for particular lost lives.[8] The extensive scholarly take-up of this aspect of Butler's work has largely retained an anthropocentric focus in asking after grievability in different contexts.[9] As James Stanescu notes, Butler's own commitment to rejecting anthropocentrism is ambivalent.[10] Regardless, the politics of mourning, which encompass Butler's concept of precarity and precarious life, are amenable to highlighting the disavowal of animality upon which dominant social orders rest and the need to remedy this orientation.[11]

The question of who is and is not mourned, especially through highly visible collective acts, points us toward the problems with personhood as a remedy for animals' present juridical abjection. As an example, consider the widespread national media coverage of a barn fire that broke out early in January 2016 at Classy Lanes Stable, a riding stable in southwestern Ontario, in the course of which forty-three racing thoroughbreds perished. Stories discussed the economic toll on the horse trainers whose livelihoods the fire had destroyed.[12] But a good number focused on the death of the forty-three horses and the human grief and other emotions that ensued.[13] Media outlets did not relegate this coverage to the back pages; indeed, the story featured in national headlines and on front pages. A memorial spread providing individual column space to pay tribute to each horse appeared on the front page of the Sports section of the Saturday edition of the *Globe and Mail*, a leading national newspaper, with the Latin equivalent of "rest in peace" as its caption.[14]

To understand how this coverage of the horses' deaths touches on the question of the appropriate legal subjectivity for animals, I draw attention to two letters to the editor that ran in the *Globe and Mail* on the same day commenting on this coverage. In the first letter, G.L. Delamer of Toronto wrote: "These horses died in terror in a barn where there was no sprinkler system. No tears shed for them will make any difference.

How about some robust legislation from the Ontario government, so this kind of scenario cannot be played out again?"

In this letter, Delamer laments the lack of fire safety standards for horse shelters. The author is clear that positive cultural responses to the horses, here in the form of human grief at their death, is insufficient absent the force of the law to guard against a recurrence. If we translate this letter into the conceptual parameters of the present text, Delamer's position aligns with the critique that although culture has an impact on how animals are treated, the law's categorization of property reduces even the most culturally favoured among them to a high level of vulnerability and precarity. We can read the letter as animal advocacy that, at a minimum, asks for better welfarist protection of horse shelters and, at a maximum (given the author's use of the term "robust legislation"), provides support for law reform that contests the horses' status as property. This latter goal, of course, has animated the present work.

The second letter, written by Vicki Fecteau, director of the CFA, states: "In the past year, there have been 49 barn fires in Canada where animals perished. In nine, the number killed is unknown. In 40 of the fires, a total of 142,469 animals died, including the 42 horses Monday night. These include cows, chickens, pigs, ducks, sheep and goats. Less than a week ago, 50,000 ducks were killed in a barn fire in Quebec. Why is it that these other barn fires rarely make the news, let alone the front page? Surely the other animals suffered as much as the horses did." The factual information Fecteau provides calls into sharp relief the "human hierarchies of being"[15] that differentiate not only among humans but among animals as well. The present work has taken seriously the impact on animals of animalization and feminization and how such cultural processes complicate and intensify the vulnerability and precariousness to which animals, as property, are exposed. The analysis has also shown why supplanting property status with personhood is a non-ideal outcome owing to personhood's exclusions of those animals that do not resemble a certain rational type of human. The liberal legalist and humanist apparatus that would grant personhood to certain animals based on their similarity to law's paradigmatic person, though revolutionary from one perspective given the current abysmal legal landscape for animals, does not in the end disrupt the exclusionary imprint of this apparatus and its insistence that beings express a certain level of rational capacity in order to matter ethically and legally.[16] In arguing for this position, this book joins the critical literature that has impugned traditional animal ethics and rights approaches for their liberal humanist premises that take Reason and the thinking and disembodied subject as ethical benchmarks.[17]

In contrast, I have argued that the cultivation of beingness as a different legal subjectivity for more-than-human animals allows us to focus on the vulnerability and precarity of all living beings without forcing animals to conform to exclusionary visions of ideal humans in order to emerge as legal subjects. Instead, both humans and animals qualify as ethical and legal subjects because of their embodiment (a trait long associated with animality and thus devalued in liberal humanism), relationality, and corresponding vulnerability. By avowing animality, beingness presses past and through liberal premises promoting human exceptionalism as well as capacity-based assessments that require certain features beyond being alive to assign moral worth. Because it expresses a non-anthropocentric departure point, beingness destabilizes inter and intra "human hierarchies of being,"[18] which rely on entwined "bestializing social logics"[19] and the power relations that animate them. Under the beingness model, animals acquire visibility in law, not because they are human-like, but because they are embodied living beings entangled in relationships of power and vulnerable to harm. Animalized and feminized animal lives matter in this matrix, not just humanized ones.

II. Implementing Beingness – First Steps

How can a beingness model supplemented by a cultural ethos that prioritizes caring and empathic responsiveness to vulnerable Others enter the legal sphere to shape the responses of legal decision-makers and those who advise them? Below I offer some preliminary suggestions as to how, at a concrete and practical level, the interspecies ethical insights I have identified as productive to shift law's ontological core toward a post-human terrain could work in practice (assuming, of course, the political will to implement beingness among legislators in a given jurisdiction). What types of practices would beingness outlaw vis-à-vis animals? And what criteria could human decision-makers follow to ensure that decisions about animals avoid anthropocentric valuations, shield animals from exploitation, reflect a decision-making process that recognizes animals' agency, and protect positive features of their lives?

A. Step 1: Codification of Prohibitions and New Legislative Principles

A new interspecies ethics grounded in feminist animal care theory and call and response ethics should generate three mutually reinforcing guiding legislative purposes and statutory interpretive directions that can then inform any public policy formulation regarding a particular social problem, eventual drafting of legislation to respond to that problem, and subsequent interpretation of that legislation. These three guiding principles are (1) a prohibition on human or corporate trade in animals or animal products, (2) a rejection of anthropocentrism and human exceptionalism, and (3) a desire to listen to and respond to the needs of vulnerable Others. This new multispecies triad of principles could be reconciled with or integrated into the current liberal legal order if need be and coexist with other classic liberal values such as freedom, equality, and dignity. The three new guiding principles would recast the anthropocentric meaning of classic liberal values to guard against valuations that exalt human or other forms of exceptionalism or otherwise reinscribe stratifying Enlightenment taxonomies that privilege human perspectives and normalize animal commodification. This triad of principles would not require expression through a constitutional amendment. Rather, laws could be enacted in all legislatures constitutionally authorized to legislate over matters of public morality, national commerce, and/or property rights that affirm the first two principles as overarching purposes for all legislation in their jurisdiction.

For example, in Canada, it is the provinces and territories (and, taking an anti-colonial perspective, all First Nations) that have jurisdiction to legislate regarding property and civil rights within their borders.[20] Provincial and territorial governments could then – relying on this authority, which arguably applies since animals are currently property – enact laws that affirm each of the three principles above. At the federal level, where the government has authority to legislate about public morality and criminal law as well as trade that crosses provincial and territorial boundaries,[21] the federal government could amend Canada's *Criminal Code* to include a provision making the trade in animals or animal products illegal. Such declaratory laws at both levels would expressly state that (1) they are to be referentially incorporated into all existing laws, and (2) laws that permit animal trade within their jurisdiction are of no force and effect. All of the principles could then be legislatively codified within general Interpretation Acts typically applicable to all legislation as well as within specific legislation in preambles or purpose sections for added emphasis; these explicit expressions of the principles would help guide judges as to legislative intent when it comes to interpretive disputes that arise in litigation regarding the scope of any of the legislative provisions.[22] As these new laws would take the form of legislative provisions that would be drafted as clearly as possible according to the principles of statutory interpretation, the legislative intent behind them would trump the common law status quo that animals are property. Administrative agencies and other bodies charged with applying these laws to their respective regulatory areas, and judges called on to interpret these laws when disputes proceed through legislation, would be obligated to follow them so as to honour legislative intent.

B. Step 2: Designing Models for Animal-Friendly Decision-Making

Of course, ample subordinate legislation (regulations, by-laws, Orders in Council) would also be required to work out the details of how industries and their human employees would have to transition into the new era in which animals are beings rather than property. Furthermore, while the first principle of the above triad prohibits certain practices, the other two principles require new legal action to ensure that anthropocentric or human exceptionalist values do not factor into decision-making and that decisions affecting animals take their needs into account and reflect consultation with animals. Policy analysts and lawmakers would therefore have to integrate animals as decision-making partners as well as integrate new animal-friendly perspectives into their decision-making to consider how issues involving animals going forward should be handled (I briefly explore one situation below as an example).

Two current decision-making models offer some guidance as to how animal-friendly decision-making (i.e., which abides by principles nos. 2 and 3 above) could work. The first is environmental impact assessment legislation. Legislatures could mandate that municipalities and administrative bodies subject all policy proposals and major regulatory decisions taken in the public interest to a "multispecies impact assessment." Legislators could also use multispecies impact assessments to gauge the likely effects of proposed laws before they are enacted to ensure their conformity with the three principles above.[23] The impact assessment model in the environmental arena is not without its flaws. Critics have pointed out that those models often fall short of the ideal and that those who follow them often struggle with the complexities of synergistic ecological impacts, low and scientifically ill-defined standards, insufficient time, funding, and expertise, and low-quality privately conducted assessments.[24] Certainly, crafting an effective multispecies impact assessment model that could avoid these problems would be important.

A second model that could be considered to generate decision-making attentive to the needs of animals is "supported decision-making." This model, presently germane to medical decision-making, advance care planning, and end-of-life care conversations in children and the law, elder law, and disability law circles, seeks to institute supportive decision-making for humans who cannot be paradigmatically autonomous in how they make decisions owing to youth, impaired cognitive functioning, or an inability to communicate their decisions to others. The model is meant to replace or at least supplement the dominant "substitute decision-making model," which relies on substitute decision-makers having knowledge of the now incapable person's wishes (not likely applicable when we are trying to figure out animals' preferences regarding their needs) or otherwise taking decisions according to their "best interests." The "substitute decision-making" model presumes a lack of capacity and agency to decide such that a substitute decision-maker must make the decision based on the "best interests" standard or previously known wishes of an adult when that person was fully capable. This model has been criticized as too paternalistic both for children of a certain age and for adults whose reasoning capacities do not approximate the paradigmatic standard of law's rational person.

As a corrective at least for adults with diminished capacity, the supported decision-making model is presented as more respectful of the agency and autonomy of the person whose wishes now need to be discerned or imagined.[25] Under the supported decision-making model, it is assumed that individuals can still participate in decision-making even if they do not possess paradigmatic capacity to make decisions and give consent under current legal standards of "capacity" and "informed consent," that is, on their own and with an ability to absorb and deliberate on information relevant to their decision and appreciate the consequences.[26] It is the standard promoted in the UN Convention of the Rights of Persons with Disabilities but is not yet mainstreamed in most liberal legal orders, where the substitute-decision making model continues to prevail.

Human decision-makers, however, could adapt the "supported decision-making" model to animals when they are trying to ensure that principle no. 3, in particular, is followed. Human decision-makers could envision animal needs by first trying to determine animals' own views about what their needs are and how they can best be satisfied, viewing animals as part of the "meaning-making or interpreting" that needs to be done.[27] At some point this exploration of what animals' views are may yield little information; decision-makers would then have to resort to a best interests model. Still, by first attempting supported decision-making, Canadian law affirms the possibility and conceptualization of animals as having worldviews and acting upon their worlds as agents.

*C. Step 3: Listening to Animals to Partner with Them
to Discern Their Needs*

No matter which model a given jurisdiction adopts, some may wonder how human decision-makers operating under a beingness legal model and thus committed to principle no. 3 (see page 168) can be sure their compassionate and empathic deliberations properly represent the perspectives of the animals themselves. Put another way, some may ask whether the outcome that feminist animal care theory or call and response ethics theorizes for animals is really what animals want for themselves. After all, how can we *know* what animals want, given the ostensibly profound communication barriers? Even if we believe in the possibility of affect attunement across species and rich communication with preverbal/non-verbal beings,[28] how can we be sure that our efforts at being responsive, at estimating animals' needs and desires, do not tend toward imperial postures of knowing what is good for Others and usurping their voices?[29] As postcolonial animal scholars have noted, no direct access to non-human voices is possible – unlike other subalterns, they cannot speak in the Spivakian sense, but are always interpreted and "given" voice through human modalities.[30]

The assumption that humans must give voice to animals raises its own imperial concerns. As Lauren Corman identifies, part of the traditional postcolonial concern in speaking for Others, stimulated by the inter-human context of Western subjects speaking for non-Western Others, is the passive object/victim status that such speaking often entails, along with misrepresentations of non-Western cultures and individuals' lives.[31] This concern seems to only intensify when the concern over speaking for Others is transposed onto the human-animal context. How can humans deeply committed to avoiding the oppression, marginalization, and exploitation of animals surmount the language barrier between humans and animals as well as the limitations that species privilege places on our ability to comprehend animals' experiences, to interpret carefully, non-imperiously, and responsively across species differences so as not to elide animals' perspectives/voices/agency?[32]

Because of the high risk of epistemic and imperial violence in silencing animals, the answer is certainly not to disengage with efforts at interspecies communication. That would risk inadvertently bolstering anthropocentric objections to including animals in governance decisions because they cannot speak our language.[33] Instead, animal law advocates must accept the paradox of attempting to free animals from human and corporate violence while also accepting the epistemological compromise of representing their interests.[34] One promising emergent model for apprehending animals' perspectives is found in the reflections of Lisa Jean Moore and Mary Kosut, who describe their efforts to turn a critical animal studies lens on urban beekeeping in New York City.[35] In their multispecies ethnography, Moore and Kosut propose an ethics of "intra-species mindfulness" for humans seeking to communicate with and learn from animals.[36] In describing this emergent idea,[37] they state that "intra-species mindfulness is a practice of speculation about non-human species that strives to resist anthropomorphic reflections. It is an attempt at getting at, and with, another species in order to move outside of our human selves – while also recognizing that both 'human' and 'other' are cultural constructions."[38] Moore and Kosut go on to describe how they marshalled the full range of their human senses to learn more about bees – "their bodies, their habitats, and their products. Getting with the bee meant acquiring new modes of embodied attention and awareness."[39] Moore and Kosut are keenly aware that what they can apprehend in this process "is filtered, diluted by humanness,"[40] and that despite their best efforts and intentions their research relationship with the bees was indelibly shaped by "inexorable domination,"[41] given human species privilege and epistemological authority in shaping, interpreting, and communicating the research.[42]

Despite this necessary incompleteness of human epistemological claims regarding the more-than-human world, Moore and Kosut's reflections instil hope that we as humans can empathize with animals, as well as listen attentively through all our senses, to try to understand animals' needs rather than assuming what they are. Legal decision-makers can also learn this embodied skill. Even judges, who are more constrained than legislative or even administrative decision-makers by the rules of evidence, can adopt Moore and Kosut's embodied approach. Of course, just as with human preverbal communicators, some needs are so transparent that we can safely assume they exist without much concern about properly apprehending animals' perspectives. We do not, for example, need to second-guess our perhaps almost immediate empathic conclusions that the separation of a female mammal from her newborn is deeply distressing and even torturous and is clearly something no typical female mammal or newborn would want. Judges' own intuitions are sufficient here, and if need be, these can be buttressed by affidavit evidence or expert testimony confirming suffering that attaches to mother–child separation in mammals. Judges should be able to take judicial notice about animal suffering as they would human suffering.[43]

Other perspective-taking may require considerably more time for us to fully understand what animals need to ensure that our human standpoint (intersectional as it, of course, is, but still almost certainly privileged by species membership and shaped by human cultural norms) does not distort or deform the perspective. As Lori Gruen has suggested in her discussion of what entangled empathy entails, we need to inform ourselves about animals' needs as well as the overall context of the situation to know how best to respond.[44] Again, uncertainty as to whether our deliberations, however non-oppressive our intentions, may in the end misrepresent animals' perspectives does not mean we should abstain from our very best non-anthropocentric efforts in trying to understand what animals wish to tell us. Decision-makers proposing legislation to regulate aspects of animals' lives have leeway for this deep perspective-taking and can benefit from the perspectives and advice of animal-friendly stakeholders. Administrative and judicial decision-makers will be more constrained in terms of time and procedural convention, but they too can incorporate the mindfulness Moore and Kosut call for into their decision-making. That listening to animals in the course of reaching decisions that will affect their lives is heretofore unheard of in the law, and that the means for doing so are equally uncharted territory, are insufficient reasons to continue with the profoundly anthropocentric approach the law currently takes to regulating and governing animals. Especially so, when we consider that the assumption that animals do not have language and exist largely as silent beings is a projection the law has placed on them to construct animals as inhuman and deny them legal subjectivity.[45]

D. An Example: Caring for Land-Based Farmed Animal Survivors

Welcoming beingness as a new legal subjectivity for animals and promoting the need for law's anthropocentric foundations to change in order to foster post-anthropocentric and overall non-exploitative values would contribute significantly to a more animal-friendly legal order. It would also help foster a legal system that guards against corrosive epistemological positions toward more-than-humans (and devalued humans). It would also recognize the enduring vulnerability of animals and other more-than-humans that arises from their long-standing legal propertied status. A change in legal subjectivity would not magically erase the culturally precarious status most animals bear. Yet the immediate implication of beingness in terms of property relations would be vast. All current animal use industries would become illegal, and the human or corporate killing of animals as well as other types of appropriation for human or corporate ends would also become illegal.[46]

That beingness would require the cessation of all animal use industries is clear. Less straightforward is how we would care for the animals that remain, including how we would manage conflict among different types of beings (such as "wild" animals) and ensure proper care for animals that remain dependent on humans. Since industries that traffic in animal bodies and body parts will be banned, any current legal disputes contesting these industry practices will become moot. Yet questions will arise regarding how humans should manage their relations with those animals that have survived the dismantling of the animal-industrial complex or that previously existed as "companion" animals and "wild" animals sharing their habitats with humans. Call and response concepts of response-ability and feminist care tradition's emphasis on compassion and empathy can help decision-makers identify how to structure relations with animals in such contexts that are not anthropocentric, that do not involve other forms of domination or exploitation, and that are responsive to the needs of all vulnerable Others. Precisely how to instil the values of non-domination, responsiveness to vulnerable Others, and rejection of anthropocentrism through revising current human-animal relations will be different for each context. And very specific considerations will need to be kept in mind regarding whether and how humans should intervene in the lives of animals that normally do not have any human contact but that suffer from predation by other animals as well as anthropogenic climate effects (consider the early 2020 Australian wildfires, in the course of which more than 3 billion animals – not counting "bats ... frogs, insects or other invertebrates" may have perished or been displaced).[47] The debate over human intervention in wild animals' lives is already a contentious one in animal ethics.[48]

The regulation that flows from a beingness model of human relationships with farmed animal, research lab, and zoo survivors, as well as companion animals and wild animals residing in or migrating through urban areas, will likely meet with more approval from animal advocates, for regulation will come into place or intensify to ensure a higher standard of care for such animals as legal beings. The details of animal care the law developed would need to draw from interdisciplinary expertise to consider what is sustainable in a specific space, for the planet and for the individual animal beings involved. It is beyond the scope of this book to set out this detailed planning. But to provide at least some sense of what beingness would mean for animals beyond precluding them from being commodified, I outline below the broad contours of legal relations for the largest group of land animals that will be affected by the change: farmed animal survivors.

We know from the preceding discussion that converting animals into beings in law would make it illegal to use them or their body parts for profit or trade. Animal use industries of all kinds would need to be phased out, with the animals living through the transition appropriately cared for and placed with sanctuaries or safe private homes.[49] Governments would have to support the care of these animals as well as help people who worked in animal use industries transition to what Kendra Coulter calls "humane labour."[50] In this section, I think through some of the implications of beingness for the farmed animals that have survived the agricultural complex once the law has granted them legal beingness. What should happen to animals that were born into animal agriculture as property but then released from it as beings?

Most obviously, because they would no longer be property, it would be illegal for intensive farming operations to keep them within their operations. It is very likely that corporations and farmers would be eager to have someone take these animals off their hands, given that they could no longer profit from their bodies and offspring. Beingness, at its base, and like personhood, could thus serve as a shield against instrumental treatment and violence. Yet it would also demand that humans respond compassionately to animals' ongoing embodied and relational needs. So legislation abiding by principles nos. 2 and 3 (see page 168) would need to be enacted to support these animals' transition from farm to home or sanctuary. It would have to detail how these animals are to be transferred, sheltered, fed, and otherwise enabled to live well.

What core apparatus would this legislation put in place? Clearly, these animals would need new places to reside and simply be. Governments and administrative agencies would have to establish publicly run farmed animal sanctuaries, and support the creation of private ones, and thereafter ensure that they operated according to the triad of principles listed above.[51] To the extent possible, sanctuaries would be located in urban environments as well as semi-rural or rural ones; this would help create multispecies communities as opposed to separate living zones for animals and people. The creation of sanctuaries will require considerable land. There must be meaningful consultation with Indigenous peoples on whose traditional territories the sanctuaries will be located. Consultation should also occur with "wild" animals, who also have an originary claim to those territories and who might be displaced by the proposed sanctuaries (the multispecies impact assessments proffered above could be deployed here). For previously farmed animals that people wish to "adopt" and bring onto their own private property, a further administrative body should be established to ensure that the human(s) seeking to take them in are suitable caregivers and companions. In all instances of deciding where the farmed animal survivors should live, how they should be housed, what food they will receive, what medical attention they need, and what opportunities they receive to enrich their experiences and lead their lives as free from human control as possible, decision-makers would be guided by primary and subordinate legislation as well as by internal guidelines and other administrative instruments that promote the purposes of principles nos. 2 and 3. They would approach the animals over whose lives they are serving as partners, advisers, and consultants when arriving at their decisions.

The amount of public resources and new space required would be considerable, given that approximately 181,600,000 farmed animals are alive at any given moment in Canada.[52] We can assume that roughly the same number of farmed animal survivors would survive and require care and rehabilitation for the rest of their lives. Taking our cue from governments that have pursued cost recovery from tobacco and opioid companies for the devastating health care costs the public purse has absorbed, money for the care of the survivors could come from the now-defunct industry through similar litigation or, better yet, corporate taxation of their plant-based operations. Large corporations have profited immensely from farming through farmland investment funds, vertical integration, and agricultural input financing, and it is not clear that bankruptcy would flow from government prohibition.[53] In 1970, there were an estimated 122,000 dairy farms in Canada; by 2000, there were only about 19,000.[54] As of 2018, there are about 10,500 farms, yet production has increased.[55] In 2013, XL Foods, Canada's largest beef processing company, was sold to the US subsidiary of a Brazilian multinational corporation, JBS SA, the world's largest meat processor.[56] In 2017, JBS SA saw net revenues of US $51.5 billion, and its US subsidiary received millions in the 2019 US "farmer bailout."[57]

A trickier issue than determining how to procure funds to support all the survivor farmed animals for the rest of their lives is whether these original farmed animal survivors should reproduce. While cows, goats, and sheep tend to have one offspring at a time, pigs and chickens can have many more offspring per year. To be sure, because of their experiences and specific breeding, not all of the female animals as farmed animal survivors will be able to reproduce or wish to do so. For example, dairy cows will likely be too weak, given what they have already endured through forced pregnancies and lactation. But the youngest animals that emerge from the agricultural food system may wish to have a family, especially given that all species, including humans, have reproductive impulses. Would a beingness model permit survivor reproduction for those animals that were inclined to mate?

In the first instance, given what principle no. 3 asserts, administrative decision-makers who regulate the care of farmed animal survivors should acknowledge that some animals will have a strong embodied need to mate and a strong relational need to start a family, whereas some animals may not. Being unable to reproduce will be experienced as a loss for at least some of the more self-aware animals, for they will grasp that they do not have offspring and perceive a loss of nurturance and kinship. For others, not being able to have sex may simply be frustrating. Moreover, the means to achieve reproductive control of animals, even contraception, are not at all benign.[58]

Yet, some relational theorists have theorized that it would be permissible for humans to regulate animals' reproduction to ensure community sustainability. In their influential account, Donaldson and Kymlicka have suggested precisely this, indicating that animals should at least be able to reproduce once but then perhaps no further in order to ensure that animal populations remain at numbers conducive to human capacities to take care of them and so as not to impose burdens on other animals.[59] Aaron Simmons suggests something similar in considering the very issue I have broached here: how to care for animals that survive the farmed animal system once it is abolished.[60] He emphasizes that, while there is no perfect solution, careful reproductive control could be conducted to prevent the misery of future offspring born in circumstances of uncontrolled reproductive autonomy.[61] Other scholars have endorsed the view that it might be defensible for humans to interfere in animals' reproductive lives where it is probable that too many offspring would result in overburdened and unsustainable multispecies communities.[62] A compromise in this case, then, would be for animals to be able to reproduce at least once to start a family and experience raising a child/children if they wish.[63] Contraception would be used thereafter.

This is still an imperfect solution, but given the drawbacks of prolonged contraceptive use, it may well be justified – that is, it may be ethical for humans to assume a measure of control over animals' reproductive lives after they have been released from agricultural systems. Moreover, the adverse greenhouse gas effects of very large animal populations would seem to support this approach. To avoid imposing more onerous reproductive surveillance on animals than we do on humans, the principles should apply to humans as well by way of educational interventions (more controlling interventions are not defensible, given humans' generally larger capacity to self-regulate their reproduction and tendency to have much fewer offspring than many other animals).[64] To avoid revivifying neocolonial narratives blaming global ills on "over-population" in the global South, such interventions for humans should start with education efforts in the global North informing people of the high planetary costs of Western consumerist lifestyles.[65] With animal populations kept at sustainable levels to optimize care, previously farmed animals and their (one-time) offspring could enjoy a high quality of life in sanctuary settings.

III. In the Meantime, Bearing Witness

The legal classification as property is a death sentence for billions of animals trapped in the world's animal agriculture and aquaculture industries and the confines of the animal industrial complex in general and for trillions of fish and other sea creatures trawled from the depths of the oceans. As this book has shown, the legal treatment of animals is very much a part of the wider cultural apparatus that permits most animals to undergo extreme levels of physical, emotional, and psychological pain, suffering, and trauma without public outcry, lamentation, or even notice. Instead, this extreme violence is widely downplayed and defended. Property as a legal status for animals is indefensible by any measure of social justice and environmental sustainability.[66] The need for law to remove animals from this abject status and assign a new legal subjectivity that does not reproduce the toxic rationalities and ontologies of Enlightenment humanism could not be more urgent. This is so whether we advert to the linkages between the confinement of animals for human consumption and zoonotic pandemics,[67] species extinction and climate change,[68] global food insecurity and hunger,[69] or the array of both harms to animals and harms to humans that degrading animality entails. The law and the human decision-makers it authorizes need to listen as best as they can to animals and include them as partners in decision-making over their lives and with respect to the overall question of how we can travel together in multispecies communities. As Donovan observes, this type of listening means "paying emotional attention, taking seriously – caring about – what they are telling us."[70] When combined with a multisensory embodied engagement of the type that Moore and Kosut envision, law through its human decision-makers can start to bear witness to the routine violence and trauma animals experience as part of instituting a new legal subjectivity and inaugurating a new era of post-anthropocentric, multispecies legalism and interspecies justice.[71]

There is so much more to be said, but I would like to end with the words of Kathryn Gillespie outlining the trajectory of the life of Sadie, a cow instrumentalized for her milk who finally found, if not freedom from human control, then at least sanctuary and human compassion. Gillespie met Sadie as part of her multispecies ethnographic fieldwork studying the dairy industry (and its spin-off industries) in the US Pacific Northwest and the lives of animals brutalized within it:[72]

> I met Sadie (a cow formerly used for dairy) at Animal Place in 2012. She had come to the sanctuary after being used first for milk-production on a large-scale dairy farm and then by a university agricultural science program as a teaching tool. By the time she reached the sanctuary, she had experienced the loss of multiple calves (taken as part of routine dairy-industry practice), she had been injured as a result of her use in the teaching program, and she was fearful and distrustful of humans. She was also pregnant. When she gave birth at the sanctuary, the calf was stillborn. For the first time, Sadie was allowed to spend time grooming and caring for her calf, although he was dead. She was given space and time to grieve. And the sanctuary caretakers grieved with her. When she had finished her ritual of tending her dead calf, they buried him at the sanctuary. Following this experience, Sadie became an adoptive mother to orphaned newborn calves who came to the sanctuary. She transformed her grief and loss into a practice of care and love. Shortly after I met Sadie, she died at Animal Place. The sanctuary community, along with tens of thousands of supporters around the world, mourned her loss.[73]

The material events of Sadie's life are briefly summarized, but their trajectory captures the profound impact that a legal sea change that moving animals from a property model to a beingness one would have for *all* brutalized feminized farmed animals like Sadie.[74] This book has sought to lay the ontological and subjectivity foundations of why and how law should one day compel and normalize the sanctuary that Sadie found by rare good fortune for all animals. Under a beingness model, animals are not relegated to the status of passive object and natural resource for legal persons to exploit. They are not held captive in intense confinement where they are subjected to complete and unimaginably painful reproductive and bodily control for human or corporate ends. Their lives will not be cut short by repeated bodily violations and immense misery and grief from the taking of their children and the appropriation and commodification of their milk. They are not prevented from engaging in activities they find meaningful and that pose no harm to themselves or others. And when animals do die, whether stillborn in their mother's womb or after a good, long life that would otherwise be theirs without human interference, they are mourned, loved, and remembered.

Notes

Introduction

1 Karen Joy Fowler, *We Are All Completely Beside Ourselves* (New York: Penguin, 2013), 302.
2 Health Canada, "Canada's Food Guide," 16 July 2019. perma.cc/6NS2 -QCYE
3 Walter Willett et al., "Food in the Anthropocene: The EAT-*Lancet* Commission on Healthy Diets from Sustainable Food Systems," *The Lancet* 393 (2019): 447.
4 *An Act to amend the Criminal Code and other Acts (ending the captivity of whales and dolphins)*, SC 2019, c. 11.
5 Jodi Lazare, "'Free Willy' law spotlights contradictions in how Canadians see animal rights," *The Conversation*, 8 July 2019. https://theconversation .com.
6 Kelly Crowe, "How many people does it take to write a guide for healthy eating? More than 26,000 and counting," *CBC News*, 9 January 2019.
7 Markus Lundström, "'We Do This Because the Market Demands It': Alternative Meat Production and the Speciesist Logic," *Agriculture and Human Values* 36.1 (2018).
8 See the websites "Fishcount," http://fishcount.org.uk and "Animal Clock," https://animalclock.org. See also the Livestock, Environment and Development Initiative, "Livestock's Long Shadow: Environmental Issues and Options" (Rome: Food and Agriculture Organization of the United Nations, 2006), iii; and Boris Worm et al., "Impacts of Biodiversity Loss on Ocean Ecosystem Services," *Science* 314.5800 (2006).
9 Paola Cavalieri, *The Animal Question: Why Non-Human Animals Deserve Human Rights* (New York: Oxford University Press, 2001), 43, 45–7; Raymond Corbey, *The Metaphysics of Apes: Negotiating the Animal-Human Boundary* (New York: Cambridge University Press, 2005), 121–2, 160–1.

10 Cavalieri, *The Animal Question*, 41–3; Corbey, *The Metaphysics of Apes*, 33–5, 121–2.
11 Cavalieri, *The Animal Question*, 78; Corbey, *The Metaphysics of Apes*, 160–3.
12 Ibid.
13 For two recent best-selling books in North American markets touting creativity as distinctly human, see Agustin Fuentes, *The Creative Spark* (Boston: E.P. Dutton, 2017); and Anthony Brandt and David Eagleman, *The Runaway Species* (New York: Catapult, 2017).
14 Maneesha Deckha, "Initiating a Non-Anthropocentric Jurisprudence: The Rule of Law and Animal Vulnerability under a Property Paradigm," *Alberta Law Review* 50.4 (2013); Irus Braverman, "Law's Underdog: A Call for More-than-Human Legalities," *Annual Review of Law and Social Science* 14 (2018): 140.
15 Marie Fox, "Rethinking Kinship: Law's Construction of the Animal Body," *Current Legal Problems* 57.1 (2004): 469; Steven M. Wise, "Legal Personhood and the Nonhuman Rights Project," *Animal Law* 17.1 (2010): 1.
16 Maneesha Deckha, "Critical Animal Studies and Animal Law," *Animal Law* 18.2 (2011–12): 208; Maneesha Deckha, "Teaching Posthumanist Ethics in Law School: The Race, Culture, and Gender Dimensions of Student Resistance," *Animal Law* 16 (2009–10): 288–9.
17 Harriet Ritvo, "On the Animal Turn," *Daedalus* 136.4 (2007). This area of study has recently been described as an "exploding" academic field in terms of the number of courses, college concentrations/programs, conferences, listservs, publications, and academic presses offering series dedicated to animal titles, and so on, that have arisen in the last decade. However, this descriptor applies to an array of academic disciplines. It is a field that arose in philosophy, developed in the social sciences, and then spread to the humanities and even natural sciences; see Shapiro and DeMello, "The State of Human-Animal Studies," *Animals and Society* 18.3 (2010): 307–10.
18 Carol J. Adams and Josephine Donovan, eds., *Animals and Women: Feminist Theoretical Explorations* (Durham: Duke University Press, 1995); idem, "Introduction," in *The Feminist Care Tradition in Animal Ethics* (New York: Columbia University Press, 2007); Greta C. Gaard, "Vegetarian Ecofeminism: A Review Essay," *Frontiers* 22.3 (2002); Marti Kheel, *Nature Ethics: An Ecofeminist Perspective* (Lanham: Rowman and Littlefield, 2008); Brian Luke, *Brutal: Manhood and the Exploitation of Animals* (Champaign: University of Illinois Press, 2007); Val Plumwood, "Androcentrism and Anthrocentrism: Parallels and Politics," *Ethics and Environment* 1.2 (1996).
19 Kay Anderson, *Race and the Crisis of Humanism* (London: Routledge, 2007); Irus Braverman, "Captive: Zoometric Operations in Gaza," *Public*

Culture 29 (2017); Karen Cardozo and Banu Subramaniam, "Assembling Asian/American Nature Cultures: Orientalism and Invited Invasions," *Journal of Asian American Studies* 16.1 (2013); Mel Y. Chen, *Animacies: Biopolitics, Racial Mattering, and Queer Affect* (Durham: Duke University Press, 2012); Stefan Dolgert, "Species of Disability: Response to Arneil," *Political Theory* 38.6 (2010); Colleen Glenney Boggs, *Animalia Americana: Animal Representations and Biopolitical Subjectivity* (New York: Columbia University Press, 2013); Megan H. Glick, *Infrahumanisms: Science, Culture, and the Making of Modern Non/personhood* (Durham: Duke University Press, 2018); Myra Hird, "Animal Transsex," *Australian Feminist Studies* 21.49 (2006); Stephanie Jenkins et al., *Disability and Animality: Crip Perspectives in Critical Animal Studies* (London: Routledge, 2020); Claire Jean Kim, "Multiculturalism Goes Imperial: Immigrants, Animals, and the Suppression of Moral Dialogue," *Du Bois Review* 4.1 (2007); idem, *Dangerous Crossings: Race, Species, and Nature in a Multicultural Age* (Cambridge: Cambridge University Press, 2015); Ruth Lipschitz, "Skin/ned Politics: Species Discourse and the Limits of 'The Human' in Nandiqha Mutambo's Art," *Hypatia* 27.3 (2012); Michael Lundblad, *The Birth of a Jungle: Animality in Progressive-Era US Literature and Culture* (New York: Oxford University Press, 2013); Kelly Oliver, *Animal Lessons: How They Teach Us to Be Human* (New York: Columbia University Press, 2009); Kelly Struthers Montford and Chloë Taylor, eds., *Colonialism and Animality: Anti-Colonial Perspectives in Critical Animal Studies* (London: Routledge, 2020); Sunaura Taylor, *Beasts of Burden: Animal and Disability Liberation* (New York: New Press, 2017); Dinesh Wadiwel, "The Sovereign Whip: Flogging, Biopolitics, and the Frictional Community," *Journal of Australian Studies* 27.76 (2003); Jennier Wolch and Jody Emel, eds., *Animal Geographies: Places, Politics, and Identity in the Nature–Culture Borderlands* (London: Verso, 1998). My own work here includes: "Toward A Postcolonial Posthumanist Feminist Theory: Centralizing Race and Culture in Feminist Work on Nonhuman Animals." *Hypatia* 27.3 (2012); "Intersectionality and Posthumanist Vision of Equality," *Wisconsin Journal of Law, Gender and Society* 23.2 (2008); "(Not) Reproducing the Cultural, Racial, and Embodied Other: A Feminist Response to Canada's Partial Ban on Sex Selection," *UCLA Women's Law Journal* 16 (2007); "The Subhuman as a Cultural Agent of Violence," *Journal of Critical Animal Studies* 8.3 (2010).

20 Nick Haslam and Steve Loughnan, "Dehumanization and Infrahumanization," *Annual Review of Psychology* 65 (2014); Mario Sainz et al., "Animalizing the Disadvantaged, Mechanizing the Wealthy: The Convergence of Socio-Economic Status and Attribution of Humanity," *International Journal of Psychology* 54.4 (2019); Mario Sainz et al., "Less

Human, More to Blame: Animalizing Poor People Increases Blame and Decreases Support for Wealth Redistribution," *Group Processes and Intergroup Relations* 23.4 (2020).

21 Braverman, "Law's Underdog," 140. As Braverman notes: "A survey of the two central American law and society journals … reveals that of 525 articles, 278 book reviews, and 131 review essays published in the decade between 2008 and 2018, only 3 … were dedicated to questions concerning nonhuman animals."

22 Deckha, "Critical Animal Studies." Exceptions include idem, "Humanizing the Nonhuman: A Legitimate Way for Animals to Escape Juridical Property Status?" In *Critical Animal Studies: Towards a Trans-Species Social Justice*, ed. John Sorenson and Atsuko Matsuoka (London: Rowman and Littlefield, 2018), 209;); Irus Braverman, ed., *Animals, Biopolitics, Law: Lively Legalities* (New York: Routledge, 2016); idem, *Wild life: The Institution of Nature* (Redwood City: Stanford University Press, 2015); Irus Braverman and Elizabeth R. Johnson, eds., *Blue Legalities: The Life and Laws of the Sea* (Durham: Duke University Press, 2020); Mathilde Cohen, "Animal Colonialism: The Case of Milk," *American Journal of Internatinal Law Unbound* 111 (2017): 267–71; Samera Esmeir, *Juridical Humanity: A Colonial History* (Redwood City, Stanford University Press, 2012); Ed Mussawir and Yoriko Otomo, "Law's Animal," in *Law and the Question of the Animal: A Critical Jurisprudence*, ed. Yoriko Otomo and Ed Mussawir (Abingdon: Routledge, 2013); Kalpana Rahita Seshadri, *HumAnimal: Race, Law, Language* (Minneapolis: University of Minnesota Press, 2012); Krithika Srinivasan, "Posthumanist Animal Studies and Zoopolitical Law," in *Critical Animal Studies: Towards Trans-species Social Justice*, ed. Atsuko Matsuoka and John Sorenson (London: Rowman and Littlefield, 2018), 234; Dinesh Wadiwel, "The War against Animals: Domination, Law and Sovereignty," *Griffith Law Review* 18.2 (2009); idem, *The War against Animals* (Leiden: Brill Publishers, 2015).

23 I have written about this divergence in views, also known as the "property debate," previously, where I have advanced the argument that a critical anti-oppressive approach for animals must favour the abolitionist side given the choice between these two options. See Deckha, "Critical Animal Studies." I present a condensed overview of this position in chapter 3.

24 See *Black's Law Dictionary*, https://www.thelawdictionary.org "person," "natural person," "artificial person," "juridical person," "body corporate."

25 Ibid.

26 For their influential writings see Gary L. Francione, *Animals, Property, and the Law* (Philadelphia: Temple University Press, 1995), idem, *Rain*

without Thunder: The Ideology of the Animal Rights Movement (Philadelphia: Temple University Press, 1996); Steven M. Wise, *Rattling the Cage: Toward Legal Rights for Animals* (Cambridge, Perseus Books, 2000); idem, *Drawing the Line: Science and the Case for Animal Rights* (Cambridge: Perseus Books, 2002). The "welfarist/abolition" debate overlaps considerably but is also different from the "welfare/rights" debate since not all rights theorists advocate abolitionism for all sentient animals as Francione and Wise do. Tom Regan's work is seen as originating and exemplifying an animal rights approach, but for an animal to be worthy of rights under Regan's approach, they must have a level of consciousness that meets his "subject of a mind test." Regan has also argued that humans should be privileged over animals in any zero sum conflict situation of harm given their higher-order consciousness. Francione vociferously contests this privileging as "welfarist" and as antithetical to the assignment of rights to animals. For a concise discussion of this divergence see Braverman, "Law's Underdog," 130.

27 Joshua St Pierre, "Cripping Communication: Speech, Disability, and Exclusion in Liberal Humanist and Posthumanist Discourse," *Communication Theory* 25.3 (2015): 331–2.

28 Matthew Calarco, "Reorienting Strategies for Animal Justice," in *Philosophy and the Politics of Animal Liberation,* ed. Paola Cavalieri (New York: Palgrave Macmillan, 2016), 54.

29 Matthew Calarco, "Identity, Difference, Indistinction," *The New Centennial Review* 11.2 (2012): 48; Braverman, "Law's Underdog," 140; idem, *Animals, Biopolitics, Law,* 3.

30 Will Kymlicka, "Connecting Domination Contracts," *Ethnic and Racial Studies* 41.3 (2017): 536–7; Glick, *Infrahumanisms,* 19.

31 Taimie L. Bryant, "Similarity or Difference as a Basis for Justice: Must Animals Be Like Humans to Be Legally Protected from Humans?," *Law and Contemporary Problems* 70.1 (2007); Sankoff, "Five Years of the 'New' Animal Welfare Regime: Lessons Learned from New Zealand's Decision to Modernize its Animal Welfare Legislation," *Animal Law* 11 (2005) (both have written about law schools).

32 The explosion of animal law courses in American law schools has not been matched elsewhere. For a discussion of the growth of animal law in the United States, see Deckha, "Critical Animal Studies."

33 Cass R. Sunstein and Martha C. Nussbaum, eds., *Animal Rights: Current Debates and New Directions* (Oxford: Oxford University Press, 2004). This collection was the only law text recently identified as a leading reader in a review of the burgeoning Human-Animal Studies literature. See Shapiro and De Mello, *The State of Human-Animal Studies,* 309. The authors in that volume largely assume a liberal foundation and do

not consider the relevance of other difference-based movements and corresponding contested social constructions within their analyses. Notable exceptions to animal law literature in this vein include Robert Garner, "Political Ideologies and the Moral Status of Animals," *Journal of Political Ideologies* 8.2 (2003), as well as the authors mentioned in nn35–6 below. See Martha Nussbaum, *Frontiers of Justice: Disability, Nationality, Species Membership* (Cambridge, MA: Harvard University Press, 2006). Martha Nussbaum's influential work on capabilities, which she has extended to animals, has criticized the dominant Rawlsian version of liberalism as a framework for helping animals, but not liberalism itself.

34 For a summary of this literature see Sue Donaldson and Will Kymlicka, *Zoopolis: A Political Theory of Animal Rights* (New York: Oxford University Press, 2011), 26.

35 Richard A. Shweder, "Shouting at the Hebrews: Imperial Liberalism v. Liberal Pluralism and the Practice of Male Circumcision," *Law, Culture and Humanities* 5.2 (2009): 247.

36 Duncan Ivison, *Postcolonial Liberalism* (Cambridge: Cambridge University Press, 2002), 16–19.

37 Liberalism, of course, is not a homogenous normative tradition. It is defensible, however, to identify some core traits important to most liberal thinkers, namely, granting equal consideration morally and legally to all persons as well as offering persons freedom of choice about most life decisions. Martha Nussbaum, "Robin West: Jurisprudence and Gender: Defending Radical Liberalism," *University of Chicago Law Review* 75.3 (2008): 994.

38 Shiraz Dossa, "Liberal Legalism: Law, Culture and Identity," *The European Legacy* 4.3 (1999): 73.

39 Ibid.

40 Ivison, *Postcolonial Liberalism*, 47–8.

41 Robin West, "Jurisprduence and Gender," *University of Chicago Law Review* 55 (1988).

42 Mark Brown, "'An Unqualified Human Good'? On Rule of Law, Globalization, and Imperialism," *Law and Social Inquiry* 43.4 (2018); Dylan Lino, "The Rule of Law and the Rule of Empire: A.V. Dicey in Imperial Context," *Modern Law Review* 81.5 (2018).

43 Jessica Eisen, "Feminist Jurisprudence for Farmed Animals," *Canadian Journal of Comparative and Constitutional Law* 5 (2019).

44 Srinivasan, "Posthumanist Animal Studies," 235.

45 Eve Darian-Smith, *Religion, Race, Rights: Landmarks in the History of Modern Anglo-American Law* (Oxford: Hart Publishing, 2010).

46 Ibid.

47 Judith Butler, *Precarious Life: The Powers of Mourning and Violence* (New York: Verso, 2006), 60–1; Margaret Denike, "The Human Rights of Others: Sovereignty, Legitimacy, and 'Just Causes' for the 'War on Terror,'" *Hypatia* 23.2 (2008): 98; Sherene Razack, *Casting Out: The Eviction of Muslims from Western Law and Politics* (Toronto: University of Toronto Press, 2008), ch. 1.
48 Ratna Kapur, "Dark Times for Liberal Intellectual Thought," *Profession* 1 (2006): 26.
49 Ibid.
50 Martha Albertson Fineman, "The Vulnerable Subject: Anchoring Equality in the Human Condition," *Yale Journal of Law and Feminism* 20.1 (2008); Dossa, "Liberal Legalism," 75.
51 Calarco, "Reorienting Strategies," 54.
52 Ibid., 54–8.
53 See *The Nonhuman Rights Project on behalf of Happy v James J Breheny & Wildlife Conservation Society*, 2019 0045164 NYSC; or visit the website, Nonhuman Rights Project, "Client, Happy" (2019), https://www.nonhumanrights.org/client-happy.
54 Joan Dunayer, "Sexist Words, Speciesist Roots," in *Animals and Women: Feminist Theoretical Explorations*, ed. Carol J. Adams and Josephine Donovan (Durham: Duke University Press, 1995), 11; Susan Kappeler, "Speciesism, Racism, Nationalism ... or the Power of Scientific Subjectivity," in *Animals and Women*, ed. Adams and Donovan, 320. As an example, consider the opening statement by Steven Wise in an article outlining the Nonhuman Rights Project, which he directs, that seeks to establish legal personhood for animals: "The defining moment for the eighteenth century slave James Somerset was when he became legally visible." Wise, "Legal Personhood," 1.
55 Ibid.
56 Maneesha Deckha, "Vulnerability, Equality, and Animals," *Canadian Journal of Women and Law* 27.1 (2015): 55; Deckha, "Intersectionality," 250–9.
57 Claire Jean Kim and Megan Glick's recent monograph projects illuminate these linkages at depth and across various contexts. Please also see arguments from my body of work: "Welfarist *and* Imperial: The Contributions of Anti-Cruelty Legislation to Civilizational Discourse," *American Quarterly* 65.3 (2013); "Postcolonial Posthumanist"; "The Subhuman"; "Intersectionality"; "The Salience of Species Difference for Feminist Legal Theory," *Hastings Women's Law Journal* 17.1 (2006); "Is Multiculturalism *Good* for Animals?" in *Multiculturalism, Race and Animals – Contemporary Moral and Political Debates*, ed. Luis Cordeiro Rodrigues and Les Mitchell (London: Palgrave, 2017), 61.

58 Of course, some liberal theorists also object to sameness logic for its anthropocentrism. See Will Kymlicka, "Social Membership: Animal Law beyond the Property/Personhood Impasse," *Dalhousie Law Journal* 40.1 (2017).

59 Wise, "Legal Personhood."

60 Deckha, "Humanizing the Nonhuman"; Jessica Eisen, "Liberating Animal Law: Breaking Free from Human-Use Typologies," *Animal Law* 17 (2010).

61 Gary L. Francione, *Animals as Persons: Essays on the Abolition of Animal Exploitation* (New York: Columbia University Press, 2009). Francione emphasizes sentience as his basis for moral valuation and has declined to align with certain campaigns that privilege certain animal species that more resemble humans in terms of intelligence and consciousness even where such campaigns are undertaken strategically to appeal to human lawmakers. Chapter 4 discusses whether sentience is still too anthropocentric a basis on which to rest our moral valuations.

62 I take this assemblage of critical theoretical concepts from Glick, *Infrahumans*, 10. This argument is accessible from many contexts such as analyses of global migration predicaments, carceral state institutions, women's reproductive rights, or even the liminal status of human children.

63 As Kelly Oliver has uncovered in her work on twentieth-century theories such as those of alterity and Otherness, many of them are harshly critical of liberalism's human subject and its values of rationality and individualism yet still fail to question human exceptionalism or the species hierarchy it sustains. Even theories committed to valuing embodied Otherness and relationality have fallen short in decentring the human subject and, quite ironically, use embodiment, affectivity, and relationality to shore up human subjectivity and its purported specialness. Oliver, *Animal Lessons*, 4.

64 Anne Schillmoller, "Gaining Ground: Towards a Discourse of Posthuman Animality: A Geophysical Journey," *Southern Cross University Law Review* 14 (2011): 55.

65 Bryant, "Similarity or Difference as a Basis for Justice"; Deckha, "Vulnerability, Equality, and Animals"; Deckha, "Initiating a Non-Anthropocentric Jurisprudence."

66 Schillmoller, "Gaining Ground," 54, 72.

67 Srinivasan, "Posthumanist Animal Studies," 235.

68 Vivienne Jabri, *The Postcolonial Subject: Claiming Politics/Governing Others in Late Modernity* (Oxford: Routledge, 2013), 3.

69 Irus Braverman, *Zooland: The Institution of Captivity* (Stanford Press, 2012); idem, *Animals, Biopolitics, Law*; David Delaney, *Law and Nature* (Cambridge: Cambridge University Press, 2003); Yoriko Otomo and Ed

Mussawir, eds., *Law and the Questions of the Animal: A Critical Jurisprudence* (Abingdon: Routledge, 2013); Dinesh Wadiwel, *The War against Animals* (Netherlands: Koninklijke Brill, 2015). None of the critical texts above centrally explore this question of law reform. Delaney appears to align himself with a critical animal studies perspective in regularly referring to the violence the law and other social institutions visit on animals. See, for example Delaney, *Law and Nature*, 216, where he refers to the "circuits of violence against animals." Braverman is more guarded, however, declining to take a position on zoos or to refer in general to conceptions of violence and exploitation in relation to animals. See Braverman, *Zooland*. Otomo and Mussawir are keen to steer their collection away from the question of reformist projects: Otomo and Mussawir, *Law and the Questions of the Animal*, 1–2. Wadiwel seems most interested in considering details about legal change, but his core question still centres on the political concept of sovereignty.

70 See Part IV.
71 Carol J. Adams and Lori Gruen, "Introduction" in *Ecofeminism: Feminist Intersections with Other Animals and the Earth* (London: Bloomsbury, 2015), 1.
72 Erika Cudworth, *Developing Ecofeminist Theory: The Complexity of Difference* (Hampshire: Palgrave Macmillan, 2005). Ecofeminist theory is diverse, and only some ecofeminists have expressed concern about animals. It is this latter group that I, following Greta Gaard, am identifying through the term "vegetarian ecofeminist." Gaard, "Vegetarian Ecofeminism," 117. For examples of vegetarian ecofeminism see Carol J. Adams, *Neither Man nor Beast: Feminism and the Defense of Animals* (New York: Continuum, 1994); idem, *The Sexual Politics of Meat: A Feminist-Vegetarian Critical Theory* (New York: Continuum, 1990); Carol J. Adams and Josephine Donovan, eds., *Beyond Animal Rights: A Feminist Caring Ethic for the Treatment of Animals* (Indianapolis: Indiana University Press, 1996) ; idem, *Animals and Women*; Donovan, "Feminism and the Treatment of Animals: From Care to Dialogue," *Signs* 31.2 (2006); Greta C. Gaard, ed., *Ecofeminism, Women, Animals, Nature* (Philadelphia: Temple University Press, 1993); Val Plumwood, *Environmental Culture: The Ecological Crisis of Reason* (London: Routledge, 2002); Plumwood, "Androcentrism"; Karen Warren, ed., *Ecofeminism: Women, Culture, Nature* (Bloomington: Indiana University Press, 1997).
73 Adams, *Neither Man nor Beast*; idem, *The Sexual Politics of Meat*; Adams and Donovan, *Beyond Animal Rights*; idem, *Animals and Women*; Gaard, *Ecofeminism*; Lisa Kemmerer and Carol J. Adams, *Sister Species: Women, Animals, and Social Justice* (Champaign: University of Illinois Press, 2011);

Plumwood, *Environmental Culture*; idem, "Androcentrism"; Warren, *Ecofeminism*.

74 Adams first articulated this groundbreaking argument in *The Sexual Politics of Meat*,; Cudworth, *Developing Ecofeminist Theory*, 4.

75 Gaard, "Vegetarian Ecofeminism," 129.

76 Ibid., 131. See also the discussion at 132–3.

77 Greta Gaard, "Ecofeminism Revisited: Rejecting Essentialism and Re-Placing Species in a Material Feminist Environmentalism," *Feminist Formations* 23.2 (2011): 35.

78 Ibid., 31–2, 39–40.

79 Adams and Gruen, "Introduction," 72; Cudworth, *Developing Ecofeminist Theory*, 6.

80 Ibid., 2.

81 Gaard, "Ecofeminism Revisited," 36.

82 Ibid., 37–8.

83 Ibid., 41.

84 Will Kymlicka and Sue Donaldson, "Animal Rights, Multiculturalism, and the Left," *Journal of Social Philosophy* 45.1 (2014): 118.

85 Ibid., 122.

86 Ibid., 125–6. Kymlicka and Donaldson, of course, do not deny that problematic racial and colonial politics inform animal advocacy, but simply contest the complete dismissal or disavowal of advocacy on this ground. Ibid. For more on this troubling rejection or diminishment of animal issues in the context of anti-racist struggle see the nuanced analyses of case studies in Kim, *Dangerous Crossings*. Kim calls for "a practice of multi-optic vision, a way of seeing that takes disparate justice claims seriously without privileging any one presumptively" as part of "a reorientation toward an *ethics of mutual avowal*" between animal advocates unreflective about race and systemic racism and anti-racist advocates unconcerned about animal oppression. Ibid., 20–1.

87 Susan Fraiman, "Pussy Panic versus Liking Animals: Tracking Gender in Animal Studies," *Critical Inquiry* 39.1 (2012): 92–3. Others have also observed the marginalization that feminist animal care theory has suffered in animal studies at large (as well as in biopolitics). See Boggs, *Animalia Americana*, 11n5; Fiona Probyn-Rapsey, Siobhan O'Sullivan, and Yvette Watt, "'Pussy Panic' and Glass Elevators: How Gender is Shaping the Field of Animal Studies," *Australian Feminist Studies* 34.100 (2019).

88 Gaard, "Vegetarian Ecofeminism," 123, 127.

89 Deckha, "Postcolonial Posthumanist." See, for example, Cudworth, *Developing Ecofeminist Theory*, 71–2.

90 Deckha, "Postcolonial Posthumanist."

91 Cathryn Bailey, "'Africa Begins at the Pyrenees': Moral Outrage,
    Hypocrisy, and the Spanish Bullfight," *Ethics and the Environment* 12.1
    (2007); Amie Breeze Harper, *Sistah Vegan: Black Female Vegans Speak out on
    Food, Identity, Health, and Society* (New York: Lantern Books, 2010); Una
    Chaudhuri and Holly Hughes, *Animal Acts: Performing Species Today* (Ann
    Arbor: University of Michigan Press, 2014); Chen, *Animacies*, 19; Donna J.
    Haraway, *When Species Meet* (Minneapolis: University of Minnesota Press,
    2008); Hird, "Animal Transsex."; Kim, *Dangerous Crossings*; Jasbir K.
    Puar, "Terrorist Assemblages: Homonationalism in Queer Times" *Social
    and Cultural Geography* 11.4 (2007): 399; Sara Salih, "Filling up the Space
    Between Mankind and Ape: Racism, Speciesism and the Androphillic
    Ape," *Ariel* 38.1 (2007); Laura Wright, *"Wilderness into Civilized Shapes":
    Reading the Postcolonial Environment* (Athens: University of Georgia Press,
    2012).
92 Deckha, "Welfarist *and* Imperial."
93 Deckha, "Critical Animal Studies."
94 Posthumanism is a term that applies to a range of fields, and a concrete
    definition has proved elusive. A working definition would understand
    it as the consolidation of those theoretical strands that question the
    traditional boundaries of the human subject, noting its machine, animal,
    monstrous, and/or alien dimensions. Posthumanism questions the
    stability of the human subject – a concept that has been foundational
    to Western thought. In contrast, human-animal studies focuses on
    relationships between humans and animals. Posthumanism thus overlaps
    but is not coterminous with human-animal studies. Nonetheless, scholars
    in both fields emphasize the constructed and contingent nature of ideas
    about humanness and species difference, charting the unstable, shifting,
    fraught, and paradoxical meaning of these terms in various contexts.
    In this goal, posthumanist and animal studies are aligned with critical
    human justice literatures (feminist, postcolonial, queer) that have
    laboured to uncover the socially constructed dimensions of differences
    previously conceived as natural and innate. Deckha, "Critical Animal
    Studies," 212–23; Cary Wolfe, "Introduction" in *What Is Posthumanism?*
    (Minneapolis: University of Minnesota Press, 2010), xv.
95 According to the website of the Institute for Critical Animal Studies, it
    is an "academic field of study dedicated to the abolition of animal and
    ecological exploitation, oppression, and domination. CAS is grounded in
    a broad global emancipatory inclusionary movement for total liberation
    and freedom." The Institute for Critical Animal Studies, "JCAS: Suggested
    Topics," perma.cc/49ZF-6LBC.
96 Many critical animal scholars situate the question of animal justice within
    the interdisciplinary, yet still anthropocentric, field of cultural studies.

Critical animal scholars have thus extended the usual scope of cultural studies, which focuses on the analysis of everyday life, by examining routine human-animal practices. Jodey Castricano, *Animal Subjects: An Ethical Reader in a Posthuman World* (Waterloo: Wilfrid Laurier University Press, 2008); idem, *Animal Subjects 2.0* (Waterloo: Wilfrid Laurier University Press Press, 2017); Haraway, *When Species Meet*; Cary Wolfe, ed., *Zoontologies: The Question of the Animal* (Minneapolis: University of Minnesota Press, 2003).

97 Donna Haraway's influential body of work on multispecies relations is exemplary of this type of critique that purports to target anthropocentrism, and is widely lauded for doing so, but justifies institutional captivity, experimentation, and agricultural death for animals. For an excellent critique of Haraway's positions on multiple forms of animal use, see Zipporah Weisberg, "The Broken Promises of Monsters: Haraway, Animals and the Humanist Legacy," *Journal of Critical Animal Studies* 7.2 (2009): 22.

98 Glick, *Infrahumanisms*, 14–15.

99 Calarco, "Reorienting Strategies," 48. As Susan Fraiman has observed, this influence is disproportionate to the actual amount of writing that Derrida devoted to animals relative to his body of work, but very likely reflective of his overall academic stature. Fraiman, "Pussy Panic versus Liking Animals," 90.

100 Calarco, "Identity," 49–50; Braverman, "Law's Underdog"; Fraiman, "Pussy Panic."

101 Schillmoller, "Gaining Ground," 55–6.

102 Ibid., 53.

103 Braverman, "Law's Underdog," 136.

104 Schillmoller, "Gaining Ground," 52.

105 Ibid.

106 Cynthia Willett, *Interspecies Ethics* (New York: Columbia University Press, 2014), 11.

107 On these points, too, then, the analysis diverges from most post-structural theory on animals, which typically channels investigation of the socially constructed realities of our concepts of human, animal, and species into an end point that denies the possibility of a stable subjectivity altogether. Boggs, *Animalia Americana*, 3–4.

108 Carol Smart, *Feminism and the Power of Law* (New York: Routledge, 1989), 5, 160.

109 Ibid., 5.

110 Ibid.

111 Ibid.

112 Ibid.

113 Ed Mussawir and Yoriko Otomo, "Law's Animal," in *Law and the Question of the Animal: A Critical Jurisprudence*, ed. Yoriko Otomo and Ed Mussawir (Abingdon: Routledge, 2013), 1.

114 Ibid., 2.

115 Matthew Chrulew, "Animals in Biopolitical Theory: Between Agamben and Negri," *New Formations* 76 (2012); Laura Hudson, "A Species of Thought: Bare Life and Animal Being," *Antipode* 43.5 (2011): 1664; Nathan Snaza, "(Im)Possible Witness: Viewing PETA's 'Holocaust on Your Plate,'" *Animal Liberation Philosophy and Politics Journal* 2.1 (2004): 12–13; Cary Wolfe, "Before the Law: Animals in a Biopolitical Context," *Sage Journal* 6.1 (2010): 20.

116 Boggs, *Animalia Americana*, 5–8; Julietta Hua and Kasturi Ray, "Rights, Affect, and Precarity: Post-Racial Formations in Carework," *Cultural Dynamics* 26.1 (2014): 10.

117 John Borrows, *Recovering Canada: The Resurgence of Indigenous Law* (Toronto: University of Toronto Press, 2002).

118 Billy Ray Belcourt, "Animal Bodies, Colonial Subjects: (Re)Locating Animality in Decolonial Thought," *Societies* 5.1 (2015): 6; Cohen, "Animal Colonialism," 268.

119 Nicoke Shukin, *Animal Capital: Rendering Life in Biopolitical Times* (Minneapolis: University of Minnesota Press, 2009).

120 Cora Diamond, "The Difficulty of Reality and the Difficulty of Philosophy," in Stanley Cavell et al, eds., *Philosophy and Animal Life* (New York: Columbia University Press 2008): 53, cited in Lynn Worsham, "Toward an Understanding of Human Violence: Cultural Studies, Animal Studies, and the Promise of Posthumanism," *Review of Education, Pedagogy, and Cultural Studies* 35.1 (2013): 58.

121 Dinesh Wadiwel, "Whipping to Win: Measured Violence, Delegated Sovereignty, and the Privatised Domination of Non-Human Life," in *Law and the Question of the Animal: A Critical Jurisprudence*, eds. Yoriko Otomo and Ed Mussawir (Abingdon: Routledge, 2013), 120.

122 Ibid., 121.

123 Victoria Ridler, "Dressing the Sow and the Legal Subjectivation of the Non-Human Animal" in *Law and the Question of the Animal: A Critical Jurisprudence*, eds. Yoriko Otomo and Ed Mussawir (Abingdon: Routledge, 2013), 107.

124 Ibid., 109.

125 Ibid., 110.

126 For leading examples of scholarship advancing such views in Canada see John Borrows, *Canada's Indigenous Constitution* (Toronto: University of Toronto Press, 2010); Gordon Christie, "Culture, Self-Determination, and Colonialism: Issues around the Revitalization of Indigenous Legal

Traditions," *Indigenous Law Journal* 6 (2007); Hadley Friedland and Val
Napoleon, "Gathering the Threads: Indigenous Legal Methodology,"
Lakehead Law Journal 1.1 (2015), as cited by Janna Promislow, "Realizing
Aboriginal Administrative Law," in *Administrative Law in Context*, ed.
Colleen M. Flood and Lorne Sossin (Toronto: Emond Montgomery, 2017),
89n6.

127 Michael Asch, John Borrows and James Tully, *Resurgence and
Reconciliation: Indigenous-Settler Relations and Earth Teachings* (Toronto:
University of Toronto Press, 2018); Mathilde Cohen, "Animal
Colonialism: The Case of Milk," *American Journal of International Law
Unbound* 111 (2017): 267–71.

128 Billy-Ray Belcourt, "Animal Bodies"; Virginia DeJohn Anderson,
Creatures of Empire: How Domestic Animals Transformed Early America
(Oxford: Oxford University Press, 2004); John Ryan Fischer, *Cattle
Colonialism: An Environmental History of the Conquest of California and
Hawai'i* (Chapel Hill: University of North Carolina Press, 2015); Kelly
Struthers Montford and Chloë Taylor, eds., *Colonialism and Animality:
Anti-Colonial Perspectives in Critical Animal Studies* (London: Routledge,
2020).

129 As an example of this argument from leading scholars in this area
discussing the Canadian context, see Taiaiake Alfred and Jeff Corntassel,
"Being Indigenous: Resurgences against Contemporary Colonialism,"
Government and Opposition 40.1 (2005); and Leanne Simpson, *Lighting the
Eighth Fire: The Liberation, Resurgence, and Protection of Indigenous Nations*
(Winnipeg: Arbeitier Ring Pub, 2008).

130 Michael Elliott, "Indigenous Resurgence: The Drive for Renewed
Engagement and Reciprocity in the Turn Away from the State," *Canadian
Journal of Political Science* 51.1 (2018): 62.

131 Val Napoleon and Hadley Friedland, "An Inside Job: Engaging with
Indigenous Legal Traditions through Stories," *McGill Law Journal* 61.4
(2016): 733. For more on what these risks are see Aaron Mills, "The
Lifeworlds of Law: On Revitalizing Indigenous Legal Orders Today,"
McGill Law Journal 61 (2016). For more on the difference between
resurgence and reconciliation theorists in the Canadian context of the
Truth and Reconciliation Commission and the value of Indigenous
engagement with present dominant systems, see Bridget Storrie, "'The
Mighty Life-Creating and Transforming Power' of Carnival: Why the
Canadian Truth and Reconciliation Commission Does Not Seem to Have
It, but Indigenous Resurgence Does," *International Journal of Transitional
Justice* 3.1 (2015). For the use of Indigenous knowledge in the academy,
see Tracey Lindberg, "Engaging Indigenous Legal Knowledge in
Canadian Legal Institutions: Four Stories, Four Teachings, Four Tips, and

Four Lessons about Indigenous Peoples in the Legal Academy," *Ottawa Law Review* 50 (2019).

132 For more on the routine brutalization of animals in various types of industries in Canada see John Sorenson, *About Canada: Animal Rights* (Toronto: Fernwood, 2010).

133 Belcourt, "Animal Bodies"; Deckha, "Animal Justice, Cultural Justice: A Posthumanist Response to Cultural Rights in Animals," *Journal of Animal Law and Ethics* 2 (2007); idem, "Postcolonial," in *Critical Terms for Animal Studies,* ed. Lori Gruen (Chicago: University of Chicago Press, 2018); idem, "Unsettling Anthropocentric Legal Systems: Reconciliation, Indigenous Laws, and Animal Personhood," *Journal of Intercultural Studies* 41.1 (2020); Brian Noble, "Treaty Ecologies: With Persons, Peoples, Animals, and the Land," in Michael Asch, John Borrows, and James Tully, eds., *Resurgence and Reconciliation: Indigenous-Settler Relations and Earth Teachings* (Toronto: University of Toronto Press, 2018).

134 Farah Godrej, *Cosmopolitan Political Thought: Method, Practice and Discipline* (London: Oxford University Press), 14.

135 Ibid., 15. Godrej uses this term to characterize her aspiration with her work in relation to equalizing traditions of political thought despite a heavily Eurocentric system at present. I believe it nicely captures my similar hope in relation to the legal status of humans and animals.

136 Calarco, "Reorienting Strategies," 28.

137 Ibid., 42.

138 Ibid., 45.

139 Ibid., 48.

140 Ibid., 50.

141 Ibid., 42–54.

142 Ibid., 42–8.

143 Ibid., 53.

144 Ibid.

145 Ibid., 54.

146 Ibid.,

147 Ibid., 54.

148 Ibid., 42, 57–8.

149 For more on this seemingly ubiquitous question posed to vegans see Gary L. Francione, "A Frequently Asked Question: What about Plants?," *Animal Rights: The Abolitionist Post* (blog), 13 December 2006, perma .cc/G8MC-K4LF. I say more about beingness's application to plants in chapter 4.

150 Chen, *Animacies*; Oliver, *Animal Lessons,* 19.

151 For sources that do, see Michael Marder, *Plant-Thinking: A Philosophy of Vegetal Life* (New York: Columbia University Press, 2013). Although I do

not address the interests or needs of other non-humans in any detail, chapter 5 does address the anticipated objection that beingness, despite best intentions, nonetheless ends up instantiating its own hierarchical standards.

152 Kim, *Dangerous Crossings*, 283–7.

153 Neel Ahuja, "Postcolonial Critique in a Multispecies World," *PMLA* 124.1 (2009): 135.

154 Chloë Taylor, "On Intellectual Generosity," *Philosophy Today* 62.1 (2018).

155 Carole Pateman, *The Sexual Contract* (Stanford: Stanford University Press, 1988); Carole Pateman and Charles Mills, *Contract and Domination* (Maiden, Polity Press, 2007); Malini Johar Schueller, "Analogy and (White) Feminist Theory: Thinking Race and the Color of the Cyborg Body," *Signs* 31.1 (2005): 65.

156 Ibid., 65.

157 Ibid., 71.

158 Ibid., 72.

159 Ibid., 82. For more on the dominance of whiteness, even in third wave feminist theorizing that purports to be diverse and to attend to race, see Rebecca L. Clark Mane, "Transmuting Grammars of Whiteness in Third Wave Feminism: Interrogating Postrace Histories, Postmodern Abstraction, and the Proliferation of Difference in Third-Wave Texts," *Signs* 38.1.

160 Other top-selling books that make similar comparisons have also attracted criticism on this front. See Charles Patterson, *Eternal Treblinka: Our Treatment of Animals and the Holocaust* (New York: Lantern Books, 2002).

161 Sheri Flannery, "The Thirteenth Amendment Won't Help Free Willy," *Scholar* 15.1 (2012–13): 32–3.

162 PETA, "PETA sues SeaWorld for Violating Orcas Constitutional Rights," perma.cc/V5DH-VPAQ ; Flannery, "The Thirteenth Amendment," 33–5. Other social media controversies not involving PETA have also erupted. See Glick's discussion of hashtag appropriations of "Black Lives Matter" in Glick, *Infrahumans*, 17–18.

163 Lipschitz, "Skin/ned Politics," 551; Louise Ridley, "Barbican's Anti-Racism Show Featuring Black People in Cages Cancelled … After Racism Claims," *Huffington Post*, 24 September 2014, http://www .huffingtonpost.co.uk/2014/09/24/anti-racism-claims-cancelled -barbican-exhibit-b- show_n_5874202.html.

164 Anna Sewell, *Black Beauty* (London: Jarrold and Sons, 1877). For an intersectional analysis of this iconic novel see Moira Ferguson, "Breaking in Englishness: Black Beauty and the Politics of Gender, Race, and Class," *Women: A Cultural Review* 5.1 (1994).

165 Alice Walker, "Am I Blue?," in *Living by the Word: Essays* (New York: Open Road Media, 2011).

166 Marjorie Spiegel's work first identified the anxiety that others have over what are very valid comparisons when practices and techniques of oppression are compared. See Marjorie Spiegel, *The Dreaded Comparison: Human and Animal Slavery* (New York: Mirror Books, 1996).

167 Laura Wright, "Orwellian Animals in Postcolonial Context: Margaret Atwood's *Oryx and Crake*," *Margaret Atwood Studies* 2.1 (2008): 9.

168 John Miller, "Introduction," in *Empire and the Animal Body: Violence, Identity and Ecology in Victorian Adventure Fiction* (London: Anthem Press, 2012), 14.

169 Cathryn Bailey, "We Are What We Eat: Feminist Vegetarianism and the Reproduction of Racial Identity," *Hypatia* 22.2 (2007); Deckha, "Is Multiculturalism *Good* for Animals?"; Kathryn Gillespie, "Placing Angola: Racialisation, Anthropocentrism, and Settler Colonialism in the Louisiana State Penitentiary's Angola Rodeo," *Antipode* 50.5 (2018); Kim, *Dangerous Crossings*; Spiegel, *The Dreaded Comparison*, 162; David Szytbel, "Can the Treatment of Animals Be Compared to the Holocaust?" *Ethics and the Environment* 11.1 (2006).

170 Worsham, "Toward an Understanding," 63–4.

171 Glick, *Infrahumans*, 9.

172 Kymlicka, "Connecting Domination Contracts," 536.

173 Ibid., 537, discussing the work of Kimberly Costello and Gordon Hodson, "Exploring the Roots of Dehumanization: The Role of Animal–Human Similarity in Promoting Immigrant Humanization," *Group Processes and Intergroup Relations* 13.1 (2010); idem, "Lay Beliefs about the Causes of and Solutions to Dehumanization and Prejudice: Do Nonexperts Recognize the Role of Human-Animal Relations?," *Journal of Applied Social Psychology* 44.4 (2014); and Kristof Dhont et al., "Social Dominance Orientation Connects Prejudicial Human-Human and Human-Animal Relations," *Personality and Individual Differences* 61 (2014).

174 Lipschitz, "Skin/ned Politics," 548. Lipschitz voices a rare concern about an eclipsing equivalency running the other way in discussing Carol J. Adams's widely influential theory about the "sexual politics of meat" within feminist animal circles. Adams, *The Sexual Politics*. Lipschitz asserts that Adams's argument is "a strategy of equivalence that marries the visual objection/fragmentation and metaphorical consumption of sexualized and racialized women to the very real slaughter and butchery of animals. In effect and practice, it denies the question of difference central to deconstructing hierarchical power relations." Lipschitz, "Skin/ned Politics," 548. I raise Lipschitz's argument not to endorse the critique about Adams's theory as I believe her argument is more nuanced than

Lipschitz suggests, but to call attention to the fact that when the parallel runs the other way – that is, when we try to demonstrate the injustice of human treatment by drawing an analogy with animals – parallel-making does not offend and perhaps is barely noticed.

175 Ahuja, "Postcolonial Critique," 149. On the perceived and actual whiteness of animal studies and advocacy see Amie Breeze Harper, "Whiteness and 'Post-Racial' Vegan Praxis," *Journal of Critical Animal Studies* 8.3 (2010); Deckha, "Toward a Postcolonial Posthumanist Feminist Theory"; Corey Lee Wrenn, "An Analysis of Diversity in Nonhuman Animal Rights Media," *Journal of Agricultural and Environmental Ethics* 29 (2016): 150.

176 For excellent discussion of this dynamic in relation to Hindu-motivated cow protection movements in India, see Yamini Narayanan, "Cow Protection as 'Casteised Speciesism': Sacralisation, Commercialization, and Politicization," *South Asia* 41.2 (2018), https://doi.org/10/1080 /00856401.2018.1419794. For other examples, see also generally the articles in the special volume of *Journal of Intercultural Studies*, titled *Animal Nationalisms: Multispecies Cultural Politics, Race, and the (Un) making of the Settler Nation-State*, edited by Kathryn Gillespie and Yamini Narayanan. That volume is summarized by Kathryn Gillespie and Yamini Narayanan, "Animal Nationalisms: Multispecies Cultural Politics, Race, and the (un)Making of the Settler Nation-State," *Journal of Intercultural Studies* 41.1 (2020), https://doi.org/10.1080/07256868.2019.1704379.

177 Yamini Narayanan's work is a model to follow in this regard. See Narayanan, ibid. See also idem, "'Cow is a Mother, Mothers Can Do Anything for Their Children!': Gaushalas as Landscapes of Anthropatriarchy and Hindu Patriarchy," *Hypatia* 34.2 (2019); and idem, "Dairy, Death, and Dharma: The Devastation of Cow Protectionism in India," *Animal Liberation*, June 18, 2017, perma.cc/395A-NMKC.

178 Patricia Hill-Collins, "Intersectionality's Definitional Dilemmas," *Annual Review of Sociology* 41.1 (2015): 2.

179 Kim, *Dangerous Crossings*, 24–60; Alice Crary, "Animals, Cognitive Disability, and Getting the World in Focus in Ethics and Social Thought: A Reply to Eva Feder Kittay and Peter Singer" *ZEMO* 139.2 (2019).

180 See, for example, Deckha, "Toward a Postcolonial Posthumanist Feminist Theory"; idem, "Humanizing the Nonhuman"; idem, "The Salience of Species."

181 Anne McClintock, *Imperial Leather: Race, Gender, and Sexuality in the Colonial Context* (New York: Routledge, 1995); Eve Darian-Smith, "Postcolonialism: A Brief Introduction," *Social and Legal Studies* 5.3 (1996): 292–3.

182 Glick, *Infrahumanisms*, 4–7.

183 Kim, *Dangerous Crossings*; Aph Ko, *Racism as Zoological Witchcraft*
(Herndon: Lantern, 2019). Aph Ko rejects intersectionality as a frame of
analysis partly since she sees it as encouraging reliance on categorical
thinking that simplifies the dynamics of oppressions and how they are
constituted. See Ko's reading and critique of intersectionality, *Racism as
Zoological Witchcraft*, 14–15, 75–86. I view my earlier work and this present
analysis, as well as the work in other self-identified "intersectional"
accounts, as cognizant of such perils and directed at what Ko promotes
as a corrective to "intersectional" accounts, that is, a "multidimensional"
analysis that recognizes how race and species are mutually co-constituted
and do not run in parallel. See Deckha, "Toward a Postcolonial
Posthumanist Feminist Theory"; "Humanizing the Nonhuman"; "The
Salience of Species Difference"; "Intersectionality and Posthumanist
Vision of Equality." I thus see a commitment to highlighting the extensive
reach of animalization and animality in both our approaches despite
the variation in terminology to describe them. I hasten to note that the
present analysis is directed at considering the widespread, multilayered
workings of anthropocentrism's animalizations in colonial legal orders
and not about advocating adherence to "intersectionality" per se.

184 Mane, "Transmuting Grammars," 79.

185 I take inspiration from Carolyn Pedwell's work in *Feminism, Culture and
Embodied Practice: The Rhetorics of Comparison* (New York: Routledge,
2010), where she examines the continuities and discontinuities between
cultural practices argued to be analogous in feminist theory through a
relational frame instead. Pedwell employs postcolonial theory, feminism,
and queer theory as main frameworks; ibid.

186 Rita Dhamoon, "Considerations on Mainstreaming Instrumentality,"
Political Research Quarterly 64.1 (2011); Glick, *Infrahumans*, 16. I note here
that Aph Ko explicity rejects intersectionality as a frame for her work,
choosing the terminology of "multilayered" analysis.

187 Godrej, *Cosmopolitan Political Thought*, 15.

188 Ibid., 13.

189 Frans de Waal, "Appendix A: Anthropomorphism and Anthropodenial,"
in *Primates and Philosophers: How Morality Evolved* (Princeton: Princeton
University Press, 2006); as discussed in Martha Nussbaum, "Compassion,"
in *Species Matters: Humane Advocacy and Cultural Theory*, ed. Marianne
DeKoven and Michael Lundblad (New York: Columbia University Press),
140.

190 Delaney, *Law and Nature*, 216. Boggs too canvasses problems with
terminology in terms of how to describe animals as well as how to
describe the fields which their academic study has produced. Boggs,
Animalia Americana, 7–9.

191 Fox, "Rethinking Kinship," 15.
192 Erica Fudge, *Animal* (London: Reaktion Books, 2002).
193 Worsham, "Toward an Understanding," citing David Wood, "Thinking with Cats," in *Animal Philosophy: Ethics and Identity*, ed. Peter Atterton and Matthew Calarco (London: Bloomsbury Academic, 2004), 133.
194 Worsham, "Toward an Understanding," 55.
195 To dilute the dichotomous effects of terms involving "non" and "other" as well as those that reference humans, Lisa Kemmerer has proffered the term "anymal" as a form of "verbal activism." "Anymal" is a contraction of "any" and "animal" and is meant to be a signifier that refers to any animal except humans. Kemmerer acknowledges that "animal" retains a dualistic meaning that continues to lump all animals into one linguistic category opposed to humans, but argues that it avoids the intensely dualistic connections of "non" and "other." Lisa Kemmerer, "Verbal Activism: Anymal," *Society and Animals* 14.1 (2006).
196 Ibid.
197 Lori Gruen and Kari Weil, "Animal Others – Editors' Introduction," *Hypatia* 27.3 (2012); Kymlicka and Donaldson, "Animal Rights"; Clare Palmer, "Colonization, Urbanization, and Animals," *Philosophy and Geography* 6.1 (2010).

1 No Escape: Anti-cruelty Laws' Property Foundations

1 Honourable Mr. Justice Rajiv Sharma writing in *Karnail Singh and others v State of Haryana*, CRR-533–2013, at para 93.
2 On the special cultural status assigned to certain companion animals and wild animals within dominant Western culture see Christine Overall, *Pets and People: The Ethics of Companion Animals* (Oxford: Oxford University Press, 2017); Rachel Nussbaum Wichert and Martha Nussbaum, "The Legal Status of Whales: Capabilities, Entitlements, and Culture," *Seqüência: Estudos Jurídicos e Políticos* 37.72 (2016). On the diverse regulation of animals depending on what kind of animal they are perceived as within the law (livestock, pest, endangered, research animal, etc.), see Irus Braverman, "Animals and Law in the American City" in *Environmental Law and Contrasting Ideas of Nature: A Constructivist Approach*, ed. Keith Hirokawa (New York: Cambridge University Press, 2014), 112. As Braverman notes, the "law classifies animals according to their relationship with humans," and these "categories for animals are not always consistent, nor are they mutually exclusive"; ibid., 113. Braverman argues that animals "jump" between these porous categories

when anthropocentric interests accumulate to prompt a regulatory change; ibid., 118.

3 Bruce Ziff, *Principles of Property Law,* 4th ed. (Toronto: Thomson Carswell, 2006) ("the common law provides that title to wild animals vests by taking possession"; 120). Wild animals are often described as public property and thus the subject of government regulation as to how they may be "taken," that is, converted to private property through acts of individual or joint possession. Hunting laws are clear examples of this type of regulation.

4 There are those that come easily to mind because their subject scope seems to be obviously focused on animals. Federally, these include the *Canadian Food Inspection Agency Act,* S.C. 1997, c. 6; the *Food and Drugs Act,* R.S.C. 1985, c. F-27; the *Health of Animals Act,* S.C. 1990, c. 21; the *Meat Inspection Act,* R.S.C. 1985, c. 25 (1st Supp.); the *Fish Inspection Act,* R.S.C. 1985, c. F-12; and the *Fisheries Act* R.S.C. 1985, c. F-14. In Ontario, these include the *Game and Fish Act,* R.S.O. 1990, c. G.1; and the *Veterinarians Act,* R.S.O. 1990, v. V.3. In British Columbia there exists the *Fur Farm Act,* R.S.B.C. 1996, c. 167; the *Fisheries Act,* R.S.B.C. 1996, c. 149; and the *Livestock Act,* R.S.B.C. 1996, c. 270, among many others. Then there are statutes that are more indirectly connected to animals, such as the *Excise Tax Act,* R.S.C. 1985, c. E-15, and the *Customs Act,* R.S.C. 1985, c. C-1 (2nd Supp.). Finally, there are in the *Criminal Code of Canada,* R.S.C. 1985, c. C-46 [the *Code*], provisions that deal with animals, such as s.444 and s.445 (injuring cattle and or other animal owned by others), s.445.01 (injuring a law enforcement, military, or service animal), ss.445.1, 445.2, and 446 (main anti-cruelty provisions), and s.447 (fighting). All these sections except s.447 are subject to the accused proving a legal justification or excuse and colour of right under s.429(2), which are common defences available for property offences.

5 The law's understanding of what constitutes cruel treatment by states against marginalized human beings also merits critical attention, provided by Colin Dayan in *The Law Is a White Dog: How Legal Rituals Make and Unmake Persons* (Princeton: Princeton University Press, 2011).

6 The *Code.* The *Code* also treats animals as property outside of these two Parts. For example, s.264.1 (uttering threats), which is housed in Part VIII directed at "Offences Against the Person and Reputation," includes threats "to kill, poison or injure an animal or bird that is the property of any person" as among the threats that are criminalized. There are other crimes involving animals that do not turn on the property status of the animal but rather on moral views regarding inappropriate sexual behaviour (i.e., bestiality). While this chapter does not include a discussion on the criminalization of bestiality, this has been the subject of

critical and legal commentary. See, for example, Erica Fudge, "Monstrous Acts: Bestiality in Early Modern England," *History Today* 50.8 (2000); Colleen Glenney Boggs, "American Bestiality: Sex, Animals, and the Construction of Subjectivity," *Cultural Critique* 76 (2010); A.D. Harvey, "Bestiality in Late-Victorian England," *Journal of Legal History* 21.3 (2000); Alphonso Lingis, "Bestiality," in *Animal Others: On Ethics, Ontology, and Animal Life,* ed. H Peter Steeves (Albany: SUNY Press, 1999).

7 The *Code*, s.322(5) reads: "For the purposes of this section, a person who has a wild living creature in captivity shall be deemed to have a special property or interest in it while it is in captivity and after it has escaped from captivity."

8 The *Code*, s.338, reads:

(1) Every one person is guilty of an indictable offence and liable to imprisonment for a term of not more than five years or is guilty of an offence punishable on summary conviction who, without the consent of the owner, (a) fraudulently takes, holds, keeps in his possession, conceals, receives, appropriates, purchases or sells cattle that are found astray, or (b) fraudulently, in whole or in part, (i) obliterates, alters or defaces a brand or mark on cattle, or (ii) makes a false or counterfeit brand or mark on cattle, is guilty of an indictable offence and liable to imprisonment for a term not exceeding five years. (2) Every person who commits theft of cattle is guilty of an indictable offence and liable to imprisonment for a term not exceeding ten years. (3) In any proceedings under this Act, evidence that cattle are marked with a brand or mark that is recorded or registered in accordance with any Act is, in the absence of any evidence to the contrary, proof that the cattle are owned by the registered owner of that brand or mark. (4) Where an accused is charged with an offence under subsection (1) or (2), the burden of proving that the cattle came lawfully into the possession of the accused or his employee or into the possession of another person on behalf of the accused is on the accused, if the accused is not the registered owner of the brand of mark with which the cattle are marked, unless it appears that possession of the cattle by an employee of the accused or by another person on behalf of the accused was without the knowledge and authority, sanction or approval of the accused.

The *Code*, s.323, also references non-humans, specifically oysters, to establish when owners' property interests in oysters will be recognized.

9 Writing about the philosophical foundation of these laws, Lesli Bisgould states: "From the outset, a concern for animals' well-being was set out, but a review of the historical record indicates that that concern has always been highly qualified and secondary to the interests of the people who owned and had a financial interest in them." Lesli Bisgould, *Animals and the Law* (Toronto: Irwin Law, 2011), 59.

10 The *Code*, s.444 read, before it was repealed,

> (1) Every one commits an offence who wilfully (a) kills, maims, wounds, poisons or injures cattle, or (b) places poison in such a position that it may easily be consumed by cattle. (2) Every one who commits an offence under subsection (1) is guilty of (a) and indictable offence and liable to imprisonment for a term of not more than five years; or (b) an offence punishable on summary conviction and liable to a fine not exceeding ten thousand dollars or to imprisonment for a term of not more than eighteen months or to both.

11 The *Code*, s.445, read, before it subsumed the then existing section 444 that had addressed cattle,

> (1) Every one commits an offence who, wilfully and without lawful excuse (a) kills, maims, wounds, poisons or injures dogs, birds or animals that are not cattle and are kept for a lawful purpose; or (b) places poison in such a position that it may easily be consumed by dogs, birds or animals that are not cattle and are kept for a lawful purpose. (2) Every one who commits an offence under subsection (1) is guilty of (a) an indictable offence and liable to imprisonment for a term of not more than five years; or (b) an offence punishable on summary conviction and liable to a fine not exceeding ten thousand dollars or to imprisonment for a term of not more than eighteen months or both.

12 Ibid.
13 "Cattle" was used to refer to many livestock animals, such as horses, cows, and mules. Offences against "cattle" were indictable, whereas those against other animals were summary offences; this distinction is revealing of the relative perceived "value" of these animals. Bisgould, *Animals and the Law*, 59, citing James Crankshaw, *The Criminal Code of Canada* (Montreal: Whiteford & Theoret, Law Publishers, 1894), 447–8. To this day the term cattle retains this broad definition; ibid., 67.
14 The *Code*, s.445.01.
15 Bisgould, *Animals and the Law*, 68. There are some cases charged under ss 444 and 445 where the harm to the animal has been understood as other than a detriment to the owner's property interest; I merely point out that such a case would be the anomaly rather than the norm. See e.g., *R. v. Sparshu* (1996), 44 Alta. L.R. (3d) 303. (Prov. Ct.); see also *R v Young*, [1997] OJ No 6214; *R v Fuller*, [1994] OJ No 4285.
16 See *R. v. Shaw*, (1988), 93 A.R. 86 (Prov. Ct.).
17 See *R. v. England*, (1924), 19 Sask. L.R. 165, [1925] 1 W.W.R. 237, 43 C.C.C.11 (C.A.); *R. v. Kokatt*, [1944] 1 W.W.R. 158, 81 C.C.C. 101 (Sask. Police Ct.); *R. v. Kroesing* (1909), 2 Alta. L.R. 275, 10 W.L.R. 649, 16 C.C.C. 312 (T.D.).
18 In this regard, they are perhaps equivalent in stature to endangered species types of legislation in conveying to the public the sense that they prioritize animals' interests over human ones and effectively protect animals. Although it is not discussed here, the *Species at Risk Act* (SC 2002, c. 29) has received similar critique for its essentially anthropocentric

204 Notes to pages 42–4

nature. See, for example, the following study, which shows the various factors, such as economics and public interest, that influence the listing of certain species over others as protected under the law: C. Scott Findlay and Stewart Elgie, "Species Listing under Canada's Species at Risk Act," *Conservation Biology* 23.6 (2009). See also Raymond A. Rogers and Christopher J.A. Wilkinson, "Policies of Extinction: The Life and Death of Canada's Endangered Species Legislation," *Policy Studies Journal* 28.1 (2000), 193.

19 Gary L. Francione, *Animals, Property, and the Law* (Philadelphia: Temple University Press, 1995).

20 Ibid., 134–60.

21 Ibid., 18.

22 Ibid.

23 Ibid., 27.

24 Ibid., 26; see also, for example, Gary L. Francione, "Reflections on *Animals, Property, and the Law* and *Rain without Thunder,*" *Law and Contemporary Problems* 70 (2007): 9; idem, "Animal Welfare and the Moral Value of Nonhuman Animals," *Law, Culture, and the Humanities* 6 (2010): 35–6.

25 Francione, *Animals, Property, and the Law*, 26.

26 Ibid.

27 Ibid.

28 Francione, *Animals, Property, and the Law*, 124–5. The Canadian mischief offence is located in s.430 of the *Code*.

29 Francione, *Animals, Property, and the Law*, 125.

30 Ibid.

31 Maneesha Deckha, "Welfarist *and* Imperial: The Contributions of Anti-Cruelty Legislation to Civilizational Discourse," *American Quarterly* 65.3 (2013): 518–19.

32 For two early and widely influential postcolonial feminist theoretical accounts of this relationship see Uma Narayan, *Dislocating Cultures: Identities, Traditions, and Third-World Feminism* (New York: Routledge, 1997); and Anne McClintock, *Imperial Leather: Race, Gender, and Sexuality in the Colonial Contest* (New York: Routledge, 1995).

33 Deckha, "Welfarist *and* Imperial," 520–5.

34 Adams, "Animals, Property, and the Law" (1996) 18 Houston J of Int'l Law 595 at 602.

35 Bisgould, *Animals and the Law*.

36 The provincial and federal anti-cruelty statutes do overlap but are not in conflict. As Bisgould explains, "while both statutes deal with the same subject matter, there is no conflict between the two and therefore no issue of paramountcy." See *R v Vaillancourt*, 2003 NSPC 59, as cited in Bisgould,

Animals and the Law, 115n86. The provincial legislation contributes to animal protection in a relatively meaningful way. This is because these laws provide an enforcement mechanism through humane societies that is more accessible than criminal prosecutions. Bisgould provides a comprehensive survey of the role of humane societies in Canada in identifying animals in distress and taking legal action against people who transgress these laws. See Bisgould, *Animals and the Law*, 97–102.

37 Ibid., 69, citing Joanne Klineberg, "Cruelty to Animals and the *Criminal Code of Canada*," in *An Introduction to Animals and the Law*, ed. Lesli Bisgould (Toronto: Law Society of Upper Canada, Continuing Legal Education, 2007), 1–3.

38 The popularity of animal hunting as a spectator sport, and part of what constituted "blood-sports," has changed significantly over the last few centuries. Until the Romantic Age in England, when sensibilities deepened regarding the suffering of animals, these sports were widely accepted and organized fights were well-attended. For a more detailed discussion, see Kathryn Shevelow, *For the Love of Animals: The Rise of the Animal Protection Movement* (New York: Henry Holt, 2008), 7–8, 39–45; Emma Griffin, *Blood Sport: Hunting in Britain since 1066* (New Haven: Yale University Press, 2007), 142; and Harriet Ritvo, *The Animal Estate* (Cambridge, MA: Harvard University Press, 1987), 125–8.

39 Janet M. Davis, "Cockfight Nationalism: Blood Sport and the Moral Politics of American Empire and Nation Building," *American Quarterly* 65.3 (2013): 551.

40 With respect to animal fighting, see Megan H. Glick, "Animal Instincts: Race, Criminality, and the Reversal of the 'Human,'" *American Quarterly* 65.3 (2013): 640. As Glick discusses, a notorious example of these dynamics is found in the case of NFL superstar Michael Vick. Ibid. For other accounts of how race and class overwhelmed public reaction and prosecution to Michael Vick's actions, see Claire Jean Kim, *Dangerous Crossings: Race, Species, and Nature in a Multicultural Age* (Cambridge University Press, 2015), 253–79; and Harlan Weaver, "'Becoming in Kind': Race, Class, Gender, and Nation in Cultures of Dog Rescue and Dogfighting," *American Quarterly* 65.3 (2013): 694–7.

41 Bisgould, *Animals and the Law*, 68.

42 The *Code*, s.446(1).

43 The *Code*, s.447.1(1)(a). This provision also applies to convictions under subsections 445(2), 445.1(2), 446(2) and 447(2).

44 By virtue of subsections 445.1(3) and 446(3), the introduction of evidence that the defendant failed to reasonably prevent pain, suffering, damage, or injury, absent contradicting evidence, is proof of the defendant's wilful infliction of the suffering or neglect to prevent it. By virtue of

subsection 445.1(4), absent evidence to the contrary, simply being present at an animal fighting activity is proof of both the *actus reus* and *mens rea* components of the offence in s.445.1(1)(b). This trumps the more general aiding and abetting provision in the *Code*, found in s.21 (Parties to Offences), where the "[m]ere presence at the scene of an offence is *not* sufficient to ground liability [emphasis mine]." Ibid.

45 The presumptions would seem to reverse the general meaning of "wilfully" as it is defined in s.429(1), which defines "wilfully" as "caus[ing] the occurrence of an event by doing an act or by omitting to do an act that is his duty to do, knowing that the act or omission will probably cause the occurrence of the event and being reckless whether the event occurs or not ..." The *Code*, s.429(1). In other words, the text suggests that a subjective inquiry approach into intent or knowledge/ awareness does not apply by virtue of the presumption provided by ss.445.1(3) and 446(3); under this reading, evidence of the *actus reus* in both ss.445.1(1)(a) and 446(1)(a) could thus establish the *mens rea*. The presumption decreases the burden of proof on the Crown so that the offence becomes one of strict liability, absent evidence to the contrary. That subsection s.445.1(1)(a) is subject to an evidentiary presumption is significant because, of all the subsections housed under s.445.1, it allows for the broadest definition of suffering.

46 Canadian anti-cruelty jurisprudence is also limited because of the small incidence of reported cases. In addition, because of the summary nature of most prosecutions, most cases are usually heard in courts of very limited jurisdiction whose resulting decisions are not reported unless the cases are appealed. See Bisgould, *Animals and the Law*, 79–81.

47 For examples of federal legislation, see the *Feeds Act*, R.S.C. 1985, c.F-9; *Animal Pedigree Act*, R.S.C.1985, c. 8 (4th Supp.); *Canada Wildlife Act*, R.S.C. 1985, c.W-9; *Canadian Food Inspection Agency Act*, S.C. 1997, c. 6; *Health of Animals Act*, S.C. 1990, c. 21; *Canada National Parks Act*, S.C. 2000, c. 32; *Pest Control Products Act*, S.C. 2002, c. 28; *Railway Safety Act*, R.S.C. 1985, c. 32 (4th Supp), s 24(1)(f); *Wild Animals and Plant Protection and Regulation of International and Interprovincial Trade Act*, S.C. 1992, c. 52. For Ontario legislation see *Animals for Research Act*, R.S.O. 1990, c. A.22; *Blind Persons' Rights Act*, R.S.O. 1990, c. B.7; *Conservation Authorities Act*, R.S.O. 1990, c. C.27; *Dog Owners Liability Act*, R.S.O. 1990, c. D.16; *Endangered Species Act*, S.O. 2007, c. 6; *Forestry Act*, R.S.O. 1990, c. F.26; *Game and Fish Act*, R.S.O. 1990, c. G.1; *Health Protection and Promotion Act*, R.S.O. 1990, c. H.7; *Highway Traffic Act*, R.S.O. 1990, c. H.8; *Protection of Livestock and poultry from Dogs Act*, R.S.O. 1990, c. L.24; *Municipal Act*, R.S.O. 1990, c. M.45; *Niagara Parks Act*, R.S.O. 1990, c. N.3; *Parks Assistance Act*, R.S.O. 1990, c. P.2; *Pesticides Act*, R.S.O. 1990, c. P.11;

Pounds Act, R.S.O., c. P.17; *Provincial Parks Act*, R.S.O., 1990, c. P.34; *Public Parks Act*, R.S.O. 1990, c. P.46; *Research Foundation Act*, R.S.O. 1990, c. R.27; *St. Clair Parkway Commission Act*, R.S.O. 1990, c. S.23; *St. Lawrence Parks Commission Act*, R.S.O. 1990 c. S.24; *Veterinarians Act*, R.S.O. 1990. c. V.3. For British Columbia legislation, see *e.g. Agricultural Produce Grading Act*, R.S.B.C. 1996, c. 11; *Animal Disease Control Act*, R.S.B.C. 1996, c. 14; *Creston Valley Wildlife Act*, R.S.B.C. 1996, c. 84; *Farming and Fishing Industries Development Act*, R.S.B.C. 1996, c. 134; *Fisheries Act*, R.S.B.C. 1996, c. 149; *Fur Farm Act*, R.S.B.C. 1996, c. 167.

48 For an overview of the oppressive treatment of animals in Canada see John Sorenson, *About Canada: Animal Rights* (Toronto: Fernwood, 2010). For an investigative first-hand account of the atrocities animals suffer even on mechanized family farms in Canada and elsewhere, see Sonia Faruqi, *Project Animal Farm: An Accidental Journey into the Secret World of Farming and the Truth about Our Food* (New York: Pegasus Books, 2014).

49 *R. v. Ménard*, (1978), 4 C.R. (3d) 333, 43 C.C.C. (2d) 458 (Que. C.A.) [*Ménard* cited to C.C.C.].

50 Two more SCC cases are relevant to this discussion, even though neither has had the effect of changing anti-cruelty jurisprudence. The first is *Harvard College v Canada (Commissioner of Patents)*, 2002 SC 76, [2002] 4 SCR 45. In this decision, the court took an unprecedented step when it acknowledged that "[i]f the line between lower and higher life forms is indefensible and arbitrary, so too is the line between human beings and other higher life forms." Ibid., 7. Though this decision questions anthropocentrism as a pillar of the Canadian legal system, it is not an anti-cruelty case, rather it presents a question of intellectual property. Even more disruptive to the systemic exploitation of animals is the dissent in *Reece and Zoocheck v Edmonton*, 2011 ABCA 238 (CanLII), 335 DLR (4th) 600, 513 AR 199 at para 162, leave denied (2012) [2011] SCCA No. 447 (QL). In applying Alberta's animal welfare legislation, Chief Justice Fraser placed the suffering of the animal in question (Lucy, an elephant) at the centre of her dissenting decision. For a discussion of the forward-thinking nature of this dissent for animals. see Deckha, "Initiating a Non-Anthropocentric Jurisprudence: The Rule of Law and Animal Vulnerability under a Property Paradigm," *Alberta Law Review* 50.2 (2013).

51 Bisgould, *Animals and the Law*, 74.

52 Ibid., 466.

53 Ibid.

54 Ibid., 467.

55 Ibid., 468.

56 Ibid., 460.

57 *R. v. Linder*, (1950), 97 C.C.C. 174, 10 C.R. 44, [1950] 1 W.W.R. 1035 [*Linder* cited to C.C.C.]; distinguished in *Ménard*; and mentioned in *R v Pacific Meat Co* (1957) BCJ no 98, 24 WWR 37 locus 40, 119 C.C.C. 237 locus 240; *R v Paish* (1977) BCJ No 924, 2 WWR 526 locus 532, 1 WCB 172; *R v Clarke* (2001) NJ No 191 locus para 48; *R v JS* (2003) NJ No 225 locus para 21, 59 WCB (2d) 228.

58 *Ford v. Wiley*, (1889), 23 Q.B.D. 203, 58 L.J.M.C. 145; mentioned most recently in *Chief Constable of Norfolk v Clayton* (1983) 2 AC 473, 2 WLR 555, 1 AII ER 984.

59 *Swan v. Saunders*, (1881), 50 L.J.M.C. 67.

60 The British Columbia Court of Appeal (BCCA) is the highest appellate court in the province of British Columbia.

61 *Criminal Code*, R.S.C. 1927, c. 36.

62 *Linder, supra* note 57 at 175.

63 *Ménard, supra* note 49 at para 463 citing *Ford, supra* note 58 at 689 and *Swan, supra* note 59 at 570.

64 *Ménard, supra* note 49 at 464.

65 A sample review of judicially reported cases since 2012 in which the accused stood trial for a charge pursuant to s 445.1 reveals three cases of severe neglect of basic needs for domestic animals over extended periods of time (see *R v Barrett*, 2015 CarswellNfld 14, 2015 CanLII 2415 (NL PC); *R v Haughton*, 2013 BCSC 1683, 2016 CarswellBC 2733; and *R v Irving*, 2013 SKPC 101, 2013 CarswellSask 431), as well as the following array of serious attacks on sentient animal bodies: kicking a cat in the chest down a flight of stairs in *R v Danfousse*, 2013 ABPC 137, 2013 CarswellAlta 866 at 16; "blunt force trauma" to a cat causing injuries that required the cat to be euthanized in *R v Habermehl*, 2013 ABPC 122, 2016 CarswellAlta 570 at 12; drowning a dog in *R v Haaksman*, 2013 ONCJ 66, 2013 CarswellOnt 2225; slitting a dog's throat with a knife in *R v Jereda*, 2015 SKPC 90, 2015 CarswellSask 335 at 1; hanging a cat upside down, slitting the animal, and letting the animal bleed out a slow death upon a couple copulating below in *R v Alcorn*, 2015 ABCA 182, 2015 CarswellAlta 948; and breaking the necks of two cats and bludgeoning them to death in *R v Marshall*, 2013 ONCJ 61, 2013 CarswellOnt 1766. A sampling of sentencing cases in which the accused pled guilty to a charge under s 445.1 reveals similarly disturbing acts involving intense levels of suffering for the animal victims: killing and evisceration of a cat and dog in *R v Bourque*, 2013 BCCA 447, 2013 CarswellBC 3094; dropping a rabbit from a balcony resulting in death in *R v Kennedy*, 2015 CarswellOnt 11987, 123 WCB (2d) 586; and throwing a dog up six flights of stairs and engaging in further actions that resulted in a "bilateral scleral hemorrhage" to the dog the next day in *R v Rowe*, 2015 ONCJ 596 at para 12, per Caldwell J.

66 *Ménard, supra* note 49 at 464. The term "without necessity" is one that previous case law had made significant to construe the meaning of then s.402(a). In *Linder, supra* note 57, Robertson J.A. cited *Ford, supra* note 58 for the meaning of "unnecessary." Robertson J.A. noted that in *Ford,* Lord Coleridge C.J. defined the term as "inflicted without necessity," and his brother, Hawkins J., added that "without necessity" meant "without good reason."

67 *Ménard, supra* note 49 at 464.

68 Ibid.

69 Ibid., 465. An elaboration of this claim can be found in chapter 16 – titled "The Philosophy of Animal Protection" – in Preece and Chamberlain, *Animal Welfare and Human Values* (Waterloo: Wilfred Laurier University Press, 1993), 283. In that chapter the authors argue in terms of "primitivism" versus "civilization" and where animal welfare is situated in this arguably artificial binary. For a discussion of the colonial elements in this common claim, and in the animal welfare movement more generally, see Ahuja, "Postcolonial Critique in a Multispecies World," *PMLA* 124.2 (2009); Deckha, "Welfarist *and* Imperial," 520–5; and Ani B. Satz, "Would Rosa Parks Wear Fur? Toward a Nondiscrimination Approach to Animal Welfare," *Journal of Animal Law & Ethics* 1.

70 Of course, it would not be difficult to argue that "mankind" also entails further stratifications along gender lines.

71 Deckha, "Welfarist *and* Imperial," 518–25. See also Samera Esmeir's discussion of British efforts in Egypt in this regard in Samera Esmeir, *Juridical Humanity: A Colonial History* (Stanford: Stanford University Press, 2012), 87, 126–40.

72 *Ménard, supra* note 48 at 465.

73 Ibid., 465 (emphasis added).

74 Ibid., 466.

75 Ibid., 464.

76 Ibid., 468.

77 Ibid.

78 Ibid., 467 (emphasis added).

79 *Ménard* was followed in *R v Mousseau,* [2011] JQ no 13401 locus para 127, 2011 QCCQ 11101; *R v McRae,* [2002] OJ No 4987 locus para 11; and *R v Amorim,* [1994] OJ No 2824 locus para 21, 26 WCB (2d) 1. This case was mentioned in more than nineteen decisions, including most recently *R v Rose,* [2009] JQ no 19387 locus para 29, 2009 QCCQ 5736; *R v McLeod,* [2011] SJ No 721 locus para 8, 2011 SKPC 180; and *R v Lyonnais,* [2012] JQ no 7321 locus para 24. It has also been mentioned in twenty-two other cases. The anthropocentric understanding of suffering has not changed where *Ménard* was mentioned but not followed. Consider, for example,

how the understanding of "unnecessary" in *Ménard* was paraphrased in *R v Clarke* (2001) CarswellNfld 189 at 52: "The reference to 'unnecessary' pain or suffering signals a legislative intent that the willful causing of any pain or suffering will not constitute an offence. Reference must be made to the extent or degree of pain and the purpose for inflicting it including any societal benefits gained. In *R v McRae* (2002) CarswellOnt 5679 at 11 the same interpretation of 'unnecessary' was extrapolated and applied systematically:

> With respect to the degree of pain or suffering caused to an animal by an accused, the Crown need prove beyond a reasonable doubt only that it caused the animal something more than "the least physical discomfort' ... Once that threshold has been met, then one must consider the means by which and the purpose for which the pain, suffering or injury was caused to decide whether it was caused 'unnecessarily' ... In determining whether or not pain, suffering or injury was caused to an animal 'unnecessarily,' it is appropriate to consider both the means employed and the purpose for which the pain, suffering or injury was caused, and also the relation between the purpose and the means ... In some cases, the purpose may be legitimate but the means employed may not be ...

80 Andrew Brighten, "Aboriginal Peoples and the Welfare of Animal Persons: Dissolving the Bill C-10B Conflict," *Indigenous Law Journal* 10.1 (2011): 47n40.

81 See, for example, Gary L. Francione, "Animals, Property, and Legal Welfarism: 'Unnecessary' Suffering and the 'Humane' Treatment of Animals," *Rutgers Law Review* 46 (1994): 723; idem, "Animals as Property," *Animal Law* 2 (1996): ii.

82 I exclude here cases where the accused pled guilty. To my knowledge there are only two such reported instances. In *R v Bocian* (1982), 16 Sask. R. 92 (Prov. Ct.), the accused had been charged with causing unnecessary suffering under s.402 because his cattle were dying of starvation due to the accused's poor managerial skills and incompetence in care during adverse winter weather. The accused received a fine of $400 and was placed on probation for two years, during which a veterinarian was ordered to inspect the animals once a month from the beginning of December to the end of March. See also *R v Paul*, [1997] BCJ No 808 (Prov Ct) cited in Bisgould, *Animals and the Law*, 78.

83 Review of all reported cases implicating s.445.1(a) or its predecessors since 1979 (cases on file with author). Bisgould has made the same observation of cases she has reviewed. Bisgould, *Animals and the Law*, 110, 75 noting the following cases as examples: *R v Marshall* 2007 BCSC 1750; *R v Sudweeks*, 2003 BCSC 1960; *R v Carter*, 2006 ABPC 341; *R v Bakic*, 2004 SKPC 134, *R v Elliott*, 2009 NSPC 5, *R v Prince*, 1995 Ont Ct Prov Div, unreported.

84 See the descriptors various courts use, *supra* note 65, for a sample set of these cases.

85 Deckha, "Welfarist *and* Imperial," 518.

86 Francione, *Animals, Property, and the Law*, 154.

87 This is a dictate the law expresses in other areas as well in relation to animals. See for example *Re Wishart Estate* (1992), 46 E.T.R. 311. In this case the owner had left a will instructing the RCMP to shoot his four horses because he feared they would be ill-treated if he was no longer able to care for them. The court invalidated this direction on the grounds of public policy that a deceased, though the owner, could not direct disposal of his property in a way that would be an *economic* waste of resources and estate assets. It was explicitly recognized that living owners have full property rights to dispose of their property as they please subject to any existing regulation, but that this property right after death is subject to public policy concerns which, of course, are of the economic utilitarian variety.

88 Further concerning in the case law post-*Ménard*, as Bisgould discusses, is the tendency of courts to relativize the treatment of animals, evaluating the seriousness of harm caused by one practice against other practices with the result that the harm at issue is minimized. Some examples of this that Bisgould points to are *R v Borges*, where the court weighed the harm caused by bullfights by comparing them to the exploitation of animals at the Calgary Stampede, and *R v Paul*, where the accused received a light sentence for killing a cat by stabbing and kicking it, because the cat's suffering was relatively short compared to the pain it was experiencing starving under the accused's care. Bisgould, *Animals and the Law*, 75–9, citing *R v Borges*, 1991 Ont Ct Prov Div, unpublished, and *R v Paul*, 1997 BCJ No 808 (Prov Ct). Bisgould also mentions *R v Pedersen*, 2005 BCPC 160 and *R v Piasentin*, 2008 ABPC 164.

89 *Mens rea*, "guilty mind," most frequently refers to criminal intent, the state of mind required for an individual to be held criminally liable. For most crimes, there are two elements of proof: the *actus reus* and the *mens rea*. The *actus reus*, "guilty act," generally refers to the conduct that constitutes the criminal act; whereas *mens rea* constitutes knowledge of the circumstances of the criminal act and foresight or intention respecting the consequences of the criminal act. There are various mental states of *mens rea*, for example, wilfulness, intent, knowledge, and recklessness. These states of mind may be proven subjectively or objectively depending on the criminal act. Lesser, regulatory offences may be strict liability offences where *mens rea* does not have to be proven in relation to

some, or all, of the *actus reus*. See CED edition (online), *Criminal Law – Offences* "Mens Rea" (I.2.(c).(i)); CED edition (online), *Criminal Law – Offences* "Actus Reus" (I.2.(b).(i).

90 *R v McHugh*, 50 C.R. 263, 51 M.P.R. 173, [1966] 1 C.C.C. 170 (N.S.C.A) [*McHugh* cited to C.C.C.]; applied in *R v McHugh* [1996] 1 C.C.C. 170, 50 C.R. 263, 51 M.P.R. 173 has been cited as providing the definition of wilfulness in *R v Dominic*, [2009] BCJ No 949 locus para 60, 2009 BCPC; *R v Hughes*, [2008] BCJ No 973 locus para 8, 2008 BCSC 676; *R v Lewis*, [2011] NJ No 251 locus para 18, among approximately twenty others.

91 *R v Radmore*, [1993] R.J.Q. 215 (C.Q.). Discussed in *R c Starnino* [1998] JQ No 4444 at paras 51–5.

92 Recall that s 446(1)(b), under which Mr Radmore was charged, is an instance of those rare human-animal interactions where the cruelty of an act is defined not by necessity but by its performance. Thus, the *Ménard* reasoning does not apply.

93 *R v Higgins* (B.), 1996 CanLII 11699 (NL SCTD).

94 Perhaps foreshadowing the disappointing result, the court describes the discipline the cat endured giving rise to the cruelty charge in an amused fashion. Ibid. at para 3.

95 *Higgins, supra* note 93 at para 3.

96 The *Code*.

97 *Higgins, supra* note 93 at para 9.

98 Ibid. at para 17.

99 Ibid. at para 10.

100 Ibid. at para 11–12.

101 Ibid. at para 16.

102 Ibid. at para 17.

103 The high *mens rea* threshold has been maintained in numerous recent cases and continues to be a barrier to applying anti-cruelty legislation in a meaningful way to protect animals. See for example, *R v Guess*, 2000 BCCA 547; and *R v Hnatiuk*, 2000 ABQB 314 (CanLII). Bisgould also cites the following cases as examples of the uncertain nature of the *mens rea* component of the offence: *R v Clarke*, 2001 CanLII 12453 (NLPC); *R v Vieira*, 2006 BCPC 288; *R v Blanchard*, 2007 CanLII 52982 (Ont SCJ). Bisgould, *Animals and the Law*, 71.

104 *R v Gerling*, 2016 BCCA 72, 2016 CarswellBC 347, para 27. This interpretation was presaged in the lower court BC decision of *R v Fountain*, 2013 BCPC 193, 2013 CarswellBC 2225.

105 *Gerling, supra* note 104, at para 27, per Chiasson J.

106 Ibid.

107 Ibid. at para 26.

108 Ibid. Justice Chiasson, speaking for the Court, also noted that the presumption in s.445.1(3) did not apply to s.445(1)(b), which relates to neglect or abandonment cases: "It is not clear to me why the presumption of proof provision, which applies to ss.446(1)(a) and 445.1(1)(a) does not apply to s.445(1)(b). This creates the need for a somewhat complex analysis of the test for *mens rea* which could be avoided." Ibid. at para 40. Indeed, the jurisprudence is confused on this point as well. Lower court decisions have previously held that because s.445(1)(b) "creates a duty of care, a purely subjective *mens rea* is not a required element of proof." *R v Bennett*, [2010] NJ No. 230 (PC), para 226 per Gorman J cited recently in *R v Barrett*, 2015 CarswellNfld 14, 2015 CanLII 2415 (NL PC), para 21. On this interpretation, the discrepancy appears to make sense because s.446(1)(b), as a duty of care negligence-based offence, is already activated through an objective test and so does not require a presumption to ensure it receives an objective reading rather than a subjective one. Yet s.429(1) applies to s.446(1)(b) and so if it always requires a subjective element for wilfulness as *Gerling* suggests, the objective nature of its *mens rea* component is superseded by s.429(1)'s subjective *mens rea*. The subjective *mens rea* standard has not worked to absolve all accused who said they were not aware that their actions would cause harm. But this positive result may be attributed to the fact that the courts in such cases have found that accused's evidence displayed awareness even though the accused denied such awareness. See, for example, *R v Parkinson*, 2016 BCPC 0103, at paras 155, 159.

109 *Parkinson, supra* note 107, at para 183, per Brown PCJ.

110 Ibid. at para 185–8. In this case the Court found that such assertions by Ms Parkinson were not credible.

111 *R v. Way*, 2016 ONCJ 126, 2016 CarswellOnt 3424.

112 Ibid. at para 28, per Horkins J.

113 Ibid. at para 31.

114 Ibid. at para 31–5, per Horkins J. The Court quotes Justice Gorham in Bennett, *supra* note 108 at para 22 directly to say that the provisions are: "*... aimed at establishing a uniform minimum level of care to be provided for those to whom it applies, and this can only be achieved if those under the duty are held to a societal, rather than a personal, standard of conduct.*" Ibid. at para 33, per Horkins J (italics in original).

115 The law has always permitted owners to kill their animals in the manner they choose even when such killing was unnecessary and the animal's life could have been saved through minimal effort of the owners to make alternative arrangements. *Miller* v *State*, 63 S.E. at 571 (Ga. Ct. App. 1909), cited in Francione, *Animals, supra note* 18 at 125 and *Cindar* v. *State*, 300 S.W. 64 at 64–5 (Tex. Crim. App. 1927). Cited ibid. at 128–9.

116 Francione, *Animals, Property, and the Law*, 128. Even *Ménard, supra* note 48 at 467, confirmed not only that the euthanasia of found stray animals is justified, but also so is the euthanasia of non-stray animals at the request of their owners.

117 Francione, *Animals, Property, and the Law*, 145–6, 153.

118 There are a few cases that do not sit entirely within the doctrine.

119 Public pressure, instigated by mainstream media coverage of the treatment of animals, also plays an important role in motivating SPCA prosecutions. For example, in August 2012, the *Toronto Star* did a series of exposes on MarineLand, a popular amusement park and aquarium in Ontario. The public outcry after these articles were published has prompted an SPCA investigation, which as of this writing has led to multiple charges being laid and prosecution pending. See Amara McLaughlin, "Marineland charged with 6 new counts of animal cruelty," *CBC News*, 9 January 2017, perma.cc/UTM3-TM75; Linda Diebel, "Inside Marineland: Star investigation: Former park employees tell of unhealthy water, chronic short staffing, and animal suffering at popular tourist attraction," *Toronto Star*, 15 August 2012, A1; "An aerial view of Marineland," *Toronto Star*, 15 August 2012, A15; "Aquarium water went bad in the afternoon," *Toronto Star*, 15 August 2012, A15; Linda Diebel, "Heartache over Smooshi," *Toronto Star*, 15 August 2012, A15; Linda Diebel, "'She finally died in our arms': Star investigation ex-employees blame short-staffing at Marineland after adult whales brutally attack baby beluga," *Toronto Star*, 16 August 2012, A1. The response to the articles was also chronicled in the *Toronto Star*. See Linda Diebel, "Marineland faces SPCA inspection: Star investigation; 'I was in tears,' says cabinet minister after reading allegations of animal suffering," *Toronto Star*, 17 August 2012, A1; Graham Slaughter, "Marineland protest gathers more supporters after Star stories," *Toronto Star*, 17 August 2012, A10; Graham Slaughter, "Singer Wants Voice Pulled from Commercials," *Toronto Star*, 17 August 2012, A10.

120 The *Code*, ss.445.1–447.1.

121 Only minor "housekeeping" changes had been made to the anti-cruelty sections of the *Code* since 1892. Canada, Department of Justice, *Crimes against Animals: A Consultation Paper* (Ottawa: Communication and Executive Services Branch, 1998), 1.

122 See Amber Prince, "What's Wrong *with Canada's Animal Cruelty Laws? Bill C-50, a Touchstone for Change* (LLM Thesis, University of Victoria Faculty of Law, 2007), UVicSPACE http://hdl.handle.net/1828/2470, 8–17, discussing the sources of the philosophic and economic theories that

underlie the original *Criminal Code* provisions. See also David Favre and Vivien Tsang, "The Development of Anti-Cruelty Laws during the 1800s," *Detroit College Law Review* (1993), discussing the way in which changes in approach to animals in the 1860s and 1870s made the adoption of animal cruelty laws possible in the United States in the first place – but also the way in which the legal approach to animals has not progressed beyond that nineteenth-century formation, particularly in comparison with the momentum in the movements for women's and children's rights over the same period of time (at 31–2).

123 For example, in a 2009 statement on its website pertaining to the *Criminal Code* anti-cruelty provisions, the Canadian Federation of Humane Societies stated that it had called for reform for over twenty-five years. Humane Canada, "Criminal Code Amendments" (2019), perma.cc /A4E9-ZQ99.

124 John Sorenson, "'Some Strange Things Happening in Our Country': Opposing Proposed Changes in Anti-Cruelty Law in Canada," *Social and Legal Studies* 12.3. (2003): 380.

125 Department of Justice, *Crimes against Animals*, 120.

126 More than 40,000 letters were received. Kim Lunman, "Animal-rights legislation faces delay in Senate," *Globe and Mail*, 22 November 2002, A10.

127 Bill C-17, *An Act to Amend the Criminal Code (Cruelty to Animals, Disarming a Peace Officer and Other Amendments) and the Firearms Act (Technical Amendments)*, 2nd Sess., 36th Parl., 1999.

128 Ibid. at cl 2, s.181.1(1)(a).

129 The original consultation paper (Department of Justice, *Crimes against Animals*) repeatedly emphasized that any proposed reform would "recognize that our society considers it acceptable to use animals in various industries and activities" (at 4) and that new provisions would "not restrict or otherwise interfere with normal and regulated activities involving animals, including hunting, fishing, and slaughter for food" (at 5). Darian M. Ibrahim argues that this focus on episodic violence in anti-cruelty legislation is the unavoidable result of the property status of animals:

> As Professor Francione has explained, economic theory tells us that rational property owners will only harm their animal property for good reason ... Therefore anticruelty statutes only need to protect against the irrational property owner – one who causes or allows harm to his property that is of no benefit to society. Viewed in this manner, the focus of anticruelty statutes on the prevention of gratuitous suffering is effectively a regulation of the irrational property owner, while the conduct of rational property owners is exempted. (Ibrahim, "The Anticruelty Statute: A Study in Animal Welfare," 187)

130 Sorenson, "'Some Strange Things Happening,'" 381–2.

131 Department of Justice, *Crimes against Animals*, 3. The consultation paper's comments give examples of studies showing links between animal abuse and mass murder, serial killings, and domestic violence. Ibid.

132 Ibid.

133 Emphasis added.

134 Emphasis added.

135 Gérald Lafrenière, Legislative Backgrounder to *Bill C-17: An Act to Amend the Criminal Code (Cruelty to Animals, Disarming a Peace Officer and Other Amendments)* and the *Firearms Act (Technical Amendments)*, March 29, 2000, perma.cc/6HCK-3V6V, at text accompanying nn8–9.

136 Bill C-17 at cl 1.

137 David Redmalm, "Pet Grief: When Is Non-Human Life Grievable," *Sociological Review* 63.1 (2015): 19.

138 The document created by the Parliamentary Services Branch to explain the bill to Parliamentarians in "plain language" said the following regarding this placement change:

> This modification is more than merely cosmetic since it would change the way the *Criminal Code* regards animals in that the cruelty to animals offences would no longer be treated, in large part, as property crimes. In fact, one of the premises of this proposed legislation 'is that all animals feel pain and are deserving of legal protection from negligence or intentional cruelty.' Thus, animals would no longer be regarded essentially as property but rather as beings that feel pain. (footnotes omitted)

See Lafreniere, "Legislative Backgrounder to *Bill C-17*." See also F.C. DeCoste, "Animals and Political Community: Preliminary Reflections Prompted by Bill C-10," *Alberta Law Review* 40 (2002): 1069, for an example of someone who opposed the changes, recognizing that their potential power lay in this symbolic shift: "The novelty of the Bill cannot ... be said to rest on the substance of the protection it provides animals overall as compared to the former regime. It does innovate however, as regards the status of animals in our *legal imaginations*" (emphasis added).

139 Bill C-17 at cl 2.

140 Brighten, "Aboriginal Peoples," 44. Section 445, for example, is limited to the protection of "dogs, birds or animals that are not cattle and are *kept for a lawful purpose* ..." The *Code*, s.555(1)(a) (emphasis added). As Brighten notes, although s.445.1(1)(a), which, it will be recalled, provides the residual catchall for all "unnecessary pain, suffering or injury" does not distinguish between domestic or wild animals through any of its wording on a literal reading, a prosecution under this provision in relation to a wild animals has never gone forward. Ibid., 44. Furthermore, Brighten notes that the Department of Justice, through testimony at committee hearings regarding amending the anti-cruelty provisions and government

reports, has formed the opinion that the anti-cruelty provisions, housed as they are in Part XI of the *Code* dealing with property crimes, do not apply to wild animals. Ibid., 44–5. Brighten aptly observes that the Department of Justice's interpretation cannot be easily reconciled with case law, including *Ménard*, where s.445.1(1)(a) was applied to stray animals, which, though not "wild," are not owned either. Ibid., 45n24. The Department of Justice in Committee Proceedings as acknowledged the discordance. Ibid., 45n26.

141 Bill C-17 at cl 2, s.182.1(8).

142 Indeed, this is how the Parliamentary Services Branch summarized the purpose of this provision in describing the Bill: Lafreniere, "Legislative Backgrounder to *Bill C-17*," 137.

143 This is a point that the Canadian Federation of Humane Societies made repeatedly in its written and oral submissions. See for example its discussion of an almost identical successor bill in Canadian Federation of Humane Societies, *Legal Analysis Re: Bill C-15B Section 15 Cruelty to Animals* (2011), https://web.archive.org/web/20110607200659/http://cfhs.ca/law/legal_analysis.

144 Bill C-17 at cl 2, s.182.2(1)(e)(f)(g) and (h). This bill would have made it an offence for anyone who

> in any manner encourages, promotes, arranges, assists at or receives money for the fighting or baiting of animals; (f) trains an animal to fight other animals; (g) builds, makes, makes, maintains, keeps or allows to be built, made, maintained or kept a cockpit or any other arena for the fighting of animals on premises he or she owns or occupies; (h) promotes, arranges, conducts, assists in, receives money for or takes part in any meeting, competition, exhibition, pastime, practice, display or event at or in the course of which captive animals are liberated by hand, trap, contrivance or any other means for the purpose of being shot when they are liberated; or (i) being the owner, occupier or person in charge of any premises, permits the premises or any part of the premises to be used in the course of an activity referred to in paragraph (e), (f) or (h).

To compare this to the provision existing at that time, recall that s.445.1(1)(b) only prohibited anyone who "in any manner encourages, aids or assists at the fighting or baiting of animals or birds." The *Code*, 445.1(1)(b) (now amended).

145 Ibid. at cl 2, s.182.1(1)(b).

146 Prince, "What's Wrong," 61–2.

147 CFHS, "Legal Analysis," 14.

148 Bill C-17 at cl 2, ss.182.1(3)–(4).

149 Ibid. at cl 2, ss.182.1(5)(a). Section 182.1(6) stipulated that a violation of a court ownership ban made under s.182.1(5)(a) would be treated as a

summary conviction carrying the traditional six months' imprisonment as well as possible liability for a fine of $2,000 or less.

150 Ibid. at cl 2, ss.182.1(5)(b).

151 Ibid. at cl 2, s.182.1(7).

152 The CFHS (a welfarist organization) and the Animal Alliance of Canada (a rights-based organization) co-drafted the Bill, which animal protection organizations generally endorsed. Georges R Dupras, *Values in Conflict: Reflections of an Animal Advocate* (Bloomington: iUniverse, 2011), 28. Note, however, as discussed above, that while large and small advocacy organizations alike ended up supporting the bill, consultation in front of the House of Commons Standing Committee on Justice and Human Rights was skewed toward national professionalized animal welfare organizations. Sorenson, "Some Strange Things Happening," 382.

153 Prince, "What's Wrong," 73–5.

154 Sorenson, "'Some Strange Things Happening,'" 378. For a sampling of some of the statements in the House detailing this resistance, see Canada, Parliament, *House of Commons Debate* [hereafter HCD] "June 3, 2002," Lipad, http://www.lipad.ca/full/2002/06/03/14/ at 14.

155 Over the years, closely drafted successor bills introduced in the House, in order, were Bill C-15, Bill C-15B, Bill C-10, Bill C-10B, *An Act to Amend the Criminal Code (Cruelty to Animals)*, 2nd Sess., 37th Parl., 2003; Bill C-22, *An Act to Amend the Criminal Code (Cruelty to Animals)*, 3rd Sess., 37th Parl., 2004; Bill C-50, *An Act to Amend the Criminal Code (Cruelty to Animals)*, 1st Sess., 38th Parl., 2005; Bill C-373, *An Act to Amend the Criminal Code (Cruelty to Animals)*, 1st Sess, 39th Parl., 2006; and Bill C-558, *An Act to Amend the Criminal Code (Cruelty to Animals)*, 2nd Sess., 39th Parl., 2008. Sorenson, "'Some Strange Things Happening,'" 378. The Senate bill that was similar to C-17 was Bill S-213, 2006. In 2002, Bill C-15B came extremely close to passing, when all parties in the House supported it, but the Senate stood in its way. It was reinstated following prorogation of Parliament in September 2002 as Bill C-10 a few months later, at which time the Senate divided the bill into two parts. *Ibid.* Bill C-10B passed all three readings in the House of Commons but met with resistance in the Senate, which eventually caused a stalemate between the two branches of Parliament.

156 Antonio Verbera, "The Politics of Animal Anti-Cruelty Legislation in Canada: An Analysis of Parliamentary Debates on Amending the Criminal Code," (2012), Electronic Theses and Dissertations, Paper 241, 7, 17.

157 See for example HCD, No 127, 25 September 2003, at 1708 (Hon. Elinor Caplan). This gives a typical example of the back-and-forth between the Senate and the House over the specifics of the animal cruelty legislation.

For a chart providing a brief summary of each bill and its main reason for demise, see Verbera, "The Politics," 17.

158 The Hansard debates reveal repeated statements to this effect both by government MPs and other parliamentarian proponents. See Prince, "What's Wrong," 76–7, 87–8, and Sorenson, "'Some Strange Things Happening,'" 383–5.

159 Prince, "What's Wrong," 89–90; Sorenson, "'Some Strange Things Happening,'" 383–5.

160 See Christina G Skibinsky, "Changes in Store for the Livestock Industry – Canada's Recurring Proposed Animal Cruelty Amendments," *Saskatchewan Law Review* 175 (2005), for a discussion of the concerns raised by the agriculture industry. See also Sorenson, "'Some Strange Things Happening,'" 386–7, for a discussion of the concerns of the medical research industry.

161 Verbera, "The Politics," 17; Bill C-10B.

162 Sorenson, "'Some Strange Things Happening,'" 379.

163 Ibid., 384.

164 Ibid., 385.

165 Ibid.

166 Ibid., 387–91. Sorenson identifies the image of the Loving Rancher, as presented during the debates, as one method of normalizing institutionalized cruelty. Again, for a sample of MPs' remarks conveying reasons for industry resistance to the bill, see *HCD*, "June 3, 2002."

167 Sorenson, "'Some Strange Things Happening,'" 386, 394–5.

168 Ibid., 386.

169 Ibid., 382.

170 Sorenson discusses the remarks made by Robert Gardiner, representative for the CFHS during the hearings before the standing committee, particularly his involvement with trapping and animal research groups. Gardiner, among other things, mentions his own involvement with an experiment that "burned the skin of pigs with a blowtorch." Ibid., 382–3.

171 Ibid., 390.

172 See ibid., 106.

173 Brighten, "Aboriginal Peoples," 47–8.

174 Ibid., 66.

175 Ibid.

176 Ibid., 48–50. When eligible according to common law tests derived by settler-colonial courts, certain practices and land claims of Indigenous peoples in Canada are protected as rights under s.35 of the Constitution Act, 1982, being Schedule B to the Canada Act 1982 (U.K.), 1982, c. 11. For an overview of the jurisprudence in this area through the lens of Indigenous critical studies, see John Borrows, "Challenging Historical

Frameworks: Aboriginal Rights, The Trickster, and Originalism," *Canadian Historical Review* 98.1 (2017).

177 Brighten, "Aboriginal Peoples," 50.

178 Deckha, "Welfarist *and* Imperial," 520–5.

179 Ibid., 525–37.

180 This premise, of course, becomes visible in the legislative speeches that MPs delivered before and after the exemption became a source of conflict between the House and the Senate. As noted above (see notes 156–7), Parliamentarians repeatedly sought to ensure that the changes would not disrupt normative industry practices.

181 Brighten, "Aboriginal Peoples," 48–50.

182 Deckha, "Welfarist *and* Imperial."

183 Brighten, "Aboriginal Peoples," 52–4, 69–70. This is not to endorse Indigenous rights to use animals in traditional ways. Such uses can be equally anthropocentric and harmful to animals, though the intent and vision of human-animal relations behind Indigenous killing may be laudable from a critical animal studies perspective. See Craig Womack, "There Is No Respectful Way to Kill an Animal," *Studies in American Indian Literatures* 25.4 (2013). For more on how to respond to cultural rights vis-à-vis animals without enacting imperialism, but still contesting the anthropocentrism that can reside in Indigenous worldviews, see Maneesha Deckha, "Animal Justice, Cultural Justice: A Posthumanist Response to Cultural Rights in Animals," *Journal of Animal Law and Ethics* 2 (2007); Greta Gaard, "Tools for a Cross-Cultural Feminist Ethics: Exploring Ethical Contexts and Contents in the Makah Whale Hunt," *Hypatia* 16.1 (2001); and Will Kymlicka and Sue Donaldson, "Animal Rights and Aboriginal Rights," in *Canadian Perspectives on Animals and the Law*, ed. Peter Sankoff, Vaughan Black, and Katie Sykes (Toronto: Irwin Law, 2015).

184 Brighten, "Aboriginal Peoples," 70.

185 Ibid., 67. Brighten is further concerned that the exemption may actually erode rather than respect Indigenous sovereignty. Ibid., 67–9.

186 Ibid. at 60.

187 Ibid.

188 Ibid.

189 Ibid., 61.

190 Ibid., 63.

191 Ibid., 63–4. For an argument as to why even Indigenous "humane" hunting methods can never be respectful, see Womack, "There Is No Respectful Way," 182.

192 For example, the Ontario *Animals for Research Act* specifically exempts scientific research activities from criminal sanctions. *Animals for Research*

Act, s.18(9): "The *Ontario Society for the Prevention of Cruelty to Animals Act* does not apply in respect of animals in the possession of the operator of a registered research facility or of a licensed operator of a supply facility." Many provincial anti-cruelty statutes also contain an explicit exclusion. Bisgould provides the example of Alberta's *Animal Protection Act*, which the author recognizes as typical of provincial legislation. This act specifies that "there is no offence if the distress results from an activity carried on in accordance with the regulations, or with reasonable and generally accepted practices of animal care, management, husbandry, hunting, fishing, trapping, pest control, or slaughter." Bisgould, *Animals and the Law*, 107, referring to *Animal Protection Act*, RSA 2000, c. A-41 at s.2(2). Other examples can be found in Manitoba's *The Animal Care Act*, CCSM, c. A84 at s.2(2), and Nova Scotia's *Animal Protection Act*, SNS 2008, c. 33 at s.21(4). The *Code* itself does not contain an explicit exclusion, but the case law has interpreted it to effectuate the same result, as I've argued above.

193 Recall that the House rejected the Senate's proposal on the basis that it wanted one standard for all Canadians. Brighten, "Aboriginal Peoples," 47–8.

194 Chronologically these were: Bill S-204, *An Act to Amend the Criminal Code (Cruelty to Animals)*, 2nd Sess., 38th Parl., 2004; Bill S-213, *An Act to Amend the Criminal Code (Cruelty to Animals)*, 2nd Sess., 38th Parl., 2006; and Bill S-203, *An Act to Amend the Criminal Code (Cruelty to Animals)*, 1st Sess., 39th Parl., 2007.

195 Bill S-203.

196 Verbera, "The Politics," 28–9.

197 Ibid., 17.

198 As Verbera notes, senators from the Progressive Conservative Party of Canada and the Conservative Alliance (as they then were), along with the Bloc Québécois, did not support any of the bills from 1999 onward that contained actual substantive amendments, however modest. Ibid., 28; Joan Bryden, "Liberals scrap over animal-cruelty bills," *Globe and Mail*, 26 February 2007, A11.

199 The *Code*, s.445.1(2). The jail times and fines for animal cruelty pursuant to s.446(2), which engages neglect, abandonment, and failure to provide the necessities of life, were increased as well, but not to the same level as for violations of the main anti-cruelty provision under s.445.1. An indictable offence under s.446(2)(a) is now punishable by two years' imprisonment, and a summary offence under s.446(2)(b) now carries a penalty of up to $5,000, although the possible incarceration time remains the same – six months. The *Code*, s.446(2).

200 Under s.447.1(1), a judge can prohibit a convicted person from owning, possessing, controlling, or residing with an animal for as long

a period as the judge chooses and, in the case of a second or further offence, for at least five years. The *Code*, ss.447.1(1) and (2).

201 *R v Munroe*, 2010 ONCJ 226, per J. O'Donnell as cited in Zeynep Husrevoglu, "Cruelty to Animals – Criminal Code Amendments: Before and After Bill S-203," *Animal Justice Review*, 20 November 2012, perma.cc /RLG8-NZRG.

202 Animal Justice Canada reviewed forty-eight reported cases before the sentencing changes came into effect and compared them with results for the ten cases reported as of 2012 (i.e., post-amendment). The analysis revealed that in the majority of pre-amendment cases the court imposed a suspended sentence coupled with two years' probation. The longest jail time meted out was eighteen months. When the ten reported cases post-amendment were examined, it was found that all cases proceeded summarily despite the possibility of proceeding by indictment. The harshest sentence imposed was found to be jail time of twelve months coupled with three years' probation and a twenty-five-year ban on owning or residing with an animal. This harshest sentence was imposed for *R v Munroe* (see above), in which the judge commented on the unprecedented magnitude of the penalty increase. The review concluded that stiffer penalties had made an impact – albeit limited – in these early post-amendment cases. Husrevoglu, "Cruelty to Animals."

203 *R v Alcorn*, 2015 ABCA 182, 2015 CarswellAlta 948. For its part, the British Columbia Court of Appeal refused to lower a sentence of nine months for the killing and evisceration and videotaping thereof a family cat and dog in *R v Bourque*, 2013 BCCA 447, 2013 CarswellBC 3094. The Ontario Court of Appeal took a similarly positive step in *R. v. Wright*, 2014 ONCA 675, in which it described the 2008 amendments as a signal that Parliament was determined to deter and punish those who engage in acts of cruelty to animals; thus, it allowed an appeal from the Crown to increase the respondent's sentence to nine months, commenting that the original sentence was "manifestly inadequate." Ibid. at para 1.

204 Ibid. at para 42.

205 Ibid. at para 3. The court classified this act as sadism. Ibid. at para 42.

206 Ibid. at para 41.

207 Ibid. at para 41.

208 Referencing Fraser CJA dissenting in *Reece and Zoocheck v Edmonton* (see note 49) that "a civilized society should show reasonable regard for vulnerable animals."

209 Brighten, "Aboriginal Peoples," n34.

210 Canadian Federation of Humane Societies, "Bill S-203," 9 June 2009, http://web.archive.org/web/20090609103648/http://cfhs.ca/law /bill_s_203/.

211 Brighten, "Aboriginal Peoples," 46.

212 In *R v Munroe*, 2012 ONSC 4768, 2012 CarswellOnt 11816, a sentencing case that involved months of the accused torturing his girlfriend's two dogs, Justice Code commented on the inadequacy of pre-2008 sentences by observing the review his colleague Justice Quantz had undertaken in *R v Connors* [2011] B.C.J. (B.C. Prov. Ct.), and relating it to the facts before him. Justice Code writes:

> Quantz J. exhaustively reviewed the case law under the old legislation, where discharges, conditional sentences, and short intermittent sentences had routinely been imposed for the cruel and sadistic killing or injuring of cats and dogs. An effective sentence of seven months imprisonment in the present case, for a first offender with Munroe's otherwise impeccable antecedents, recognizes the change in the appropriate range of sentence brought about by the April 17, 2008 legislative reforms. (*R v Munroe*, 2012, para 96, Code J.)

The reforms also led to a seven-month incarceration period at the Alberta Court of Appeal despite the appellate court's recognition of Parliament's intent to stiffen penalties.

213 *R v Perrin*, 2012 NSPC 134, 2012 CarswellNS 1092, para 3 per Joskins PCJ.

214 One court has partly attributed Parliament's intention to raise the penalties in the 2008 amendments to the growing awareness that "cruelty to animals presages other more chilling possible adult behaviours." *R v Chailler*, 26 Aug 2013 unreported (121450597P1), p. 6, as cited by *R v C*, 2015 ABPC 65, 2015 CarswellAlta 536, para 22, per Judge GJ Gaschler. Justice Gashler, citing *Habermehl*, at p. 2, also attributed the legislative change to "widespread concerns that the Criminal Code provisions concerning cruelty to animals had fallen drastically out of step with current social values ..." *R v C*, para 23.

215 See the cased mentioned in nn200–2 and 211–13. See also *R v SAS*, 2011 BCPC 470 (CanLII) where the accused received six months for killing a cat to spite his girlfriend.

216 *Perrin* (see note 213) at paras 75, 77. The accused also had to pay a victim surcharge of $100. Ibid. at para 78. The Court applied a ten-year ban regarding his ability to own or have custody of an animal. *Ibid* at para 79.

217 Ibid. at paras 31–49.

218 Ibid. at paras 48–9, likening it to previous offences described as such by Judge MJ Brecknell in *R v Pederson*, [2005] BCJ No 985 (BCPC) at para 49.

219 Ibid. at paras 53, 70.

220 *R v Helfer*, 19 June 2014, unreported, Ontario Court of Justice.

221 *R v Alcorn*, ABPC December, 2014, unreported, (130018757P1), aff'd *Alcorn*, see n64.

222 *Chailler*, n213

223 *R v Munroe*, 2012, see n211.

224 *R v McKinnon*, ABPC 7 October 2014, unreported (140370248P1).

225 *R v Chalmers*, ABPC 23 April 2013, unreported (110779394P1).

226 *R v Rodgers*, 2012 OJ No. 6287.

227 *R v Tremblay*, 2012 BCPC 410 (CanLII).

228 *Connors*, see n211.

229 *R v Anderson*, ABPC 29 November 2012, unreported (110049731P1).

230 *Habermehl*, see n64.

231 *Connors*, see n211, para 38.

232 The *Code*, s.718. Section 718.2 sets out specific criteria for courts to consider, including the presence of "relevant aggravating or mitigating circumstances relating to the offence or the offender." Ibid., s.781.2(a).

233 At least one court, in *obiter*, has observed and registered disagreement with this valuation. In *R v Tremblay*, (see note 227), a case involving a "protracted, savage and excruciating assault" of his girlfriend's dog (para 6), the court remarked:

> If Mr. Tremblay had attacked a human being in the same way he attacked King, the appropriate charge might have been aggravated assault, contrary to section 268 of the *Criminal Code*. Aggravated assault is an indictable, rather than hybrid, offence carrying a maximum sentence of 14 years' imprisonment. A moral philosopher might conclude that an assault on an animal is no less worthy of denunciation, and should not attract a lesser punishment, than a similar assault on a human being. However, Parliament has clearly espoused a contrary view, and that is a matter for Parliament, not for me.
> (Ibid. at para 22, per Goudge J)

The 2015 case of *R v Rowe*, 2015 ONCJ 596, 2015 CarswellOnt 16365, involving sentencing for a man who threw his dog up a flight of six stairs and then attacked him the next day, also contains *obiter* remarks from the judge that show resistance to lenient results. In *Rowe*, both sides had agreed that the offender should receive only sixty days of incarceration; since the offender had already served 40 days pre-trial he had effectively served all of his sentence on a 1.5 ratio applied to time served. Ibid. at paras 7–8. The judge went along with this joint submission as to the proper custodial period for sentence but remarked that "60 days is on the lower end of the acceptable range." Ibid., para 9, per Justice Cladwell. He further imposed a three-year probationary period and a four-year ban under s.447.1. Ibid. at paras 14–15. Justice Caldwell also made other remarks that press against the propertied view of animals although, again, in a non-consequential way. He observed that

> (a)nimals, particularly very small animals such as Fendi, are extremely vulnerable creatures given in part their size, inability to articulate verbally, and the fact that they are totally subject to the control of their owners. There is no question that they experience both fear and pain. Further, Mr. Rowe tossed Fendi up the stairs as if she was an inanimate object … I find that Mr. Rowe should have no contact absolutely with Fendi over the term of his probation.

I am told that it is Fendi that will be penalized as permanent alternative care arrangements will need to be found. I find it difficult, however, to see how it is in Fendi's interests to be returned to Mr. Rowe's care or for him to have contact with her given what occurred. (ibid. at paras 33–5)

234 Section 718.2(b) of the *Code* states that "a sentence should be similar to sentences imposed on similar offenders for similar offences committed in similar circumstances." A case that illustrates this pressure is *R v Haaksman*, 2013 ONCJ 66, 2013 CarswellOnt 2225 involving sentencing of two accused for the drowning of a companion animal dog. Justice J.G. Griffin decided upon incarceration periods of three months for one of the accused and two months for the other but only after noting that in three cases involving much more violent acts (compared to deliberately drowning the dog by attaching a cinder block to his body before throwing him in a lake) with many more extensive injuries to the animals involved, the convicted parties only received custodial sentences of six months. Ibid., pp. 10, 13. It is clear that Justice Griffin struggled to apply the sentencing provisions in this case, in which the two men convicted were of somewhat diminished capacity and lacking in life skills. Ibid., p. 12. He observed before reaching his conclusion on sentencing that the two men would be vulnerable in prison just as the dog was vulnerable, intimating the problems with a carceral approach in general. Ibid., p. 12. For a discussion of how longer jail terms for animal cruelty does not serve animals or broader social justice goals, see Justin Marceau, *Beyond Cages: Animal Law and Criminal Punishment* (Cambridge: Cambridge University Press, 2019).

235 For examples of other cases where the acts were considered egregious but the sentences were extremely lenient see *Habermehl* (note 64).

236 *Perrin* (see note 213), at para 47, per Justice Hoskins. See also *Camardi* (note 214).

237 The *Code*, s.781.03. This provision adopts language identical to that in ss.718.01 and 718.02, where Parliament has entered the same instruction for offences against children and peace or other justice system officers/participants. Ibid., ss.718.01, 718.02.

238 In the seventy-four reported cases since *Ménard* (see note 49), involving charges made under s.445.1(a) or its historical antecedents for physical acts of aggression (as opposed to neglect of animals), one considers a crow (*R v SJ*, 2003 CarswellNfld 222) and two consider horses (*R v M(M)*, 2002 CarswellOnt 3007; *R v Paish*, [1977] 2 WWR 526); the rest concern domestic dogs and cats that are someone's companion animals. The heightened concern for companion animals is also evinced by judicial remarks such as those of Justice St Pierre in *R v Whitlock*, 2013 BCPC 153, 2013 CarswellBC 1859, that "pets are people's soul mates and, you know, even surrogate children." Ibid. at para 83. It is worth noting that Justice St Pierre made these comments in the context of affirming audience

members' strong reactions to the actions of the offender, who had beaten his dog to death, given that "the connections obviously that people form with their animals are the longest and strongest and most powerful relationships in many people's lives." Ibid. He proceeded, however, to state that such emotions do not excuse the vigilantism anyone might be contemplating conducting to register disgust once the offender was back in the community. Justice St Pierre only imposed a custodial sentence of sixty days in jail. Ibid. at paras 83–5.

239 Socially acceptable physical discipline for dogs and cats is not treated as abuse. See e.g. *R v Kyle*, 2015 ONJC 375, 2015 CarswellOnt 10598, where swatting the nose of dog to teach him a lesson was not contested but the use of a cattle prod on dogs by a doggy day care owner was in *R v Sanaee*, 2016 ABCA 289, 2016 CarswellAlta 1843.

240 Bill C-558, introduced by NDP MP Penny Priddy on 4 June 2008, died on the Order Paper in the fall of 2008 when Parliament prorogued for the upcoming election. Bill C-558, *An Act to Amend the Criminal Code (Cruelty to Animals)*, 2nd Sess., 39th Parl., 2008. Almost immediately after the election, on 1 December 2008, Bill C-229 was introduced by Liberal MP Mark Holland and was re-introduced a further two times. Bill C-229, *An Act to Amend the Criminal Code (Cruelty to Animals)*, 3rd Sess., 40th Parl., 2008. In June 2011, NDP MP Peggy Nash unsuccessfully introduced Bill C-232. Bill C-232, *An Act to Amend the Criminal Code (Cruelty to Animals)*, 1st Sess., 40st Parl., 2011. Later that year in September, Liberal MP Hedy Fry introduced two bills (Bill C-274 and Bill C-277). These were consolidated into Bill C-558, *An Act to Amend the Criminal Code (Cruelty to Animals)*, 2nd Sess., 41st Parl., 2011. Verbera, "The Politics," 18.

241 A coalition of nine animal protection organizations, at least five of them non-welfarist (Animal Alliance of Canada, Animal Alliance Environment Voters Party of Canada, Canadian Coalition for Farm Animals, International Fund for Animal Welfare, and Zoocheck), supported the bill. See International Fund for Animal Welfare, "New bill would make significant improvement to animal welfare laws in Canada," 3 March 2016, http://web.archive.org/web/20160502150725/http://www.ifaw.org/canada/news/new-bill-would-make-significant-improvements-animal-welfare-laws-canada.

242 In 2015, Canada imported over 300,000 pounds of shark fins according to a report by the *Globe and Mail*. Meanwhile, Australia and ten states in the United States have banned fin importation. Canada, Parliament, *House of Commons Debate*, 42nd Parl, 1st Sess., Vol. 148, No. 83 (28 September 2016) at 5245 (Nathaniel Erskine-Smith). It would have still been possible to import detached shark fins where the importer received ministerial approval on the basis that the importation was for research

or conservation purposes. *Bill C-246, Modernizing Animal Protections Act,* R.S., c. C-46, 1st Sess., 42nd Parl., 2016, s.12(2).

243 This would have occurred through amendments to the *Canada Consumer and Product Safety Act*, SC 2010, c. 21. Bill C-246, cl 13.

244 This would have occurred through amendments to the *Textile Labelling Act*, R.S.C. 1985, c T-10. Ibid., cl 12.

245 See note 242 at 5245 (Nathaniel Erskine-Smith).

246 *HCD*, 42nd Parl., 1st Sess., Vol. 148, No. 51 (9 May 2016) at 3035–6 (Nathaniel Erskine-Smith). See Bill C-246 (note 252), ss.3–4.

247 See note 242 at 5237 (Sheila Malcolmson); see also note 242 at 5238 (Arif Virani). MP Malcolmson also pointed out the overwhelming public support for such a ban in Canada. Ibid.

248 See note 246 at 3035–6 (Nathaniel Erskine-Smith).

249 See samples of the debate in the House at *HCD*, 42nd Parl., 1st Sess., Vol. 148, No 51 (9 May 2016).

250 Kim, *Dangerous Crossings*, 102–3; David Grimm, *Citizen Canine: Our Evolving Relationships with Cats and Dogs* (New York: Public Affairs, 2014); Andrew Jensen Kerr, "Pedagogy in Translation: Teaching Animal Law in China," *Asian Journal of Legal Education* 1.1 (2014): 34–5, 38. Of course, some businesses are invested in the trade in shark fins and legally challenged a by-law in Toronto that had taken effect at the municipal level for being *ultra vires* municipal jurisdiction. The challenge was successful and has led to the repeal of the ban in Toronto and a handful of other Ontario cities that have passed similar bans. Bans in British Columbia in several cities surrounding Vancouver and on Vancouver Island are still in place. For a detailed outline of these developments see Animal Justice, "Issues: Shark Finning," perma.cc/BEP9-UZ8W.

251 This is not to suggest that all humanized animals would receive similar treatment if the legitimated human use of an animal worked to trump its culturally favourable cultural status. Consider that shelters may release stray dogs that are not claimed by their owners after several days to research facilities, besides destroying them. *Animals for Research Act*, s 20.

252 Peter Sankoff and Camille Labchuk, "The battle to pass Canada's new shark fin import ban," *Animal Justice*, 24 June 2019 (podcast).

253 Kim, *Dangerous Crossings*, 117–21.

254 See note 242 at 5240 (Larry Miller).

255 Ibid.; see also note 246 at 3039 (Robert Sopuck).

256 See note 242 at 5241 (Larry Miller); note 246 at 3039 (Robert Sopuck).

257 See note 242 at 5240 (Larry Miller). The standard of gross negligence is created by the addition of the word "recklessly," so the opening of the proposed general anti-cruelty provision would read: "Everyone commits an offence who, willfully or recklessly ..." Opponents argue that, like

"brutally or viciously," the term "recklessly" is undefined and therefore the scope of criminal prosecution is left too broad, potentially including anyone who is "clumsy, incompetent, or unlucky." See note 245 at 3039 (Robert Sopuck).

258   See note 242 at 5240 (Larry Miller).

259   Ibid.; see also note 241 at 5244 (Bob Zimmer).

260   *R. v. D.L.W.*, [2016] 1 SCR 402, 2016 SCC 22 (CanLII). The issue before the court was the definition of bestiality in the *Code*, which the majority held pursuant to statutory interpretive principles pivoted on penetration. Animal Justice, a national organization pursuing legal protections and enforcement of existing laws for animals, acquired intervener status in the case and argued that "bestiality' should cover all types of sexual activity between humans and an animal, given animals' vulnerable and non-consenting status in these acts. See the Sankoff and Labchuk, "Factum of the Intervenor," perma.cc/7LYY-JZTZ, paras 2–3.

261   See note 242 at 5238 (Arif Virani); see also note 242 at 5245 (Nathaniel Erskine-Smith).

262   See note 246 at 3035–6 (Nathaniel Erskine-Smith).

263   Ibid.

264   Ibid.

265   See note 242 at 5245 (Nathaniel Erskine-Smith).

266   See note 242 at 5238 (Arif Virani).

267   Member Nathaniel Erskine-Smith, who introduced this bill, sought to clarify misinterpretation of it among its opponents during second reading. In his remarks, he clarified that "[w]hen I introduced the bill I said the bill would bring our laws into the 21st century. I overstated the case. This is a basket of modest measures, all things considered, to improve our animal protection laws." He sought to allay fears that the bill would give animals rights by reminding his audience that the legislation was identical to earlier versions of the bill that had received support from the Cattlemen's Association and the Dairy Farmers of Canada. He also allied himself with "farmers, fishermen, and anglers against animal cruelty" to press forward the point that the bill "is about ending animal abuse, not ending animal use." See note 242 at 5245 (Nathaniel Erskine-Smith). For other examples see note 242 at 5237 (Sheila Malcolmson). Her closing remarks read:

> In conclusion, I want to say again that this bill is not about hunting and fish-
> ing. If it were, I would not support it. This is about animal abuse, not animal
> use. The bill applies to criminal abuse, not to lawful activities involving
> animals. My riding is built on commercial fisheries. It is full of hunters and
> anglers doing vital preservation work, and our riding is very dependent on
> recreational and sport fisheries. Because I do not want anyone to fear that

lawful activities like those would ever be affected by this bill, there is an amendment we would propose in committee to clarify that this would not affect lawful hunting and fishing.

268 Jodi Lazare, "'Free Willy' law spotlights contradictions in how Canadians see animal right," *The Conversation*, 8 July 2019, https://theconversation.com.

269 *An Act to amend the Criminal Code and other Acts (ending the captivity of whales and dolphins)*, SC 2019, c. 11.

270 Ibid., c. 11, s.2.

271 Ibid., c. 11, s.2; amended the *Code*, s.445.2(3)–(3.1). The bill also demands that all cetacean performance facilities be licensed. Ibid., s.445.2(4). The penalties are the same as those currently available for a violation of s.445.1 of the *Code*. Ibid., s.445.2(5). The two existing facilities in Canada that house cetaceans are MarineLand and the Vancouver Aquarium. Lazare, "'Free Willy' law."

272 See the sponsor and response speeches made in the Senate during second reading of the bill that evince this elevated cultural status: Canada, Parliament, *Debates of the Senate* [hereafter *CDS*], 42nd Parl., 1st Sess., Vol. 150, No 8 (27 January 2016) 1530 (Hon. Wilfred P Moore); *CDS*, 42nd Parl, 1st Sess., Vol. 150, No. 22 (22 March 2016), 1505 (Hon. Janis G. Johnson).

273 Ontario banned the possession and breeding of orcas in 2015 through an amendment to its anti-cruelty law. *Ontario Society for the Prevention of Cruelty to Animals Act*, RSO 1990, c. O-36, s.11.3.1(1). The amendment, however, permitted the continued possession of orcas already in possession on 22 March 2015. Ibid. at s.11.3.1(2). The statute also lets anyone who acquired an orca after this date but before the amendment received Royal Assent to continue to possess the orca until six months after the amendment came into effect. Ibid., s.11.3.1(3). The Vancouver Parks Board voted in March 2017 to enact a by-law that would prevent the importation and display of cetaceans in the City of Vancouver. The deaths in late 2016, nine days apart, of a mother orca and her adult calf at the aquarium galvanized public petitions and protest. Before the vote, the aquarium had agreed to phase out captivity of cetaceans by 2029, but also announced that it would add to its existing population of three cetaceans following the death of the mother-child dyad by building whale pools and adding whales to their complement. CBC News, "Vancouver Park Board votes to end display of cetaceans at aquarium," 9 March 2017, perma.cc/2X6K-QS2X. For more on the context in which the decision was taken see the full internal recommendation to the Park Board chair and commissioners: General Manager's Office, Vancouver Board of Parks and Rec, "Recommendation," 3 March 2017, perma.cc/KJ5N-TDXN.

274 Thomas Walkom, "Senate bill to free the whales faces a rough ride,"
    Toronto Star, 20 March 2017, perma.cc/Y3QU-R3KC.

275 The Senate bill, S-238, *An Act to Amend the Fisheries Act and the
    Wild Animal and Plant Protection and Regulation of International and
    Interprovincial Trade Act (importation and exportation of shark fins),*
    42nd Parl., 1st Sess., was proposed by the Honourable Michael L.
    MacDonald, a Conservative senator. Review of the House and Senate
    debate demonstrates widespread cross-party support for the bill and
    disapproval of shark finning. See *CDS,* 42nd Parl., 1st Sess.,
    Vol. 150, No. 121 (16 May 2017), 1510–35 and 1615–25 (Hon Michael L.
    Macdonald); *CDS,* 42nd Parl., 1st Sess., Vol. 150, No. 131 (13 June 2017),
    2045–100 (Hon. Rosa Galvez); *HCD,* 42nd Parl., 1st Sess., Vol. 148,
    No. 395 (1 April 2019), 1830 (Mr Fin Donnelly).There were some
    concerns about the legal implications of the bill for international trade
    obligations and sustainable fisheries; however, these were raised while
    the bill was decidedly supported in principle: *HCD,* 42nd Parl, 1st
    Sess., Vol. 148, No. 395 (1 April 2019) 1845–51 (Mr Sean Casey); *HCD,*
    42nd Parl,. 1st Sess., Vol. 148, No. 407 (1 May 2019) 1820–30 (Mr Toddy
    Doherty). Bill S-238 did not go to third reading. Instead the provisions
    of the bill were inserted into Bill C-68, *An Act to amend the Fisheries Act
    and other Acts In consequence,* 1st Sess., 42nd Parl., 2019, through senate
    amendment. Bill C-68 received Royal Assent on 21 June 2019.

276 The new provisions broaden the scope of animal fighting offences to
    include a wider range of activities. This includes encouraging, promoting,
    arranging and assisting at, receiving money for, or taking part in the
    fighting or baiting of animals and prohibiting any of these activities
    with respect to the training, transporting, or breeding of animals for
    fighting or baiting. Furthermore, the prohibition of cockpits has been
    amended to include the building, keeping, or maintaining of any arena
    for the purposes of fighting any animal. See Bill C-84, *An Act to amend the
    Criminal Code (bestiality and animal fighting),* 1st Sess., 42nd Parl., 2019, s
    2–4; *HCD,* 42nd Parl., 1st Sess., Vol. 148, No. 344 (29 October 2018), 1205
    (Jody Wilson Raybould).

277 Bill C-84. Hansard analysis demonstrates that the bill was largely
    critiqued for not being passed quickly enough or for not going far
    enough. See *HCD,* 42nd Parl., 1st Sess., Vol. 148, No. 344 (29 October
    2018), 1220 (Hon. Michelle Rempel); 1222, (Mr Alistair MacGregor).
    While there was some concern over the form of the provisions, the House
    unanimously voted for the bill to pass third reading: 276 Yay, 0 Nay: *Vote
    No.1311,* 1st Sess., 42nd Parl. (8 May 2019), sitting no. 412 (Mr Lametti).

278 See for example *Ontario Society for the Prevention of Cruelty to Animals
    Act,* note 272, and *Society for the Prevention for Cruelty to Animals Act,*

RSNB 1973, c. S-12. Legislation in two of the territories – the Northwest Territories and Nunavut – only covers dogs; see *Dog Act*, RSNWT 1998, c. D-7.

279 Animal Legal Defense Fund, "2012 Canadian Animal Protection Law Rankings," http://www.aldf.org. For 2012, Manitoba, British Columbia, Ontario, and Nova Scotia received top rankings for legislation containing a wide range of protections, strong enforcement regimes, and high penalties. Prince Edward Island, the Northwest Territories, Quebec, and Nunavut were ranked last, primarily due to the limited range of the territorial legislation.

280 *Ontario Society for the Prevention of Cruelty to Animals Act*.

281 Ibid. at ss.11.1(2)(a), 11.2(6)(a)-(c). Agricultural operations are exempt from following the regulated standards of care (which deal with the provision of food, water, ventilation, space, light, and sanitary conditions) as long as they are following "reasonable and generally accepted practices." See also *Animals for Research Act*, s 18(9), which holds that the owners of registered research facilities are not subject to the provisions of the *Ontario Society for the Prevention of Cruelty to Animals Act*.

282 Ontario O Reg 60/09, s.2(8).

283 *Animal Protection Act*, RSA 2000, c. A-41.

284 *Prevention of Cruelty to Animals Act*, RSBC 1996, C. 372. Prior to the proposed amendments, BC had placed sixth on the Animal Legal Defense Fund's ranking of provincial animal protection laws. See Animal Legal Defense Fund, "Rankings." Although the PCAA provided a wide range of protections for animals, the report indicated that standards of care were ill-defined, that mandatory reporting by veterinarians was lacking, and that prohibitions had been weakened by the limitation of coverage to the owner of the animal. Penalties were set at a maximum of $5,000 or six months' imprisonment for a first offence and $10,000, six months' imprisonment, or both for a second offence. Ibid. at 7.

285 For a representative sample of media coverage, see Pemberton, "SPCA probes 'execution' of 100 sled dogs," *Vancouver Sun*, 1 February 2011, A1; Sunny Dhillon, "Sled dogs' mass gravesite kept secret," *Globe and Mail*, 2 February 2011, S1; Maneesha Deckha, "Law must see animals as more than 'property,'" *Times-Colonist*, 3 February 2011, A10; and Adrian Morrow, "A killing without cruelty is no crime," *Globe and Mail*, 2 February 2011, S2.

286 See Deckha, "Law must see." The sled-dog touring company, Outdoor Adventures, has since claimed that there was no link between the cull and a tourism slump following the Olympics: Pemberton, "Owner takes 'moral responsibility' for dog cull; Outdoor Adventures' Joey Houssian wants to keep business going," *Times-Colonist*, 8 February 2011, A8.

287 Ibid.
288 WorkSafeBC, "Review Decision," 25 January 2011, R0119660 http://web
      .archive.org/web/20110304013214/http://www.cbc.ca/bc/news/bc
      -110131-worksafebc-whistler-dog-cull.pdf.
289 Ibid. The employee, Robert Todd Fawcett, who carried out these acts
      on behalf of his employer also faced animal cruelty charges under
      the *Code* with respect to nine of the dogs' deaths. Despite the court's
      agreement that the suffering for these nine dogs was "horrific" and the
      recognition that multiple aggravating factors were present to create
      moral blameworthiness, Mr Fawecett received a monetary fine of $1,500,
      three years' probation, and 200 hours of community service as his entire
      sentence. No incarceration period or lifetime ban was imposed. *R v
      Fawcett*, 2012 BCPC 421 (CanLII), paras, 2, 21, 32, 51 per Merrick J. Justice
      Merrick prefaced his sentencing decision with the commentary that he
      realized the case had engaged national attention and rightly so and that
      many would expect the maximum incarceration period of five years
      to apply. Ibid. at para 3. He also stated that he had to apply the *Code*'s
      sentencing principles in ss.718 to 718.2 and that he "hope(d) by hearing
      the detailed submissions of counsel, that the community is aware that
      such a sentence would simply be contrary to the principles of sentencing
      and is not a supportable sentence based on the principles of sentencing
      and the circumstances of Mr. Fawcett." Ibid. The Court listed several
      mitigating circumstances including medical evidence that Mr Fawcett
      had entered a dissociative state in conducting the killings after previously
      trying to convince his owner not to "retire" the dogs in such a manner
      and trying to find other homes for them. Ibid. at paras 13, 16–17. About
      the $1,500 amount of the fine, Merrick J said the following:

> … the fine in no way relates to anything other than I have concluded that
> denunciation and deterrence require a fine and that a fine must be commen-
> surate with your ability to pay and in no way relates to the suffering, that is
> to say, the quantum or the level of fine in no way is in any way based on the
> level of pain or suffering because if I were to do that, the amount of fine that
> I would impose would be astronomical and would never be paid in your
> lifetime, your children's lifetime, or your grandchildren's lifetime. (ibid. at
> para 21)

Thus, here again is a case where a reader can observe a judge struggling
with applying a sentence that conforms to the general principles of
sentencing but also meets legitimate community expectations regarding
the horror of treating dogs and cats in certain ways. Despite Justice
Merrick's characterization of the nine dogs as "living beings" (para 19)
who suffered, and the duty to apply the *Code*'s principles of sentencing
so as to encourage non-incarceration options wherever appropriate,

it is the welfarist apparatus behind s.445.1 as a provision that permits $1,500, three years' probation, and 200 hours of community service to be sufficient punishment for the taking of nine lives.

290 Fawcett, see note 288, at Exhibit 1, Statement of Agreed Facts [Exhibit 1], para 47. The details in Exhibit 1 are graphic and chilling to say the least but also confounding given Fawcett's perception of the dogs as friends and his history of taking care of them. In para 47, the facts reveal a website blog that Fawcett kept where he wrote the following about killing: "Some I missed, had to chase around with blood everywhere, some I had to slit their throats because it was the only way to keep them calm in my arms. 1 had one still alive in a pit I dug for a mass burial. I carried them all one by one so as to at least give them some kind of respect. Day 2 was no different."

291 Coverage of the sled dog killings was international in scope, so much so that Premier Christy Clark described the incident as giving BC a "terrible black eye" internationally; Pemberton, "BC to toughen animal cruelty penalties: Report on killed sled dogs makes several proposals," *National Post,* 6 April 2011, A7. For examples of international coverage, see Jeremy Hainsworth, "100 Dogs in Canada Killed after Business Slows," *Associated Press,* 1 February 2011, http://abcnews .go.com/International/wireStory?id=12807719; Joanna Zelman, "100 Sled Dogs Killed in BC Due to Slump in Tourism," *Huffington Post,* 31 January 2011, perma.cc/YB5C-42QA ; "Sled dogs culled after Winter Olympics," *Daily Telegraph,* 2 February 2011, 18; Nance Carter, "PTSD cited after slaughter of 100 dogs," *Long Island Examiner,* 2 February 2011; and "Probe into dog slaughter – CANADA" *The Age,* 4 February 2011, 13. The public reaction also had an international component. The coverage garnered the attention of the Ian Somerhalder Foundation, a conservation and animal rights group created by an American actor, and the foundation spearheaded a petition that was eventually submitted to the Task Force with more than 50,000 signatures; see IS Foundation, "Save the sled dog: Reform British Columbia's anti-cruelty to animals law," *Change,* http:// web.archive.org/web/20190802181156/https://www.change.org/p /save-the-sled-dog-reform-british-columbias-anti-cruelty-to-animals -law. By early February, 40,000 people had joined a Facebook page calling for a boycott of the tour company: Jim Fox, "Killing of dogs is investigated," *St Petersburg* Times, 6 February, 2011, 11A. See also Darryl Crane, "Social media vigil for sled dogs found in Whistler," *Invermere Valley Echo,* 26 April 2011), 1, discussing the way social media were used to involve participants from locations like South Africa, Sweden, and Washington, DC, in the planned sled dog vigil. And the push to ban dogsledding stretched beyond BC: Manning, "Activists target dog sled

rides after Canada dog deaths," *Fairbanks Daily News-Miner,* 8 February 2011.

292 British Columbia, Sled Dog Task Force, *Sled Dog Task Force Report* (Victoria: Ministry of Agriculture, 2011), 5.

293 Ibid, 24–5.

294 Ibid.

295 Office of the Premier, "Premier announces Canada's toughest animal cruelty laws," April 5, 2011, Ministry of Agriculture, https://archive.news .gov.bc.ca/releases/news_releases_2009-2013/2011PREM0030-000340 .htm.

296 *Prevention of Cruelty to Animals Act,* ss.15.1, 15.2, and 24.1.

297 Ibid., s.22.1.

298 *Sled Dog Standard of Care Regulation,* BC Reg 21/2012. Part 2, for example, lays out standards for such matters as containment areas, release from such areas, the size of pens and the length of tethers, and frequency of feeding. Ibid., ss.3, 5, 6, 8(1), 12.

299 Ibid. See also Pemberton, "SPCA probes 'execution.'" The SPCA has estimated, however, that the investigation into the sled dog deaths themselves could cost as much as $225,000: Laura Kane, "RCMP appeals for calm as sled-dog exhumations begin," *Times-Colonist,* 3 May 2011, A5.

300 *Sled Dog Standard of Care Regulation.*

301 Sunny Dhillon, "BC crackdown won't ban sled dog culls," *Globe and Mail,* 6 April 2011, A8.

302 The Sled Dog Standard of Care Regulation attempts to avoid the situation that led to the public outcry by outlining "standards" for killing sled dogs under Part 4 – Killing Sled Dogs. For example, under subsections 21(1) and (2), owners are still able to kill sled dogs as long as they try to rehome them first and record their efforts to do so. Furthermore, ss.21(4) and (5) together try to effectuate an immediate death for the sled dog that is to be killed, though they also leave room for a death where suffering is still involved.

303 There may also be some positive impact on the treatment of companion animals. Although the report focused on the treatment of sled dogs, the strengthened standards of care, increased penalties, and further funding for the SPCA will all benefit companion animals, for they, unlike "industrial" animals, are not the subject of general exemptions under the legislation.

304 *Sled Dog Task Force Report,* 23–4. While the report indicates that some of the public feedback was related to animal welfare in general, recommendations on this topic are limited to a call for "minimum evidence-based standards" of treatment. Recommendations for the dog

sled industry specifically included a call for certification and a working group to establish stronger regulation. The report led to the enactment of the Sled Dog Standard of Care Regulation.

305 Ibid., 17.

306 Ibid.

307 Francione, *Animals, Property, and the Law*, 26.

308 Ibid., 45–56.

309 In February 2012 the provincial government announced the creation of the "Sled-Dog Code of Practice". British Columbia Ministry of Agriculture, "The Sled-Dog Code of Practice," 30 January 2012, Ministry of Agriculture, perma.cc/5U4D-67E7. The Code of Practice is described as a best-practices guide, whereas the Sled Dog Standard of Care Regulation contains mandatory care standards. As noted above, these are welfarist in nature.

310 For example, see Charity Intelligence Canada, "BC SPCA," 19 June 2019, perma.cc/F8A7-3DFQ. The BC SPCA does not receive operational funding from the BC government, though it received a $5 million capital grant in 2015 to replace old facilities. It receives some federal support through employment grants, but overall the BC SPCA is funded mostly by private donations. The OSPCA receives $5.75 million in provincial funding annually; however, the OSPCA says this is not sufficient to carry out enforcement duties. See CBC News, "OSPCA tells Ontario government it will no longer enforce animal cruelty laws," *CBC News*, 4 March 2019.

311 *Bogaerts v Attorney General of Ontario* 2019 ONSC 41, [2019] OJ No 5, at para 94.

312 CBC News, "OSPCA tells."

313 Ibid.

314 BBC News, "Canadian man sorry."

315 Troubling political appetite for an increasingly carceral state is also likely a factor in the Canadian context, as it is south of the border. The United States, with many more jurisdictions legislating on cruelty, has tended to focus reform in this area on the creation of stiffer penalties. The changes in the United States also came earlier and often include even higher penalties than those in Canada. Marceau, *Beyond Cages*. A broader comparison of Canada with the United States in non-criminal legal areas suggests that the stagnation highlighted in this chapter is present throughout the Canadian legal landscape. Maneesha Deckha, "Property on the Borderline: A Comparative Analysis of the Legal Status of Animals in Canada and the United States," *Cardozo Journal of International & Comparative Law* 20.2 (2012).

2 What's Wrong with Personhood?

1 Colleen Glenney Boggs, *Animalia Americana: Animal Representations and Biopolitical Subjectivity* (New York: Columbia University Press, 2013), 27.
2 Elizabeth Stein and Steven M. Wise, "Memorandum of Law in Support of Petition For Habeas Corpus," in *The Nonhuman Rights Project on behalf of Happy v James J Breheny & Wildlife Conservation Society,* N.Y.S.18 45164 (Sup. Ct. 2019) at 25 perma.cc/HP75-R49D.
3 Paola Cavalieri and Peter Singer, *The Great Ape Project: Equality beyond Humanity* (New York: St Martin's Griffin, 1996); see also, GAP Project, "World Declaration on Great Primates," perma.cc/4BVD-GFQ8.
4 See, generally, ibid.
5 Angus Taylor, *Animals and Ethics* (Toronto: Broadview Press, 2003), 176.
6 "Declaration signed on great apes," *BBC News,* 12 September 2005, perma.cc/D4HC-U9MZ .
7 See, generally, Wesley J. Smith, "Let Great Apes Be Apes," *Human Life Review* 32.3–4 (2006): 147.
8 Nora Ellen Groce and Jonathan Marks, "The Great Ape Project and Disability Rights Ominous Undercurrents of Eugenics in Action," *American Anthropology* 102.4 (2000), 818.
9 See, for example, Marc Bekoff, "Deep Ethology, Animal Rights, and the Great Ape/Animal Project: Resisting Speciesism and Expanding the Community of Equals," *Journal of Agricultural and Environmental Ethics* 10.3 (1997): 269.
10 Nonhuman Rights Project, "What Is The Nonhuman Rights Project?," perma.cc/CV6N-629D.
11 James Gorman, "Rights group is seeking status of 'legal person' for captive chimpanzee," *New York Times,* 2 December 2013, perma.cc /N7YH-JGCR; Charles Siebert, "Should a chimp be able to sue its owner?," *New York Times Magazine,* 23 April 2014, perma.cc/Z98R -4LF5 ; Andrew Westoll, "Are animals people, too? Soon, a chimpanzee could walk into a courtroom as a thing, and walk out as a person," *National Post,* 19 August 2016, perma.cc/4CPF-D2VZ ; Alan Yuhas, "Chimpanzee representatives argue for animals' rights in New York court," *The Guardian,* 27 May 2015, perma.cc/J5MA-MDC6. See also the documentary *Unlocking the Cage,* directed by Chris Hegedus and D.A. Pennebaker (New York: Pennebaker Hegedus Films, 2016); Leslie Felperin, "Unlocking the Cage Review – exemplary animal rights documentary," *The Guardian,* 16 June 2016, http://www .theguardian.com; Amy Kaufman, "The lawyer fighting for animal rights in 'Unlocking the Cage' asks: 'What kind of being are you?,'" *Los Angeles Times,* 24 June 2016, http://www.latimes.com; Chris Knight, "Unlocking

the Cage is an uneven journey, though heartening if you too believe animals deserve legal protection," *National Post*, 19 August 2016, http://news.nationalpost.com.

12 Leah Edgerton, "What is the most effective way to advocate legally for nonhuman animals?," *Animal Charity Evaluators*, 29 August 2016, perma .cc/GD8Z-XYBQ .

13 Gary L. Francione, "The Abolition of Animal Exploitation." in *The Animal Rights Debate: Abolition or Regulation?*, ed. Gary L. Francione and Robert Garner (New York: Columbia University Press, 2010), 1. A separate debate has emerged surrounding the term "abolitionism" itself and whether animal advocates should use it. Claire Jean Kim, a critical race and animal studies scholar, has argued that "abolitionism" has been appropriated from the specific history of African Americans and the movement to end slavery and that animal advocates use the term today in ways that diminish the ongoing effects of this history and the systemic and distinctive anti-black racist discrimination it has produced. See Claire Jean Kim, "Abolitionism," in *Critical Terms in Animal Studies*, ed. Lori Gruen (Chicago: Chicago University Press, 2018), 15–32.

14 David Delaney, *Law and Nature* (Cambridge: Cambridge University Press, 2003), 222.

15 Ibid., 226.

16 Ibid., 222.

17 James Kim, "Petting Asian America" *MELUS* 36.1 (2011): 137.

18 See Gary L. Francione, *Animals, Property, and the Law* (Philadelphia: Temple University Press, 1995), 28, 254.

19 Robert Garner, "A Defense of a Broad Animal Protectionism," in *The Animal Rights Debate: Abolition or Regulation?*, ed. Gary L. Francione and Robert Garner (New York: Columbia University Press, 2010), 103.

20 Jason Wyckoff, "The Animal Rights Debate: Abolition or Regulation? – By Gary L. Francione and Robert Garner," *Journal of Applied Philosophy* 28.4 (2011).

21 See, generally, Jonathan R. Lovvorn, "California Proposition 2: A Watershed Moment for Animal Law,"*Animal Law* 15.2 (2009).

22 Gary L. Francione, "What to Do on Proposition 2," *Animal Rights: The Abolitionist Approach*, 2 September 2008, perma.cc/S3DH-HR6C.

23 Garner, "A Defense," 143.

24 Cass R. Sunstein and Martha C. Nussbaum, *Animal Rights: Current Debates and New Directions* (New York: Oxford University Press, 2004), 253.

25 Ibid., 261.

26 Alisdair Cochrane, "Ownership and Justice for Animals," *Utilitas* 21.4 (2009): 426; David Favre, "Integrating Animal Interests Into Our Legal System" *Animal Law* 10 (2004).

27 Favre, "Integrating," 88. Robert Garner has also defended the position that property status is not a bar to meaningful legal change for animals. For Garner, the principle of treating animal interests with equal consideration is what matters and a propertied legal status does not prevent this. See Garner, "A Defense," 128–35. For a critical animal studies critique of Garner's view, see Maneesha Deckha, "Critical Animal Studies and the Property Debate in Animal Law," in *Animal Subjects 2.0: An Ethical Reader in a Posthuman World*, ed. Jodey Castricano and Lauren Corman (Waterloo: Wilfrid Laurier University Press, 2016), 51–5.

28 See generally David Favre, "Living Property: A New Status For Animals Within the Legal System," *Marquette Law Review* 93.3 (2010).

29 Ibid., 1069.

30 Eileen E. Gillese, *The Law of Trusts*, 3rd ed. (Toronto: Irwin Law Inc, 2014), 8.

31 David Favre, "Equitable Self-Ownership for Animals," *Duke Law Journal* 50.2 (2000): 494–5.

32 Ibid., 495.

33 For a more thorough development of the argument in this section as well as more detailed reviews of the various positions in the debate, see Deckha, "Critical Animal Studies," 45–80.

34 Debra Satz, "Voluntary Slavery and the Limits of the Market," *Law and Ethics of Human Rights* 3.1 (2009). Satz discusses contemporary examples of slavery, called today perhaps more euphemistically "debt bondage, attached labor, serfdom, and debt slavery" (ibid., 87). She distinguishes these from "formally free contractual labor" of the employee-employer kind (ibid.).

35 Ibid., citing Pranab Bardhan, *The Economic Theory of Agrarian Institutions* (Oxford: Clarendon Press, 1991), ch. 12.

36 For arguments to this effect even in the non-companion animal context and so where animals are exploited for profit, see Deborah Heath and Anne Meneley, "The Naturecultures of Foie Gras: Techniques of the Body and a Contested Ethics of Care," *Food, Culture, and Society* 13.3 (2010).

37 Satz, *Why Some Things Should Not Be for Sale*, ch. 8.

38 The literature on whether to commodify human tissue is vast. For discussion of the divergent feminist views on the topic, see generally Donna Dickenson, "Commodification of Human Tissue: Implications for Feminist and Development Ethics," *Developing World Bioethics* 2.1 (2002); Joan Raphael-Leff, "Gift of Gametes – Unconscious Motivation, Commodification and Problematics of Genealogy," *Feminist Review* 94 (2010).

39 Delaney, *Law and Nature*, 222.
40 Saru Matambanadzo, "Embodying Vulnerability," *Duke Journal of Gender Law and Policy* 20.1 (2012): 65. Matambanadzo notes the reductive nature of this tracing, pointing to Etruscan and Greek etymological origins that suggest the word more properly connotes the face. She argues that this connotation is more reflective of the ethical responsibility that personhood should compel from others. Here she illuminatingly draws from Barbara Johnson's connection of personhood as face to Emmanuel Levinas's influential theory of the face (ibid. at 65–6), citing Barbara Johnson, *Person and Things* (Cambridge, MA: Harvard University Press, 2008), 182–3.
41 Katherine Barber, "The Last Word," *Performing Arts and Entertainment in Canada* 32.3 (1999); John E. Stoll, "Mask, Persona, Personality," *Sewanee Review* 92.1 (1984).
42 John Thomas Noonan, *Persons and Masks of the Law: Cardozo, Holmes, Jefferson, and Wythe as Makers of the Masks* (New York: Farrar, Straus and Giroux, 1976), 22.
43 David DeGrazia, "On the Question of Personhood Beyond Homo Sapiens," in *In Defense of Animals: The Second Wave*, ed. Peter Singer (Malden: Blackwell, 2006).
44 Rebecca J. Huss, "Valuing Man's and Woman's Best Friend: The Moral and Legal Status of Companion Animals," *Marquette Law Review* 86.1 (2002), 72, 74.
45 Ibid. at 71–8.
46 Ibid. at 77.
47 Ngaire Naffine, *Law's Meaning of Life: Philosophy, Religion, Darwin, and the Legal Person* (Oxford: Oxford University Press, 2001), 21–2. For a further discussion of this "empty shell" categorization of personhood, see Matambanadzo, "Embodying Vulnerability," 67–8.
48 Also well-known is the writing and legal activism of Steven M. Wise. Wise, however, only advocates for personhood for animals that demonstrate a certain level of cognitive capacity, whereas Francione champions personhood for all sentient animals, a much larger group. See Steven Wise, *Rattling the Cage: Towards Legal Rights for Animals* (Cambridge, MA: Perseus Books, 2000); and *Drawing the Line: Science and the Case for Animal Rights* (Cambridge, MA: Perseus Books, 2002). As Naffine remarks in discussing Wise's views, he is thus aligned with the Rationalist view of legal personhood. Naffine, *Law's Meaning*, 132. Interestingly, Naffine suggests that Francione "is perhaps closer to the Religionists, in that he finds innate value (perhaps even a divine spark) in all living beings": ibid., 136). I would respectfully disagree with this estimation given Francione's consistent grounding of animals'

recognition in their sentience in his body of work. See Gary L. Francione, *Animals as Persons: Essays on the Abolition of Animal Exploitation* (New York: Columbia University Press, 2008).

49 Naffine, *Law's Meaning*, 44–61.

50 Ibid., 61–3.

51 Paola Cavalieri, *The Animal Question: Why Nonhuman Animals Deserve Human Rights* (Oxford: Oxford University Press, 2001), see especially 38–40. Cavalieri has also articulated this position in other work. See Cavalieri, "The Animal Debate: A Reexamination" in Singer, *In Defense of Animals*.

52 Cavalieri, *The Animal Question*, 38 (emphasis in original).

53 Ibid., 117.

54 See, for example, Angela Campbell, "Could a Chimpanzee or Bonobo Take the Stand?," *Animal Law* 8 (2002); Luis E. Chiesa, "Of Persons and the Criminal Law: (Second Tier) Personhood as a Prerequisite for Victimhood," *Pace Law Review* 28 (2007–8): 773–8; DeGrazia, "On the Question of Personhood," 44–6; Rowan Taylor, "A Step at a Time: New Zealand's Progress Toward Hominid Rights" *Animal Law* 7 (2001); Roger S. Fouts, "Apes, Darwinian Continuity, and the Law" *Animal Law* 10 (2004), 107–12. The role of "science" is significant in this debate, as many theorists cite studies that "prove" the possession of certain capacities in certain animals. See, for example, Kyle Ash, "International Animal Rights: Speciesism and Exclusionary Human Dignity" *Animal Law* 11 (2005), 212–13; Lesley J Rogers and Gisela Kaplan, "Think or be Damned: The Problematic Case of Higher Cognition in Animals and Legislation for Animal Welfare," *Animal Law* 12 (2005–6), 160–80.

55 Rogers and Kaplan, "Think or Be Damned," 182–5; Camden J. McDaris, "Legal Protection Only for Those Who Are Most Like 'Us': What Animal Activists Can Learn from the Early Women's Movement about Society's Resistance to Acknowledging Rights," *Journal of Animal Law* 2 (2006).

56 Naffine, *Law's Meaning*, 59.

57 Ibid., 61.

58 Ibid., 29.

59 Tucker Culbertson, "Animal Equality, Human Dominion, and Fundamental Interdependence," *Journal of Animal Law* 5 (2009), 42.

60 Anna Grear, "Deconstructing *Anthropos*: A Critical Legal Reflection on 'Anthropocentric' Law and Anthropocene 'Humanity'" *Law and Critique* 26.3 (2015), 232; Drucilla Cornell, "Rethinking Legal Ideals after Deconstruction" in *Law's Madness*, ed. Sarat et al. (Ann Arbor: University of Michigan Press, 2003), 147.

61 Grear, "Deconstructing *Anthropos*," 231.

62 Ibid., 234.

63 Ibid., 234.
64 Ibid., 231–3.
65 Ibid., 235.
66 Matthew Calarco, "Identity, Difference, Indistinction," *New Centennial Review* 11.3 (2012), 46.
67 Anna Grear, "The Vulnerable Living Order: Human Rights and the Environment in a Critical and Philosophical Perspective," *Journal of Human Rights and the Environment* 2 (2011), 26.
68 Matthew Calarco, "Reorienting Strategies for Animal Justice," in *Philosophy and the Politics of Animal Liberation*, ed. Paola Cavalieri (London: Palgrave Macmillan, 2016), 54–5.
69 Ciméa Barbato Bevilaqua, "Chimpanzees in Court: What Difference Does It Make?," in *Law and the Questions of the Animal: A Critical Jurisprudence*, ed. Yoriko Otomo and Ed Mussawir (Oxford: Routledge, 2013), 80.
70 Calarco, "Reorienting Strategies for Animal Justice," 56–7.
71 Grear, "The Vulnerable Living Order," 26.
72 Ibid., 32.
73 Sheryl Hamilton has demonstrated the constructedness and inflexible exclusionary dimensions of personhood as a legal category across a range of beings in *Impersonations: Troubling the Person in Law and Culture* (Toronto: University of Toronto Press, 2009).
74 Ibid., 23.
75 Grear, "Deconstructing *Anthropos*," 236.
76 Colin Dayan, *The Law Is a White Dog: How Legal Rituals Make and Unmake Persons* (Princeton: Princeton University Press, 2011).
77 Ibid., 40, 132.
78 Ibid., 72.
79 Ibid., ch. 3, "Punishing the Residue."
80 Ibid., 71, 115.
81 Dehumanization can also occur through mechanization. The theorists I discuss and my overall analysis focuses on dehumanization through animalization, that is, where humans are seen to be subhuman because they lack traits associated with human exceptionalism. For more on the different modalities of dehumanization, see Steve Loughnan and Nick Haslam, "Animals and Androids: Implicit Associations between Social Categories and Nonhumans," *Psychological Science* 18 (2007); Steve Loughnan, Nick Haslam, and Yoshihisa Kashima, "Understanding the Relationship between Attribute-Based and Metaphor-Based Dehumanization," *Group Processes and Intergroup Relations* 12.6 (2009); and Steve Loughnan, Nick Haslam, Robbie M. Sutton, and Bettina Spencer, "Dehumanization and Social Class; Animality in the Stereotypes of 'White Trash,' 'Chavs,' and 'Bogans,'" *Social Psychology* 45.1 (2014).

82 Dayan, *The Law Is a White Dog*, 73, citing an interview Dayan had with the Arizona Department of Corrections spokesperson discussing super-maximum security units. See ibid., 73n4. See also ibid., 26–33, 116–24.

83 Phillip Atiba Goff et al., "Not Yet Human: Implicit Knowledge, Historical Dehumanization, and Contemporary Consequences," *Journal of Personality and Social Psychology* 94.2 (2008); Tarik Kochi, "Species War: Law, Violence and Animals," *Law, Culture, and Humanities* 5.3 (2009).

84 American slavery and the Jewish Holocaust are obvious examples – see Dayan, *The Law Is a White Dog*, 115, 118–33 – but also consider the Rwandan Genocide, the dispossession of Indigenous peoples in settler countries, and projects of forced sterilization, medical experimentation, and public health. See Kay Anderson, *Race and the Crisis of Humanism* (London: Routledge, 2007), 12; E.N. Anderson and Barbara A. Anderson, *Warning Signs of Genocide: An Anthropological Perspective* (Lanham: Lexington Books, 2013), 67; Megan H. Glick, "Of Sodomy and Cannibalism: Dehumanisation, Embodiment, and the Rhetorics of Same-Sex and Cross-Species Contagion," *Gender and History* 23.2 (2011), 268–9.

85 Samera Esmeir, "On Making Dehumanization Possible," *PMLA* 121.5 (2006), 1544.

86 Ibid. For a full discussion of the trajectory of juridical humanity in Egypt, see Samera Esmeir, *A Juridical Humanity: A Colonial History* (Stanford: Stanford University Press, 2012).

87 Esmeir, "Dehumanization," 1545–9; idem, *Juridical Humanity*, 4.

88 Esmeir, "Dehumanization," 1548. Esmeir explains that in the late nineteenth-century British colonial era, law played handmaiden to colonialism through ideologies that celebrated the rule of law and the establishment of an independent judiciary as features of a proper civilization that would humanize Britain's colonial subjects, who had been subhumanized by their home states and cultures. Esmeir is concerned that international human rights law has perpetuated this racialized civilizational logic through human rights "campaigns (that) effectively transform humanity into a legal status to be granted to citizens of the global south": ibid., 1545.

89 Sara Ahmed, "Problematic Proximities: Or Why Critiques of Gay Imperialism Matter," *Feminist Legal Studies* 19.2 (2011), 131.

90 Andreja Zevnik, "Becoming-Animal, Becoming-Detainee: Encountering Human Rights Discourse in Guantanamo," *Law and Critique* 22.2 (2011), 157. See also, Jasbir K. Puar, *Terrorist Assemblages: Homonationalism in Queer Times* (Durham: Duke University Press, 2007), 13–15; Sherene Razack, *Casting Out: The Eviction of Muslims from Western Law and Politics* (Toronto: University of Toronto Press, 2008), 60–1.

91 Rebecca Scott, "Body Worlds' Plastinates, the Human/Nonhuman Interface, and Feminism," *Feminist Theory* 12.2 (2011), citing Carol Quillen, "Feminism Theory, Justice, and the Lure of the Human," *Signs* 27.1 (2001); Natasha Marhia, "Some Humans Are More Human Than Others: Troubling the 'Human' in Human Security from a Critical Feminist Perspective," *Security Dialogue* 44 (2013): 23–6.

92 Ngaire Naffine, "Liberating the Legal Person" *Canadian Journal of Law and Society* 26.1 (2011), 199, 203.

93 The emphatic division of entities and beings into either persons or property is evidence of Euro-American law's binary classification system. It is useful to note, however, that an entity can sometimes straddle these two categories. Francione and Dayan point us toward the historical example of the legal status of slaves. A contemporary example is corporations, which have the legal subjectivity of persons but can also be sold as property. On this latter point see Naffine, *Law's Meaning*, 48. Naffine adds, presumably contemplating embryos, fetuses, and the comatose in the last clause, that "humans too can possess an ambiguous legal status, especially at the margins of life" (ibid.). With this comment, Naffine seeks to draw our attention to the "clustered" nature of the two concepts in law and to the ways that the typical attributes of one can sometimes attach to the other. Consider, for example, the ability of humans to sell some of their body tissue and biological services on the market, thus propertizing parts of what is normally simply personified.

94 Delaney, *Law and Nature*, 223.

95 Glenney Boggs, *Animalia Americana*, 42.

96 Indeed, some of those who oppose personhood for animals emphasize this very point, suggesting that our humanity would be lost if animals lost their property status, for it is through their commodification that we concretize our humanity and thus our personhood. See Naffine, *Law's Meaning*, 142.

97 Marie Fox, "Rethinking Kinship: Law's Construction of the Animal Body," *Current Legal Problems* 57.1 (2004), 480, 483.

98 Cary Wolfe and Jonathan Elmer, "Subject to Sacrifice: Ideology, Psychoanalysis, and the Discourse of Species in Jonathan Demme's The Silence of the Lambs," in *Animal Rites: American Culture, The Discourse of Species, and Posthumanist Theory,* ed. Cary Wolfe (University of Chicago Press, 2003), 101.

99 Ibid.

100 Maneesha Deckha, "Humanizing the Nonhuman: A Legitimate Way for Animals to Escape Juridical Property Status?," in *Critical Animal Studies: Towards a Trans-Species Social Justice,* ed. John Sorenson and Atsuko Matsuoka (London: Rowman and Littlefield, 2018), 209–33.

101 Chimpanzees and cetaceans are humanized animals and figure prominently in these campaigns. Both are listed as endangered under the Convention on International Trade in Endangered Species of Wild Fauna and Flora. See *Convention on International Trade in Endangered Species of Wild Fauna and Flora, Appendix I*, 4 April 2017, 993 U.N.T.S. 243. Globally, for example, it is estimated that there are fewer than 200,000 chimpanzees. Library and Information Service, "Chimpanzee: Pan troglodytes Factsheet," *National Primate Research Center* (2006), perma.cc/7JNH-AM7B. Farmed animals greatly outstrip this number. In the United States alone, it is estimated that 9 billion animals are killed annually, a figure that includes "8.5 billion chickens, 30 million cattle, 100 million pigs and 250 million turkeys." John Rossi and Samual A. Garner, "Industrial Farm Animal Production: A Comprehensive Moral Critique," *Journal of Agriculture and Environmental Ethics* (2014), 492, citing Humane Society of the United States, *An HSUS Report: The Welfare of Intensively Confined Animals in Battery Cages, Gestation Crates, and Veal Crates* (2013), perma.cc/9ZHS-LXN8; and Aysha Akhtar, "The Need to Include Animal Protection in Public Health Policies," *Journal of Public Health Policy* 34.4 (2013).

102 Bevilaqua, "Chimpanzees in Court," 83–4.

103 Sue Donaldson and Will Kymlicka, *Zoopolis: A Political Theory of Animal Rights* (Oxford: Oxford University Press, 2011), 30.

104 Bevilaqua, "Chimpanzees in Court," 80–1.

105 As Bevilaqua notes, the genetic argument is particularly powerful given the precedent of recognizing DNA as proof of kinship and relationship status: ibid., 82.

106 Ibid., 85.

107 For discussions of personhood in Indigenous cosmologies around the globe, see Katie Glaskin, "Anatomies of Relatedness: Considering Personhood in Aboriginal Australia," *American Anthropologist* 114.2 (2012); Markus Fraundorfer, "The Rediscovery of Indigenous Thought in the Modern Legal System: The Case of the Great Apes," *Global Policy Volume* 9.1 (2018), 18, 20–3 (discussing Amerindian perspectivism in particular); Maureen Trudelle Schwartz, *Molded in the Image of Changing Woman: Navajo Views on the Human Body and Personhood* (Phoenix: University of Arizona Press, 1997); Evan M. Mwangi, *The Postcolonial Animal: African Literature and Posthuman Ethics* (Ann Arbor: University of Michigan Press, 2019). For a discussion of attributions of personhood to non-humans in Asian and African societies, see James L. Smith, "I, River?: New Materialism, Riparian Non-Human Agency and the Scale of Democratic Reform," *Asia Pacific Viewpoint* 58.1 (2017), 104–8; Yunxiang

Yan, "Doing Personhood in Chinese Culture," *Cambridge Anthropology* 35.2 (2017); and John L. Comaroff and Jean Comaroff, "On Personhood: An Anthropological Perspective from Africa," *Social Identities: Journal for the Study of Race, Nation, and Culture* 7.2 (2001).

108 While being mindful of not entrenching a stark binary between Western and non-Western conceptions, it is still productive to note the differences in hegemonic attributes of personhood that prevail in certain societies, including differences between Western and non-Western societies. Glaskin, "Anatomies of Relatedness," 298. Richard Baxstrom, "Force, Dwelling, and the Personhood of Things in Urban Malaysia," *Comparative Studies of South Asia, Africa and the Middle East* 37.3 (2017).

109 I cannot complete this analysis here in this present study.

110 Notable here in the liberal tradition is the work of Donaldson and Kymlicka, who argue for a relational theory of rights for all animals, including citizenship rights for domesticated animals. See Donaldson and Kymlicka, *Zoopolis*.

3 Toward a Post-Anthropocentric Legal Ontology

1 Jasbir Puar, ed., "Precarity Talk: A Virtual Roundtable with Lauren Berlant, Judith Butler, Bojana Cvejic, Isabell Lorey, and Ana Vujanovic" *The Drana Review* 56.4 (2012): 170.

2 Irina Aristarkhova, "Thou Shall Not Harm All Living Beings: Feminism, Jainism, and Animals," *Hypatia* 27.3 (2012): 637.

3 Paul Rekret, "A Critique of New Materialism: Ethics and Ontology," *Subjectivity* 9.3 (2016).

4 Donna J. Haraway, *When Species Meet* (Minneapolis: University of Minnesota Press, 2008); Kelly Oliver, *Earth and World: Philosophy after the Apollo Missions* (New York: Columbia University Press, 2015).

5 As the discussion proceeds below, the continuities with many Indigenous and other non-Western relational worldviews regarding appropriate interspecies relations will become obvious to readers familiar with these "alternative" worldviews and epistemologies. See, for example Neil Dalal and Chloë Taylor, *Asian Perspectives on Animal Ethics: Rethinking the Nonhuman* (London: Routledge, 2014); Christopher G. Framarin, "The Moral Standing of Animals and Plants in the Manusmriti," *Philosophy East and West* 64.1 (2014); Kai Horsthemke, *Animals and African Ethics* (London: Palgrave Macmillan, 2015); Val Plumwood, *Environmental Culture: The Ecological Crisis of Reason* (London: Routledge, 2002); Rod Preece, *Animals and Nature: Cultural Myths, Cultural Realities* (Vancouver: UBC Press, 1999); Margaret Robinson, "Animal Personhood in Mi'kmaq Perspective" *Societies* 4.4 (2014); Amba J. Septie, "More Than Stories,

More Than Myths: Animal/Human/Nature(s) in Traditional Ecological Worldviews," *Humanities* 6.4 (2017). I do not, however, draw primarily from these worldviews and epistemologies in this chapter, for three principal reasons. First, I do not wish to conflate all Indigenous and other non-Western worldviews into one general iteration, for this would obscure the immense diversity of these traditions, given the space limitations of this chapter. Although generalizations are required in any type of analysis, and I have defended various types (e.g., using the categories of the West, non-West) in the introduction to this work, each ontological worldview merits an in-depth excavation for the purposes of this chapter that is not feasible to present. Although such a strategy can be critically productive at times, I do not wish to pick from a smattering of non-Western ontologies to discuss legal cultural change. For more about the challenges of discussing distinct Indigenous and non-Western cultural teachings and lifeways in homogeneous and fragmented ways, see Val Napoleon and Hadley Friedland, "An Inside Job: Engaging with Indigenous Legal Traditions through Stories," *McGill Law Journal* 61.4 (2016): 739. Second, I expect that if I were to draw more closely from Indigenous and other non-Western epistemologies to chart the cultural shifts that are necessary if Canadian law is to move toward non-hierarchical valuations of animals and a more robust interspecies view of legal and surrounding orders, some might wonder – and hope that I address – whether Indigenous subsistence or community needs–based killing of animals may be justified if done from a position of respect and responsibility for animals rather than Western law's subordinating stance. This is a question that I have taken up elsewhere and do not wish to revisit in this analysis. See Maneesha Deckha, "Animal Justice, Cultural Justice: A Posthumanist Response to Cultural Rights in Animals," *Journal of Animal Law and Ethics 2* (2007); and Maneesha Deckha, "Postcolonial," in *Critical Terms for Animal Studies*, ed. Lori Gruen (Chicago: University of Chicago Press, 2018). Instead, I would like to focus in this chapter on the conceptual resources that feminist and feminist-inspired theories make available to produce the foundational cultural shifts in Canadian law that I call for here, demonstrating that there are conceptual resources internal to Western theorizations that we can harness in the shared project among Indigenous, other non-Western, and critical literatures aimed at unsettling the colonial human-centredness of Canadian law and cultivating a non-domination ethic of care and responsibility.

6 Moreover, while general ecofeminist and feminist ethic-of-care theories share synergies, they should be seen distinctly. Ecofeminist theory is a branch of feminist thought that draws connections between the oppression of women and the oppression of nature, arguing that in

order to understand these oppressions properly they must be seen as intertwined. Some ecofeminists adopt a caring ethic toward the earth and the environment in articulating how political transformation should proceed, but others do not, resisting the ability of a care ethic to generate a transformative feminist praxis. Sherilyn MacGregor, "From Care to Citizenship," *Ethics and the Environment* 9.1 (2004); Catriona Sandilands, *The Good-Natured Feminist: Ecofeminism and the Quest for Democracy* (Minneapolis: University of Minnesota Press, 1999).

7 Greta C. Gaard, "Vegetarian Ecofeminism: A Review Essay," *Frontiers* 22.3 (2002): 118.

8 For a summary of the tenets of feminist ethic-of-care theory for animals, see Carol Adams and Josephine Donovan, eds., "Introduction," in *The Feminist Care Tradition in Animal Ethics* (New York: Columbia University Press, 2007).

9 This follows Josephine Donovan's terminology primarily due to ease of reference. Josephine Donovan, "Feminism and the Treatment of Animals: From Care to Dialogue," *Signs* 31.2 (2006): 306.

10 Susan Fraiman, "Pussy Panic versus Liking Animals: Tracking Gender in Animal Studies," *Critical Inquiry* 39.1 (2012). Some of this classic and new posthumanist scholarship on animals continues to value reasoning ability as a mark of personhood and/or moral worth. See Tom Regan, *The Case for Animal Rights* (Berkeley: University of California Press, 1983), 164; Steven M. Wise, *Rattling the Cage: Toward Legal Rights for Animals* (Boston: Da Capo Press, 2000),131.

11 Adams and Donovan, "Introduction," 2–3; Gaard, "Vegetarian Ecofeminism," 123.

12 Lori Gruen, *Entangled Empathy: An Alternative Ethic for Our Relationship with Animals* (New York: Lantern Press, 2015), 34.

13 Donovan, "Feminism and the Treatment of Animals," 306; Marti Kheel, "The Liberation of Nature: A Circular Affair," in *Beyond Animal Rights: A Feminist Caring Ethic for the Treatment of Animals,* ed. Carol J. Adams and Josephine Donovan (New York: Continuum, 1996), 27.

14 Carol J. Adams, "Caring About Suffering: A Feminist Exploration," in *The Feminist Care Tradition in Animal Ethics*, ed. Carol J. Adams and Josephine Donovan (New York: Columbia University Press, 2007), 198, 201–2.

15 Adams and Donovan, "Introduction," 3.

16 Gaard, "Vegetarian Ecofeminism," 119, 121.

17 Josephine Donovan, "Attention to Suffering: Sympathy as a Basis for Ethical Treatment of Animals," in Adams and Donovan, *The Feminist Care Tradition*, 185.

18 Ibid., 190; Gaard, "Vegetarian Ecofeminism," 121.

19 Josephine Donovan, "Animal Rights and Feminist Theory," in Adams and Donovan, *The Feminist Care Tradition*, 75; idem, "Attention to Suffering," 190.

20 Donovan, "Feminism and the Treatment of Animals," 308.

21 Donovan, "Attention to Suffering," 187–8; Gaard, "Vegetarian Ecofeminism," 123.

22 Donovan, "Attention to Suffering," 180.

23 Donovan, "Feminism and the Treatment of Animals," 309–11.

24 Gruen, *Entangled Empathy*.

25 Ibid., 3.

26 Earlier in her scholarship, Gruen had termed "entangled empathy" as "engaged empathy": "Empathy involves a transfer of affect, and eventually, a cognitive engagement with the perspective of the 'object' of empathy. When an individual is emotionally and cognitively empathizing with another they are practicing in what I will call 'engaged empathy.'" Lori Gruen, "Attending to Nature: Empathetic Engagement with the More than Human World," *Ethics and the Environment* 14.2 (2009): 27.

27 Gruen, *Entangled Empathy*, 5.

28 Ibid., 25, 61; idem, "Attending to Nature," 30.

29 Ibid., "Attending to Nature," 32.

30 Ibid., 33.

31 Gruen, *Entangled Empathy*, 5; Carol Cohn, "'Maternal Thinking' and the Concept of 'Vulnerability' in Security Paradigms, Policies, and Practices," *Journal of International Political Theory* 10.1 (2013): 47n5, discussing Sara Ruddick, *Maternal Thinking: Toward a Politics of Peace* (Boston: Beacon Press, 1989).

32 Gruen, *Entangled Empathy*, 59–60.

33 Kamalini Ramdas, "Feminist Care Ethics, Becoming Area," *Society and Space* 34.5 (2016): 846.

34 Fiona Robinson, "Stop Talking and Listen: Discourse Ethics and Feminist Care Ethics in International Political Theory," *Millennium: Journal of International Studies* 39.3 (2011): 847.

35 For an explanation of how feminist animal care theory overlaps with virtue ethics but is also distinct from it, see Nancy M. Williams, "The Ethics of Care and Humane Meat: Why Care Is Not Ambiguous about 'Humane' Meat," *Journal of Social Philosophy* 46.2 (2015): 274.

36 T.J. Kasperbauer, "Rejecting Empathy for Animal Ethics," *Ethical Theory and Moral Practice* 18.4 (2015): 821–2.

37 Ibid.

38 Renata Grossi, "Understanding Law and Emotion," *Emotion Review* 7.1 (2015): 55. Grossi encapsulates the major contours of the field when she writes that law and emotion "seeks to illuminate the affective features

of legal problems; investigate these features through interdisciplinary analysis; and integrate resulting understandings into practical, normative proposals": ibid.

39 Ibid., 56.

40 This is a position not yet articulated within law and emotion scholarship, though Heather Conway and John Stannard have argued for better legal valuation within property law of the emotions people feel for other non-human objects, including companion animals. Heather Conway and John Stannard, "Property and Emotions," *Emotion Review* 8.1 (2016): 38.

41 Susan Bandes, *The Passions of Law* (New York: New York University Press, 1999), as cited in ibid., 41–2.

42 Donovan, "Feminism and the Treatment of Animals," 307–10.

43 It is because of this distinction that Nedelsky, in speaking about the relationship between her relational theory project and an ethic of care, declines to accept the characterization of her work as part of ethic-of-care scholarship. See Jennifer Nedelsky, *Law's Relations: A Relational Theory of Self, Autonomy, and Law* (New York: Oxford University Press, 2011), 87.

44 Sherilyn MacGregor, *Beyond Mothering Earth: Ecological Citizenship and the Politics of Care* (Vancouver: UBC Press, 2006), 60, citing leading ethic-of-care theorists J.B. Elshtain, *Public Man, Private Woman: Women in Social and Political Thought* (Princeton: Princeton University Press, 1981); Nel Noddings, *Caring: A Feminine Approach to Ethics and Moral Education* (Berkeley: University of California Press, 1984); and Sara Ruddick, *Maternal Thinking*.

45 MacGregor, *Beyond Mothering Earth*, 79.

46 Ibid.

47 Maria Drakopoulou, "The Ethic of Care, Female Subjectivity and Feminist Legal Scholarship" *Feminist Legal Studies* 8.2 (2000): 205.

48 Ibid. at 207–15.

49 Ibid.

50 Carol Gilligan, *In a Different Voice: Psychological Theory and Women's Development* (Cambridge, MA: Harvard University Press, 1982), 73.

51 See the authors cited in Adams and Donovan, "Introduction," 2.

52 Some ecofeminists who advocate for an ethic of care contest the disavowal of the feminine as the only way to avoid essentialism, arguing that it is possible to revere feminine capacities in the Earth's and women's life-giving abilities without investing in gender binaries or dualisms. See Lori J. Swanson, "A Feminist Ethic That Binds Us to Mother Earth," *Ethics and the Environment* 20.2 (2015): 83 at 87.

53 Nedelsky explains her reluctance to associate her theory with an ethic of care – which she tells us it is often assumed to be – at the close of the chapter in which she introduces the relational framework. Nedelsky,

Law's Relations, 87–9. Her reasons for distinguishing her work from ethic-of-care theory are both continuous and discontinuous from mine.

54 Greta Gaard, "Ecofeminism Revisited: Rejecting Essentialism and Re-Placing Species in a Material Feminist Environmentalism," *Feminist Formations* 23.2 (2011): 26; Nadine Levy, "Towards a New Environmental Ethic in Contemporary Feminist Theory," *Hecate* 38.1–2 (2012): 11–14n4.

55 Adams and Donovan, "Introduction."

56 Aristarkhova, "Thou Shall Not Harm," 640–1.

57 Ibid., 642.

58 Ibid., 644.

59 Ibid., 643.

60 Grossi, "Understanding Law and Emotion," 55. Josephine Donovan discusses this more conventional criticism of emotions in Donovan, "Animal Rights."

61 Eleni Panagiotarakou, "Who Loves Mosquitoes?: Care Ethics, Theory of Obligation, and Endangered Species," *Journal of Agricultural and Environmental Ethics* 29 (2016): 1057.

62 Kathy Rudy, *Loving Animals: Toward a New Animal Advocacy* (Minneapolis: University of Minnesota Press, 2011), xi–xii.

63 Ibid., x.

64 It is important to note that Rudy does not locate her work in feminist ethic-of-care theory. She describes the work of Carol Adams, Josephine Donovan, and other theorists in this field as emphasizing standpoint theory for animals, that is, advocating a theoretical position in which we consider animals' experiences and see the world from their perspective: ibid., 35. Rudy attests that she finds the principle theoretically compelling in the "abstract" but not in practice; for Rudy, she must fall in love with an individual animal, "and when that happens, a part of [her] own subjectivity shifts and somehow belongs to that animal": ibid. Rudy's resistance to an ethic-of-care tradition is not germane to my analysis here, so I do not pursue this point further.

65 Ibid., xiii.

66 Ibid.

67 Ibid.

68 Ibid., xiii.

69 Ibid., xii.

70 See her discussion of these industries, ibid., chs. 2–5.

71 Ibid.

72 Ibid., xxx.

73 Elisa Aaltola, "Loving Animals: Toward a New Animal Advocacy," *Times Higher Education Supplement* 20.20 (2011); M.A. Betz, "Rudy, Kathy. Loving Animals: Toward a New Animal Advocacy," *Choice* 49.6 (2012).

For more favourable reviews of Rudy's book see Nancy Bent, "Loving Animals: Toward a New Animal Advocacy," *American Library Association* 108.1 (2011); Lisa Gerber, "Book Review: Loving Animals: Toward a New Animal Advocacy," *SAGE* 25.1 (2012); Kyrille Goldbeck, "Rudy, Kathy. Loving Animals: Toward a New Animal Advocacy," *Library Journal* 136.14 (2011); Tora Holmberg, "Narrative, Affect, Love, and Confusion: Review of Kathy Rudy, Loving Animals: Toward a New Animal Advocacy," *Humanimalia* 3.2 (2012); and Anna Peterson, "Kathy Rudy: Loving Animals: Toward a New Animal Advocacy," *Journal of Agriculture and Environmental Ethics* 25.5 (2012).

74 Robert Garner, *A Theory of Justice for Animals: Animal Rights in a Nonideal World* (New York: Oxford University Press, 2013); Martha Craven Nussbaum, *Frontiers of Justice: Disability, Nationality, Species Membership* (Cambridge, MA: Harvard University Press, 2006); Regan, *The Case for Animal Rights*.

75 Kelly Oliver, *Animal Lessons: How They Teach Us to Be Human* (New York: Columbia University Press, 2009).

76 Oliver, *Earth & World*, 4–5.

77 Ibid., 5.

78 Ibid.

79 Cynthia Willett, *Interspecies Ethics* (New York: Columbia University Press, 2014), 11.

80 Oliver, *Animal Lessons*. Oliver terms this teaching function of animals "animal pedagogy" (5).

81 Ibid., 5.

82 Willett, *Interspecies Ethics*, 10. As Willett further observes, the response ethics tradition "aimed to replace not only modern self-legislating reason but also classical virtue ethics' self-discipline and self-cultivation as the proper site for ethics. For response ethics, the direct and compelling source of obligation is not rational principle, individual preference, or character virtue, but the overpowering draw of the vulnerable other and is *erotic* in this nonreductive and nonsexual use of this ancient Greek term."

83 Oliver, *Animal Lessons*, 5.

84 Willett, *Interspecies Ethics*, 10.

85 Oliver, *Animal Lessons*, 141–2.

86 Ibid., 303.

87 Ibid., 306.

88 Ibid., 21, 305.

89 Willett, *Interspecies Ethics*, 11.

90 Oliver, "Animal Ethics," 269.

91 Ibid., 280.

92 Ibid., 270.

93 Ibid., 304–6; Oliver, "Animal Ethics," 280. "Response-ability" for Oliver is part of the "witnessing structure" that facilitiates our subjectivities and takes shape through our unconscious. See Oliver, "Witnessing and Testimony," 83–6, for a fuller exposition of the concept, its emphasis on the unconscious, and its relevance to the meaning of subjectivity in phenomenonology and psychoanalysis. Although Donna Haraway's use of the term response-ability in relation to ethical relations with animals is perhaps much better known to animal scholars, I wish to signal my strong preference for Oliver's non-domination conceptualization. I read Oliver's use of the term as denoting a non-violent responsibility toward animals that is categorically different from what Haraway suggests by "response-ability" in her writings despite both scholars' emphasis on emphasizing how our subjectivities and selves emerge through relations with others including animal others. For example, despite her ostensible disavowal of human exceptionalism, Haraway's "response-ability" is part of an overall ethical stance where she classifies animals imprisoned in research laboratories as "workers," celebrates the co-mingling of subjectivities of human lab technician with the confined animals that can come when the humans who experiment on animals or otherwise work with them "share" their suffering, and generally condones experimenting on animals for human purposes. See Haraway, *When Species Meet*, 71–2. She similarly focuses on the conditions by which animals become food and whether we perceive those animals properly as agents rather than fungible units; "response-ability" toward animals leads her to sympathize with rather than oppose hunting and the consumption of hunted animals by affluent individuals in the West as an example of "killing well" and "eating well." Ibid, 296–9. For an incisive and comprehensive critique of Haraway's ethical positions vis-à-vis animals see Zipporah Weisberg, "The Broken Promises of Monsters: Haraway, Animals, and the Humanist Legacy," *Journal of Critical Animal Studies* 7.2 (2009): 22.

94 Oliver, "Animal Ethics," 280.

95 Oliver, *Animal Lessons*, 304. Oliver reinforces all of these points in *Earth and World*.

96 Oliver, *Animal Lessons*, 305.

97 Oliver, *Animal Lessons*, 40.

98 Ibid., 306.

99 Jonathan K. Crane et al., "Beastly Morality: Untangling Possibilities," in *Beastly Morality: Animals as Ethical Agents*, ed. Jonathan K Crane (New York: Columbia University Press, 2016), 256–61.

100 Ibid., 257.

101 Ibid., 257.

102 Willett, *Interspecies Ethics*, 13.
103 Ibid., 15.
104 Ibid., 13.
105 Ibid.
106 Ramdas, "Feminist Care Ethics," 846, citing Emily Beausoleil, "Mastery of Knowledge or Meeting of Subjects? The Epistemic Effects of Two Forms of Political Voice," *Contemporary Political Theory* 15.1 (2016): 17–18; Lorraine Code, "Feminist Epistemologies and Women's Lives," in *The Blackwell Guide to Feminist Philosophy*, ed. Linda M. Alcoff and Eva Kittay (Malden: Blackwell, 2007), 223.
107 Ramdas, "Feminist Care Ethics," 846.
108 Oliver, *Earth and World*; Willett, supra note 78 at 140.
109 Willett, *Interspecies Ethics*, 94.
110 Kelly Oliver, "The Plight of Ethics," *Journal of Speculative Philosophy* 26.2 (2012): 130.
111 Jennifer McWeeny, "Topographies of Flesh: Women, Nonhuman Animals, and the Embodiment of Connection and Difference," *Hypatia* 29:2 (2014): 271. McWeeny draws from Carol Adams and Karen Davis's intersectional analysis of the gendered nature of animal objectification, and Simone de Beauvoir and Maurice Merleau-Ponty's theorizations of the flesh, as well as Maria Lugones's postcolonial analysis of gender relations: ibid., 271–2.
112 McWeeny does not rule out attending to "trees, rocks and ecosystems" as participants and subjects of intercorporeal exchanges: ibid., 283.
113 Ibid., 273.
114 Ibid., 273.
115 Ibid., 271.
116 Ibid., 275.
117 Ibid.
118 Ibid., 277.
119 Ibid.
120 Ibid., 279.
121 Ibid., 278.
122 Ibid., 278–9, 282.
123 Ibid., 282.
124 Ibid.
125 Ibid., 284.
126 Ralph R. Acampora, *Corporal Compassion: Animal Ethics and Philosophy of Body* (Pittsburgh: University of Pittsburgh Press, 2006), 5–6, 24.
127 Ibid., 74.
128 Ibid., 3–4.
129 Ibid., 4.

130 Ibid., 5.
131 Ibid.
132 Ibid., 75.
133 Ibid., 124.
134 Ibid., 76.
135 Ibid.
136 Ibid., 93–4.
137 Ibid., 79–80.
138 Ibid., 123.
139 Ibid., 79–80.
140 Ibid., 125.
141 Ibid., 132.
142 Ibid., 44.
143 Ibid., 74.
144 Ibid.
145 Ibid., 78.
146 Ibid., 84.
147 Ibid., 6.
148 Ibid., 77.
149 Ibid., 78, 82, 114. Acampora distinguishes empathy from symphysis
     as follows: "Empathy is a force that builds bridges of identification
     across separation, whereas symphysis is a state or condition of merging
     through commonality (shy of total fusion) – empathy establishes atomic
     or molecular connections as external relations, but internally relational
     symphysis has no atoms to begin with": ibid., 78.
150 Carol J. Adams and Lori Gruen, "Introduction," in *Ecofeminism: Feminist
     Interactions with Other Animals and the Earth,* ed. Adams and Gruen (New
     York: Bloomsbury Academic, 2014), 3; Deane Curtin, "Compassion and
     Being Human," in Adams and Gruen, *Ecofeminism,* 49; Gruen, *Entangled
     Empathy,* ch. 3.
151 Gruen, *Entangled Empathy,* 33.
152 Ibid., 29.
153 Ibid., 30.
154 Ibid., 34.
155 Ibid.
156 Ibid., 34.
157 Ibid., 113, citing Marilyn Frye, *The Politics of Reality* (Trumanburg:
     Crossing Press, 1983), 67.
158 Gruen, *Entangled Empathy,* 125.
159 Ibid., 114.
160 Ibid., 133.
161 Ibid., 122.

162 See, for example, Michael Asch, John Borrows, and James Tully, eds., *Resurgence and Reconciliation: Indigenous–Settler Relations and Earth Teachings* (Toronto: University of Toronto Press, 2018).

163 For more on the continuities and tensions between a no-killing ethic for animals and the rights of Indigenous peoples, see my summative discussions in "Unsettling Anthropocentric Legal Systems: Reconciliation, Indigenous Laws, and Animal Personhood" *Journal of Intercultural Studies* 41.1 (2020); and "Postcolonial" in *Critical Terms*, ed. Gruen. For an Indigenous feminist account that reaches similar conclusions about the author's own Indigenous heritage, see Margaret Robinson, "Animal Personhood in Mi'kmaq Perspective," *Societies* 4 (2014): 672–88. For an argument about the tight colonial juridical and mainstream cultural association between Indigenous cultures and legal orders in settler colonies such as Canada with hunting, fishing, and trapping rights, and the impasse this presents for seeing Indigenous sovereignty and justice claims and the pursuit of decolonization as aligned with animal justice claims, see Maneesha Deckha, "Veganism, Dairy, and Decolonization," *Journal of Human Rights and the Environment* 11.2 (2020): 247–8, 263–5. As noted in the introduction to this monograph, the remaining question of what the implications of beingness are for Indigenous rights in Canada and elsewhere requires a nuanced analysis that the present analysis cannot attempt.

4 Beingness: A New Legal Subjectivity for Animals

1 Ciméa Barbato Bevilaqua, "Chimpanzees in Court: What Difference Does It Make?," in *Law and the Questions of the Animal: A Critical Jurisprudence,* ed. Yoriko Otomo and Ed Mussawir (Oxford: Routledge, 2013), 84.

2 Judith Butler, *Precarious Life: The Powers of Mourning and Violence* (New York: Verso, 2006), 33.

3 Thus, the concept is not meant to be exclusive to non-human animals; it could also be extended to other non-human candidates, notably plants. I briefly address the application of beingness to other non-humans in the next chapter. For a fascinating discussion of plant ontologies and the ethical and moral responses this demands of humans according to long-standing accounts of who/what should matter in the social order, see Michael Marder, *Plant-Thinking: A Philosophy of Vegetal Life* (New York: Columbia University Press, 2013).

4 See Anna Grear, "Challenging Corporate 'Humanity': Legal Disembodiment, Embodiment and Human Rights," *Human Rights Law Review* 7.3 (2007): 515–20.

5 Sabine Lennkh, "The Animal: A Subject of Law: A Reflection on the Aspects of the Austrian and German Juridical Systems," *International Journal for the Semiotics of Law* 24.3 (2011): 337.
6 Ibid., 312, n15, 319.
7 Ibid., 309. Judicial readings of other promising constitutional and legislative references to animals' dignity in European jurisdictions have also been disappointing. See Margot Michel and Eveline Schneider Kayasseh, "The Legal Situation of Animals in Switzerland: Two Steps Forward, One Step Back – Many Steps to Go," *Journal of Animal Law* 7 (2011): 3.
8 Alexandra Isfahani-Hammond, "Of She-Wolves and Mad Cows: Animality, Anthropophagy and the State of Exception in Cláudio Assis's Amerola manga," *Luso-Brazilian Review* 48.2 (2011): 145.
9 Isabel Karpin and Roxanne Mykitiuk, "Feminist Legal Theory as Embodied Justice," in *Transcending the Boundaries of Law: Generations of Feminism and Legal Theory*, ed. Martha Fineman (New York: Routledge, 2011), 115.
10 For a sampling of this vast literature see Debra Bergoffen and Gail Weiss, "Embodying the Ethical – Editors' Introduction," *Hypatia* 26.3 (2011): 453; Fiona Kumari Campbell, *Contours of Ableism: The Production of Disability and Abledness* (Basingstoke: Palgrave Macmillan, 2009), 160–95; Rosemarie Garland-Thomson, "Feminist Disability Studies," *Signs* 30.2 (2005), 1558; Stella Gonzalez-Arnal, Gill Jagger and Kathleen Lennon, eds., *Embodied Selves* (Basingstoke: Palgrave Macmillan, 2012); Paddy McQueen, "Invited Review Essay," *Hypatia* 27:2 (2012): 338; Lynn Meskell and Robert W. Preucel, *A Companion to Social Archaeology* (Malden: Blackwell, 2004), 92; Lisa Jean Moore and Mary Kosut, *The Body Reader: Essential Social and Cultural Readings* (New York: New York University Press, 2010); Margrit Shildrick, *Dangerous Discourses of Disability, Subjectivity and Sexuality* (Basingstoke: Palgrave Macmillan, 2009); Margrit Shildrick and Roxanne Mykitiuk, *Ethics of the Body: Postconventional Challenges* (Cambridge, MA: MIT Press, 2005).
11 This is not to say that the body as metaphor has not had purchase in the law. As Saru Matambanadzo has shown in her work on corporations, the body "serves an important expressive purpose, describing implicit attributes of legal persons and indicating what sorts of creatures law makers feel a legal person should be. Non-human entities, individuals or collectives that do not possess a recognizable physical body must be rendered conceptually corporeal and embodied through the use of the body as metaphor in order to be recognized as persons." Saru Matambanadzo, "The Body, Incorporated," *Tulsa Law Review* 87.3 (2013).

12 Oliver, "Bodies Against the Law: Abu Ghraib and the War on Terror," *Continential Philosophy Review* 42.1 (2009): 64.

13 Ibid., 65–6, 74–5.

14 Ibid., 78.

15 Kelly Oliver, *Animal Lessons: How They Teach Us to Be Human* (New York: Columbia University Press, 2009); idem, "Bodies"; idem, "What Is Wrong with (Animal) Rights?," *Journal of Speculative Philosophy* 22.3 (2008): 220; idem, "Conflicted Love," *Hypatia* 15.3 (2000).

16 Oliver, *Animal Lessons*, 191.

17 Jennifer Nedelsky, *Law's Relations: A Relational Theory of Self, Autonomy, and Law* (New York: Oxford University Press, 2011), 163, 193. See also idem, "Relations of Freedom and Law's Relations," *Politics & Gender* 8.2 (2012).

18 Henson explains this dynamic as such: in "capitalism's drive towards self-preservation," it exploits and sacrifices. One way in which capitalism makes exploitation and sacrifice of animals acceptable is by dehumanizing them. The human is considered different from the animal because the human aspect of the human is tied to the political realm rather than the natural realm; thus the human is tied to their rights rather than to their body. Henson, "Species of Thought," 1660, 1664.

19 Shildrick, "Beyond the Body of Bioethics," 15.

20 She cites land enclosures, Indigenous dispossession, other colonialisms, corporate empires, anthropogenic climate change, and global economic disparity as examples. Grear, "Vulnerability," 46.

21 Kathryn Gillespie, "Placing Angola: Racialisation, Anthropocentrism, and Settler Colonialism in the Louisiana State Penitentiary's Angola Rodeo," *Antipode* 50.5 (2018); Glenney Boggs, *Animalia Americana*, 9; Grear, "Vulnerability," 45; Oliver, Animal Ethics, 27.

22 Henson, "Species of Thought," 1664.

23 David Delaney, *Law and Nature* (New York: Cambridge University Press, 2003), 216; Henson, "Species of Thought," 1664. As Henson further explains: "Because humanness is made a political, conceptual category rather than a biological fact, certain humans can be defined as no longer fully human or deserving of 'human rights.' Today, with the widespread animalization of many, what is seen to constitute 'the human' is becoming increasingly amorphous, difficult to locate, and abstract. As those banned or marked as outside the political realm are silenced, the (biologized) animal comes to mark the refugee, the 'illegal' migrant, the prisoner, and the slum dweller." Ibid. See also Oliver, Animal Ethics, 271–2.

24 Ann V. Murphy, "Corporeal Vulnerability," *Hypatia* 26.3 (2011): 575.

25 Bergoffen and Weiss, "Embodying the Ethical," 459.
26 Suvadip Sinha and Amit R. Baishya, "Introduction," in *Postcolonial Animalities*, ed. Suvadip Sinha and Amit R. Baishya (New York: Routledge, 2019).
27 Sundhya Walther, "Fables of the Tiger Economy: Species and Subalternity in Aravind Adiga's White Tiger," *MFS Modern Fiction Studies* 60.3 (2014).
28 See the comprehensive albeit anthropocentric discussion of law's response to marginalized bodies in Karpin and Mykitiuk, "Feminist Legal Theory."
29 Nedelsky, *Law's Relations*, 190.
30 Grear, "Vulnerability," 47; Zakiyyah Iman Jackson, "Animal: New Directions in the Theorization of Race and Posthumanism" *Feminist Studies* 39.3 (2013): 672, discussing Sylvia Wynter, "Unsettling the Coloniality of Being/Power/Truth/Freedom: Toward the Human, after Man, Its Overrepresentation – an Argument," *The New Centennial Review* 3.3 (2003); Mayo Moran, *Rethinking the Reasonable Person: An Egalitarian Reconstruction of the Objective Standard* (Oxford University Press, 2003), 9–10, 14; Ngaire Naffine, *Law's Meaning of Life: Philosophy, Religion, Darwin, and the Legal Person* (Oxford: Hart, 2009), 76–7.
31 See, for example, Susan Bordo, *The Flight of Objectivity: Essays on Cartesianism and Culture* (Albany: SUNY Press, 1987), 9; Fiona Kumari Campbell, "Inciting Legal Fictions: 'Disabilities' Date with Ontology and the Ableist Body of the Law," *Griffith Law Review* 10.1 (2001): 46–7; Drucilla Cornell, *The Philosophy of the Limit* (New York: Routledge, 1992), 107; Eve Darian-Smith and Peter Fitzpatrick, *Laws of the Postcolonial* (Ann Arbor: University of Michigan Press, 1999), 79; Rosemarie Garland-Thomson, "Misfits: A Feminist Materialist Disability Concept," *Hypatia* 26.3 (2011); Isabel Karpin and Roxanne Mykitiuk, "'Going out on a limb': Prosthetics, Normalcy, and Disputing the 'Therapy/Enhancement' Distinction,'" *Medical Law Review* 16.3 (2008), 413; Nedelsky, *Law's Relations*, 163–4; Linda Steele and Leanne Dowse, "Gender, Disability Rights, and Violence Against Medical Bodies," *Australian Feminist Studies* 31.88 (2016): 193–4.
32 Sunaura Taylor, "Animal Crips," in *Disability and Animality: Crip Perspectives in Critical Animal Studies*, ed. Stephanie Jenkins, Kelly Struthers Montford, and Chloë Taylor (London: Routledge, 2020), 18–24; Kelly Somers and Karen Soldatic, "Productive Bodies: How Neoliberalism Makes and Unmakes Disability in Human and Non-human Animals," in Jenkins, Struthers, Montford, and Taylor, *Disability and Animality*, 37–41.
33 Sunaura Taylor, *Beasts of Burden: Animals and Disability Liberation* (New York: New Press, 2017); Taylor, "Disability and Interdependence," in

Messy Eating: Conversations on Animals as Food, ed. Samantha King et al. (New York: Fordham University Press).

34 Taylor, *Beasts of Burden.*
35 Nedelsky, *Law's Relations,* 166–7.
36 Butler, *Precarious Life,* 26.
37 Judith Butler, *Gender Trouble* (New York: Routledge, 2000).
38 Butler, *Precarious Life,* 26.
39 Ibid., 27.
40 Nedelsky's work in *Law's Relations* is focused on humans, but in a coda to her chapter discussing the multidimensional self and her creative and interactive capacity, she specifically affirms the extension of a relational approach to all beings that have the capacity for creative interaction: 194–9. Nedelsky maintains that any relational approach that allows violence against animals and other non-humans to continue will undermine its own aims in addition to drawing its own exclusionary boundaries. At the same time, Nedelsky admits that she preserves the language of equality and premise about equality that ground her relational approach for humans only, preferring a language of "incalculable, intrinsic worth for other entities as a starting point" for rethinking human–non-human relations: 195. She justifies this difference in wording because of pragmatic issues regarding familiar language when thinking about humans but also because she admits she is uncertain about what equal relations with animals would look like and is not yet prepared to be as absolutist in her claims about animals as she is with humans. Nedelsky hopes that her relational arguments will ultimately catalyse more non-anthropocentric attention to animals and other non-humans, but again, she is forthright that her choice to reserve equality for humans only in the present moment counters such a move. She chooses it nonetheless for her present work because she sees equality as an indispensable linguistic and conceptual tool to make intelligible to her readers what she wants to say about liberal legalism as a whole in her book. Nedelsky does indicate that she hopes to transcend this linguistic compromise in future work, addressing the implications of her relational approach beyond intrahuman justice questions: 199. Thus, it would seem fair to summarize Nedelsky's stance on animals and other non-humans as a desire to include them equally in the future but not just yet. I say more about Butler's take on non-human animals later in this chapter.
41 Marc Bekoff and Jessica Pierce, *Wild Justice: The Moral Lives of Animals* (Chicago: University of Chicago Press, 2009).
42 Ibid., iv.
43 Ibid., iv, xi.

44 Ibid., iv, xii. In this they join other leading ethologists who have written extensively about animal intelligence and emotions that place human exceptionalism in context. See, in particular, two recent works of Frans de Waal: *Are We Smart Enough to Know How Smart Animals Are?* (New York: W.W. Norton, 2017); and *Mama's Last Hug: Animal Emotions and What They Tell Us about Ourselves* (New York: W.W. Norton, 2019).

45 Bekoff and Pierce, *Wild Justice*, 56.

46 Ibid., 59.

47 Ibid., 107.

48 Cynthia Willett, *Interspecies Ethics* (New York: Columbia University Press, 2014).

49 Willett references de Waal's work thirteen times in her index. Ibid., 218.

50 Ibid., 132.

51 Ibid., 139.

52 Ibid., 48–51, 75–6.

53 Ibid., 31.

54 Carol Adam and Lori Gruen, eds., *Ecofeminism: Feminist Intersections with Animals and the Earth* (New York: Bloomsbury, 2014); Lori Gruen and Kari Weil, "Animal Others – Editors' Introduction" *Hypatia* 27.3 (2012); Gruen, "A Few Thoughts on the Future of Environmental Philosophy," *Ethics and the Environment* 12.2 (2007); idem, "Conflicting Values in a Conflicted World: Ecofeminism and Multicultural Environmental Ethics," *Women and Environments International Magazine* 52–3 (Fall 2001); idem, "On the Oppression of Women and Animals," *Environmental Ethics* 18.4 (1996).

55 Gruen, *Entangled Empathy*.

56 Ibid., 59.

57 Ibid., 60, citing Karen Barad, *Meeting the Universe Halfway* (Durham: Duke University Press, 2007), as well as Adam Kleinmann, "Intra-actions: An interview with Karen Barad", *Mousse Magazine* 34.1–2 (2012).

58 Gruen, *Entangled Empathy*, 59. For historical arguments to this effect see Christopher Watts, ed., *Relational Archaeologies: Humans, Animals, Things* (New York: Routledge, 2013).

59 Gruen, *Entangled Empathy*, 58–61.

60 Estair Van Wagner, "Putting Property in its Place: Relational Theory, Environmental Rights and Land Use Planning," *Revue Générale De Droit* 43 (2013): 280.

61 Taimie L. Bryant, "Denying Animals Childhood and Its Implications for Animal-Protective Law Reform" *Law, Culture, and the Humanities* 6.1 (2010).

62 I explain more precisely how this would occur in the Conclusion.

63 Lisa C. Knisely, "Oppression, Normative Violence, and Vulnerability: The Ambiguous Beauvoirian Legacy of Butler's Ethics," *philoSOPHIA* 2.2 (2012). See, for example, Eva Feder Kittay, "Human Dependency and

Rawlsian Equality," in *Feminists Rethink the Self*, ed. Diana T. Meyers
(Boulder: Westview Press, 1997); Sara Ruddick, *Maternal Thinking*.

64 Martha Albertson Fineman, "Equality, Autonomy, and the Vulnerable
Subject in Law and Politics," in *Vulnerability: Reflections on a New Ethical
Foundation for Law and Politics*, ed. Fineman and Anna Grear (Surrey:
Ashgate, 2013), 20; Ani Satz, "Animals as Vulnerable Subjects: Beyond
Interest Convergence, Hierarchy, and Property" *Animal Law* 16.1 (2009):
79.

65 Alice Kuzniar, "Where Is the Animal after Post-Humanism?: Sue Coe and
the Art of Quivering Life," *New Centennial Review* 11.2 (2007): 27.

66 Shahrzad Fouladvand and Tony Ward, "Human Trafficking,
Vulnerability, and the State," *Journal of Criminal Law* 83:1 (2019): 39. See
also Martha Albertson Fineman, "The Vulnerable Subject: Anchoring
Equality in the Human Condition," *Yale Journal of Law and Feminism*
20.1 (2008); idem, "Vulnerability and the Institution of Marriage" *Emory
Law Journal* 64.6 (2015); idem, "Vulnerability and Inevitable Inequality,"
Oslo Law Review 4.4 (2017). See also the Vulnerability and Human
Condition Initiative (VHC), established by Fineman in 2008. The VHC
is an academic space, hosting scholars and workshops, that imagines
alternative modes of state responsibility focused on the universal
vulnerability of human beings and our reliance on social relationships
and institutions. The initiative proposes that the "vulnerable legal
subject" displace the liberal legal subject that dominates law and policy
and shapes our social relationships and institutions. VHC, perma.cc
/AHV9-XBPH .

67 Grear, "Vulnerability," 49.

68 Nayeli Urquiza Haas, "Book Review: M.A. Fineman and A. Grear (eds):
Vulnerability: Reflections on a New Ethical Foundation for Law and
Politics (London: Ashgate, 2013)," *Feminist Legal Studies* 22 (2014): 338.

69 Anna Grear has also affirmed the "theoretical potency" of vulnerability
to transform law into a transspecies paradigm given that vulnerability
inheres in non-human entities as well. Grear, "Vulnerability," 50. Angela
Harris makes a similar argument in favour of thinking about human
relations with nature or the environment. Angela P. Harris, "Vulnerability
and Power in the Age of the Anthropocene," *Washington & Lee Journal* 6.1
(2015): 109.

70 Satz proposes a model of equality for animals that draws from American
Equal Protection Doctrine. She engages with liberal legal orders in
order to find a practical alternative to current rights-based models. Satz,
"Animals as Vulnerable Subjects," 110–11.

71 Joshua Tray Barnett, "Thinking Ecologically with Judith Butler" *Culture,
Theory, and Critique* 59.1 (2018): 22.

72 Puar, "Precarity Talk," 163–77. Butler identifies precarity as "the politically induced condition in which certain populations suffer from failing social and economic networks ... becoming differentially exposed to injury, violence, and death." Butler, *Precarious Life*, 53, as cited in Nayeli Urquiza Haas, "The Semiotic Fractures of Vulnerable Bodies," *International Journal for the Semiotics of Law* 30.4 (2017): 554.

73 Rob Cover, "Sexual Ethics, Masculinity and Mutual Vulnerability," *Australian Feminist Studies* 29.82 (2014): 436.

74 Butler, *Precarious Life*, 30.

75 Ibid., 42–3.

76 Ibid.

77 Ibid., 43.

78 Fineman, "Equality," 16.

79 Murphy, "Corporeal Vulnerability," 577. Although Butler and Fineman diverge on this point, they agree on others, namely, the need to supplant liberal individualism with an alternative model that is rooted in humanness rather than the politics of difference/identify politics. Ibid., 578.

80 Butler, *Precarious Life*, 31–4, 44–5.

81 Knisely, "Oppression," 145. Knisely notes other scholarly influences on Butler's body of work on vulnerability, arguing in particular that Simone de Beauvoir's ethics has shaped her thinking. Ibid., 147.

82 Chloë Taylor, "The Precarious Lives of Animals: Butler, Coetzee, and Animal Ethics," *Philosophy Today* 52.1 (2008): 60.

83 Ibid., 20.

84 Ibid., 29.

85 Ibid., 30.

86 Tula Brannelly, "Sustaining Citizenship: People with Dementia and the Phenomenon of Social Death," *Nursing Ethics* 18.5 (2011): 662; Kim, *Dangerous Crossings*; Ko, *Racism as Zoological Witchcraft*; Alexander G. Weheliye, *Habeas Viscus: Racializing Assemblages, Biopolitics, and Black Feminist Theories of the Human* (Durham: Duke University Press, 2014).

87 Puar, "Precarity Talk," 170.

88 Taylor, "The Precarious Lives," 60.

89 Ibid.

90 Ibid.

91 Puar, "Precarity Talk," 67.

92 Jasbir Puar's previous work on these questions may be found in the special volume titled "Interspecies" that she co-edited with Julie Livingston in *Social Text* 29.1 (2011); and Jasbir Kin Puar, "'I Would Rather

be a Cyborg than a Goddess': Becoming Intersectional in Assemblage Theory," *philoSOPHIA* 2.1 (2012).

93 Puar, "Precarity Talk," 170–1.

94 Ibid. at 173–4.

95 As referenced in the Introduction, Megan H. Glick says more about such pitfalls with humanization language or with any discourse that relies on the human as an innocent ethical category. See Megan H. Glick, *Infrahumanisms: Science, Culture, and the Making of Modern Non/personhood* (Durham: Duke University Press, 2018). See also my "Subhuman as a Cultural Agent of Violence," *Journal of Critical Animal Studies* 8.3 (2010).

96 Glenney Boggs, *Animalia Americana*, 24.

97 See Maneesha Deckha, "Initiating a Non-Anthropocentric Jurisprudence: The Rule of Law and Animal Vulnerability under a Property Paradigm," *Alberta Law Review* 50.4 (2013); *Reece v Edmonton (City)*, 2011 ABCA 238 (CanLII), 335 DLR (4th) 600, 513 AR 199, Chief Justice Fraser's dissent at 88. For discussion of how companion animals' status as property renders them vulnerable, see Marie Fox and Mo Ray, "No Pets Allowed?: Companion Animals, Older People, and Residential Care," *Medical Humanities* 45.2 (2019); Nicole R. Pallotta, "Chattel of Child: The Liminal Status of Companion Animals in Society and Law," *Social Sciences* 8.5 (2019). For a moving representation of such precarity in fiction, see Andre Alexis, *Fifteen Dogs: An Apologue* (Toronto: Coach House, 2015).

98 Rob Nixon, *Slow Violence and the Environmentalism of the Poor* (Cambridge, MA: Harvard University Press, 2011), 63–4.

99 Taylor, "The Precarious Lives," 60.

100 James Stanescu, "Species Trouble: Judith Butler, Mourning, and the Precarious Lives of Animals," *Hypatia* 27.3 (2012).

101 Grear, "Vulnerability"; Harris, "Vulnerability and Power."

102 Wendy Rogers, Catriona Mackenzie, and Susan Dodds, "Why Bioethics Needs a Concept of Vulnerability," *International Journal of Feminist Approaches to Bioethics* 5.2 (2012): 32.

103 Henson, "Species of Thought," 1674; Oliver, "Animal Ethics," 271; Taylor, "The Precarious Lives," 66.

104 Other criticisms of the argument may, of course, also inhere, but I focus here on those that are most salient to the blend of theoretical frameworks in which I've housed beingness. For further criticisms of, for example, vulnerability that I do not address, see Danielle Petherbridge, "What's Critical about Vulnerability?: Rethinking Interdependence, Recognition, and Power," *Hypatia* 31.1 (2016): 590–1.

105 Elizabeth V. Spelman, *Fruits of Sorrow: Framing Our Attention to Suffering* (Boston: Beacon Press, 2001), 1.

106 Carol Cohn, "'Maternal Thinking' and the Concept of 'Vulnerability' in Security Paradigms, Policies, and Practices," *Journal of International Political Theory* 10.1 (2013): 53, 55, 62–3.

107 Ibid.

108 Alyson Cole, "All of Us Are Vulnerable, but Some Are More Vulnerable than Others: The Political Ambiguity of Vulnerability Studies, an Ambivalent Critique," *Journal of Philosphy and Social Theory* 17.2 (2016): 263.

109 Ibid., 268; Rebecca M.F. Hewer, "A Gossamer Consensus: Discourses of Vulnerability in the Westminster Prostitution Policy Subsystem," *Social and Legal Studies* 28.2 (2019): 228; Haas, "The Semiotic Fractures," 548–52.

110 Petherbridge, "What's Critical about Vulnerability?," 591; Cohn, "'Maternal Thinking,'" 62.

111 Taimie L. Bryant, "Animals Unmodified: Defining Animals/Defining Human Obligations to Animals" *University of Chicago Legal Forum* (2006): 144.

112 Ibid.

113 Ibid.

114 Kuzniar, "Where Is the Animal?," 33.

115 Willett, *Interspecies Ethics*, 85.

116 Matthew Calarco, "Animal Studies," *The Year's Work in Critical and Cultural Theory* 24.1 (2016).

117 Haas, "The Semiotic Fractures," 553.

118 Fouladvand and Ward, "Human Trafficking," 40.

119 Spelman, *Fruits of Sorrow*, 61–2; Hewer, "A Gossamer Consensus," 228; Haas, "The Semiotic Fractures," 553, 559; Cole, "All of Us Are Vulnerable," 265, 273; Fouladvand and Ward, "Human Trafficking," 49.

120 Kelly Oliver explains the problems with recognition at length as well as the witnessing structure she creates to retheorize subjectivity in *Witnessing: Beyond Recognition* (Minneapolis: Minneapolis University Press, 2001).

121 Ibid., 79.

122 Bettina Stumm, "Witnessing Others in Narrative Collaboration: Ethical Responsibility beyond Recognition," *Biography* 37.3 (2014): 768, 777, 780.

123 Oliver, *Witnessing*, 78.

124 Furthermore, it may be that vulnerability and the recognition thereof is a prerequisite for transformative political action. See Ewa Plonowska Ziarek, "Feminist Reflections on Vulnerability: Disrespect, Obligation, Action" *SubStance* 42.3 (2013): 81. Drawing from Levinas and Arendt, Ziarek argues that an ethics infused by recognition of the vulnerability of

the Other is a catalyst for feminist praxis that can transcend the current dominant and reductive discourses on vulnerability that speak about vulnerability of human populations through the frame of biopower or, alternatively, through a liberal individualist frame that sees vulnerability as an attribute of individual human beings to be alleviated through self-help programs and initiatives. Ibid., 81–2.

125 Malini Johar Schueller, "Decolonizing Global Theories Today: Hardt and Negri, Agamben, Butler," *Interventions* 11.2 (2009).

126 Ibid., 249–50.

127 Ibid., 237.

128 Ibid., 252.

129 Others have also noted the Eurocentrism of these global theories. For another critique of Agamben see Glenney Boggs, *Animalia Americana*, 13–16.

130 Schueller, "Decolonizing Global Theories Today," 246.

131 Ibid., 237. Schueller acknowledges the anti-imperial impulse of all the global theories she unpacks.

132 Ibid.

133 Ibid., 247.

134 Ibid.

135 Ibid., 248.

136 Ibid., 248–9.

137 Ibid., 249.

138 Ibid.

139 Ibid.

140 Paola Cavalieri, "The Animal Debate," in *In Defense of Animals: The Second Wave*, ed. Peter Singer (Malden: Blackwell, 2006), 54.

141 McWeeny, "Topographies of Flesh," 283.

5 Liberal Humanism Repackaged?

1 Erica Fudge, *Animal* (London: Reaktion, 2002).

2 Kelly Oliver, "The Right to Remain Silent," in *Animal Lessons: How They Teach Us to Be Human* (New York: Columbia University Press, 2009), 27–8.

3 Gary L. Francione, "A Frequently Asked Question: What about Plants?," *Animal Rights: The Abolitionist Post* (blog), 13 December 2006, perma.cc /G8MC-K4LF .

4 Matthew Calarco, "Identity, Difference, Indistinction," *New Centennial Review* 11.2 (2012). See the discussion in the Introduction.

5 *The Oxford English Dictionary*, s.v. "animal," perma.cc/SL2D-HCCB.

6 Ibid.

7 Taimie L. Bryant, "Animals Unmodified: Defining Animals/Defining Human Obligations to Animals," *University of Chicago Legal Forum* (2006). For examples of theorists who have explicitly addressed this question of line-drawing and settled on sentience see Gary L. Francione, *Animals as Persons: Essays on the Abolition of Animal Exploitation* (New York: Columbia University Press, 2008); Ani Satz, "Would Rosa Parks Wear Fur?," *Journal of Animal Law and Ethics* 1 (2006): 153.

8 Anna Grear explains how this holds true even for legal personhood for corporations through what is termed, paradoxically, the embodiment theory of corporate personality. Anna Grear, "Challenging Corporate Humanity," *Human Rights Law Review* 7.3 (2007)

9 See for example, Frans de Waal, *Are We Smart Enough to Know How Smart Animals Are?* (New York: W.W. Norton, 2017).

10 Bryant, "Animals Unmodified," 165.

11 Ibid., 169. She asks the same set of questions about another planetary life form that is not sentient: coral. Ibid., 168–70.

12 Myra Hird makes a similar point about bacteria, crediting these microorganisms with evolutionary and scientific progress and imploring animal studies scholars to afford them ethical protection. Hird regards the advocacy focus on larger organisms as exhibiting sameness logic since larger animals are more human-like than bacteria. Hird, "Meeting with the Microcosmos," *Society and Space* 28.1 (2010): 36.

13 Bryant, "Animals Unmodified," 169–70.

14 Ibid., 166; Taimie L. Bryant, "Similarity or Difference as a Basis for Justice: Must Animals Be Like Humans to Be Legally Protected from Humans," *Animal Law and Policy* 70.1 (2007): 217.

15 John Miller, *Empire and the Animal Body: Violence, Identity, and Ecology in Victorian Adventure Fiction* (London: Anthem Press, 2012), 17.

16 Astrida Neimanis, "No Representation without Colonisation? (or, Nature Represents Itself)," *Somatechnics* 5:1 (2015).

17 Bryant, "Animals Unmodified," 165–6.

18 David J. Gunkel, "A Vindication of the Rights of Machines," *Philosophy and Technology* 27.1 (2014).

19 Ibid., 115.

20 Ibid., 119.

21 Ibid.

22 For samples of these genres, see Karen Barad, "Posthumanist Performativity: Toward an Understanding of How Matter Comes to Matter," *Signs* 28.3 (2003); Susanne Beck, "The Problem of Ascribing Legal Responsibility in the Case of Robotics," *Artificial Intelligence and Society* 31 (2016); Argyro Karanasiou and Dimitri Pinotsis, "Towards a Legal Definition of Machine Intelligence: The Argument for Artificial

Personhood in the Age of Deep Learning," *International Conference on Aritifical Intelligence and Law* 17 (2017); Nicola Liberati and Shoji Nagataki, "Vulnerability under the Gaze of Robots: Relations among Humans and Robots," *Artificial Intelligence and Society* (2018), doi.org/10.1007 /s00146-01800849-1; Luciana Parisi, *Abstract Sex: Philosophy, Technology, and Mutations of Desire* (London: Continuum, 2004); Steven Shakespeare, "Articulating the Inhuman: God, Animal, Machine," in *Beyond Human: From Animality to Transhumanism*, ed. Charlie Blake, Claire Molloy, and Steven Shakespeare (London: Continuum, 2012); Anneke Smelik and Nina Lykke, eds., *Bits of Life* (Seattle: University of Washington Press, 2008).

23 Gunkel, "A Vindication," 119–22.

24 Ibid., 122.

25 Ibid., 123.

26 Ibid., 123. Gunkel sets his focus on a theory that is even more inclusive of biocentrism, namely, Information Ethics. Information Ethics draws from Floridi's notion that bioethics and environmental ethics are an incomplete innovation because they replace biocentrism with animocentrism and thus continue to exclude entities such as technology or other types of artifacts. Information Ethics is more inclusive because it replaces biocentrism with ontocentrism. It focuses on the existence of all entities rather than on life, and on the destruction of informational objects rather than on suffering. Therefore, according to Information Ethics, an entity is deserving of ethical consideration if it exists as a coherent body of information.

27 Ibid., 124.

28 Ibid., 124.

29 Calarco, "Identity, Difference, Indistinction," 58.

30 Gunkel, "A Vindication," 124.

31 Ibid., 124–5.

32 Ibid., 125.

33 Ibid.

34 Ibid., 125–6.

35 David Gunkel and Debra Hawhee, "Virtual Alterity and the Reformatting of Ethics," *Journal of Mass Media Ethics* 18.3–4 (2003): 177.

36 Gunkel, "A Vindication," 126.

37 Gayatri Chakravarthy Spivak, *In Other Worlds: Essays in Cultural Politics* (New York: Routledge, 1998).

38 Gunkel, "A Vindication," 127.

39 Ibid.

40 Ibid., citing John Llewellyn, *Emmanuel Levinas: The Genealogy of Ethics* (London: Routledge, 1995), 4.

41 Gunkel, "A Vindication," 128. Gunkel is aware that Levinas himself declined to consider faces that were not human as Others to which he must respond. This limit of Levinas's ethic of Otherness is more manageable, though, as his theory does not pivot on anthropocentrism, but merely assumes it.

42 Neimanis, "No Representation," 16, 150.

43 Bryant, "Animals Unmodified," 169–70.

44 Ibid., 173.

45 Ani Satz, "Animals as Vulnerable Subjects: Beyond Interest-Convergence, Hierarchy, and Property," *Animal Law* 16.1 (2009): 110.

46 Ibid., 110–16.

47 Alice Crary, "Animals, Cognitive Disability, and Getting the World in Focus in Ethics and Social Thought: A Reply to Eva Feder Kittay and Peter Singer," *ZEMO* 139.2 (2019).

48 Hird, "Meeting with the Microcosmos."

49 Kelly Oliver, "What Is Wrong with (Animal) Rights?," *Journal of Speculative Philosophy* 22.3 (2008): 222.

50 Ibid.

51 Hird, "Meeting with the Microcosmos," 36–8, as discussed in Zipporah Weisberg, "The Trouble with Posthumanism: Bacteria Are People Too," in *Critical Animal Studies: Thinking the Unthinkable*, ed. John Sorenson (Toronto: Canadian Scholars' Press, 2014), 108.

52 Ibid.

53 Weisberg, "The Trouble with Posthumanism," 109.

54 Ibid.

55 Lori Gruen, *Entangled Empathy* (Brooklyn: Lantern Books, 2015), 65–6. Gruen writes: "Acknowledging our entanglements with the bacteria in our guts and having our perspectives altered when we realize we exist with others [that] have been on Earth for thousands of years, highlight connections. But these connections aren't clearly or obviously ethical ones. And if they are, the values that flow through them are different from those we focus on when we are empathizing with the wellbeing of an other": ibid., 65. Gruen appears to ascribe "wellbeing" only to those animals that are sentient: ibid., 65, 70).

56 Ibid., 71. I would hasten to add here that we should not be too quick to dimiss the possible sentience of plants, given evidence coming forward regarding the consciousness of plants and their protective attitudes toward themselves and other plants (capacities that have not been associated with plants in Western epistemologies) as well as long-standing perspectives in some non-Western cultures regarding plant sentience and intentionality. For more on the consciousness of plants, see Michael Marder, *Plant-Thinking: A Philosophy of Vegetal Life* (New

York: Columbia University Press, 2013). For more on culturally variable beliefs in plant aptitudes, see Bethany Ojalehto, Douglas L. Medin, and Salino G. Garcia, "Conceptualizing Agency: Folkpsychological and Folkcommunicative Perspectives on Plants," *Cognition* 162 (2017).

57 Gruen's comment above endorsing "loving regard for and commitment to other-than-sentient nature" suggests that plants are not sentient. There is emerging work that suggests plants may be sentient as well as critical scholarship that challenges as human hubris any claim not being plants ourselves, that they are not.

58 For accounts of the value of vegetal life that give focused attention to the anthropocentric, gendered, and racist violence of settler colonialism vis-à-vis vegetal life, see Catriona Sandilands, *The Good-Natured Feminist: Ecofeminism and the Quest for Democracy* (Minneapolis: University of Minnesota Press, 1999); Robin Wall Kimmerer, *Braiding Sweetgrass: Indigenous Wisdom, Scientific Knowledge, and the Teachings of Plants* (Minneapolis: Milkweed Editions, 2013); Dan Bousfield, "Settler Colonialism in Vegetal Worlds: Exploring Progress and Resilience at the Margins of the Anthropocene," *Settler Colonial Studies* 10.1 (2020), https://doi.org/10.1080/2201473X.2019.160429. For a post-structuralist monograph treatment of the intentionality of plants, see Marder, *Plant-Thinking*.

59 Gary L. Francione, "Debate with Professor Michael Marder on Plant Ethics," *Animal Rights: The Abolitionist Post* (blog), 8 June 2012, perma .cc/7DF4-G82M .

60 Ibid.

61 Ibid.

62 Ibid.

63 Marder, *Plant-Thinking*, 185.

64 Ibid., 185.

65 Ibid., 184.

66 Ibid., 184.

67 Ibid., 185.

68 Stefan Knauss, "Conceptualizing Human Stewardship in the Anthropocene: The Rights of Nature in Ecuador, New Zealand, and India," *Journal of Agricultural and Environmental Ethics* 31.6 (2018).

69 Roughly 8 million tonnes enter the Earth's oceans annually. Paul Hond, "Plastic, Plastic Everywhere," *Columbia Magazine* (2019), perma.cc /F6X5-P875.

70 Astrida Neimanis, "Feminist Subjectivity, Watered," *Feminist Review* 103 (2013). To be sure, we can also think seriously about the entirety of the planet's surfaces along this line – mountain ranges and land in general as living and in need of protection from human and corporate

capitalist schemes. But the question of how best to decommodify land, which humans and non-aquatic animals need to live, and its mediation by settler-colonial histories of private ownership, and now decolonizing efforts meant to recognize human Indigenous claims in land, is too complex to be taken up, even to sketch a brief answer.

71 Here, I define "living" as referring to entities that breathe through a respiratory system. I include only born living forms, so embryos or fetuses not yet born would not count where their interests clash with the females in which they are located. I do so largely for the reasons advanced by Jennifer Nedelsky in "Property in Potential Life? A Relational Approach to Choosing Legal Categories," *Canadian Journal of Law and Jurisprudence* 6.2 (1993); Judith Jarvis Thomson, "A Defense of Abortion," *Philosophy and Public Affairs* 1.1 (1971). This is not to say there should be no respect afforded embryos or fetuses short of full legal subjectivity. See Maneesha Deckha, "Legislating Respect: A Pro-choice Feminist Legal Analysis of Embryo Research Restrictions in Canada," *McGill Law Journal* 58.1 (2012). I also recognize that classifying entities as "living" or even "sentient" is a deeply culturally contingent practice and that in Western epistemologies, anthropocentric epistemic violence has been enacted against entities such as mountains and rocks through their relegation to the realm of passive object rather than agentic subject. I do not seek to fortify the passive representation of these naturalized entities with the present argument; rather, I grapple with the question of harm and conflict reduction where exploitation of non-humans is at stake. For more on the agential capacities of matter (particularly mountains) commonly assumed to be inanimate in dominant Western epistemologies, see Guillermo Salas Carreno, "Mining and the Living Materiality of Mountains in Andean Societies," *Journal of Material Culture* 22.2 (2016); Julie Cruickshank, *Do Glaciers Listen? Local Knowledges, Colonial Encounters, and Social Imagination* (Vancouver: UBC Press, 2005); and Bryanne Young, "Intimacies of Rock: Ethnographic Considerations of Posthuman Performativity in Canada's Rocky Mountains," *Cultural Studies/Critical Methodologies* 16.1 (2016).

72 Stacy Alaimo, "Jellyfish Science, Jellyfish Aesthetics: Posthuman Reconfigurations of the Sensible," in *Thinking with Water*, ed. Cecelia Chen, Janine MacLeod and Astrida Neimanis (Montreal and Kingston: McGill-Queen's University Press, 2013); idem, *Bodily Natures: Science, Environment, and the Material Self* (Bloomington: Indiana University Press, 2010); idem, "Trans-Corporeal Feminisms and the Ethical Space of Nature," in *Material Feminisms*, ed. Stacy Alaimo and Susan Hekman (Bloomington: Indiana University Press, 2008);); Stacy Alaimo and Susan Hekman, "Introduction: Emerging Models of Materiality in Feminist

Theory," in Alaimo and Hekman, *Material Feminisms*; Jane Bennett, *Vibrant Matter: A Political Ecology of Things* (Durham: Duke University Press, 2010); Karen Barad, *Meeting the Universe Halfway: Quantum Physics and the Entanglement of Matter and Meaning* (Durham: Duke University Press, 2007).

73 Francione, "Debate with Professor Michael Marder." For a fuller exposition of Marder's views about plants see his *Plant-Thinking*; as well as his article "Is It Ethical to Eat Plants?"

74 I realize giving more details and case studies about how such assessments may occur is necessary, but I leave the lengthy discussion this would entail for another time.

75 I thank my colleague Gillian Calder for raising this query with me.

76 Claire Young and Susan Boyd, "Losing the Feminist Voice? Debates on the Legal Recognition of Same Sex Partnerships in Canada," *Feminist Legal Studies* 14.2 (2006): 230–1.

77 Indeed, this dynamic is apparent (albeit, I would argue, more acceptable) in Canada if we compare the status of corporations and the rights they are afforded as persons against those of humans. This is not to argue, of course, that corporations should have more rights than they currently do. For a critique of the expansive set of rights corporations already hold, see Grear, "Challenging Corporate Humanity," 517–21.

Conclusion

1 James Stanescu, "Species Trouble: Judith Butler, Mourning, and the Precarious Lives of Animals," *Hypatia* 27.3 (2012): 576.

2 Nancy M. Williams, "The Ethics of Care and Humane Meat: Why Care Is Not Ambiguous about 'Humane' Meat," *Journal of Social Philosophy* 46.2 (2015): 271.

3 Dinesh Wadiwel, *The War against Animals* (Leiden: Brill Publishers, 2015).

4 According to Agriculture and Agri-Food Canada slaughter reports, more than 800 million land animals were killed for food in 2017. See Animal Justice, "Canada killed more Than 800 million land animals for food in 2017" (blog), 17 April 2018, perma.cc/SBW2-UY8E. It is estimated that more than 55 billion land and aquatic animals die each year to support the US food supply; see Animal Clock, https://animalclock.org. It is projected that 30 to 50 per cent of all species will be headed toward extinction by 2050. See: C.D. Thomas et al., "Extinction Risk from Climate Change," *Nature* 427 (2004). Currently, 99 per cent of threatened species are at risk from anthropogenic activities, largely those driving habitat loss, introduced species spread, and climate change. See "Endangered

Species," *Encyclopædia Britannica*, 2009, https://www.britannica.com /science/endangered-species.

5 Wadiwel, *The War against Animals* (Leiden: Brill Publishers, 2015); Lynn Worsham, "Toward an Understanding of Human Violence: Cultural Studies, Animal Studies, and the Promise of Posthumanism," *Review of Education, Pedagogy and Cultural Studies* 35.1 (2013).

6 Ibid.

7 Ibid.

8 Judith Butler, *Precarious Life: The Powers of Mourning and Violence* (London: Verso, 2004), 20. See also idem, *Frames of War: When Is Life Grievable?* (New York: Verso, 2009).

9 For animal scholars who have extended Butler's theory of grievability to animals, see Anat Pick, "Turning to Animals between Love and Law," *New Formations* 76 (2012); Stanescu, "Species Trouble"; Chloë Taylor, "The Precarious Lives of Animals: Butler, Coetzee, and Animal Ethics," *Philosophy Today* 52.1 (2008).

10 Stanescu, "Species Trouble," 571, 576. He insists that the richness of Butler's body of work provides sufficient kernels of thought that we can piece together into a vegan ethic that retrieves animals from the margins of her work. As he notes, other notable feminist scholars have lamented the dominant focus on humans that Butler continues to deliver despite the trans-species applicability of her theoretical commitments. Ibid., 571.

11 Ibid., 574–6; Taylor, "The Precarious Lives," 61.

12 See, for example, Ben Spurr, "Death of 43 racehorses in stable fire devastates Ontario's race community," *Toronto Star*, 5 January 2016, perma.cc/MSB4-J7P6; Tony Saxon, "Multimillion-dollar loss: More than 40 racehorses die in Classy Lane Stable fire in Puslinch," *The Record*, 6 January 2016, perma.cc/9MPH-TATP.

13 See, for example, Richard Warnica, "It's just crazy': Ontario community reeling after at least 40 racehorses killed in massive fire" *National Post*, 5 January 2016, perma.cc/6JXJ-8M4Q. One article also reported that firefighters covered the horses in yellow blankets after death just as they would human bodies. Liam Casey, "Stable rebuilds after fire killed 43 horses," *National Post*, 16 March 2016, https://www.pressreader.com /canada/national-post-latest-edition/20160514/281642484393458; Robert MacLeod and Tu Thanh Ha, "Trainer watches in horror as 42 horses die in Ontario stable fire," *Globe and Mail*, 5 January 2016, perma.cc/8QC4 -TPFM.

14 Robert MacLeod, "Requiescat in Pace," *Globe and Mail*, 5 January 2016, perma.cc/95DQ-Z4NY. One of the racetracks where many of the horses were frequently raced held a memorial for them: see "Woodbine

Racetrack pays tribute to 43 horses killed in barn fire," *InsideToronto.com*, 8 January 2016, perma.cc/6WLS-795V.

15 Anna Grear, "Deconstructing *Anthropos*: A Critical Legal Reflection on 'Anthropocentric' Law and Anthropocene 'Humanity,'" *Law and Critique* 26 (2015): 231.

16 Although current litigation efforts such as the set of lawsuits brought forward by the Nonhuman Rights Project to liberate animals through declarations of legal personhood may stake their claims more heavily on animals' sentience rather than on their cognitive capacities, demonstrating that animals are similar to humans is still important to this litigation, as is working within the established parameters of personhood as a legal category. As such, this type of litigation retains a solid humanist orientation. For reflections on how litigation for humanized animals can proceed without promoting liberal humanist standards, see Maneesha Deckha, "Humanizing the Nonhuman: A Legitimate Way for Animals to Escape Juridical Property Status?," in *Critical Animal Studies: Towards a Trans-Species Social Justice*, ed. John Sorenson and Atsuko Matsuoka (London: Rowman and Littlefield, 2018), 209–33, see Deckha, "Humanizing the Nonhuman."

17 Zakiyyah Iman Jackson, "Animal: New Directions in the Theorization of Race and Posthumanism," *Feminist Studies* 39.3 (2013): 676.

18 Grear, "Deconstructing *Anthropos*," 231.

19 Jackson, "Animal," 674.

20 The *Constitution Act, 1867*, ss.92(13), 30 & 31 Victoria, c 3 (U.K.).

21 The *Constitution Act, 1867*, ss.91(1A), (27), 30 & 31 Victoria, c 3 (U.K.).

22 For example, see Canada's federal interpretation act: *Interpretation Act*, R.S.C., 1985, c. I-21. The Supreme Court of Canada endorsed the modern approach to statutory interpretation in *Re Rizzo & Rizzo Shoes Ltd.* [1998] SCJ No.2, [1998] 1 SCR 27, at 41. Under the modern approach, judges may consider interpretation acts, purpose sections, and preambles when interpreting ambiguous words in a statute and determining the object of an act and the intention of Parliament. See Ruth Sullivan, *Sullivan on the Construction of Statutes*, 6th ed, (Toronto: LexisNexis, 2014).

23 Andrew J. Wright et al., "Myth and Momentum: A Critique of Environmental Impact Assessments," *Journal of Environmental Protection* 4 (2013).

24 Ibid.

25 The supported decision-making model involves a series of relationships, practices, agreements, and arrangements to assist an individual with a disability in making and communicating decisions about his or her life. When a person has limited capacity, supported decision-making can significantly enhance their self-determination and dignity, allowing

them to participate in decisions that impact their lives through a process that enhances their legal capacity. This model challenges traditional views about agency and capacity by seeking recognition of, and legal mechanisms to legitimize, the interdependent nature of all decision-making and the potential for shared capacity. See Krista James and Lauren Watts, "Understanding the Lived Experiences Supported Decision Making in Canada: Legal Capacity, Decision-Making, and Guardianship," *Law Commission of Ontario* (2014), perma.cc/6B8X-MRLV; Michelle Browning, Christine Bigby, and Jacinta Douglas "Supported Decision Making: Understanding How Its Conceptual Link to Legal Capacity Is Influencing the Development of Practice," *Research* and *Practice in Intellectual Developmental Disabilities* 1.1 (2014).

26 Ibid.
27 Clemens Driessen, "Comment: Caring for Captive Communities by Looking for Love and Loneliness, or against an Overly Individualist Liberal Animal Ethics," in *Animal Ethics in the Age of Humans*, ed. Bernice Bovenkerk and Jozef Keulartz (New York: Springer, 2016), 322; Driessen, "Comment," 322.
28 Cynthia Willett, "Affect Attunement in the Caregiver-Infant Relationship and across Species: Expanding the Ethical Scope of Eros," *philoSOPHIA* 2.2 (2012), 112, citing Cynthia Willett, *Maternal Ethics and Other Slave Moralities* (New York: Routledge Press, 1995), 24–30.
29 Astrida Neimanis, "No Representation without Colonisation? (or, Nature Represents Itself)," *Somatechnics* 5:1 (2015).
30 Cynthia Huff and Joel Haefner, "His Master's Voice: Animalographies, Life Writing, and the Posthuman," *Biography* 35.1 (2012), 155.
31 Lauren Corman, "The Ventriloquist's Burden: Animal Advocacy and the Problem of Speaking for Others," in *Animal Subjects 2.0*, ed. Jodey Castricano and Lauren Corman (Waterloo: Wilfrid Laurier University Press, 2017), 473–5, 481. As Corman notes, and cites as generative of her own work, a widely influential essay illustrating these concerns in the context of Western feminist representations of non-Western women is Chandra Talpade Mohanty's "Under Western Eyes: Feminist Scholarship and Colonial Discourses," *Feminist Review* 30 (1988), cited in Corman, "The Ventriloquist's Burden."
32 Even within animal advocacy, the problematic presumption prevails that animals are "voiceless." Corman, "The Ventriloquist's Burden," 482–7.
33 Rafi Youatt critically discusses this "language objection" more fully in "Interspecies Relations, International Relations: Rethinking Anthropocentric Politics" *Millennium* 43.1 (2014): 214–19.
34 Neimanis, "No Representation."

35 Lisa Jean Moore and Mary Kosut, "Among the Colony: Ethnographic Fieldwork, Urban Bees and Intra-Species Mindfulness," *Ethnography* 15.4 (2013): 519, 534–5.

36 Ibid., 520.

37 Moore and Kosut indicate that their proposal is still at a "larval state": ibid., 530. The authors resist the term "embryonic" and with it the dominance of mammalian representation when considering non-human models the mindfulness of which they are seeking to articulate.

38 Ibid.

39 Ibid.

40 Ibid., 525.

41 Ibid.

42 Ibid.

43 Judicial notice is a legal doctrine that allows a judge to make a finding of fact without a party proving said fact through evidence. It is an exception to the rule of formal proof that requires parties to present evidence to establish all facts in a trial. In Canada, judicial notice may be used where a fact is "so notorious or generally accepted as to not be the subject of debate among reasonable persons or capable of immediate and accurate demonstration by resort to readily accessible source of indisputable accuracy": *R v Spence* [2005] 3 SCR 458, 2005 SCC 71 (CanLii) at 53.

44 Lori Gruen, *Entangled Empathy: An Alternative Ethic for Our Relationships with Animals* (Brooklyn: Lantern Books, 2015), 46–7.

45 Jackson, "Animal," 675, discussing the main argument of Kalpana Rahita Seshadri, *HumAnimal: Race, Law, Language* (Minneapolis: University of Minnesota Press, 2012).

46 Assisted death or euthanasia for animals and Indigenous rights to subsistence hunting might be legitimate exceptions: the former as an option to alleviate suffering in animals that are catastrophically injured or dying, and the latter to properly acknowledge Indigenous worldviews regarding relations with animals. To carefully work out the merits of these potential exceptions will take considerably more space than I have here, so I leave them aside in the present analysis.

47 Sophie Lewis, "Over 1 billion animals feared dead in Australian wildfires," *CBC News*, 7 January 2020, perma.cc/NN2N-7EN3.

48 Eleni Panagiotarakou, "Who Loves Mosquitoes? Care Ethics, Theory of Obligation, and Endangered Species," *Journal of Agriculture & Environmental Ethics* 29 (2016): 1059–62.

49 Given the numbers, this transition and phasing out would have to be thoroughly planned. Detailing this plan is not the purpose of the present work. For hope that such a transformation is possible, see [Staff Writers], "Former 'Slaughter-Free Dairy' Farmer: No Such Thing as Humane

Dairy," *Free from Harm*, 20 September 2018, perma.cc/Y6DB-C7H4. The phasing out of all animal-use industries raises the question of whether everyone would have to become vegan. This, too, is an expansive question that I can't properly consider here. For some discussion of why eating some animal products (for those who wish) might still be possible even after the law regards animals as beings, see John Milburn's work on "clean milk," "Death-Free Dairy? The Ethics of Clean Milk," *Journal of Agricultural and Environmental Ethics* 31 (2018), and his article with Bob Fischer on consuming chicken eggs, "In Defence of Backyard Chickens," *Journal of Applied Philosophy* 36.1 (2017).

50 Kendra Coulter, "Beyond Human to Humane: A Multispecies Analysis of Care Work, Its Repression, and Its Potential," *Studies in Social Justice* 10.2 (2016): 215. Coulter defines humane jobs as "jobs that benefit both people and animals." To shift workforces and economies to away from destructive practices and industries, "humane alternatives must be created which are about helping not harming others" Ibid. There might also be compensation in such situations for the workers, given their precarity in the capitalist system. That argument is for another project. I am inclined to say, however, that there would be no compensation for the humans or corporations who ran these farms, although there could be retraining.

51 For further discussion of best practices for sanctuaries to guard against human domination within them, see Sue Donaldson and Willand Kymlicka, "Farmed Animal Sanctuaries: The Heart of the Movement?," *Politics and Animals* 1.1 (2015).

52 Statistics Canada. "Table 32-10-0155-01 Selected livestock and poultry, historical data," perma.cc/8VYE-R23T. This is a conservative estimate as it reflects 2016 census day totals for cattle, calves, pigs, sheep, lambs, hens, chickens, and turkeys only.

53 Cathy Holtslander, "Losing Our Grip: 2015 Update" (Canada: National Farmers Union, 2015), perma.cc/XCA9-8DA4.

54 Marlene Werry, "A Snapshot of the Canadian Dairy Industry," Ontario, Ministry of Agriculture Food and Rural Affairs (2003), https://web .archive.org/web/20090925024649/http://www.omafra.gov.on.ca /english/livestock/dairy/facts/snapshot.htm.

55 Statistics Canada, "Canada's Dairy Industry at a Glance" (2018) perma .cc/V7S9-T4M6.

56 JBS purchased a 75,000-capacity feedlot, 6,600 acres of farmland, and two meatpacking plants in Canada. JBS works in meat processing, but its parent company, J&F Investmentos, has a diverse portfolio that includes marketing, sales generation, real estate, publishing, and waste management. Holtsander, "Losing Our Grip," 15.

57 Results for the Fourth Quarter and Year Ended, March 31, 2017, perma .cc/3VNC-6XCF; [n.a.], "Among the Beneficiaries of Trump's Tariff

Bailout for Farmers? A Brazilian-Owned Meat Company," *Mother Jones*, 16 May 2019, perma.cc/7QVW-JBZ4.

58 Aaron Simmons, "Animals, Freedom, and the Ethics of Veganism," in *Animal Ethics in the Age of Humans*, ed. Bernice Bovenkerk and Jozef Keulartz (New York: Springer, 2016), 275.

59 Sue Donaldson and Will Kymlicka, *Zoopolis: A Political Theory of Animal Rights* (Oxford: Oxford University Press, 2011), 146.

60 Simmons, "Animals, Freedom," 275–6.

61 Ibid., 275.

62 T.J. Kasperbauer, "Should Captive Primates Have Reproductive Rights?," in Bovenkerk and Keulartz, *Animal Ethics*, 286.

63 Ibid., 290. Donaldson and Kymlicka have also endorsed the opportunity for animals to have a chance to reproduce at least once in order to honour their reproductive autonomy. See Sue Donaldson and Will Kymlicka, "Comment: Between Wild and Domesticated: Rethinking Categories and Boundaries in Response to Animal Agency," in Bovenkerk and Keulartz, *Animal Ethics*, 238.

64 Kasperbauer, "Should Captive Primates."

65 An individual in North America consumes, on average, around 90 kilograms of natural resources each day, while an individual in Africa consumes only 10. See S. Giljum et al., *Overconsumption? Our Use of the World's Natural Resources* (Brussels: Friends of the Earth Europe, 2009), perma.cc/UW7N-WTG8.

66 On this latter point, see especially Probyn-Ramsay et al, "A Sustainable Campus: The Sydney Declaration on Interspecies Sustainability," *Animal Studies Journal* 5.1 (2016).

67 See Michael Greger, "The Human/Animal Interface: Emergence and Resurgence of Zoonotic Infectious Diseases," *Critical Reviews in Microbiology* 33.4 (2007); Jan Dutkiewicz, Astra Taylor, and Troy Vettesse, "The Covid-19 pandemic shows we must transform the global food system," *The Guardian*, 16 April 2020, perma.cc/UH2G-R3XK.

68 Joseph Poore and T. Nemeck, "Reducing food's environmental impacts through producers and consumers," *Science* 360 (2018) 987.

69 Intergovernmental Panel on Climate Change (IPCC), "Climate Change and Land: An IPCC Special Report on Climate Change, Desertification, Land Degradation, Sustainable Land Management, Food Security, and Greenhouse Gas Fluxes in Terrestrial Ecosystems," (2020), https://www.ipcc.ch/srccl.

70 Josephine Donovan, "Feminism and the Treatment of Animals: From Care to Dialogue," *Signs* 31.2 (2006): 305.

71 Kathryn Gillespie, "Witnessing Animal Others: Bearing Witness, Grief, and the Political Function of Emotion," *Hypatia* 31.3 (2016): 572. See also my discussion of the overall benefits of bearing witness for animals even when they continue to die in Deckha, "The Save Movement and

Farmed Animal Suffering: The Advocacy Benefits of Bearing Witness as a Template for Law," *Canadian Journal of Constitutional and Comparative Law* 5 (2019): 77.

72 Ibid., 572. For Gillespie's full ethnographic treatment, see her book *The Cow with Ear Tag #1389* (Chicago: University of Chicago Press, 2018).

73 Ibid., 583–4. Gillespie contrasts the grievability of Sadie's life now with the death of a steer still ensnared in propertied exchanges as part of animal agriculture, whose death was not grieved and was treated as pure economic loss. Ibid., 584.

74 See also Maria Elena Garcia's reflections on her grief after an encounter with normalized animal suffering and death in her fieldwork on guinea pigs in Peru and the silence she kept to comport with mainstream expectations regarding the inappropriateness of grief as a response to the suffering and death of farmed animals. Maria Elena Garcia, "Death of a Guinea Pig: Grief and the Limits of Multispecies Ethnography in Peru," *Environmental Humanities* 11.2 (2019): 351–72. Gillespie reflects on how we can become more responsive to animals at the end of their lives in "Provocation from the Field: A Multispecies Doula Approach to Death and Dying," *Animal Studies Journal* 9.1 (2020).

Bibliography

Legislation: Canada

Agricultural Produce Grading Act, R.S.B.C. 1996, c. 11.
An Act to amend the Criminal Code and other Acts (ending the captivity of whales and dolphins), SC 2019, c. 11.
Animal Care Act, CCSM, c. A84.
Animal Disease Control Act, R.S.B.C. 1996, c. 14.
Animal Pedigree Act, R.S.C. 1985, c. 8 (4th Supp.).
Animal Protection Act, RSA 2000, c. A-41.
Animal Protection Act, SNS 2008, c. 33.
Animals for Research Act, R.S.O. 1990, c. A.22.
Bill C-15, Bill C-15B, Bill C-10, Bill C-10B *An Act to Amend the Criminal Code (Cruelty to Animals)*, 2nd Sess., 37th Parl., 2003.
Bill C-17, *An Act to Amend the Criminal Code (Cruelty to Animals, Disarming a Peace Officer and Other Amendments) and the Firearms Act (Technical Amendments)*, 2nd Sess., 36th Parl., 1999.
Bill C-22, *An Act to Amend the Criminal Code (Cruelty to Animals)*, 3rd Sess., 37th Parl., 2004.
Bill C-50, *An Act to Amend the Criminal Code (Cruelty to Animals)*, 1st Sess., 38th Parl., 2005.
Bill C-68, *An Act to amend the Fisheries Act and other Acts In consequence*, 1st Sess., 42nd Parl., 2019.
Bill C-84, *An Act to amend the Criminal Code (bestiality and animal fighting)*, 1st Sess., 42nd Parl., 2019.
Bill C-229, *An Act to Amend the Criminal Code (Cruelty to Animals)*, 3rd Sess., 40th Parl., 2008.
Bill C-232, *An Act to Amend the Criminal Code (Cruelty to Animals)*, 1st Sess., 40st Parl., 2011.
Bill C-373, *An Act to Amend the Criminal Code (Cruelty to Animals)*, 1st Sess., 39th Parl., 2006.

Bill C-246, *Modernizing Animal Protections Act, R.S., c. C-46*, 1st Sess., 42nd Parl., 2016.

Bill C-558, *An Act to Amend the Criminal Code (Cruelty to Animals)*, 2nd Sess., 39th Parl., 2008.

Bill C-558, *An Act to Amend the Criminal Code (Cruelty to Animals)*, 2nd Sess., 41st Parl., 2011.

Bill S-203, *An Act to Amend the Criminal Code (Cruelty to Animals)*, 1st Sess., 39th Parl., 2007.

Bill S-204, *An Act to Amend the Criminal Code (Cruelty to Animals)*, 2nd Sess., 38th Parl., 2004.

Bill S-213, *An Act to Amend the Criminal Code (Cruelty to Animals)*, 2nd Sess., 39th Parl., 2006.

Bill S-238, *An Act to Amend the Fisheries Act and the Wild Animal and Plant Protection and Regulation of International and Interprovincial Trade Act (importation and exportation of shark fins)*, 1st Sess., 42nd Parl, 2017.

Blind Persons' Rights Act, R.S.O. 1990, c. B.7.

Canada Consumer and Product Safety Act, S.C. 2010, c. 21.

Canada National Parks Act, S.C. 2000, c. 32.

Canada Wildlife Act, R.S.C. 1985, c.W-9.

Canadian Food Inspection Agency Act, S.C. 1997, c. 6.

Conservation Authorities Act, R.S.O. 1990, c. C.27.

Creston Valley Wildlife Act, R.S.B.C. 1996, c. 84.

Criminal Code of Canada, R.S.C. 1985, c. C-46.

Customs Act, R.S.C. 1985, c. C-1 (2nd Supp.).

Dog Act, R.S.N.W.T. 1998 c. D-7.

Dog Owners Liability Act, R.S.O. 1990, c. D.16.

Endangered Species Act, S.O. 2007, c. 6.

Excise Tax Act, R.S.C. 1985, c. E-15.

Farming and Fishing Industries Development Act, R.S.B.C. 1996, c. 134.

Feeds Act, R.S.C. 1985, c. F-9.

Fish Inspection Act, R.S.C. 1985, c. F-12.

Fisheries Act, R.S.B.C. 1996, c. 149.

Fisheries Act, R.S.C. 1985, c. F-14.

Food and Drugs Act, R.S.C. 1985, c. F-27.

Forestry Act, R.S.O. 1990, c. F.26.

Fur Farm Act, R.S.B.C. 1996, c. 167.

Game and Fish Act, R.S.O. 1990, c. G.1.

Health of Animals Act, S.C. 1990, c. 21.

Health Protection and Promotion Act, R.S.O. 1990, c. H.7.

Highway Traffic Act, R.S.O. 1990, c. H.8.

Interpretation Act, R.S.C., 1985, c. I-21.

Livestock Act, R.S.B.C. 1996, c. 270.

Meat Inspection Act, R.S.C. 1985, c. 25 (1st Supp.).
Municipal Act, R.S.O. 1990, c. M.45.
Niagara Parks Act, R.S.O. 1990, c. N.3.
Ontario Society for the Prevention of Cruelty to Animals Act, R.S.O. 1990 c. O-36.
Parks Assistance Act, R.S.O. 1990, c. P.2.
Pest Control Products Act, S.C. 2002, c. 28.
Pesticides Act, R.S.O. 1990, c. P.11.
Pounds Act, R.S.O. c. P.17.
Prevention of Cruelty to Animals Act, R.S.B.C. 1996 c. 372.
Provincial Parks Act, R.S.O. 1990, c. P.34.
Protection of Livestock and Poultry from Dogs Act, R.S.O. 1990, c. L.24.
Public Parks Act, R.S.O. 1990, c. P.46.
Railway Safety Act, R.S.C. 1985, c. 32 (4th Supp.).
Research Foundation Act, R.S.O. 1990, c. R.27.
Sled Dog Standard of Care Regulation, B.C. Reg 21/2012.
Society for the Prevention for Cruelty to Animals Act, R.S.N.B. 1973 c. S-12.
Species at Risk Act, S.C. 2002, c. 29.
Standards of Care and Administrative Standards Regulation, Ontario O Reg 60/09.
St. Clair Parkway Commission Act, R.S.O. 1990, c. S.23.
St. Lawrence Parks Commission Act, R.S.O. 1990, c. S.24.
Textile Labelling Act, R.S.C. 1985, c. T-10.
Veterinarians Act, R.S.O. 1990, c. V.3.
Wild Animals and Plant Protection and Regulation of International and Interprovincial Trade Act, S.C. 1992, c. 52.

Legislation: Foreign and International

Constitution Act, 1867, 30 & 31 Victoria, c. 3 (U.K.).
Convention on International Trade in Endangered Species of Wild Fauna and Flora, 4 April 2017, 993 U.N.T.S. 243: https://cites.org/eng/app/appendices.php.

Jurisprudence: Canada

Bogaerts v Attorney General of Ontario 2019 ONSC 41, [2019] OJ No 5.
Chief Constable of Norfolk v Clayton (1983) 2 AC 473, 2 WLR 55, 1 AII ER 984.
Ford v Wiley, (1889), 23 Q.B.D. 203, 58 L.J.M.C. 145.
Harvard College v Canada (Commissioner of Patents), 2002 SC 76, [2002] 4 SCR 45.
Re Wishart Estate, (1992) 46 E.T.R. 311.
R v Alcorn, ABPC December 2014, unreported, (130018757P1).
R v Alcorn, 2015 ABCA 182, 2015 CarswellAlta 948.
R v Amorim, [1994] OJ No 2824, 26 WCB (2d) 1.
R v Anderson, ABPC 29 November 2012, unreported (110049731P1).

R v Bakic, 2004 SKPC 134.

R v Barrett, 2015 CarswellNfld 14, 2015 CanLII 2415 (NL PC).

R v Bennett, 2010 NJ No. 230 (PC).

R v Blanchard, 2007 CanLII 52982 (Ont SCJ).

R v Bocian (1982), 16 Sask R 92 (Prov Ct).

R v Borges, 1991 Ont Ct Prov Div, unpublished.

R v Bourque, 2013 BCCA 447, 2013 CarswellBC 3094.

R v C, 2015 ABPC 65, 2015 CarswellAlta 536.

R v Carter, 2006 ABPC 34.

R v Chailler, 26 August 2013, unreported (121450597P1).

R v Chalmers, ABPC 23 April 2013, unreported, (110779394P1).

R v Clarke (2001) NJ No 191, CarswellNfld 189, 2001 CanLII 12453 (NLPC).

R v Connors 2011 NLCA 74 (CanLII).

R v Danfousse, 2013 ABPC 137, 2013 CarswellAlta 866.

R v D.L.W., [2016] 1 SCR 402, 2016 SCC 22 (CanLII).

R v Dominic, [2009] BCJ No 949, 2009 BCPC.

Reece v Edmonton (City), 2011 ABCA 238 (CanLII), 335 DLR (4th) 600, 513 AR 199.

R v Elliott, 2009 NSPC 5.

R v England, (1924), 19 Sask. L.R. 165, [1925] 1 W.W.R. 237, 43 C.C.C.11 (C.A.).

R v Fawcett, 2012 BCPC 421 (CanLII).

R v Fountain, 2013 BCPC 193, 2013 CarswellBC 2225.

R v Fuller, [1994] OJ No 4285.

R v Gerling, 2016 BCCA 72, 2016 CarswellBC 347.

R v Guess, 2000 BCCA 547.

R v Haaksman, 2013 ONCJ 66, 2013 CarswellOnt 2225.

R v Habermehl, 2013 ABPC 122, 2016 CarswellAlta 570.

R v Haughton, 2013 BCSC 1683, 2016 CarswellBC 2733.

R v Helfer, 19 June 2014, unreported, OCJ.

R v Higgins (B.), 1996 CanLII 11699 (NL SCTD).

R v Hnatiuk, 2000 ABQB 314 (CanLII).

R v Hughes, [2008] BCJ No 973, 2008 BCSC 676.

R v Irving, 2013 SKPC 101, 2013 CarswellSask 431.

R v Jereda, 2015 SKPC 90, 2015 CarswellSask 335.

R v JS, (2003) NJ No 225 locus para 21, 59 WCB (2d) 228.

R v Kennedy, 2015 CarswellOnt 11987, 123 WCB (2d) 586.

R v Kokatt, [1944] 1 W.W.R. 158, 81 C.C.C. 101 (Sask. Police Ct.).

R v Kroesing, (1909), 2 Alta. L.R. 275, 10 W.L.R. 649, 16 C.C.C. 312 (T.D.).

R v Kyle, 2015 ONJC 375, 2015 CarswellOnt 10598.

R v Lewis, [2011] NJ No 251.

R v Linder, (1950), 97 C.C.C. 174, 10 C.R. 44, [1950] 1 W.W.R. 1035.

R v Lyonnais, [2012] JQ no 7321.

R v Marshall 2007 BCSC 1750.

R v Marshall, 2013 ONCJ 61, 2013 CarswellOnt 1766.

R v McHugh, 1966 50 C.R. 263, 51 M.P.R. 173, [1966] 1 C.C.C. 170 (N.S.C.A).

R v McHugh, [1996] 1 C.C.C. 170, 50 CR 263, 51 M.P.R. 173.

R v McKinnon, ABPC 7 October 2014, unreported (140370248P1).

R v McLeod, [2011] SJ No 721, 2011 SKPC 180.

R v McRae, [2002] OJ No 4987, CarswellOnt 5679.

R v Ménard, (1978), 4 C.R. (3d) 333, 43 C.C.C. (2d) 458 (Que. C.A.).

R v M(M), 2002 CarswellOnt 3007.

R v Mousseau, [2011] JQ no 13401, 2011 QCCQ 11101.

R v Munroe, 2010 ONCJ 226.

R v Munroe, 2012 ONSC 4768, 2012 CarswellOnt 11816.

R v Pacific Meat Co (1957) BCJ no 98, 24 WWR 37 locus 40, 119 C.C.C. 237 locus 240.

R v Paish (1977) BCJ No 924, 2 WWR 526, 1 WCB 172.

R v Parkinson, 2016 BCPC 0103, at paras 155, 159.

R v Paul, [1997] BCJ No 808 (Prov Ct).

R v Pedersen, 2005 BCPC 160, BCJ No 985.

R v Perrin, 2012 NSPC 134, 2012 CarswellNS 1092.

R v Piasentin, 2008 ABPC 164.

R v Prince, 1995 Ont Ct Prov Div, unreported.

R v Radmore, [1993] R.J.Q. 215 (C.Q.).

R v Rodgers, 2012 OJ No. 6287.

R v Rose, [2009] JQ no 19387, 2009 QCCQ 5736.

R v Rowe, 2015 ONCJ 596, 2015 CarswellOnt 16365.

R v Sanaee, 2016 ABCA 289, 2016 CarswellAlta 1843.

R v SAS, 2011 BCPC 470 (CanLII).

R v Shaw, (1988), 93 A.R. 86 (Prov. Ct.).

R v SJ, 2003 CarswellNfld 222.

R v Sparshu (1996), 44 Alta. L.R. (3d) 303. (Prov. Ct.).

R v Spence [2005] 3 SCR 458, 2005 SCC 71 (CanLii).

R v Starnino [1998] JQ No 4444.

R v Sudweeks, 2003 BCSC 1960.

R v Tremblay, 2012 BCPC 410 (CanLII).

R v Vaillancourt, 2003 NSPC 59.

R v Vieira, 2006 BCPC 288.

R v Way, 2016 ONCJ 126, 2016 CarswellOnt 3424.

R v Whitlock, 2013 BCPC 153, 2013 CarswellBC 1859.

R v. Wright, 2014 ONCA 675.

R v Young, [1997] OJ No 6214.

Reece and Zoocheck v Edmonton, 2011 ABCA 238 (CanLII), 335 DLR (4th) 600, 513 AR 199, leave denied (2012) [2011] SCCA No 447 (QL).

Swan v. Saunders, (1881), 50 L.J.M.C. 67.

Jurisprudence: Foreign

Cindar v. *State*, 300 S.W. 64 (Tex. Crim. App. 1927).
Karnail Singh and others v State of Haryana, CRR-533–2013.
Miller v *State*, 63 S.E. at 571 (Ga. Ct. App. 1909).
The Nonhuman Rights Project on behalf of Happy v James J Breheny & Wildlife Conservation Society, NYSC 45164 2019.

Government Publications

British Columbia Ministry of Agriculture. "The Sled-Dog Code of Practice." 30 January 2012. Ministry of Agriculture. http://www.gov.bc.ca/agri/down/sled_dog_code_of_practice.pdf.
British Columbia Sled Dog Task Force. *Sled Dog Task Force Report*. Victoria: Ministry of Agriculture, 2011.
Canada, Parliament. *Debates of the Senate*, 42nd Parl., 1st Sess., Vol. 150, No. 8, 27 January 2016.
– *Debates of the Senate*, 42nd Parl., 1st Sess., Vol. 150, No. 22, 22 March 2016.
– *Debates of the Senate*, 42nd Parl., 1st Sess., Vol. 150, No. 121, 16 May 2017.
– *Debates of the Senate*, 42nd Parl., 1st Sess., Vol. 150. No. 131, 13 June 2017.
– *House of Commons Debates*, 42nd Parl., 1st Sess., Vol. 148, No. 51, 9 May 2016.
– *House of Commons Debates*, 42nd Parl., 1st Sess., Vol. 148, No. 83, 28 September 2016.
– *House of Commons Debates*, 42nd Parl., 1st Sess., Vol. 148, No. 344, 29 October 2018.
– *House of Commons Debates*, 42nd Parl., 1st Sess., Vol. 148, No. 395, 1 April 2019.
– *House of Commons Debates*, 42nd Parl., 1st Sess., Vol. 148, No. 407, 1 May 2019.
– *House of Commons Debates*, 37th Parl., 1st Sess., No. 197, 3 June 2002.
– *House of Commons Debates*, 37th Parl, 2nd Sess., No. 127, 25 September 2003.
– *House of Commons Vote No. 1311*, 1st Sess, 42nd Parl, 8 May 2019), sitting no. 412.
Department of Justice. *Crimes against Animals: A Consultation Paper*. Ottawa: Communication and Executive Services Branch, 1998.
General Manager's Office, Vancouver Board of Parks and Rec. "Recommendation." 3 March 2017. http://parkboardmeetings.vancouver.ca/2017/20170308/REPORT-CetaceansAtVancouverAquarium-ReferralReportBack-20170308.pdf.
Health Canada. "Canada's Food Guide." 16 July 2019. https://food-guide.canada.ca/en.

Lafrenière, Gérald. "Legislative Backgrounder to *Bill C-17: An Act to Amend the Criminal Code (Cruelty to Animals, Disarming a Peace Officer and Other Amendments)* and the *Firearms Act (Technical Amendments)*." 29 March 2000. Parliament of Canada. http://www.lop.parl.gc.ca/About/Parliament /LegislativeSummaries/bills_ls.asp?lang=E&ls=C17&Parl=36&Ses=2#(9).

The Livestock, Environment, and Development Initiative. "Livestock's Long Shadow: Environmental Issues and Options." Rome: Food and Agriculture Organization of the United Nations, 2006, at iii.

Office of the Premier. "Premier announces Canada's toughest animal cruelty laws" [News release 2011PREM0030-000340]. 5 April 2011. British Columbia Ministry of Agriculture. https://archive.news.gov.bc.ca/releases/news _releases_2009-2013/2011PREM0030-000340.htm.

Statistics Canada. "Canada's Dairy Industry at a Glance." 2018. https://www .dairyinfo.gc.ca/index_e.php?s1=cdi-ilc&s2=aag-ail.

– "Table 32-10-0155-01: Selected livestock and poultry, historical data." https://www150.statcan.gc.ca/t1/tbl1/en/tv.action?pid=3210015501.

Werry, Marlene. "A Snapshot of the Canadian Dairy Industry." 2003. Ontario, Ministry of Agriculture, Food, and Rural Affairs. https://web.archive.org /web/20090925024649/http://www.omafra.gov.on.ca/english/livestock /dairy/facts/snapshot.htm.

WorkSafeBC. "Review Decision." 25 January 2011. R0119660. http://web .archive.org/web/20110304013214/http://www.cbc.ca/bc/news/bc -110131-worksafebc-whistler-dog-cull.pdf.

Secondary Materials: Edited Collections

Adams, Carol J. "Caring about Suffering: A Feminist Exploration." In *The Feminist Care Tradition in Animal Ethics*, ed. Carol J. Adams and Josephine Donovan. New York: Columbia University Press, 2007, 198.

Adams, Carol J., and Josephine Donovan, eds. *Animals and Women: Feminist Theoretical Explorations*. Durham: Duke University Press, 1995.

– *Beyond Animal Rights: A Feminist Caring Ethic for the Treatment of Animals*. Indianapolis: Indiana University Press, 1996.

– "Introduction." In *The Feminist Care Tradition in Animal Ethics*, ed. Carol J. Adams and Josephine Donovan. New York: Columbia University Press, 2007.

Adams, Carol J., and Lori Gruen. "Introduction." In *Ecofeminism: Feminist Interactions with Other Animals and the Earth*, ed. Adams and Gruen. New York: Bloomsbury Academy, 2014.

Alaimo, Stacy. "Jellyfish Science, Jellyfish Aesthetics: Posthuman Reconfigurations of the Sensible." In *Thinking with Water*, ed. Cecelia Chen, Janine MacLeod, and Astrida Neimanis. Montreal and Kingston: McGill-Queen's University Press, 2013, 139.

– "Trans-Corporeal Feminisms and the Ethical Space of Nature." in *Material Feminisms*, ed. Stacy Alaimo and Susan Hekman, Bloomington: Indiana University Press, 2008.

Alaimo, Stacy, and Susan Hekman. "Introduction: Emerging Models of Materiality in Feminist Theory." in *Material Feminisms*, ed. Alaimo and Hekman. Bloomington: Indiana University Press, 2008.

Asch, Michael, John Borrows, and James Tully, eds. *Resurgence and Reconciliation: Indigenous–Settler Relations and Earth Teachings*. Toronto: University of Toronto Press, 2018.

Bevilaqua, Ciméa Barbato. "Chimpanzees in Court: What Difference Does It Make?" In *Law and the Questions of the Animal: A Critical Jurisprudence*, ed. Yoriko Otomo and Ed Mussawir. Oxford: Routledge, 2013, 71.

Braverman, Irus. "Animals and Law in the American City." In *Environmental Law and Contrasting Ideas of Nature: A Constructivist Approach*, ed. Keith Hirokawa. New York: Cambridge University Press, 2014, 112.

Braverman, Irus, ed. *Animals, Biopolitics, Law: Lively Legalities*. New York: Routledge, 2016.

Braverman, Irus, and Elizabeth R Johnson, eds. *Blue Legalities: The Life and Laws of the Sea*. Durham: Duke University Press, 2020.

Calarco, Matthew. "Reorienting Strategies for Animal Justice." In *Philosophy and the Politics of Animal Liberation*, ed. Paola Cavalieri, London: Palgrave Macmillan, 2016, 45.

Cavalieri, Paola. "The Animal Debate." In *In Defense of Animals: The Second Wave*, ed. Peter Singer. Malden: Blackwell, 2006, 54.

Code, Lorraine. "Feminist Epistemologies and Women's Lives." In *The Blackwell Guide to Feminist Philosophy*, ed. Linda M. Alcoff and Eva Kittay. Malden: Blackwell 2007, 211.

Corman, Lauren. "The Ventriloquist's Burden: Animal Advocacy and the Problem of Speaking for Others." In *Animal Subjects 2.0: An Ethical Reader in a Posthuman World*, ed. Jodey Castricano and Lauren Corman. Waterloo: Wilfrid Laurier University Press, 2017, 473.

Cornell, Drucilla. "Rethinking Legal Ideals after Deconstruction." In *Law's Madness*, ed. Austin Sarat et al. Ann Arbor: University of Michigan Press, 2003, 147.

Crane, Jonathan K., et al. "Beastly Morality: Untangling Possibilities." In *Beastly Morality: Animals as Ethical Agents*, ed. Jonathan K Crane. New York: Columbia University Press, 2016, 251.

Curtin, Deane. "Compassion and Being Human." In *Ecofeminism: Feminist Interactions with Other Animals and the* Earth, ed, Carol J. Adams and Lori Gruen. New York: Bloomsbury Academy, 2014, 39.

Deckha, Maneesha. "Critical Animal Studies and the Property Debate in Animal Law." In *Animal Subjects 2.0: An Ethical Reader in a Posthuman*

World, ed. Jodey Castricano and Lauren Corman. Waterloo: Wilfrid Laurier University Press, 2016, 45.

– "Humanizing the Nonhuman: A Legitimate Way for Animals to Escape Juridical Property Status?" In *Critical Animal Studies: Towards a Trans-Species Social Justice*, ed. John Sorenson and Atsuko Matsuoka. London: Rowman and Littlefield, 2018, 209.

– "Is Multiculturalism *Good* for Animals?" In *Multiculturalism, Race and Animals – Contemporary Moral and Political Debates*, ed. Luis Cordeiro Rodrigues and Les Mitchell. London: Palgrave Macmillan, 2017, 61.

– "Postcolonial." In *Critical Terms for Animal Studies*, ed. Lori Gruen. Chicago: University of Chicago Press, 2018, 160.

DeGrazia, David. "On the Question of Personhood beyond Homo sapiens." In *In Defense of Animals: The Second Wave*, ed. Peter Singer. Malden: Blackwell, 2006, 40.

Diamond, Cora. "The Difficulty of Reality and the Difficulty of Philosophy." In *Philosophy and Animal Life* , ed. Stanley Cavell et al. New York: Columbia University Press 2008, 43.

Donaldson, Sue, and Will Kymlicka. "Comment: Between Wild and Domesticated: Rethinking Categories and Boundaries in Response to Animal Agency." In *Animal Ethics in the Age of Humans*, ed. Bernice Bovenkerk and Jozef Keulartz. New York: Springer, 2016, 225.

Donovan, Josephine. "Animal Rights and Feminist Theory." In *The Feminist Care Tradition in Animal Ethics*, ed. Carol J. Adams and Josephine Donovan. New York: Columbia University Press, 2007, 58.

– "Attention to Suffering: Sympathy as a Basis for Ethical Treatment of Animals." In *The Feminist Care Tradition in Animal Ethics*, ed. Carol J. Adams and Josephine Donovan. New York: Columbia University Press, 2007, 174.

Driessen, Clemens. "Comment: Caring for Captive Communities by Looking for Love and Loneliness, or Against an Overly Individualist Liberal Animal Ethics." In *Animal Ethics in the Age of Humans*, ed. Bernice Bovenkerk and Jozef Keulartz. New York: Springer, 2016, 321.

Dunayer, Joan. "Sexist Words, Speciesist Roots." in *Animals and Women: Feminist Theoretical Explorations*, ed. Carol J. Adams and Josephine Donovan. Durham: Duke University Press, 1995, 11.

Fineman, Martha Albertson. "Equality, Autonomy, and the Vulnerable Subject in Law and Politics." In *Vulnerability: Reflections on a New Ethical Foundation for Law and Politics*, ed. Martha Albertson Fineman and Anna Grear, Surrey: Ashgate, 2013, 13.

Francione, Gary L. "The Abolition of Animal Exploitation." In *The Animal Rights Debate: Abolitions or Regulation*, ed. Gary L. Francione and Robert Garner. New York: Columbia University Press, 2010, 1.

Gaard, Greta C., ed. *Ecofeminism, Women, Animals, Nature*. Philadelphia: Temple University Press, 1993.

Garner, Robert. "A Defense of a Broad Animal Protectionism." In *The Animal Rights Debate: Abolition or Regulation?*, ed. Gary L. Francione and Robert Garner. New York: Columbia University Press, 2010, 103.

Grear, Anna. "Vulnerability, Advanced Global Capitalism, and Co-symptomatic Injustice: Locating the Vulnerable Subject." In *Vulnerability: Reflections on a New Ethical Foundation for Law and Politics*, ed. Martha Albertson Fineman and Anna Grear. Surrey: Ashgate, 2013, 41.

Jenkins, Stephanie, Kelly Struthers Montford, and Chloë Taylor. *Disability and Animality: Crip Perspectives in Critical Animal Studies*. London: Routledge, 2020.

Kappeler, Susan. "Speciesism, Racism, Nationalism ... or the Power of Scientific Subjectivity." In *Animals and Women: Feminist Theoretical Explorations*, ed. Carol J. Adams and Josephine Donovan, Durham: Duke University Press, 1995, 320.

Karpin, Isabel, and Roxanne Mykitiuk. "Feminist Legal Theory as Embodied Justice." In *Transcending the Boundaries of Law: Generations of Feminism and Legal Theory*, ed. Martha Fineman. New York: Routledge, 2011, 115.

Kasperbauer, T.J. "Should Captive Primates Have Reproductive Rights?" In *Animal Ethics in the Age of Humans*, ed. Bernice Bovenkerk and Jozef Keulartz. New York: Springer, 2016, 279.

Kheel, Marti. "The Liberation of Nature: A Circular Affair." In *Beyond Animal Rights: A Feminist Caring Ethic for the Treatment of Animals*, ed. Carol J. Adams and Josephine Donovan. New York: Continuum, 1996, 17.

Kim, Claire Jean. "Abolitionism." In *Critical Terms in Animal Studies*, ed. Lori Gruen. Chicago: University of Chicago Press, 2018, 15.

Kittay, Eva Feder. "Human Dependency and Rawlsian Equality." In *Feminists Rethink the Self*, ed. Diana T. Meyers, Boulder: Westview Press, 1996, 219.

Klineberg, Joanne. "Cruelty to Animals and the *Criminal Code of Canada*." In *An Introduction to Animals and the Law*, ed. Lesli Bisgould.Toronto: Law Society of Upper Canada, Continuing Legal Education, 2007, 69.

Kymlicka, Will, and Sue Donaldson. "Animal Rights and Aboriginal Rights." In *Canadian Perspectives on Animals and the Law*, ed. Peter Sankoff, Vaughan Black & Katie Sykes. Toronto: Irwin Law, 2015, 159.

Lingis, Alphonso. "Bestiality." In *Animal Others: On Ethics, Ontology, and Animal Life*, ed. H. Peter Steeves. Albany: SUNY Press, 1999, 37.

McKittrick, Katherine, ed. *Sylvia Wynter: On Being Human as Praxis*. Durham: Duke University Press, 2015.

Montford, Kelly Struthers, and Chloë Taylor, eds. *Colonialism and Animality: Anti-Colonial Perspectives in Critical Animal Studies*. London: Routledge, 2020.

Moore, Lisa Jean, and Mary Kosut, eds. *The Body Reader: Essential Social and Cultural Readings*. New York: NYU Press, 2010.

Mussawir, Ed, and Yoriko Otomo. "Law's Animal." In *Law and the Question of the Animal: A Critical Jurisprudence*, ed. Yoriko Otomo and Ed Mussawir. Abingdon: Routledge, 2013.

Noble, Brian. "Treaty Ecologies: With Persons, Peoples, Animals, and the Land." In *Resurgence and Reconciliation: Indigenous–Settler Relations and Earth Teachings*, ed. Michael Asch, John Borrows, and James Tully, Toronto: University of Toronto Press, 2018, 318.

Nussbaum, Martha. "Compassion." In *Species Matters: Humane Advocacy and Cultural Theory*, ed. Marianne DeKoven and Michael Lundblad, New York: Columbia University Press, 2011, 139.

Otomo, Yoriko, and Ed Mussawir, eds. *Law and the Questions of the Animal: A Critical Jurisprudence*. Abingdon: Routledge, 2013.

Promislow, Janna, and Naiomi Metallic. "Realizing Aboriginal Administrative Law." In *Administrative Law in Context*, ed. Colleen M. Flood and Lorne Sossin, Toronto: Emond Montgomery, 2018, 87.

Ridler, Victoria. "Dressing the Sow and the Legal Subjectivation of the Non-human Animal." In *Law and the Question of the Animal: A Critical Jurisprudence*, ed. Yoriko Otomo and Ed Mussawir, Abingdon: Routledge, 2013, 102.

Ruddick, Sara. *Maternal Thinking: Toward a Politics of Peace*. Boston: Beacon Press, 1989.

Shakespeare, Steven. "Articulating the Inhuman: God, Animal, Machine." In *Beyond Human: From Animality to Transhumanism*, ed. Charlie Blake, Claire Molloy, and Steven Shakespeare. London: Continuum, 2012, 227.

Shildrick, Margrit. "Beyond the Body of Bioethics: Challenging the Conventions." In *Ethics of the Body: Postconventional Challenges*, ed. Margrit Shildrick and Roxanne Mykitiuk. Cambridge, MA: MIT Press, 2005.

Shildrick, Margrit, and Roxanne Mykitiuk eds. *Ethics of the Body: Postconventional Challenges*. Cambridge, MA: MIT Press, 2005, 1.

Sinha, Suvadip, and Amit R. Baishya. "Introduction." In *Postcolonial Animalities*, ed. Sinha and Baishya. New York: Routledge, 2019.

Smelik, Anneke, and Nina Lykke, eds. *Bits of Life*. Seattle: University of Washington Press, 2008.

Simmons, Aaron. "Animals, Freedom, and the Ethics of Veganism." In *Animal Ethics in the Age of Humans*, ed. Bernice Bovenkerk and Jozef Keulartz. New York: Springer, 2016, 265.

Somers, Kelly, and Karen Soldatic. "Productive Bodies: How Neoliberalism Makes and Unmakes Disability in Human and Non-human Animals." In *Disability and Animality: Crip Perspectives in Critical Animal Studies*, ed. Stephanie Jenkins, Kelly Struthers Montford, and Chloë Taylor. London: Routledge, 2020.

Srinivasan, Krithika. "Posthumanist Animal Studies and Zoopolitical Law." In *Critical Animal Studies: Towards Trans-species Social Justice*, ed. Atsuko Matsuoka and John Sorenson. London: Rowman and Littlefield, 2018, 234.

Taylor, Sunaura. "Animal Crips." In *Disability and Animality: Crip Perspectives in Critical Animal Studies*, ed. Stephanie Jenkins, Kelly Struthers Montford and Chloë Taylor. London: Routledge, 2020.

– "Disability and Interdependence." In *Messy Eating: Conversations on Animals as Food*, ed. Samantha King et al. New York: Fordham University Press, 2019.

Warren, Karen, ed. *Ecofeminism: Women, Culture, Nature*. Bloomington: Indiana University Press, 1997.

Wadiwel, Dinesh. "Whipping to Win: Measured Violence, Delegated Sovereignty, and the Privatised Domination of Non-Human Life." In *Law and the Question of the Animal: A Critical Jurisprudence*, ed. Yoriko Otomo and Ed Mussawir, Abingdon: Routledge, 2013, 116.

Watts, Christopher, ed. *Relational Archaeologies: Humans, Animals, Things*. New York: Routledge, 2013.

Weisberg, Zipporah. "The Trouble with Posthumanism: *Bacteria Are People Too*." In *Critical Animal Studies: Thinking the Unthinkable*, ed. John Sorenson. Toronto: Canadian Scholars' Press, 2014, 93.

Wolch, Jennifer, and Jody Emel, eds. *Animal Geographies: Places, Politics, and Identity in the Nature-Culture Borderlands*. London: Verso, 1998.

Wolfe, Cary, ed. *Zoontologies: The Question of the Animal*. Minneapolis: University of Minnesota Press, 2003.

Wolfe, Cary, and Jonathan Elmer. "Subject to Sacrifice: Ideology, Psychoanalysis, and the Discourse of Species in Jonathan Demme's *The Silence of the Lambs*." In *Animal Rites: American Culture, The Discourse of Species, and Posthumanist Theory*, ed. Cary Wolfe. Chicago: University of Chicago Press, 2003, 97.

Wood, David. "Thinking with Cats." In *Animal Philosophy: Ethics and Identity*, ed. Peter Atterton and Matthew Calarco. London: Bloomsbury Academic, 2004, 129.

Secondary Materials: Journal Articles

Aaltola, Elisa. "Loving Animals: Toward a New Animal Advocacy." *Times Higher Education Supplement* 20.20 (2011): 58.

Adams, Robert. "Animals, Property, and the Law" (1996) 18 Houston J of Int'l Law 595.

Ahmed, Sara. "Problematic Proximities: Or Why Critiques of Gay Imperialism Matter" (2011) 19:2 Fem Leg Stud 119.

Ahuja, Neel. "Postcolonial Critique in a Multispecies World." *PMLA* 124.2 (2009): 556.

Akhtar, Aysha. "The Need to Include Animal Protection in Public Health Policies." *Journal of Public Health Policy* 34.4 (2013): 549.

Alfred, Taiaiake, and Jeff Corntassel. "Being Indigenous: Resurgences against Contemporary Colonialism" *Government and Opposition* 40.4 (2005): 587.

Aristarkhova, Irina. "Thou Shall Not Harm All Living Beings: Feminism, Jainism, and Animals" *Hypatia* 27.3 (2012): 636.

Ash, Kyle. "International Animal Rights: Speciesism and Exclusionary Human Dignity" (2005) 11 Animal L 195.

Bailey, Cathryn. "'Africa Begins at the Pyrenees': Moral Outrage, Hypocrisy, and the Spanish Bullfight" *Ethics and Environment* 12.1 (2007): 23.

– "We Are What We Eat: Feminist Vegetarianism and the Reproduction of Racial Identity." *Hypatia* 22.2 (2007): 39.

Bain, Paul, et al. "Attributing Human Uniqueness and Human Nature to Cultural Groups: Distinct Forms of Subtle Dehumanization." *Group Processes and Intergroup Relations* 12.6 (2009): 789. https://doi.org/10.1177/1368430209340415.

Barad, Karen. "Posthumanist Performativity: Toward an Understanding of How Matter Comes to Matter." *Signs* 28.3 (2003): 80.

Barber, Katherine. "The Last Word." *Performing Arts and Entertainment Canada* 32.3 (1999): 46.

Barnett, Joshua Tray. "Thinking Ecologically with Judith Butler." *Culture Theory and Critique* 59.1 (2018): 20.

Bastian, Brock, and Nick Haslam. "Experiencing Dehumanization: Cognitive and Emotional Effects of Everyday Dehumanization." *Basic and Applied Social Psychology* 33.4 (2011): 295. https://doi.org/10.1080/01973533.2011.614132.

Baxstrom, Richard. "Force, Dwelling, and the Personhood of Things in Urban Malaysia" *Comparative Studies of South Asia, Africa, and the Middle East* 37.3 (2017): 437.

Beausoleil, Emily. "Mastery of Knowledge or Meeting of Subjects? The Epistemic Effects of Two Forms of Political Voice" *Contemporary Political Theory* 15.1 (2016): 16.

Beck, Susanne. "The Problem of Ascribing Legal Responsibility in the Case of Robotics." *AI and Society* 31 (2016): 473.

Bekoff, Marc. "Deep Ethology, Animal Rights, and the Great Ape/Animal Project: Resisting Speciesism and Expanding the Community of Equals." *Journal of Agricultural and Environmental Ethics* 10.3 (1997): 269.

Belcourt, Billy Ray. "Animal Bodies, Colonial Subjects: (Re)Locating Animality in Decolonial Thought." *Societies* 5.1 (2015): 1.

Bent, Nancy. "Loving Animals: Toward a New Animal Advocac." *American Library Association* 108.1 (2011): 16.

Bergoffen, Debra, and Gail Weiss. "Embodying the Ethical – Editors' Introduction," *Hypatia* 26.3 (2011): 453.

Betz, M.A. "Rudy, Kathy. Loving Animals: Toward a New Animal Advocacy." *Cho'ice* 49.6 (2012): 1075.

Boggs, Colleen Glenney. "American Bestiality: Sex, Animals, and the Construction of Subjectivity." *Cultural Critique* 76 (2010): 98.

Borrows, John. "Challenging Historical Frameworks: Aboriginal Rights, the Trickster, and Originalism." Canadian Historical Review 98.1 (2017): 114.

Bousfield, Dan. "Settler Colonialism in Vegetal Worlds: Exploring Progress and Resilience at the Margins of the Anthropocene." *Settler Colonial Studies* 10.1 (2020): 15. https://doi.org/10.1080/2201473X.2019.1604297.

Brannelly, Tula. "Sustaining Citizenship: People with Dementia and the Phenomenon of Social Death." *Nursing Ethics* 18.5 (2011): 662. https://doi.org/10.1177/0969733011408049.

Braverman, Irus. "Captive: Zoometric Operations in Gaza." *Public Culture* 29 (2017): 191.

– "Law's Underdog: A Call for More-than-Human Legalities." *The Annual Review of Law and Social Science* 14 (2018): 127.

Brighten, Andrew. "Aboriginal Peoples and the Welfare of Animal Persons: Dissolving the Bill C-10B Conflict" (2011) 10:1 Indigenous LJ 39.

Brown, Mark. "'An Unqualified Human Good'? On Rule of Law, Globalization, and Imperialism." *Law and Social Inquiry* 43.4 (2018): 1391.

Browning, Michelle, Christine Bigby, and Jacinta Douglas. "Supported Decision Making: Understanding How Its Concept Link to Legal Capacity Is Influencing the Development of Practice." *Research and Practice in Intellectual Developmental Disabilities* 1.1 (2014): 34.

Bryant, Taimie L. "Animals Unmodified: Defining Animals / Defining Human Obligations to Animals" (2006) U Chi Legal Forum 165.

– "Denying Animals Childhood and Its Implications for Animal-Protective Law Reform" *Law, Culture, and the Humanities* 6.1 (2010): 56.

– "Similarity or Difference as a Basis for Justice: Must Animals Be like Humans to Be Legally Protected from Humans" (2007) 70:1 Animal L & P 207.

Calarco, Matthew. "Animal Studies." *The Year's Work in Critical and Cultural Theory* 24.1 (2016): 24.

– "Identity, Difference, Indistinction" *CR: The New Centennial Review* 11.2 (2012): 41.

Campbell, Angela. "Could a Chimpanzee or Bonobo Take the Stand?" (2002) 8 Animal L 243.

Cardozo, Karen, & Banu Subramaniam. "Assembling Asian/American Nature Cultures: Orientalism and Invited Invasions." *Journal of Asian American Studies* 16.1 (2013): 1.

Carreno, Guillermo Salas. "Mining and the Living Materiality of Mountains in Andean Societies." *Journal of Material Culture* 22.2 (2016): 133.

Chiesa, Luis E. "Of Persons and the Criminal Law: (Second Tier) Personhood as a Prerequisite for Victimhood" (2007–2008) 28 Pace L R 759.

Christie, Gordon. "Culture, Self-Determination, and Colonialism: Issues around the Revitalization of Indigenous Legal Traditions" (2007) 6 Indigenous LJ 13.

Chrulew, Matthew. "Animals in Biopolitical Theory: Between Agamben and Negri." *New Formations* 76.76 (2012): 53.

Cochrane, Alisdair. "Ownership and Justice for Animals" (2009) 21:4 Utilitas 424.

Cohen, Mathilde. "Animal Colonialism: The Case of Milk" (2017) AJIL Unbound 111: 267.

Cohn, Carol. "'Maternal Thinking' and the Concept of 'Vulnerability' in Security Paradigms, Policies, and Practice." *Journal of International Political Theory* 10.1 (2013): 46.

Cole, Alyson. "All of Us Are Vulnerable, but Some Are More Vulnerable than Others: The Political Ambiguity of Vulnerability Studies, an Ambivalent Critique." *Journal of Philosophy and Social Theory* 17.2 (2016): 260.

Comaroff, John L., and Jean Comaroff. "On Personhood: An Anthropological Perspective from Africa." *Social Identities: Journal for the Study of Race, Nation, and Culture* 7.2 (2001): 267.

Conway, Heather, and John Stannard. "Property and Emotions." *Emotion Review* 8.1 (2016): 38.

Costello, Kimberly, and Gordon Hodson. "Exploring the Roots of Dehumanization: The Role of Animal–Human Similarity in Promoting Immigrant Humanization." *Group Processes and Intergroup Relations* 13.1 (2010): 3. https://doi.org/10.1177/1368430209347725.

– "Lay Beliefs about the Causes of and Solutions to Dehumanization and Prejudice: Do Nonexperts Recognize the Role of Human-Animal Relations?" *Journal of Applied Social Psychology* 44.4 (2014): 278. https://doi.org/10.1111/jasp.12221.

Coulter, Kendra. "Beyond Human to Humane: A Multispecies Analysis of Care Work, Its Repression, and Its Potential." *Studies in Social Justice* 10.2 (2016): 199.

Cover, Rob. "Sexual Ethics, Masculinity, and Mutual Vulnerability." *Australian Feminist Studies* 29.82 (2014): 435.

Crary, Alice. "Animals, Cognitive Disability, and Getting the World in Focus in Ethics and Social Thought: A Reply to Eva Feder Kittay and Peter Singer." *Journal for Ethics and Moral Philosophy* 39.2 (2019): 139.

Culbertson, Tucker. "Animal Equality, Human Dominion, and Fundamental Interdependence." (2009) 5 J Animal L 33.

Darian-Smith, Eve. "Postcolonialism: A Brief Introduction." *Social and Legal Studies* 5.3 (1996): 291.

Davis, Janet M. "Cockfight Nationalism: Blood Sport and the Moral Politics of American Empire and Nation Building." *American Quarterly* 65.3 (2013): 549.

Deckha, Maneesha. "Animal Justice, Cultural Justice: A Posthumanist Response to Cultural Rights in Animals." *Journal of Animal Law and Ethics* 2 (2007): 189.

– "Critical Animal Studies and Animal Law" (2011–12) 18:2 Animal L. 207.

– "Initiating a Non-Anthropocentric Jurisprudence: The Rule of Law and Animal Vulnerability under a Property Paradigm." *Alberta Law Review* 50.4 (2013): 783.

– "Intersectionality and Posthumanist Vision of Equality" (2008) 23:2 Wis J L Gender & Soc 249.

– "Legislating Respect: A Pro-choice Feminist Legal Analysis of Embryo Research Restrictions in Canada" (2012) 58:1 McGill L J 199.

– "(Not) Reproducing the Cultural, Racial, and Embodied Other: A Feminist Response to Canada's Partial Ban on Sex Selection" (2007) 16 UCLA Women's LJ 1.

– "Property on the Borderline: A Comparative Analysis of the Legal Status of Animals in Canada and the United States" (2012) 20:2 Cardozo J Intl & Comparative L 313.

– "Teaching Posthumanist Ethics in Law School: The Race, Culture, and Gender Dimensions of Student Resistance" (2009–2010) 16 Animal L. 287.

– "The Salience of Species Difference for Feminist Legal Theory" (2006) 17:1 Hastings Women's L J 1.

– "The Save Movement and Farmed Animal Suffering: The Advocacy Benefits of Bearing Witness as a Template for Law" (2019) 5 Can J Constitutional & Comp L77.

– "The Subhuman as a Cultural Agent of Violence" *Journal of Critical Animal Studies* 8.3 (2010): 28.

– "Toward a Postcolonial Posthumanist Feminist Theory: Centralizing Race and Culture in Feminist Work on Nonhuman Animals." *Hypatia* 27.3 (2012): 527.

– "Unsettling Anthropocentric Legal Systems: Reconciliation, Indigenous Laws, and Animal Personhood." *Journal of Intercultural Studies* 41.1 (2020): 77.

– "Veganism, Dairy, and Decolonization." *Journal of Human Rights and the Environment* 11.2 (2020): 244.

– "Vulnerability, Equality, and Animals" (2015) 27:1 Can J Women & L 47.

– "Welfarist *and* Imperial: The Contributions of Anti-Cruelty Legislation to Civilizational Discourse." *American Quarterly* 65.3 (2013): 515.

DeCoste, F.C. "Animals and Political Community: Preliminary Reflections Prompted by Bill C-10" (2002) 40 Alta L Rev 1057.

Denike, Margaret. "The Human Rights of Others: Sovereignty, Legitimacy, and 'Just Causes' for the 'War on Terror.'" *Hypatia* 23.2 (2008): 95.

Dhamoon, Rita. "Considerations on Mainstreaming Instrumentality," *Political Research Quarterly* 64.1 (2011): 230.

Dhont, Kristof, et al. "Social Dominance Orientation Connects Prejudicial Human-Human and Human-Animal Relations." *Personality and Individual Differences* 61 (2014): 105.

Dickenson, Donna. "Commodification of Human Tissue: Implications for Feminist and Development Ethics." *Developing World Bioethics* 2.1 (2002): 55.

Dolgert, Stefan. "Species of Disability: Response to Arneil." *Political Theory* 38.6 (2010): 859.

Donaldson, Sue, and Will Kymlicka. "Farmed Animal Sanctuaries: The Heart of the Movement?" *Politics and Animals* 1.1 (2015): 50.

Donovan, Josephine. "Feminism and the Treatment of Animals: From Care to Dialogue." *Signs* 31.2 (2006): 305.

Dossa, Shiraz. "Liberal Legalism: Law, Culture and Identity." *The European Legacy* 4.3 (1999): 73.

Drakopoulou, Maria. "The Ethic of Care, Female Subjectivity, and Feminist Legal Scholarship." (2000) 8:2 Fem L Stud 199.

Eisen, Jessica. "Feminist Jurisprudence for Farmed Animals" (2019) 5 Can J Comp & Constitutional L 111.

– "Liberating Animal Law: Breaking Free from Human-Use Typologies" (2010) 17 Animal L 59.

Elliott, Michael. "Indigenous Resurgence: The Drive for Renewed Engagement and Reciprocity in the Turn Away from the State." *Canadian Journal of Political Science* 51.1 (2018): 61.

Esmeir, Samera. "On Making Dehumanization Possible." *PMLA* 121.5 (2006): 1544.

Favre, David. "Equitable Self-Ownership for Animals" (2000) 50:2 Duke LJ 473.

– "Integrating Animal Interests Into Our Legal System" (2004) 10 Animal L 87.

– "Living Property: A New Status for Animals within the Legal System" (2010) 93:3 Marq L Rev 1021.

Favre, David, and Vivien Tsang, "The Development of Anti-Cruelty Laws during the 1800's" (1993) Det CL Rev 1.

Ferguson, Moria. "Breaking in Englishness: Black Beauty and the Politics of Gender, Race, and class." *Women: A Cultural Review* 5.1 (1994): 34.

Findlay, C. Scott, and Stewart Elgie. "Species Listing under Canada's Species at Risk Act." *Conservation Biology* 23.6 (2009): 1609.

Fineman, Martha Albertson. "The Vulnerable Subject: Anchoring Equality in the Human Condition" (2008) 20:1 Yale JL & Feminism 1.
- "Vulnerability and the Institution of Marriage" (2015) 64:6 Emory LJ 2089.
- "Vulnerability and Inevitable Inequality" (2017) 4:4 Oslo L Rev 133.
Fischer, Bob, and Josh Milburn. "In Defence of Backyard Chickens." *Journal of Applied Philosophy* 36.1 (2017): 108. https://doi.org/10.1111/japp.12291.
Flannery, Sheri. "The Thirteenth Amendment Won't Help Free Willy." *Scholar* 15.1 (2012–2013): 29.
Fouladvand, Shahrzad, and Tony Ward. "Human Trafficking, Vulnerability, and the State" (2019) 83:1 J Crim L 39.
Fouts, Roger S. "Apes, Darwinian Continuity, and the Law" (2004) 10 Animal L 99.
Fox, Marie. "Rethinking Kinship: Law's Construction of the Animal Body" (2004) 57:1 Curr Legal Probs 469.
Fox, Marie, and Mo Ray, "No Pets Allowed? Companion Animals, Older People, and Residential Care." *Medical Humanities* 45.2 (2019): 211.
Francione, Gary L. "Animals as Property" (1996) 2 Animal L i.
- "Animals, Property and Legal Welfarism: 'Unnecessary' Suffering and the 'Humane' Treatment of Animals" (1994) 46 Rutgers L Rev 721.
- "Animal Welfare and the Moral Value of Nonhuman Animals." *Law, Culture, and the Humanities* 6 (2010): 24.
- "Reflections on *Animals, Property and the Law* and *Rain without Thunder*." *Law and Contemporary Problems* 70 (2007): 9.
Fraiman, Susan. "Pussy Panic versus Liking Animals: Tracking Gender in Animal Studies." *Critical Inquiry* 39.1 (2012): 89.
Framarin, Christopher G. "The Moral Standing of Animals and Plants in the Manusmriti." *Philosophy East and West* 64.1 (2014): 192.
Fraundorfer, Markus. "The Rediscovery of Indigenous Thought in the Modern Legal System: The Case of the Great Apes." *Global Policy* 9.1 (2018): 17.
Friedland, Hadley, and Val Napoleon, "Gathering the Threads: Indigenous Legal Methodology" (2015) 1:1 Lakehead LJ 16.
Fudge, Erica. "Monstrous Acts: Bestiality in Early Modern England." *History Today* 50.8 (2000): 20.
Gaard, Greta. "Ecofeminism Revisited: Rejecting Essentialism and Re-Placing Species in a Material Feminist Environmentalism." *Feminist Formations* 23.2 (2011): 26.
- "Tools for a Cross-Cultural Feminist Ethics: Exploring Ethical Contexts and Contents in the Makah Whale Hunt." *Hypatia* 16.1 (2001): 1.
- "Vegetarian Ecofeminism: A Review Essay." *Frontiers* 22.3 (2002): 117.
Garcia, Maria Elena. "Death of a Guinea Pig: Grief and the Limits of Multispecies Ethnography in Peru." *Environmental Humanities* 11.2 (2019): 351.

– "The Taste of Conquest: Colonialism, Cosmopolitics, and the Dark Side of Peru's Gastronomic Boom." *Journal of Latin American and Caribbean Anthropology* 18.3 (2013): 505.

Glaskin, Katie. "Anatomies of Relatedness: Considering Personhood in Aboriginal Australia." *American Anthropologist* 114.2 (2012): 297.

Glick, Megan H. "Animal Instincts: Race, Criminality, and the Reversal of the 'Human.'" *American Quarterly* 65.3 (2013): 639.

– "Of Sodomy and Cannibalism: Dehumanisation, Embodiment, and the Rhetorics of Same-Sex and Cross-Species Contagion." *Gender and History* 23.2 (2011): 266.

Garland-Thomson, Rosemarie. "Feminist Disability Studies." *Signs* 30.2 (2005): 1557.

– "Misfits: A Feminist Materialist Disability Concept" *Hypatia* 26.3 (2011): 591.

Garner, Robert. "Political Ideologies and the Moral Status of Animals." *Journal of Political Ideologies* 8.2 (2003): 233.

Gerber, Lisa. "Book Review: Loving Animals: Toward a New Animal Advocacy." *SAGE* 25.1 (2012): 102.

Gillespie, Kathryn. "Placing Angola: Racialisation, Anthropocentrism, and Settler Colonialism at the Louisiana State Penitentiary's Angola Rodeo." *Antipode* 50.5 (2018): 1267. https://doi.org/10.1111/anti.12393.

– "Provocation from the Field: A Multispecies Doula Approach to Death and Dying." *Animal Studies Journal* 9.1 (2020). http://dx.doi.org/10.14453/asj.v9i1.2.

– "Witnessing Animal Others: Bearing Witness, Grief, and the Political Function of Emotion." *Hypatia* 31.3 (2016): 572.

Gillespie, Kathryn, and Yamini Narayanan. "Animal Nationalisms: Multispecies Cultural Politics, Race, and the (un)Making of the Settler Nation-State." *Journal of Intercultural Studies* 41.1 (2020): 1.

Goff, Phillip Atiba, et al. "Not Yet Human: Implicit Knowledge, Historical Dehumanization, and Contemporary Consequences." *Journal of Personality and Social Psycholology* 94.2 (2008): 292.

Goldbeck, Kyrille. "Rudy, Kathy. Loving Animals: Toward a New Animal Advocacy" *Library Journal* 136.14 (2011): 127.

Grear, Anna. "Challenging Corporate 'Humanity': Legal Disembodiment, Embodiment, and Human Rights." (2007) 7:3 Human Rights L Rev 511.

– "Deconstructing *Anthropos*: A Critical Legal Reflection on 'Anthropocentric' Law and Anthropocene 'Humanity'" (2015) 26 Law and Critique 225 at 231.

– "The Vulnerable Living Order: Human Rights and the Environment in a Critical and Philosophical Perspective" (2011) 2 J Hum Rts & Env't 23.

Greger, Michael. "The Human/Animal Interface: Emergence and Resurgence of Zoonotic Infectious Diseases." *Critical Reviews in Microbiology* 33.4 (2007) 243.

Groce, Nora Ellen, and Jonathan Marks. "The Great Ape Project and Disability Rights: Ominous Undercurrents of Eugenics in Action." *American Anthropologist* 102.4 (2000): 818.

Grossi, Renata. "Understanding Law and Emotion." *Emotion Review* 7.1 (2015): 55.

Gruen, Lori. "Attending to Nature: Empathetic Engagement with the More Than Human World." *Ethics and the Environment* 14.2 (2009): 23.

– "A Few Thoughts on the Future of Environmental Philosophy." *Ethics and the Environment* 12.2 (2007): 124.

– "Conflicting Values in a Conflicted World: Ecofeminism and Multicultural Environmental Ethics." *Women and Environments International Magazine* 52–3 (Fall 2001): 16.

– "On the Oppression of Women and Animals" *Environmental Ethics* 18.4 (1996): 441.

Gruen, Lori, and Kari Weil, "Animal Others – Editors' Introduction." *Hypatia* 27.3 (2012): 477.

Gunkel, David J. "A Vindication of the Rights of Machines" *Philosophy and Technology* 27.1 (2014): 113.

Gunkel, David, and Debra Hawhee. "Virtual Alterity and the Reformatting of Ethics." *Journal of Mass Media Ethics* 18.3–4 (2003): 173.

Haas, Nayeli Urquiza. "Book Review: M.A. Fineman and A. Grear, eds, Vulnerability: Reflections on a New Ethical Foundation for Law and Politics (London: Ashgate, 2013)" (2014) 22 Fem. Leg. Stud. 335.

– "The Semiotic Fractures of Vulnerable Bodies" (2017) 30:4 Int'l J Sem L 543 at 554.

Haraway, Donna. "Anthropocene, Capitalocene, Plantationocene, Chthulucene: Making Kin." *Environmental Humanities* 6.1 (2015): 159.

Harper, Amie Breeze. "Whiteness and 'Post-Racial' Vegan Praxis." *Journal of Critical Animal Studies* 8.3 (2010): 7.

Harris, Angela P. "Vulnerability and Power in the Age of the Anthropocene." *Washington and Lee Journal of Energy, Climate, and the Environment* 6.1 (2015): 98.

Harvey, A.D. "Bestiality in Late-Victorian England" (2000) 21:3 J Legal Hist 85.

Haslam, Nick. "Dehumanization: An Integrative Review." *Personality and Social Psychology Review* 10.3 (2006): 252. https://doi.org/10.1207/s15327957pspr1003_4.

Haslam, Nick, and Steve Loughnan. "Dehumanization and Infrahumanization." *Annual Review of Psychology* 65 (2014): 399. https://dx.doi.org/10.1146/annurev-psych-010213-115045.

Heath, Deborah, and Anne Meneley. "The NatureCultures of Foie Gras: Techniques of the Body and a Contested Ethics of Care." *Food, Culture, and Society* 13.3 (2010): 440.

Henson, Laura. "Species of Thought: Bare Life and Animal Being." *Antipode* 43.5 (2011): 1659.

Hewer, Rebecca, MF. "A Gossamer Consensus: Discourses of Vulnerability in the Westminster Prostitution Policy Subsystem" (2019) 28:2 Soc & Leg Stud 227.

Hill-Collins, Patricia. "Intersectionality's Definitional Dilemmas." *Annual Review of Sociology* 41.1 (2015): 1.

Hird, Myra. "Animal Transsex." *Australian Feminist Studies* 21.49 (2006): 35.

– "Meeting with the Microcosmos." *Environment and Planning D: Society and Space* 28.1 (2010): 36.

Holmberg, Tora. "Narrative, Affect, Love, and Confusion: Review of Kathy Rudy, Loving Animals. Toward a New Animal Advocacy." *Humanimalia* 3.2 (2012): 12.

Hua, Julietta, and Kasturi Ray. "Rights, Affect, and Precarity: Post-Racial Formations in Carework." *Cultural Dynamics* 26.1 (2014): 9.

Hudson, Laura. "A Species of Thought: Bare Life and Animal Being." *Antipode* 43.5 (2011): 1659.

Huff, Cynthia, and Joel Haefner. "His Master's Voice: Animalographies, Life Writing, and the Posthuman." *Biography* 35.1 (2012): 153.

Huss, Rebecca J. "Valuing Man's and Woman's Best Friend: The Moral and Legal Status of Companion Animals" (2002) 86:1 Marq L Rev 47.

Ibrahim, Darian M. "The Anticruelty Statute: A Study in Animal Welfare" (2006) 1 J Animal L & Ethics 175.

Isfahani-Hammond, Alexandra. "Of She-Wolves and Mad Cows: Animality, Anthropophagy and the State of Exception in Cláudio Assis's Amerola manga." *Luso-Brazilian Review* 48.2 (2011): 129.

Jackson, Zakiyyah Iman. "Animal: New Directions in the Theorization of Race and Posthumanism." *Feminist Studies* 39.3 (2013): 669.

– "Outer Worlds: The Persistence of Race in Movement 'beyond the Human.'" *Gay and Lesbian Quarterly* 21.2 (2015): 215.

Kapur, Ratna. "Dark Times for Liberal Intellectual Thought." *Profession* 1 (2006): 22.

Karanasiou, Argyo, and Dimitri Pinotsis. "Towards a Legal Definition of Machine Intelligence: The Argument for Artificial Personhood in the Age of Deep Learning" *ICAIL* 17 (2017): 119.

Karpin, Isabel, and Roxanne Mykitiuk. "'Going out on a limb': Prosthetics, Normalcy, and Disputing the 'Therapy/Enhancement' Distinction'" (2008) 16:3 Medical L Rev 413.

Kasperbauer, T.J. "Rejecting Empathy for Animal Ethics" *Ethical Theory and Moral Practice* 18.4 (2015): 817.

Kemmerer, Lisa. "Verbal Activism: Anymal" *Society and Animals* 14.1 (2006): 9.

Kerr, Andrew Jensen. "Pedagogy in Translation: Teaching Animal Law in China." *Asian Journal of Legal Education* 1.1 (2014): 33.

Kim, Claire Jean. "Multiculturalism Goes Imperial: Immigrants, Animals, and the Suppression of Moral Dialogue." *Du Bois Review* 4.1 (2007): 233.

Kim, James. "Petting Asian America." *MELUS* 36.1 (2011): 135.

Knauss, Stefan. "Conceptualizing Human Stewardship in the Anthropocene: The Rights of Nature in Ecuador, New Zealand, and India." *Journal of Agricultural and Environmental Ethics* 31.6 (2018): 703.

Knisely, Lisa C. "Oppression, Normative Violence, and Vulnerability: The Ambiguous Beauvoirian Legacy of Butler's Ethics." *philoSOPHIA* 2.2 (2012): 145.

Kochi, Tarik. "Species War: Law, Violence, and Animals." *Law, Culture, and the Humanities* 5.3 (2009): 353.

Kumari Campbell, Fiona. "Inciting Legal Fictions: 'Disabilities' Date with Ontology and the Ableist Body of the Law" (2001) 10:1 Griffith L Rev 42.

Kuzniar, Alice. "Where Is the Animal after Post-Humanism?: Sue Coe and the Art of Quivering Life." *CR: The New Centennial Review* 11.2 (2007): 17.

Kymlicka, Will. "Connecting Domination Contracts." *Ethnic and Racial Studies* 41.3 (2017): 532.

– "Social Membership: Animal Law beyond the Property/Personhood Impasse" (2017) 40:1 Dalhousie L J 123.

Kymlicka, Will, and Sue Donaldson. "Animal Rights, Multiculturalism, and the Left." *Journal of Social Philosophy* 45.1 (2014): 116.

Lennkh, Sabine. "The Animal: A Subject of Law: A Reflection on the Aspects of the Austrian and German Juridical Systems" (2011) 24:3 Int'l J Sem L. 307.

Levy, Nadine. "Towards a New Environmental Ethic in Contemporary Feminist Theory." *Hecate* 38.1–2 (2012): 9.

Liberati, Nicola, and Shoji Nagataki. "Vulnerability under the Gaze of Robots: Relations among Humans and Robots." *AI and Society* (2018). https://doi.org/10.1007/s00146-018-0849-1.

Lindberg, Tracey. "Engaging Indigenous Legal Knowledge in Canadian Legal Institutions: Four Stories, Four Teachings, Four Tips, and Four Lessons about Indigenous Peoples in the Legal Academy" (2019) 50 Ottawa L Rev 119.

Lino, Dylan. "The Rule of Law and the Rule of Empire: A.V. Dicey in Imperial Context" (2018) 81:5 Modern L Rev 739.

Lipschitz, Ruth. "Skin/ned Politics: Species Discourse and the Limits of 'The Human' in Nandiqha Mutambo's Art." *Hypatia* 27.3 (2012): 546.

Livingston, Julie, and Jasbir K. Puar. "Interspecies." *Social Text* 29.1 (2011): 3.

Loughnan, Steve, and Nick Haslam. "Animals and Androids: Implicit Associations between Social Categories and Nonhumans." *Psychological Science* 18 (2007): 116. https://doi.org/10.1111/j.1467-9280.2007.01858.x.

Loughnan, Steve, Nick Haslam, and Yoshihisa Kashima. "Understanding the Relationship between Attribute-Based and Metaphor-Based Dehumanization." *Group Processes and Intergroup Relations* 12.6 (2009): 747. https://doi.org/10.1177/1368430209347726.

Loughnan, Steve et al. "Dehumanization and Social Class: Animality in the Stereotypes of 'White Trash,' 'Chavs,' and 'Bogans.'" *Social Psychology* 45.1 (2014): 54. https://doi.org/10.1027/1864-9335/a000159.

Lovvorn, Jonathan R. "California Proposition 2: A Watershed Moment for Animal Law" (2009) 15:2 Animal L 149.

Lundström, Markus. "'We Do This Because the Market Demands It': Alternative Meat Production and the Speciesist Logic." *Agriculture and Human Values* 36:1 (2018): 127.

MacGregor, Sherilyn. "From Care to Citizenship." *Ethics and the Environment* 9.1 (2004): 1085.

Mane, Rebecca L. Clark. "Transmuting Grammars of Whiteness in Third Wave Feminism: Interrogating Postrace Histories, Postmodern Abstraction, and the Proliferation of Difference in Third-Wave Texts." *Signs* 38.1 (2012): 71.

Marder, Michael. "Is It Ethical to Eat Plants?" Parallas 19.1 (2013): 29.

Marhia, Natasha. "Some Humans Are More *Human* Than Others: Troubling the 'Human' in Human Security from a Critical Feminist Perspective." *Security Dialogue* 44 (2013): 19.

Matambanadzo, Saru. "The Body, Incorporated" (2013) 87:3 Tul L Rev 457.

– "Embodying Vulnerability" (2012) 20:1 Duke J of Gender L & Policy 45 at 65.

McDaris, Camden J. "Legal Protection Only for Those Who Are Most Like 'Us': What Animal Activists Can Learn from the Early Women's Movement about Society's Resistance to Acknowledging Rights" (2006) 2 J of Ani L 159.

McQueen, Paddy. "Invited Review Essay." *Hypatia* 27.2 (2012): 338.

McWeeny, Jennifer. "Topographies of Flesh: Women, Nonhuman Animals, and the Embodiment of Connection and Difference." *Hypatia* 29.2 (2014): 269.

Michel, Margot, and Eveline Schneider Kayasseh. "The Legal Situation of Animals in Switzerland: Two Steps Forward, One Step Back – Many Steps to Go" (2011) 7 J Animal L 1.

Milburn, Josh. "Death-Free Dairy? The Ethics of Clean Milk." *Journal of Agricultural and Environmental Ethics* 31 (2018): 261. https://doi.org/10.1007/s10806-018-9723-x.

Mills, Aaron. "The Lifeworlds of Law: On Revitalizing Indigenous Legal Orders Today" (2016) 61 McGill L J 847.

Mohanty, Chandra Talpade. "Under Western Eyes: Feminist Scholarship and Colonial Discourses." *Feminist Review* 30 (1988): 61.

Moore, Lisa Jean, and Mary Kosut. "Among the Colony: Ethnographic Fieldwork, Urban Bees, and Intra-Species Mindfulness." *Ethnography* 15.4 (2013): 516.

Murphy, Ann V. "Corporeal Vulnerability." *Hypatia* 26.3 (2011): 575.

Naffine, Ngaire. "Liberating the Legal Person" (2011) 26:1 CJLS 193.

Napoleon, Val, and Hadley Friedland, "An Inside Job: Engaging with Indigenous Legal Traditions through Stories" (2016) 61:4 McGill LJ 725.

Narayanan, Yamini. "'Cow Is a Mother, Mothers Can Do Anything for Their Children!": Gaushalas as Landscapes of Anthropatriarchy and Hindu Patriarchy." *Hypatia* 34.2 (2019): 195.

– "Cow Protection as 'Casteised Speciesim': Sacralisation, Commercialization, and Politicization." *South Asia* 41.2 (2018): 331.

– "Dairy, Death, and Dharma: The Devastation of Cow Protectionism in India." *Animal Liberation*, 18 June 2017.

Nedelsky, Jennifer. "Property in Potential Life? A Relational Approach to Choosing Legal Categories" (1993) 6:2 Can J L & Jurisprudence 343.

– "Relations of Freedom and Law's Relations." *Politics and Gender* 8.2 (2012): 231.

Neimanis, Astrida. "Feminist Subjectivity, Watered." *Feminist Review* 103 (2013): 23.

– "No Representation without Colonisation? (Or, Nature Represents Itself)." *Somatechnics* 5.1 (2015): 135.

Nussbaum, Martha. "Robin West: Jurisprudence and Gender: Defending Radical Liberalism" (2008) 75:3 U Chicago L Rev 985.

Ojalehto, Bethany, Douglas L. Medin, and Salino G, Garcia. "Conceptualizing Agency: Folkpsychological and Folkcommunicative Perspectives on Plants." *Cognition* 162 (2017): 103.

Oliver, Kelly. "Animal Ethics: Toward an Ethics of Responsiveness." *Research in Phenomenology* 40 (2010): 267.

– "Bodies against the Law: Abu Ghraib and the War on Terror." *Continental Philosophy Review* 42.1 (2009): 63.

– "Conflicted Love" *Hypatia* 15.3 (2000): 1.

– "The Plight of Ethics." Journal of Speculative Philosophy 26.2 (2012): 118.

– "What Is Wrong with (Animal) Rights?" *Journal of Speculative Philosophy* 22.3 (2008): 214.

– "Witnessing and Testimony." *Parallax* 10.1 (2004): 78.

Pallotta, Nicole R. "Chattel of Child: The Liminal Status of Companion Animals in Society and Law." *Social Sciences* 8.5 (2019): 158.

Palmer, Clare. "Colonization, Urbanization, and Animals." *Philosophy and Geography* 6.1 (2010): 48.

Panagiotarakou, Eleni. "Who Loves Mosquitoes? Care Ethics, Theory of Obligation, and Endangered Species" *Journal of Agricultural and Environmental Ethics* 29 (2016): 1057.

Peterson, Anna. "Kathy Rudy: Loving Animals: Toward a New Animal Advocacy" *Journal of Agricultural and Environmental Ethics* 25.5 (2012): 787.

Petherbridge, Danielle. "What's Critical about Vulnerability?: Rethinking Interdependence, Recognition, and Power." *Hypatia* 31.1 (2016): 589.

Pick, Anat. "Turning to Animals between Love and Law." *New Formations* 76 (2012): 68.

Plumwood, Val. "Androcentrism and Anthrocentrism: Parallels and Politics." *Ethics and Environment* 1.2 (1996): 119.

Poore, Joseph, and Thomas Nemecek, "Reducing Food's Environmental Impacts through Producers and Consumers," *Science* 360:6392 (2018).

Probyn-Rapsey, Fiona, et al. "A Sustainable Campus: The Sydney Declaration on Interspecies Sustainability." *Animal Studies Journal* 5.1 (2016): 110.

Probyn-Rapsey, Fiona, Siobhan O'Sullivan, & Yvette Watt. "'Pussy Panic' and Glass Elevators: How Gender Is Shaping the Field of Animal Studies." *Australian Feminist Studies* 34.100 (2019): 198.

Puar, Jasbir K. "'I Would Rather Be a Cyborg than a Goddess': Becoming Intersectional in Assemblage Theory." *philoSOPHIA* 2.1 (2012): 49.

– "Precarity Talk: A Virtual Roundtable with Lauren Berlant, Judith Butler, Bojana Cveji, Isabell Lorey, Jasbir Puar, and Ana Vujanovic." *TRD: The Drama Review* 56.4 (2012): 163.

– "Terrorist Assemblages: Homonationalism in Queer Times." *Social and Cultural Geography* 11.4 (2007): 399.

Quillen, Carol. "Feminism Theory, Justice, and the Lure of the Human." *Signs* 27.1 (2001): 88.

Ramdas, Kamalini. "Feminist Care Ethics, Becoming Area." *Environment and Planning D: Society and Space* 34.5 (2016): 843.

Raphael-Leff, Joan. "Gift of Gametes – Unconscious Motivation, Commodification, and Problematics of Genealogy." *Feminist Review* 94 (2010): 117.

Redmalm, David. "Pet Grief: When Is Non-Human Life Grievable." *The Sociological Review* 63.1 (2015): 19.

Rekret, Paul. "A Critique of New Materialism: Ethics and Ontology." *Subjectivity* 9.3 (2016): 225.

Ritvo, Harriet. "On the Animal Turn." *Daedalus* 136.4 (2007): 118.

Robinson, Fiona. "Stop Talking and Listen: Discourse Ethics and Feminist Care Ethics in International Political Theory." *Millennium: Journal of International Studies* 39.3 (2011): 845.

Robinson, Margaret. "Animal Personhood in Mi'kmaq Perspective." *Societies* 4.4 (2014): 672.

Rogers, Lesley H., and Gisela Kaplan. "Think or Be Damned: The Problematic Case of Higher Cognition in Animals and Legislation for Animal Welfare" (2005–2006) 12 Animal L 151.

Rogers, Raymond A., & Christopher J.A. Wilkinson. "Policies of Extinction: The Life and Death of Canada's Endangered Species Legislation." *Policy Studies Journal* 28.1 (2000): 190.

Rogers, Wendy, Catriona Mackenzie, and Susan Dodds. "Why Bioethics Needs a Concept of Vulnerability." *International Journal of Feminist Approaches to Bioethics* 5.2 (2012): 11.

Rossi, John, and Samuel A Garner. "Industrial Farm Animal Production: A Comprehensive Moral Critique." *Journal of Agricultural and Environmental Ethics* 27 (2014): 479.

St Pierre, Joshua. "Cripping Communication: Speech, Disability, and Exclusion in Liberal Humanist and Posthumanist Discourse." *Communication Theory* 25.3 (2015): 330.

Sainz, Mario, et al. "Animalizing the Disadvantaged, Mechanizing the Wealth: The Convergence of Socio-Economic Status and Attribution of Humanity." *International Journal of Psychology* 54.4 (2019): 423. https://doi.org/10.1002/ijop.12485.

– "Less Human, More to Blame: Animalizing Poor People Increases Blame and Decreases Support for Wealth Redistribution." *Group Processes and Intergroup Relations* 23.4 (2020): 546. https://doi.org/10.1027/1864-9335/a000159.

Salih, Sara. "Filling Up the Space between Mankind and Ape: Racism, Speciesism, and the Androphillic Ape." *Ariel* 38.1 (2007): 95.

Sankoff, Peter. "Five Years of *the* 'New' Animal Welfare Regime: Lessons Learned from New Zealand's Decision to Modernize Its Animal Welfare Legislation" (2005) 11 Animal L. 7.

Satz, Ani. "Animals as Vulnerable Subjects: Beyond Interest-Convergence, Hierarchy, and Property" (2009) 16:1 Animal L. 65.

– "Would Rosa Parks Wear Fur?" (2006) 1 J of Animal L & Ethics 139.

Satz, Debra. "Voluntary Slavery and the Limits of the Market" (2009) 3:1 L & Ethics of Human Rights 87.

Schillmoller, Anne. "Gaining Ground: Towards a Discourse of Posthuman Animality: A Geophysical Journey" 14 Southern Cross U L Rev 41.

Schueller, Malini Johar. "Analogy and (White) Feminist Theory: Thinking Race and the Color of the Cyborg Body." *Signs* 31.1 (2005): 63.

– "Decolonizing Global Theories Today: Hardt and Negri, Agamben, Butler." *Interventions* 11.2 (2009): 235.

Scott, Rebecca. "Body Worlds' Plastinates, the Human/Nonhuman Interface, and Feminism." *Feminist Theory* 12.2 (2011): 169.

Septie, Amba J. "More Than Stories, More Than Myths: Animal/Human/Nature(s) in Traditional Ecological Worldviews." *Humanities* 6.4 (2017): 78.

Shapiro, Kenneth, and Margo DeMello. "The State of Human-Animal Studies." *Animals and Society* 18.3 (2010): 307.

Shweder, Richard A. "Shouting at the Hebrews: Imperial Liberalism v. Liberal Pluralism and the Practice of Male Circumcision." *Law, Culture, and the Humanities* 5.2 (2009): 247.

Skibinsky, Christina G. "Changes in Store for the Livestock Industry – Canada's Recurring Proposed Animal Cruelty Amendments" (2005) 68 Sask L Review 175.

Smith, James L. "I, River?: New Materialism, Riparian Non-Human Agency and the Scale of Democratic Reform." *Asia Pacific Viewpoint* 58.1 (2017): 99.

Smith, Wesley J. "Let Great Apes Be Apes." *The Human Life Review* 32.3–4 (2006): 147.

Snaza, Nathan. "(Im)Possible Witness: Viewing PETA's 'Holocaust on Your Plate.'" *Animal Liberation Philosophy and Policy Journal* 2.1 (2004): 1.

Sorenson, John. "'Some Strange Things Happening in Our Country': Opposing Proposed Changes in Anti-Cruelty Law in Canada." *Social and Legal Studies* 12.3 (2003): 377.

Stanescu, James. "Species Trouble: Judith Butler, Mourning, and the Precarious Lives of Animals" *Hypatia* 27.3 (2012): 567.

Steele, Linda, and Leanne Dowse. "Gender, Disability Rights, and Violence against Medical Bodies." *Australian Feminist Studies* 31.88 (2016): 187.

Stoll, John E. "Mask, Persona, Personality." *The Sewanee Review* 92.1 (1984): xiii.

Storrie, Bridget. "'The Mighty Life-Creating and Transforming Power' of Carnival: Why the Canadian Truth and Reconciliation Commission Does Not Seem to Have It, but Indigenous Resurgence Does." *International Journal of Transitional Justice* 3.1 (2015): 469.

Stumm, Bettina. "Witnessing Others in Narrative Collaboration: Ethical Responsibility beyond Recognition." *Biography* 37.3 (2014): 768.

Swanson, Lori J. "A Feminist Ethic That Binds Us to Mother Earth." *Ethics and the Environment* 20.2 (2015): 83.

Szytbel, David. "Can the Treatment of Animals Be Compared to the Holocaust?" *Ethics and the Environment* 11.1 (2006): 97.

Tallbear, Kim. "An Indigenous Reflection on Working beyond the Human/Not Human." *Gay and Lesbian Quarterly* 21.2 (2015): 230.

Taylor, Chloë. "On Intellectual Generosity." *Philosophy Today* 62.1 (2018): 3.

– "The Precarious Lives of Animals: Butler, Coetzee, and Animal Ethics." *Philosophy Today* 52.1 (2008): 60.

Taylor, Rowan. "A Step at a Time: New Zealand's Progress toward Hominid Rights" (2001) 7 Animal L 35.

Thomas, C.D., et al. "Extinction Risk from Climate Change." *Nature* 427 (2004).

Thomson, Judith Jarvis. "A Defense of Abortion." *Philosophy and Public Affairs* 1.1 (1971): 47.

Van Wagner, Estair. "Putting Property in Its Place: Relational Theory, Environmental Rights, and Land Use Planning" (2013) 43 RGD 275.

Wadiwel, Dinesh. "The Sovereign Whip: Flogging, Biopolitics, and the Frictional Community." *Journal of Australian Studies* 27.76 (2003): 117.

– "The War against Animals: Domination, Law, and Sovereignty" (2009) 18:2 Griffith L Rev 283.

Walther, Sundhya. "Fables of the Tiger Economy: Species and Subalternity in Aravind Adiga's The White Tiger." *Modern Fiction Studies* 60.3 (2014): 579.

Weaver, Harlan. "'Becoming in Kind': Race, Class, Gender, and Nation in Cultures of Dog Rescue and Dogfighting." *American Quarterly* 65.3 (2013): 689.

Weisberg, Zipporah. "The Broken Promises of Monsters: Haraway, Animals, and the Humanist Legacy." *Journal of Critical Animal Studies* 7.2 (2009): 22.

West, Robin. "Jurisprduence and Gender" (1988) 55 U Chicago L Rev 1.

Wichert, Rachel Nussbaum, and Martha Nussbaum., "The Legal Status of Whales: Capabilities, Entitlements, and Culture." *Seqüência: Estudos Jurídicos e Políticos* 37.72 (2016): 19.

Willett, Cynthia. "Affect Attunement in the Caregiver–Infant Relationship and across Species: Expanding the Ethical Scope of Eros." *philoSOPHIA* 2.2 (2012): 111.

Willett, Walter, et al. "Food in the Anthropocene: the EAT-*Lancet* Commission on Healthy Diets from Sustainable Food Systems." *The Lancet* 393 (2019): 447.

Williams, Nancy M. "The Ethics of Care and Humane Meat: Why Care Is Not Ambiguous about 'Humane' Meat." *Journal of Social Philosophy* 46.2 (2015): 264.

Wise, Steven M. "Legal Personhood and the Nonhuman Rights Project" (2010) 17:1 Animal L. 1.

Wolfe, Cary. "Before the Law: Animals in a Biopolitical Context." *Sage Journal* 6.1 (2010): 8.

Womack, Craig. "There Is No Respectful Way to Kill an Animal." *Studies in American Indian Literatures* 25.4 (2013): 11.

Worm, Boris, et al. "Impacts of Biodiversity Loss on Ocean Ecosystem Services." *Science* 314.5800 (2006): 787.

Worsham, Lynn. "Toward an Understanding of Human Violence: Cultural Studies, Animal Studies, and the Promise of Posthumanism." *Review of Education, Pedagogy, and Cultural Studies* 35.1 (2013): 51.

Wrenn, Corey Lee. "An Analysis of Diversity in Nonhuman Animal Rights Media." *Journal of Agricultural and Environmental Ethics* 29 (2016): 143.

Wright, Andrew J., et al. "Myth and Momentum: A Critique of Environmental Impact Assessments." *Journal of Environmental Protection* 4 (2013): 72.

Wright, Laura. "Orwellian Animals in Postcolonial Context: Margaret Atwood's *Oryx and Crake*." *Margaret Atwood Studies* 2.1 (2008): 3.

Wyckoff, Jason. "The Animal Rights Debate: Abolition or Regulation? – By Gary L. Francione & Robert Garner." *Journal of Applied Philosophy* 28.4 (2011): 415.

Wynter, Sylvia. "Unsettling the Coloniality of Being/Power/Truth/Freedom: Toward the Human, after Man, Its Overrepresentation – An Argument." *CR: The New Centennial Review* 3.3 (2003): 257.

Youatt, Rafi. "Interspecies Relations, International Relations: Rethinking Anthropocentric Politics." *Millennium* 43.1 (2014): 207.

Young, Bryanne. "Intimacies of Rock: Ethnographic Considerations of Posthuman Performativity in Canada's Rocky Mountains." *Cultural Studies/ Critical Methodologies* 16.1 (2016): 75.

Young, Claire, and Susan Boyd. "Losing the Feminist Voice? Debates on the Legal Recognition of Same Sex Partnerships in Canada" (2006) 14:2 Fem Legal Stud 213.

Yunxiang Yan. "Doing Personhood in Chinese Culture." *Cambridge Anthropology* 35.2 (2017): 1.

Zevnik, Andreja. "Becoming-Animal, Becoming-Detainee: Encountering Human Rights Discourse in Guantanamo." *Law Critique* 22.2 (2011): 157.

Ziarek, Ewa Plonowska. "Feminist Reflections on Vulnerability: Disrespect, Obligation, Action." *SubStance* 42.3 (2013): 67.

Secondary Materials: Monographs

Acampora, Ralph R. *Corporal Compassion: Animal Ethics and Philosophy of Body.* Pittsburgh: University of Pittsburgh Press, 2006.

Adams, Carol J. *Neither Man nor Beast: Feminism and the Defense of Animals.* New York: Continuum, 1994.

– *The Sexual Politics of Meat: A Feminist-Vegetarian Critical Theory.* New York: Continuum, 1990.

Alaimo, Stacy. *Bodily Natures: Science, Environment, and the Material Self.* Bloomington: Indiana University Press, 2010.

Alexis, Andre. *Fifteen Dogs.* Toronto: Coach House Books, 2015.

Anderson, E.N., and Barbara A. Anderson, *Warning Signs of Genocide: An Anthropological Perspective.* Lanham: Lexington Books, 2013.

Anderson, Kay. *Race and the Crisis of Humanism.* London: Routledge, 2007.

Anderson, Virginia DeJohn. *Creatures of Empire: How Domestic Animals Transformed Early America.* Oxford: Oxford University Press, 2006.

Bandes, Susan. *The Passions of Law.* New York: NYU Press, 1999.

Barad, Karen. *Meeting the Universe Halfway: Quantum Physics and the Entanglement of Matter and Meaning.* Durham: Duke University Press, 2007.

Bardhan, Pranab. *The Economic Theory of Agrarian Institutions.* Oxford: Clarendon Press, 1991.

Bekoff, Marc, and Jessica Pierce. *Wild Justice: The Moral Lives of Animals.* Chicago: University of Chicago Press, 2009.

Bennett, Jane. *Vibrant Matter: A Political Ecology of Things.* Durham: Duke University Press, 2010.

Bisgould, Lesli. *Animals and the Law.* Toronto: Irwin Law, 2011.

Bordo, Susan. *The Flight of Objectivity: Essays on Cartesianism and Culture.*
Albany: SUNY Press, 1987.

Borrows, John. *Canada's Indigenous Constitution.* Toronto: University of Toronto
Press, 2010.

– *Recovering Canada: The Resurgence of Indigenous Law.* Toronto: University of
Toronto Press, 2002.

Brandt, Anthony, and David Eagleman. *The Runaway Species.* New York:
Catapult, 2017.

Braverman, Irus. *Wild Life: The Institution of Nature.* Stanford: Stanford
University Press, 2015.

– *Zooland: The Institution of Captivity.* Stanford: Stanford University Press, 2012.

Butler, Judith. *Frames of War: When Is Life Grievable?* New York: Verso, 2009.

– *Gender Trouble.* New York: Routledge, 2000.

– *Precarious Life: The Powers of Mourning and Violence.* London: Verso, 2004.

Campbell, Fiona Kumari. *Contours of Ableism: The Production of Disability and
Abledness.* Basingstoke: Palgrave Macmillan, 2009.

Castricano, Jodey. *Animal Subjects: An Ethical Reader in a Posthuman World.*
Waterloo: Wilfrid Laurier University Press, 2008.

– *Animal Subjects 2.0.* Waterloo: Wilfrid Laurier University Press, 2017.

Cavalieri, Paola. *The Animal Question: Why Non-Human Animals Deserve Human
Rights* (New York: Oxford University Press, 2001.

Cavalieri, Paola, and Peter Singer. *The Great Ape Project: Equality beyond
Humanity.* New York: St Martin's Griffin, 1996.

Chaudhuri, Una, and Holly Hughes. *Animal Acts: Performing Species Today.*
Ann Arbor: University of Michigan Press, 2014.

Chen, Mel Y. *Animacies: Biopolitics, Racial Mattering, and Queer Affect.* Durham:
Duke University Press, 2012.

Corbey, Raymond. *The Metaphysics of Apes: Negotiating the Animal-Human
Boundary.* New York: Cambridge University Press, 2005.

Cornell, Drucilla. *The Philosophy of the Limit.* New York: Routledge, 1992.

Crankshaw, James. *The Criminal Code of Canada.* Montreal: Whiteford &
Theoret, Law Publishers, 1894.

Cruickshank, Julie. *Do Glaciers Listen? Local Knowledges, Colonial Encounters,
and Social Imagination.* Vancouver: UBC Press, 2005.

Cudworth, Erika. *Developing Ecofeminist Theory: The Complexity of Difference.*
Hampshire: Palgrave Macmillan, 2005.

Dalal, Neil, and Chloë Taylor. *Asian Perspectives on Animal Ethics: Rethinking
the Nonhuman.* London: Routledge, 2014.

Darian-Smith, Eve. *Religion, Race, Rights: Landmarks in the History of Modern
Anglo-American Law.* Oxford: Hart, 2010.

Darian-Smith, Eve, and Peter Fitzpatrick. *Laws of the Postcolonial.* Ann Arbor:
University of Michigan Press, 1999.

Dayan, Colin. *The Law Is a White Dog: How Legal Rituals Make and Unmake Persons*. Princeton: Princeton University Press, 2011.

Delaney, David. *Law and Nature*. New York: Cambridge University Press, 2003.

de Waal, Frans. *Are We Smart Enough to Know How Smart Animals Are?* New York: W.W. Norton, 2017.

– *Mama's Last Hug: Animal Emotions and What They Tell Us about Ourselves*. New York: W.W. Norton, 2019.

– *Primates and Philosophers: How Morality Evolved*. Princeton: Princeton University Press, 2006.

Donaldson, Sue, and Will Kymlicka. *Zoopolis: A Political Theory of Animal Rights*. Oxford: Oxford University Press, 2011.

Dupras, Georges R. *Values in Conflict: Reflections of an Animal Advocate*. Bloomington: iUniverse, 2011.

Elshtain, J.B. *Public Man, Private Woman: Women in Social and Political Thought* Princeton: Princeton University Press, 1981.

Esmeir, Samera. *A Juridical Humanity: A Colonial History*. Stanford: Stanford University Press, 2012.

Faruqi, Sonia. *Project Animal Farm: An Accidental Journey into the Secret World of Farming and the Truth about Our Food*. New York: Pegasus Books, 2014.

Fishcer, John Ryan. *Cattle Colonialism: An Environmental History of the Conquest of California and Hawai'i*. Chapel Hill: University of North Carolina Press, 2015.

Fowler, Karen Joy. *We Are All Completely Beside Ourselves*. New York: Penguin, 2013.

Francione, Gary L. *Animals as Persons: Essays on the Abolition of Animal Exploitation*. New York: Columbia University Press, 2008.

– *Animals, Property, and the Law*. Philadelphia: Temple University Press, 1995.

– *Rain without Thunder: The Ideology of the Animal Rights Movement*. Philadelphia: Temple University Press, 1996.

Frye, Marilyn. *The Politics of Reality*. Trumanburg: Crossing Press, 1983.

Fudge, Erica. *Animal*. London: Reaktion, 2002.

Fuentes, Agustin. *The Creative Spark*. Boston: E.P. Dutton, 2017.

Garner, Robert. *A Theory of Justice for Animals: Animal Rights in a Nonideal World*. New York: Oxford University Press, 2013.

Gillese, Eileen E. *The Law of Trusts*, 3rd ed. Toronto: Irwin Law, 2014.

Gillespie, Kathryn. *The Cow with Ear Tag #1389*. Chicago: University of Chicago Press, 2018.

Gilligan, Carol. *In a Different Voice: Psychological Theory and Women's Development*. Cambridge, MA: Harvard University Press, 1982.

Glenney Boggs, Colleen. *Animalia Americana: Animal Representations and Biopolitical Subjectivity*. New York: Columbia University Press, 2013.

Glick, Megan H. *Infrahumanisms: Science, Culture, and the Making of Modern Non/personhood*. Durham: Duke University Press, 2018.

Godrej, Farah. *Cosmopolitan Political Thought: Method, Practice, and Discipline*. London: Oxford University Press.

Gonzalez-Arnal, Stella, Gill Jagger, and Kathleen Lennon, eds. *Embodied Selves*. Basingstoke: Palgrave Macmillan, 2012.

Griffin, Emma. *Blood Sport: Hunting in Britain since 1066*. New Haven: Yale University Press, 2007.

Grimm, David. *Citizen Canine: Our Evolving Relationships with Cats and Dogs*. New York: Public Affairs, 2014.

Gruen, Lori. *Entangled Empathy: An Alternative Ethic for Our Relationships with Animals*. Brooklyn: Lantern Books, 2015.

Hamilton, Sheryl. *Impersonations: Troubling the Person in Law and Culture*. Toronto: University of Toronto Press, 2009.

Haraway, Donna J. *When Species Meet*. Minneapolis: University of Minnesota Press, 2008.

Harper, Amie Breeze. *Sistah Vegan: Black Female Vegans Speak out on Food, Identity, Health, and Society*. New York: Lantern Books, 2010.

Horsthemke, Kai. *Animals and African Ethics*. London: Palgrave Macmillan, 2015.

Ivison, Duncan. *Postcolonial Liberalism*. Cambridge: Cambridge University Press, 2002.

Jabri, Vivienne. *The Postcolonial Subject: Claiming Politics/Governing Others in Late Modernity*. Oxford: Routledge, 2013.

Johnson, Barbra. *Person and Things*. Cambridge, MA: Harvard University Press, 2008.

Kemmerer, Lisa, and Carol J. Adams. *Sister Species: Women, Animals, and Social Justice*. Champaign: University of Illinois Press, 2011.

Kimmerer, Robin Wall. *Braiding Sweetgrass: Indigenous Wisdom, Scientific Knowledge, and the Teachings of Plants*. Minneapolis: Milkweed Editions, 2013.

Kheel, Marti. *Nature Ethics: An Ecofeminist Perspective*. Lanham: Rowman and Littlefield, 2008.

Kim, Claire Jean. *Dangerous Crossings: Race, Species, and Nature in a Multicultural Age*. Cambridge: Cambridge University Press, 2015.

Ko, Aph. *Racism as Zoological Witchcraft*. Herndon: Lantern. 2019.

Llewellyn, John. *Emmanuel Levinas: The Genealogy of Ethics*. London: Routledge, 1995.

Luke, Brian. *Brutal: Manhood and the Exploitation of Animals*. Champaign: University of Illinois Press, 2007.

Lundblad, Michael. *The Birth of a Jungle: Animality in Progressive-Era U.S. Literature and Culture*. New York: Oxford University Press, 2013.

MacGregor, Sherilyn. *Beyond Mothering Earth: Ecological Citizenship and the Politics of Care*. Vancouver: UBC Press, 2006.

Marceau, Justin. *Beyond Cages: Animal Law and Criminal Punishment*. Cambridge: Cambridge University Press, 2019.

Marder, Michael. *Plant-Thinking: A Philosophy of Vegetal Life*. New York: Columbia University Press, 2013.

McClintock, Anne. *Imperial Leather: Race, Gender, and Sexuality in the Colonial Contest*. New York: Routledge, 1995.

Meskell, Lynn, and Robert W. Preucel. *A Companion to Social Archaeology*. Malden: Blackwell, 2004.

Miller, John. *Empire and the Animal Body: Violence, Identity, and Ecology in Victorian Adventure Fiction*. London: Anthem Press, 2012.

Moran, Mayo. *Rethinking the Reasonable Person: An Egalitarian Reconstruction of the Objective Standard*. Oxford: Oxford University Press, 2003.

Naffine, Ngaire. *Law's Meaning of Life: Philosophy, Religion, Darwin, and the Legal Person* Oxford: Hart, 2009.

Narayan, Uma. *Dislocating Cultures: Identities, Traditions, and Third-World Feminism*. New York: Routledge, 1997.

Nedelsky, Jennifer. *Law's Relations: A Relational Theory of Self, Autonomy, and Law*. New York: Oxford University Press, 2011.

Nixon, Rob. *Slow Violence and the Environmentalism of the Poor*. Cambridge, MA: Harvard University Press, 2011.

Noddings, Nel. *Caring: A Feminine Approach to Ethics and Moral Education*. Berkeley: California: University of California Press, 1984.

Noonan, John Thomas. *Persons and Masks of the Law: Cardozo, Holmes, Jefferson, and Wythe as Makers of the Masks*. New York: Farrar, Straus and Giroux, 1976.

Nussbaum, Martha. *Frontiers of Justice: Disability, Nationality, Species Membership*. Cambridge, MA: Harvard University Press, 2006.

Oliver, Kelly. *Animal Lessons: How They Teach Us to Be Human*. New York: Columbia University Press, 2009.

– *Earth and World: Philosophy after the Apollo Missions*. New York: Columbia University Press, 2015.

– *Witnessing: Beyond Recognition*. Minneapolis: Minneapolis University Press, 2001.

Overall, Christine. *Pets and People: The Ethics of Companion Animals*. Oxford: Oxford University Press, 2017.

Parisi, Luciana. *Abstract Sex: Philosophy, Technology, and Mutations of Desire*. London: Continuum, 2004.

Pateman, Carole. *The Sexual Contract*. Stanford: Stanford University Press, 1988.

Pateman, Carole, and Charles Mills. *Contract and Domination*. Malden: Polity Press, 2007.

Patterson, Charles. *Eternal Treblinka: Our Treatment of Animals and the Holocaust*. New York: Lantern Books, 2002.

Pedwell, Carolyn. *Feminism, Culture and Embodied Practice: The Rhetorics of Comparison*. New York: Routledge, 2010.

Plumwood, Val. *Environmental Culture: The Ecological Crisis of Reason*. London: Routledge, 2002.

Preece, Rod. *Animals and Nature: Cultural Myths, Cultural Realities*. Vancouver: UBC Press, 1999.

Preece, Rod, and Lorna Chamberlain. *Animal Welfare and Human Values*. Waterloo: Wilfrid Laurier University Press, 1993.

Puar, Jasbir K. *Terrorist Assemblages: Homonationalism in Queer Times*. Durham: Duke University Press, 2007.

Razack, Sherene. *Casting Out: The Eviction of Muslims from Western Law and Politics*. Toronto: University of Toronto Press, 2008.

Regan, Tom. *The Case for Animal Rights*. Berkeley: University of California Press, 1983.

Ritvo, Harriet. *The Animal Estate*. Cambridge, MA: Harvard University Press, 1987.

Ruddick, Sara. *Maternal Thinking: Toward a Politics of Peace*. Boston: Beacon Press, 1989.

Rudy, Kathy. *Loving Animals: Toward a New Animal Advocacy*. Minneapolis: University of Minnesota Press, 2011.

Sandilands, Catriona. *The Good-Natured Feminist: Ecofeminism and the Quest for Democracy*. Minneapolis: University of Minnesota Press, 1999.

Satz, Debra. *Why Some Things Should Not Be for Sale: The Moral Limits of Markets*. Oxford: Oxford University Press, 2010.

Schwartz, Maureen Trudelle. *Molded in the Image of Changing Woman: Navajo Views on the Human Body and Personhood*. Phoenix: University of Arizona Press, 1997.

Seshadri, Kalpana Rahita. *HumAnimal: Race, Law, Language*. Minneapolis: University of Minnesota Press, 2012.

Sewell, Anna. *Black Beauty*. London: Jarrold and Sons, 1877.

Shevelow, Kathryn. *For the Love of Animals: The Rise of the Animal Protection Movement*. New York: Henry Holt, 2008).

Shildrick, Margrit. *Dangerous Discourses of Disability, Subjectivity, and Sexuality*. Basingstoke: Palgrave Macmillan, 2009.

Shukin, Nicole. *Animal Capital: Rendering Life in Biopolitical Times*. Minneapolis: University of Minnesota Press, 2009.

Simpson, Leanne. *Lighting the Eighth Fire: The Liberation, Resurgence, and Protection of Indigenous Nations*. Winnipeg: Arbeiter Ring, 2008.

Smart, Carol. *Feminism and the Power of Law*. New York: Routledge, 1989.

Sorenson, John. *About Canada: Animal Rights*. Toronto: Fernwood, 2010.

Spelman, Elizabeth V. *Fruits of Sorrow: Framing Our Attention to Suffering*. Boston: Beacon Press, 2001.

Spiegel, Marjorie. *The Dreaded Comparison: Human and Animal Slavery*. New York: Mirror Books, 1996.

Spivak, Gayatri Chakravorty. *In Other Worlds: Essays in Cultural Politics*. New York: Routledge, 1998.

Sullivan, Ruth. *Sullivan on the Construction of Statutes*, 6th ed. Toronto: LexisNexis, 2014.

Sunstein, Cass R., and Martha C. Nussbaum. *Animal Rights: Current Debates and New Directions*. New York: Oxford University Press, 2004.

Taylor, Angus. *Animals and Ethics*. Toronto: Broadview Press, 2003.

Taylor, Sunaura. *Beasts of Burden: Animal and Disability Liberation*. New York: New Press, 2017.

Wadiwel, Dinesh. *The War against Animals*. Leiden: Brill, 2015.

Walker, Alice. "Am I Blue?" In *Living by the Word: Essays*. New York: Open Road Media, 2011.

Weheliye, Alexander G. *Habeas Viscus: Racializing Assemblages, Biopolitics, and Black Feminist Theories of the Human*. Durham: Duke University Press, 2014.

Willett, Cynthia. *Interspecies Ethics*. New York: Columbia University Press, 2014.

– *Maternal Ethics and Other Slave Moralities*. New York: Routledge, 1995.

Wise, Steven M. *Drawing the Line: Science and the Case for Animal Rights*. Cambridge, MA: Perseus Books, 2002.

– *Rattling the Cage: Toward Legal Rights for Animals*. Boston: Da Capo Press, 2000.

Wolfe, Cary. *What Is Posthumanism?* Minneapolis: University of Minnesota Press, 2010.

Wright, Laura. *"Wilderness into Civilized Shapes": Reading the Postcolonial Environment*. Athens: University of Georgia Press, 2012.

Ziff, Bruce. *Principles of Property Law*, 4th ed. Toronto: Thomson Carswell, 2006.

Secondary Materials: News Sources

n.a. "Among the beneficiaries of Trump's tariff bailout for farmers? A Brazilian-owned meat company." *Mother Jones*, 16 May 2019. https://www.motherjones.com/food/2019/05/among-the-beneficiaries-of-trumps-tariff-bailout-for-farmers-a-brazilian-owned-meat-company.

– "Probe into dog slaughter – CANADA." *The Age*, 4 February 2011, 13.

– "Sled dogs culled after Winter Olympics." *Daily Telegraph*, 2 February 2011, 18.

BBC News. "Canadian man sorry for butchering and eating pet pig Molly," 27 February 2018. http://www.bbc.com/news/world-us-canada-43216143.

– "Declaration signed on great apes," 12 September 2005. http://news.bbc.co.uk/2/hi/science/nature/4232174.stm.

Bryden, Joan. "Liberals scrap over animal-cruelty bills." *Globe and Mail*, 26 February 2007, A11.

Carter, Nance. "PTSD cited after slaughter of 100 dogs." *Long Island Examiner*, 2 February 2011.

Casey, Liam. "Stable rebuilds after fire killed 43 horses." *National Post*, 16 March 2016. https://www.pressreader.com/canada/national-post-latest-edition/20160514/281642484393458.

CBC News. "OSPCA tells Ontario government it will no longer enforce animal cruelty laws," 4 March 2019. https://www.cbc.ca/news/canada/toronto/ospca-ontario-animal-cruelty-laws-1.5042073.

– "Vancouver Park Board votes to end display of cetaceans at aquarium," 9 March 2017. http://www.cbc.ca/news/canada/british-columbia/vancouver-park-board-votes-to-end-display-of-cetaceans-at-aquarium-1.4018872.

Crane, Darryl. "Social media vigil for sled dogs found in Whistler." *Invermere Valley Echo*, 26 April 2011, 1.

Crowe, Kelly. "How many people does it take to write a guide for healthy eating? More than 26,000 and counting." *CBC News,* 9 January 2019.

Deckha, Maneesha. "Law must see animals as more than 'property.'" *The Times-Colonist*, 3 February 2011, A10.

Dhillon, Sunny. "BC crackdown won't ban sled-dog culls." *Globe and Mail*, 6 April 2011, A8.

– "Sled dogs' mass gravesite kept secret." *Globe and Mail*, 2 February 2011, S1.

Diebel, Linda. "An aerial view of Marineland." *Toronto Star*, 15 August 2012, A15.

– "Aquarium water went bad in the afternoon." *Toronto Star*, 15 August 2012, A15.

– "Heartache over Smooshi," *Toronto Star*, 15 August 2012, A15.

– "Inside Marineland: Star investigation; former park employees tell of unhealthy water, chronic short staffing, and animal suffering at popular tourist attraction." *Toronto Star*, 15 August 2012, A1.

– "Marineland faces SPCA inspection: Star investigation; 'I was in tears,' says cbinet minister after reading allegations of animal suffering." *Toronto Star*, 17 August 2012, A1.

– "'She finally died in our arms': Star investigation ex-employees blame short-staffing at Marineland after adult whales brutally attack baby beluga." *Toronto Star*, 16 August 2012, A1.

Dutkiewicz, Jan, Astra Taylor, and Troy Vettesse. "The Covid-19 pandemic shows we must transform the global food system." *The Guardian,* 16 April 2020. https://www.theguardian.com/commentisfree/2020/apr/16/coronavirus-covid-19-pandemic-food-animals.

Gorman, James. "Rights group is seeking status of 'legal person' for captive chimpanzee." *New York Times*, 2 December 2013.

Hainsworth, Jeremy. "100 dogs in Canada killed after business slows." *Associated Press*, 1 February 2011. http://abcnews.go.com/International/wireStory?id=12807719.

Hond, Paul. "Plastic, plastic everywhere." *Columbia Magazine*, 2019. https://magazine.columbia.edu/article/plastic-plastic-everywhere.

Felperin, Leslie. "*Unlocking the Cage* review – exemplary animal rights documentary." *The Guardian*, 16 June 2016.

Fox, Jim. "Killing of dogs is investigated." *St Petersburg Times*, 6 February 2011, 11A.

"Joaquin Phoenix's Oscars speech in full: 'We feel entitled to artificially inseminate a cow and steal her baby'" [video]. 10 February 2020. *The Guardian*. https://www.theguardian.com/film/2020/feb/10/joaquin-phoenixs-oscars-speech-in-full.

Kane, Laura. "RCMP appeals for calm as sled-dog exhumations begin." *Times-Colonist*, 3 May 2011, A5.

Kaufman, Amy. "The lawyer fighting for animal rights in 'Unlocking the Cage' asks: 'What kind of being are you?'" *Los Angeles Times*, 24 June 2016. https://www.latimes.com/entertainment/movies/la-et-mn-unlocking-the-cage-feature-20160617-snap-story.html.

Knight, Chris. "Unlocking the Cage is an uneven journey, though heartening if you too believe animals deserve legal protection." *National Post*, 19 August 2016. https://nationalpost.com/entertainment/movies/unlocking-the-cage-is-an-uneven-journey-though-heartening-if-you-too-believe-animals-deserve-legal-protection

Kleinmann, Adam. "Intra-actions: An interview with Karen Barad." *Mousse Magazine* 34, nos. 1–2 (2012): 76.

Lazare, Jodi. "'Free Willy' law spotlights contradictions in how Canadians see animal rights." *The Conversation*, .8 July 2019. https://theconversation.com.

Lewis, Sophie. "Over 1 billion animals feared dead in Australian wildfires." *CBS News*, 7 January 2020. www.cbsnews.com.

Lunman, Kim. "Animal-rights legislation faces delay in Senate." *Globe and Mail*, 22 November 2002, A10.

MacLeod, Robert. "Requiescat in Pace." *Globe and Mail*, 5 January 2016. www.globeandmail.com.

MacLeod, Robert, and Tu Thanh Ha. "Trainer watches in horror as 42 horses die in Ontario stable fire." *Globe and Mail*, 5 January 2016. www.globeandmail.com.

Manning, Sue. "Activists target dog sled rides after Canada dog deaths." *Fairbanks Daily News-Miner*, 8 February 2011.

McLaughlin, Amara. "Marineland charged with 6 new counts of animal cruelty." *CBC News*, 9 January 2017. http://www.cbc.ca/news/canada /hamilton/marineland-charged-with-6-counts-animal-cruelty-1.3927659.

Morrow, Adrian. "A killing without cruelty is no crime." *Globe and Mail*, 2 February 2011, S2.

Pemberton, Kim. "BC to toughen animal cruelty penalties; Report on killed sled dogs makes several proposals." *National* Post, 6 April 2011, A7.

– "Owner takes 'moral responsibility' for dog cull; Outdoor Adventures' Joey Houssian wants to keep business going." *Times-Colonist*, 8 February, 2011, A8.

– "SPCA probes 'execution' of 100 sled dogs." *Vancouver Sun*, 1 February 2011, A1.

Ridley, Louise. "Barbican's anti-racism show featuring black people in cages cancelled ... after racism claims." *Huffington Post*, 24 September 2014. http://www.huffingtonpost.co.uk/2014/09/24/racism-claims-cancelled -barbican-exhibit-b-show_n_5874202.html.

Saxon, Tony. "Multimillion-dollar loss: More than 40 racehorses die in Classy Lane Stable fire in Puslinch." *The Record*, 6 January 2016. http://www .therecord.com/news-story/6220059-multimillion-dollar-loss-more-than -40-racehorses-die-in-classy-lane-stable-fire-in-puslinch.

Siebert, Charles. "Should a chimp be able to sue its owner?" *New York Times*, 23 April 2014. https://www.nytimes.com/2014/04/27/magazine/the -rights-of-man-and-beast.html.

Slaughter, Graham. "Marineland protest gathers more supporters after Star stories." *Toronto Star*, 17 August 2012, A10.

– "Singer wants voice pulled from commercials." *Toronto Star*, 17 August 2012, A10.

Spurr, Ben. "Death of 43 racehorses in stable fire devastates Ontario's race community." *Toronto Star*, 5 January 2016. https://www.thestar.com/news /canada/2016/01/05/at-least-43-racehorses-die-in-ontario-stable-fire.html.

Walkom, Thomas. "Senate bill to free the whales faces a rough ride." *Toronto Star*, 20 March 2017. https://www.thestar.com/opinion/commentary/2017/03/19 /senate-bill-to-free-the-whales-faces-a-rough-ride-walkom.html.

Warnica, Richard. "It's just crazy': Ontario community reeling after at least 40 racehorses killed in massive fire." *National Post*, 5 January 2016. http:// news.nationalpost.com/news/canada/at-least-43-racehorses-die-in -ontario-barn-fire-at-classy-lane-stables-training-centre.

Westoll, Andrew. "Are animals people, too? Soon, a chimpanzee could walk into a courtroom as a thing, and walk out as a person." *National Post*, 19 August 2016. ationalpost.com/entertainment/movies/are-animals-people -too-soon-a-chimpanzee-could-walk-into-a-courtroom-as-a-thing-and-walk -out-as-a-person.

"Woodbine Racetrack pays tribute to 43 horses killed in barn fire." *Inside Toronto*, 8 January 2016. https://www.insidetoronto.com/news-story /6224212-woodbine-racetrack-pays-tribute-to-43-horses-killed-in-barn-fire.

Yuhas, Alan. "Chimpanzee representatives argue for animals' rights in New York court." *The Guardian*, 27 May 2015. https://www.theguardian.com /us-news/2015/may/27/chimpanzee-animals-rights-new-york-court.

Zelman, Joanna. "100 sled dogs killed in BC due to slump in tourism." *Huffington Post*, 31 January 2011. http://www.huffingtonpost.com/2011 /01/31/100-sled-dogs-slaughtered_n_816462.html.

Secondary Materials: Reference Books

Black's Law Dictionary. "person," "natural person," "artificial person," "juridical person," "body corporate." https://www.thelawdictionary.org.

CED edition (online). *Criminal Law – Offences* "Mens Rea" (I.2.(c).(i)).

– *Criminal Law – Offences* "Actus Reus" (I.2.(b).(i)).

Encyclopædia Britannica. "Endangered Species." 2009. http://www.britannica .com/EBchecked/topic/186738/endangered-species.

Oxford English Dictionary, s.v. "animal." http://www.oxforddictionaries .com/definition/english/animal.

Secondary Materials: Blogs and Webpages

"Animal Clock." https://animalclock.org.

Animal Justice. "Canada killed more than 800 million land animals for food in 2017" (blog), 17 April 2018, perma.cc/SBW2-UY8E.

– "Issues: Shark finning" (2019), http://www.animaljustice.ca/issues/shark -finning.

Animal Legal Defense Fund. "2012 Canadian animal protection law rankings." http://www.aldf.org.

CFHS (Canadian Federation of Humane Societies). "Bill S-203," 9 June 2009 http://web.archive.org/web/20090609103648/http://cfhs.ca/law/bill_s_203.

– "Criminal Code Amendments." *Humane Canada* (2019). https://humanecanada .ca/our-work/focus-areas/animals-and-the-law/history-of-criminal-code -amendments.

– "Legal Analysis Re: Bill C-15B Section 15 Cruelty to Animals" (2011). https://web.archive.org/web/20110607200659/http://cfhs.ca/law/legal _analysis.

Charity Intelligence Canada. "BC SPCA," 19 June 2019. https://www .charityintelligence.ca/charity-details/10-bc-spca.

Edgerton, Leah. "What is the most effective way to advocate legally for nonhuman animals?" *Animal Charity Evaluators*, 29 August 2016. https://

animalcharityevaluators.org/blog/what-is-the-most-effective-way-to
-advocate-legally-for-nonhuman-animals.

"Fishcount." http://fishcount.org.uk.

Francione, Gary L. "A Frequently Asked Question: What about Plants?" *Animal Rights: The Abolitionist Post* (blog), 13 December 2006, perma.cc/G8MC-K4LF.

– "Debate with Professor Michael Marder on plant ethics." *Animal Rights: The Abolitionist Approach* (blog), 8 June 2012, perma.cc/7DF4-G82M.

– "What to do on Proposition 2." *Animal Rights: The Abolitionist Approach*, 2 September 2018. http://www.abolitionistapproach.com/what-to-do-on -proposition-2.

GAP Project. "World Declaration on Great Primates." *GAP Project*. http:// www.projetogap.org.br/en/world-declaration-on-great-primates.

Husrevoglu, Zeynep. "Cruelty to animals – Criminal Code amendments: Before and after Bill S-203." *Animal Justice Review*, 20 November 2012. http://www.animaljustice.ca/blog/cruelty-to-animals-criminal-code -amendments-before-and-after-bill-s-203.

International Fund for Animal Welfare. "New bill would make significant improvement to animal welfare laws in Canada." 3 March 2016. http:// web.archive.org/web/20160502150725/http://www.ifaw.org/canada /news/new-bill-would-make-significant-improvements-animal-welfare -laws-canada.

IS Foundation. "Save the sled dog: Reform British Columbia's anti-cruelty to animals law." *Change*. http://web.archive.org/web/20190802181156 /https://www.change.org/p/save-the-sled-dog-reform-british-columbias -anti-cruelty-to-animals-law.

Nonhuman Rights Project. "What Is Nonhuman Rights Project?," https://web .archive.org/web/20160201002322/http://www.nonhumanrightsproject .org/overview.

PETA. "PETA sues SeaWorld for violating orcas' constitutional rights," perma. cc/V5DH-VPAQ.

[Staff writers]. "Former 'slaughter-free dairy' farmer: No such thing as humane dairy." *Free From Harm*, 20 September 2018. https://freefromharm .org/animal-farmer-turned-vegan/former-slaughter-free-dairy-farmer-no -such-thing-as-humane-dairy.

Vulnerability and Human Condition Initiative (2019). http://web.gs.emory .edu/vulnerability.

Other Materials

Giljum, S, et al. "Overconsumption? Our use of the world's natural resources" (2009). Brussels: Friends of the Earth Europe. http://www.foeeurope.org /publications/2009/Overconsumption_Sep09.pdf.

Holtslander, Cathy. "Losing Our Grip: 2015 Update." Canada: National Farmers Union (2015). https://www.nfu.ca/wp-content/uploads/2018/07/Losing -Our-Grip-2015-Update-Web-Version.pdf.

Humane Society of the United States. "An HSUS Report: The Welfare of Intensively Confined Animals in Battery Cages, Gestation Crates, and Veal Crates" (2013). https://www.humanesociety.org/sites/default/files/docs /hsus-report-animal-welfare-of-intensively-confined-animals.pdf.

Intergovernmental Panel on Climate Change (IPCC). "Climate Change and Land: An IPCC Special Report on Climate Change, Desertification, Land Degradation, Sustainable Land Management, Food Security, and Greenhouse Gas Fluxes in Terrestrial Ecosystems." (2020). https://www .ipcc.ch/srccl/.

James, Krista, and Lauren Watts. "Understanding the Lived Experiences of Supported Decision-Making in Canada: Legal Capacity, Decision-Making, and Guardianship." Law Commission of Ontario, March 2014. https:// www.lco-cdo.org/wp-content/uploads/2014/03/capacity-guardianship -commissioned-paper-ccel.pdf.

JBS. "Results for the Fourth Quarter and Year Ended, March 31, 2017," 28 March 2018. https://jbss.infoinvest.com.br/enu/4523/4Q17%20 Earnings%20Release%20%28Final%29.pdf.

Library and Information Service, National Primate Research Center. "Chimpanzee: *Pan troglodytes* factsheet" (2006). http://pin.primate .wisc.edu/factsheets/entry/chimpanzee/cons.

Prince, Amber. "What's Wrong with Canada's Animal Cruelty Laws? Bill C-50, a Touchstone for Change." LLM Thesis, University of Victoria Faculty of Law, 2007. http://hdl.handle.net/1828/2470.

Sankoff, Peter, and Camille Labchuk. "The battle to pass Canada's new shark fin import ban" [podcast]. Animal Justice, 24 June 2019.

– "Factum of the Intervenor" in *R. v. D.L.W.*, [2016] 1 SCR 402, 2016 SCC 22 (CanLII). http://www.scc-csc.ca/WebDocuments-DocumentsWeb/36450 /FM030_Intervener_Animal-Justice.pdf.

Stein, Elizabeth, and Steven M. Wise. "Memorandum of Law in Support of Petition For Habeas Corpus." In *The Nonhuman Rights Project on behalf of Happy v James J Breheny & Wildlife Conservation Society*, NYSC 45164 2019.

Unlocking the Cage (2016). New York: Pennebaker Hegedus Films, 2016.

Verbera, Antonio. "The Politics of Animal Anti-Cruelty Legislation in Canada: An Analysis of Parliamentary Debates on Amending the Criminal Code" (2012). Electronic Theses and Dissertations.

Index

Printed and bound by CPI Group (UK) Ltd, Croydon, CR0 4YY

13/04/2025

14656518-0002